Living Insects of the World

Living Insects

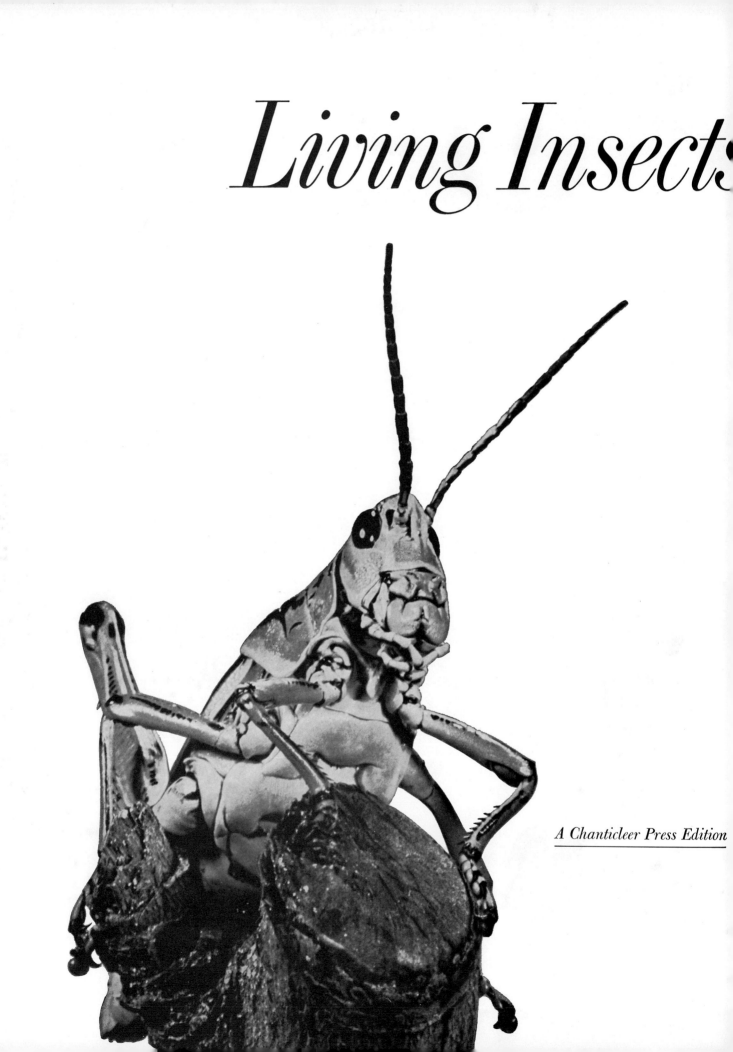

A Chanticleer Press Edition

of the World

by ALEXANDER B. KLOTS

Associate Professor of Biology at The City College of New York
and Research Associate of the American Museum of Natural History

and ELSIE B. KLOTS

With photographs by

ANDREAS FEININGER

EDWARD S. ROSS

ALEXANDER B. KLOTS

and others

Line drawings by

SU ZAN NOGUCHI SWAIN

DOUBLEDAY & COMPANY Inc.

Garden City, New York

Published by Doubleday & Company, Inc., New York, N.Y.

Fourth Printing 1975

Planned, prepared and produced by Chanticleer Press, Inc., New York

THE WORLD OF NATURE SERIES

Living Mammals of the World by Ivan T. Sanderson

Living Reptiles of the World by Karl P. Schmidt
and Robert F. Inger

Living Birds of the World by E. Thomas Gilliard

Living Insects of the World by Alexander B. Klots
and Elsie B. Klots

*The Lower Animals: Living Invertebrates of the
World* by Ralph Buchsbaum and Lorus J. Milne,
in collaboration with Mildred Buchsbaum
and Margery Milne

Living Fishes of the World by Earl S. Herald

Living Amphibians of the World by Doris M. Cochran

ISBN: 0–385–06873–5

Library of Congress Catalog Card No. 59–9100

Printed by Kingsport Press, Kingsport, Tennessee

Contents

Photographic Credits : *Color*

INCLUDING GEOGRAPHIC SOURCES OF PHOTOGRAPHS

The name in <u>*italics*</u> *indicates the area in which the photograph was taken,*
wherever such information was available.

PLATE

1 Roman Vishniac
2 Alexander B. Klots—*New York*
3 D. Dwight Davis—*California*
4 Edward S. Ross
5 Andreas Feininger—*U.S.A.*
6, 7 Ross E. Hutchins—*Mississippi*
8–10 Edward S. Ross—*Peru*
11 Andreas Feininger—*U.S.A.*
12 Heinrich Schäfer—*Germany*
13 Andreas Feininger—*California*
14 Edward S. Ross—*California*
15, 16 Andreas Feininger—*U.S.A.*
17 Edward S. Ross
18 Alexander B. Klots—*New York*
19 Edward S. Ross—*California*
20 Alexander B. Klots—*Connecticut*
21 Edward S. Ross—*Peru*
22 Andreas Feininger—*U.S.A.*
23 Ross E. Hutchins
24 David C. Stager—*New Jersey*
25 Andreas Feininger—*U.S.A.*
26 Harald Schultz—*Brazil*
27 John Gerard: Monkmeyer
28 Edward S. Ross—*Eastern Peru*
29 David C. Stager—*New Jersey*
30–33 Andreas Feininger—*U.S.A.*
34 Ross E. Hutchins
35 Alexander B. Klots—*New York*
36 Ross E. Hutchins
37 Alexander B. Klots—*New York*
38 Edward S. Ross—*Pennsylvania*
39 Andreas Feininger—*U.S.A.*
40 Alexander B. Klots—*New York*
41 Edward S. Ross—*California*
42 Andreas Feininger—*U.S.A.*
43 J. W. Kamp
44 Edward S. Ross—*Peru*
45 Fritz Goro: *Life* Magazine
46 Andreas Feininger—*U.S.A.*
47 Edward S. Ross
48 Alexander B. Klots—*Iowa*
49 A. B. Klots—*New Mexico*
50 Andreas Feininger—*U.S.A.*
51 Alexander B. Klots—*New York*
52 Alexander B. Klots—*Connecticut*
53 Louis Carrano
54 Edward S. Ross—*Peru*
55 Alexander B. Klots—*Connecticut*

PLATE

56 Andreas Feininger—*U.S.A.*
57 Edward S. Ross—*Peru*
58 Andreas Feininger—*U.S.A.*
59 Edward S. Ross—*California*
60, 61 Andreas Feininger—*U.S.A.*
62, 63 Heinrich Schäfer
64 Harald Schultz—*Brazil*
65 S. Beaufoy—*England*
66–67 A. B. Klots—*Connecticut*
68 Eliot Porter
69 Alexander B. Klots—*New York*
70 Andreas Feininger—*U.S.A.*
71 Hal H. Harrison: National Audubon
72 Alexander B. Klots
73 Alexander B. Klots—*New York*
74, 75 Andreas Feininger—*U.S.A.*
76 Edward S. Ross
77 Eliot Porter—*New Hampshire*
78 Eliot Porter
79 Andreas Feininger—*U.S.A.*
80 Alexander B. Klots—*Connecticut*
81 John Markham—*England*
82, 83 A. B. Klots—*Connecticut*
84 Alexander B. Klots—*New Jersey*
85 Lynwood M. Chace
86 Günther Olberg
87 Alexander B. Klots—*Connecticut*
88 Alexander B. Klots—*New York*
89 Andreas Feininger—*U.S.A.*
90 Eliot Porter—*New Hampshire*
91 Andreas Feininger—*U.S.A.*
92 Alexander B. Klots—*New York*
93 John Markham—*England*
94 Alexander B. Klots—*Connecticut*
95 Alexander B. Klots—*New York*
96 Edward S. Ross—*Eastern Peru*
97 Andreas Feininger—*U.S.A.*
98 Alexander B. Klots—*Connecticut*
99 S. Beaufoy—*England*
100 Alexander B. Klots—*Bahamas*
101 John H. Gerard: Monkmeyer
102–104 Alexander B. Klots—*Connecticut*
105 Andreas Feininger—*U.S.A.*
106 John H. Gerard: Monkmeyer
107–110 Edward S. Ross—*Eastern Peru*

PLATE

111 Lynwood M. Chace—*North America*
112 Harald Schultz—*South America*
113 Eliot Porter—*New Mexico*
114 Sam Beaufoy—*Europe*
115–118 Edward S. Ross—*Eastern Peru*
119 Alexander B. Klots—*Connecticut*
120 Andreas Feininger—*U.S.A.*
121 Fran Hall: National Audubon
122 Andreas Feininger—*U.S.A.*
123 Ross E. Hutchins
124–126 Alexander B. Klots—*Connecticut*
127 Alexander B. Klots—*New York*
128 Ross E. Hutchins—*Mississippi*
129 Andreas Feininger—*U.S.A.*
130 Grace Thompson: National Audubon—*Texas*
131 Alexander B. Klots—*Connecticut*
132 David C. Stager
133 Eliot Porter—*New Mexico*
134 Edward S. Ross
135 David C. Stager
136 Alexander B. Klots—*Connecticut*
137 Eliot Porter—*New Mexico*
138 Alexander B. Klots—*New York*
139 Alexander B. Klots—*Connecticut*
140 Ross E. Hutchins—*Mississippi*
141 T. C. Schnierla—*Panama*
142 Andreas Feininger—*U.S.A.*
143 Alexander B. Klots—*Connecticut*
144 David C. Stager—*New Jersey*
145–146 Ross E. Hutchins—*Mississippi*
147 Grace Thompson: National Audubon—*Texas*
148 Alexander B. Klots—*Connecticut*
149 Alexander B. Klots—*New York*
150 Andreas Feininger—*U.S.A.*
151–152 Grace Thompson: National Audubon—*Texas*

Photographic Credits : *Black-and-White*

Preface

IT has been far from easy to plan and write a book in non-technical language to cover so vast, so varied and so pervasive a group as the insects. There are more species of insects than of all other animals and plants combined. Some are simple and primitive in both structure and behavior; and many live in a wide variety of habitats and feed on almost anything they encounter. The majority, however, are highly evolved and delicately attuned to very special and restricted ways of life. Some form true societies of a magnitude and complexity unsurpassed by those of any other animals, man himself included. Many are major pests in our homes or in forestry, industry and agriculture; and many others are responsible for the transmission of some of the most harmful diseases of man and his domestic animals. On the other hand, a great many are essential to our economy as the sources of various useful products, as weed destroyers, as our chief agents of control of harmful insects, or as the essential pollinators of many of our most valuable plants. The lives of even the most urbanized human beings are far more intimately associated with and affected by the insects than is generally realized.

In general, we have followed a taxonomic sequence in presenting the material in this book. In so doing we have been forced to omit many groups that are not without special interest but are very small in size or limited in distribution; and we have had to make many arbitrary choices from among numerous nomenclatorial variants. In the interest of the average reader, who is not concerned with the complexities that have developed with our expanding and evolving taxonomy, we have tended to select a relatively simple, and in some ways highly conservative, system of classification, and to use the best-established and most widely adopted names. We have followed the most recent large textbook, that of Imms, as revised by Richards and Davies, more than any other. When numbers of species within a group have been given they are in approximate round numbers and represent the more conservative estimates of specialists.

Many of the details of insect development and structure are not widely known, but are nevertheless essential for an understanding of insect life and classification. We have accordingly prepared a short digest of these, which will explain most of the special terms used. This will be found in an appendix (page 291).

We have sought to eschew the spectacular and to avoid making dramatic comparisons of insects and man. The temptation in this area is great because insects *are* spectacular and insects *do* put man to shame in any mathematical tabulation of their skills. That a house fly hums in the key of F and beats its wings 20,700 strokes a minute; that a particular beetle is able to pull 42.7 times its own weight; or that a caterpillar has some 4000 muscles (and a man but 792), are interesting items in themselves but contribute little to the broad story we have tried to tell.

Despite a total between us of several score years of study and experience with insects in several continents, we have drawn very heavily on the knowledge of many others, gleaned from dozens of books and thousands of articles. We have also been materially aided by many of our colleagues, specialists in particular groups, who have given us advice and information. We are highly appreciative of the great contribution made by the photographers and the illustrators without whose work, as selected by the editors, this book would not have been possible. We only hope that we ourselves have not committed too many errors, and that those that have slipped in will be regarded with tolerance.

ALEXANDER BARRETT KLOTS
ELSIE BROUGHTON KLOTS

Pelham, New York

Living Insects of the World

INTRODUCTION

All life, both plant and animal, began in the water. For countless ages it remained there, slowly differentiating and slowly evolving in size and complexity. Meanwhile the land lay bare and lifeless, subject only to surging, elemental physical forces. Gradually life crept up onto the land, doubtless at first in the narrow intertidal zone of the seacoasts. The green plants must have been the pioneers, for animals cannot exist in a world where there have been no chlorophyl-bearing plants to manufacture food; but in time both plants and animals solved the special problems of land life and populated the whole of the new environment, reaching even high mountain tops and barren deserts far removed from their ancestral home in the water.

The adage that "nature abhors a vacuum" is not merely a popular saying but an expression of a fundamental law of life. Wherever a vacant area exists in which life can conceivably survive, the ecologic vacuum attracts some form of life that colonizes the area and, in time, attains success there. Many forms may fail, but eventually one succeeds. It was thus when the green plants emerged from the water onto the bare land, and it was thus when many of the animal groups followed them, and with them created the world of terrestrial life.

Nearly every one of the great animal phyla—the major groups of the animal kingdom—sent at least some immigrants to the land. Only a few, such as the sponges and the jellyfish and their kin, were too primitive and lacked the necessary means of adaptation. But nearly every other phylum has today some members that live in or on land, even though the representation in some cases may be small. Flatworms, and roundworms; leeches and earthworms; roaches, butterflies and spiders; frogs and snakes; birds and mammals—all have, in varying degrees, evolved from originally aquatic ancestors, and all have clearly recognizable "cousins" still living in the water, the descendants of more conservative stocks that stayed in the ancestral home.

Three of the phyla—the roundworms, the earthworms and the molluscs—have attained a high degree of terrestrial success, as is attested by their great numbers, wide distribution and relative security on land. But two others, the arthropods and the chordates, have been far more successful than these or any others, and between them almost completely dominate animal land life. The arthropods are chiefly represented on land by the insects, although they also include such lesser groups as the millipedes and centipedes, and the spiders and their relatives. Of the chordates, four groups of the vertebrates—amphibians, reptiles, birds and mammals—have become successful earth-dwellers, matching the insects in everything but sheer numbers, extending to nearly every practicable environment and exploiting nearly every possible source of food.

Inevitably there has been, is and always will be competition between these two major groups. This is not as great as might be expected, however, owing chiefly to the marked disparity in size of the individual insect and the individual vertebrate. Because of their larger size many vertebrates can and do live solely by catching insects, but the reverse is very rare—it is "news" when an insect catches a vertebrate. But because of their smaller size many insects can and do live as parasites, either actual or social, upon vertebrates. There is constant competition for food between members of the two groups, of course, although seldom does this effect either vitally. In general, the two groups coexist, each in its own "sphere of influence," with far less friction and competition than we might expect. Because of the complexities and self-limitations of the balances of nature that have evolved in all environments, wars of extinction between insects and vertebrates, including man, take place only in the imagination of the uninformed or in the pages of sensational writers. An appreciation of this, such as we shall try to transmit here, is the key to understanding the world of insects and man's contact with it.

CHAPTER I

The Background of the Insect World

A FOSSIL SCORPION FLY

INSECTS are the dominant animals in the land world today. Nearly everywhere they are abundant, invading a multitude of environments and exploiting almost all possible food supplies. Yet the details of their early evolution are lost in the mists of antiquity. This is due in part to the fact that the first insects were doubtless small, fragile creatures that disintegrated long before they could become fossilized; and in part to the almost total absence of rocks that contain fossils of the land animals from the period when insects were beginning to appear. It is quite probable that some of the early members of the group of marine arthropods known as trilobites, which are first recorded in the rocks of the Cambrian period, perhaps 400 million years ago, were allied to the ancestral insects. At any rate they are the only known arthropods from that period that could have evolved into insects, the others being too definitely committed in other directions. The trilobites lasted for some 140 million years and then became extinct, but the span of their existence largely covers the long blank period of early insect evolution.

Although a number of specimens of doubtful identity are known, there are no fossils unquestionably recognized as insects from earlier than the Carboniferous period, some 175 million years after the beginning of the Cambrian. By this time the land plants were highly evolved and successful, forming the great pteridophyte forests that eventually became transformed into much of our coal and oil. The abundant food supply that they created, as yet utilized by no great group of animals, offered an unparalleled opportunity. We know that the vertebrates were taking advantage of it, for they had successfully made the move onto land, as is shown by the fossil remains of amphibians and primitive reptiles from this period. Their early land evolution is better documented than that of the insects.

Suddenly in the rocks of the Carboniferous we find unmistakable insect fossils—and they are the remains of highly evolved, already winged insects of a number of well-differentiated orders. Such complex animals do not spring into being overnight or in the course of a mere few million years. They must have been evolving for scores of millions of

[11

years—as the vertebrates and spiders had been doing during the same time. But the detailed record of this has not yet been found. If it still exists, it is in the rocks now deeply covered by the oceans, and thus beyond our reach.

Most of the Carboniferous insects belonged to groups that have since become extinct, either by simply dying out or by evolving into something quite different. To the humble and much maligned roaches, however, belongs the distinction of having a "family tree" clearly recognizable in even these earliest records; for typical roaches occur, even commonly, in Carboniferous strata. The immediate precursors of our present-day dragonflies are also known from this period, although they differ sufficiently from their descendants to be regarded as a distinct order, the Protodonata. Some of them reached a size unthought of in modern insects, the gigantic dragonfly *Meganeura monyi* from the coal measures of Commentry in France having had a wing expanse of approximately thirty-six inches. The Carboniferous strata in which fossil insects have been found are widespread, the best known in North America being at Mazon Creek, Illinois, many Pennsylvania localities and several mines in New England and eastern Canada. Many other fossils that are associated with those of the insects, often in the same pieces of rock, tell us much about the rich flora and the other animal life of the times.

We have many and highly varied insect fossils from the Permian period, which succeeded the Carboniferous. They have been found abundantly in Kansas, Russia and Australia, enabling us to make world-wide comparisons. Some are marvelously detailed, showing not only the veins of the wings and patches of color in the wing membranes but even the tiny spines no more than a hundredth of an inch long that covered the wings of some of the species. The Permian insects are particularly significant since they agree in showing us many details of the early evolution of a number of the modern insect orders as well as of a number of other groups that subsequently became extinct. The large Protodonata lasted well into the Permian, being found in the same rocks as the first known true Odonata, their more progressive "cousins" that have survived as the modern dragonflies. By the end of the Permian, perhaps 225 million years ago, the insects were abundantly established along approximately the lines they have followed down to the present.

Coming down practically to modern times (geologically speaking) the insects of the mid-Tertiary period, some 25 to 35 million years ago, were very similar to those of today. One of the most famous sources of their fossils is at Florissant, Colorado, where countless numbers of insects fell into an ancient lake and became buried in its muds, along with the plants, fishes and other inhabitants of the region. Beautifully preserved fossils were formed as the layers of mud changed into paper-thin layers of shale. Even butterflies have been found with the patterns of their wings showing plainly, although not in the original colors. One of these would fit into a modern genus, and perhaps, with a bit of stretching of the imagination, into a modern species.

Enormous numbers of insects are known from Baltic and other amber of the Tertiary. This is the fossilized resin of coniferous trees; inside of masses of this resin many insects (Plate 132), as well as seeds, pollen grains and all kinds of small objects were caught. The preservation is so exquisite that one can see as clearly as on a microscope slide the smallest details of the structure of the specimen. We once obtained in Denmark a small piece of amber that contained a very modern-looking cranefly. On examining it more closely we saw that we had not only the cranefly but two other flies as well; and then we found that on the cranefly were two tiny mites that had been riding about on it, just as modern mites do on craneflies and other insects today. At least one of the ants found in Baltic amber belongs to a species that, it is claimed, still exists in Asia; and three others are so similar to three species that live in the Baltic region today that William Morton Wheeler admitted his inability to tell them apart. Despite their age of 20 to 35 million years, the Florissant and Baltic amber insects bring the group right down to modern times.

Note: All necessary technical terms are explained in the Appendix, page 291.

CHAPTER II

The Most Primitive Insects

(Subclass Apterygota)

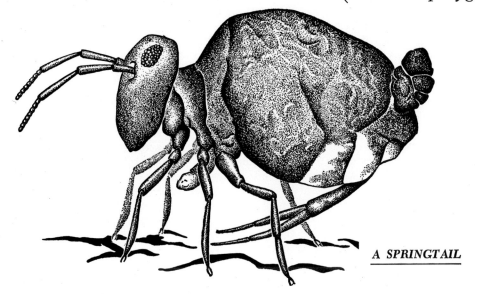

A SPRINGTAIL

THIS most primitive group of insects consists of small wingless creatures that are of great scientific interest since in some respects they are much like the ancestral stock of all insects. They are world-wide in distribution but number only about twelve hundred to fifteen hundred species, of which the great majority are members of the most specialized order, the springtails. Since their small size and secretive habits enable them to escape detection, there are doubtless many more still to be discovered, especially in the largely unexplored tropics. All evidence indicates that their winglessness is a primitive condition and that their ancestors never developed wings. They are almost completely without metamorphosis, at least of the conventional insect type; and many of them have, still preserved and functional, some of the paired abdominal appendages that have been almost entirely lost in the higher insects. Their mouthparts are chiefly modifications of the primitive biting type. Three orders are usually recognized.

THE BRISTLETAILS
—Order Thysanura

These small insects (Plate 1) get their name from the three slender bristle-like appendages, two of which are cerci, that stream out behind the abdomen of some of the commonest of the species.

The single pair of antennae, extending forward, is often similarly long and bristle-like. The legs are long and slender and well adapted for running. Vestiges of some of the paired appendages are found on a number of abdominal segments in some of the species.

The majority live in sheltered, damp places such as under dead bark, beneath stones and logs and in the leaf mold, feeding upon plant detritus. Two species of the family Lepismatidae, however, have invaded man's houses and sometimes become minor pests because of their fondness for glue, paste or nearly anything that contains starch. These are: the little silverfish or fish moth, *Lepisma saccharina,* which is covered with tiny scales that rub off at a touch; and the firebrat, *Thermobia domestica,* noted for its preference for extremely warm, even hot places, such as around chimneys and heating flues, where it lives in temperatures that would discourage other insects.

Bristletails have a strong negative tropism to light, and so make forays from the narrow cracks in which they live only under cover of darkness. Consequently they are seldom seen unless exposed by the sudden opening of a closet door or the turning on of a light; even then, their small size (with their long hairlike appendages they are no more than an inch in length), slender form, neutral color and speed in getting to shelter enable them to escape the eye so readily as to make one wonder if they were really there at all.

The Lepismatidae and Machilidae have compound eyes; but the Campodeidae and Japygidae do not, and are sometimes placed in a separate order, the Diplura, because of this as well as for their distinctive mouthparts. *Campodea staphyliniformis* is a pale whitish species about a quarter of an inch long that may sometimes be found under stones or damp bark. *Japyx* has the cerci short and curved instead of long and bristlelike, and looks like a miniature earwig.

THE PROTURANS
—Order Protura

These soft-bodied, minute insects, known only since 1907 when they were discovered in the soil in Italy, have been collected in Europe, India, the United States and Canada. Fewer than fifty species have been described. In some ways they are exceedingly primitive and simple, but much of their simplicity is degenerative.

They have neither eyes nor antennae, but walk with the forelegs held up in front as though being used as tactile organs. Their mouthparts are not of the primitive biting type but are modified for piercing and sucking. The abdomen is long and slender, with a pair of appendages on each of the first three segments. The newly hatched larva has nine abdominal segments but acquires three more by the time it becomes an adult. This phenomenon of increasing the number of segments during development is almost unheard of in insects but is characteristic of such primitive arthropod groups as the centipedes and millipedes and of many annelid worms.

THE SPRINGTAILS
—Order Collembola

The springtails constitute the great majority of the Apterygota and are the most specialized of these generally primitive insects. They are as completely world-wide as any group can be, for they occur abundantly in all of the major continents as well as in the far Arctic and Antarctic regions; in the latter they are the only insects known except for a few bird parasites.

Most of the species are only a few millimeters or less in length. The compound eyes are vestigial in some and altogether absent in others. The mouthparts, sometimes adapted for biting and sometimes for sucking, are usually retracted into the head capsule. The partial fusion of the segments of the thorax is a marked departure from the conventional insect form; but their most distinctive specializations are on the short, reduced abdomen that is made up of only five or six segments. Here, on the under surface, is a unique mechanism that, employing the suddenly released force of a strong spring under great tension, enables the insect to leap straight into the air for a distance of perhaps dozens of times its own length.

Springtails live in a great variety of habitats but chiefly in moist or wet places, where they may become a nuisance, especially around maple sap buckets, in mushroom beds or on young seedlings. They probably feed on decaying plant or animal matter, possibly also on algae and diatoms. *Podura aquatica* is very commonly seen on the surface of quiet pools, in masses perhaps an inch or two in diameter and containing hundreds of individuals. The mass seems to be in constant motion as individuals spring into the air and then drop back, while others slip beneath the surface of the water only to pop up into the assemblage again in a few seconds. The little dark *Anurida maritima* is similarly found along the northern seacoasts, often forming masses on the surface of tidal pools. One of the most unusual species is *Achorutes nivicola,* which occurs in enormous numbers on the surface of the snow, not only in winter in temperate regions, but in the far Arctic and on the snow fields of great glaciers. The ability of this tiny insect to remain active, find food, thrive and reproduce in such a seemingly impossible environment is still far from understood.

Other species occur in equally unusual environments: *Entomobrya mawsoni,* for example, lives beneath stones in the penguin rookeries of Macquarie Island, and species of *Axelsonia* have been found living in barnacle shells. Members of the family Sminthuridae can thrive in somewhat drier places, some occasionally reaching sufficient abundance in gardens to be minor pests, especially under conditions of very high relative humidity. In all, some fifteen hundred species and ten or more families have been described.

CHAPTER III

Roaches, Mantids, Locusts and their kin

(Order Orthoptera)

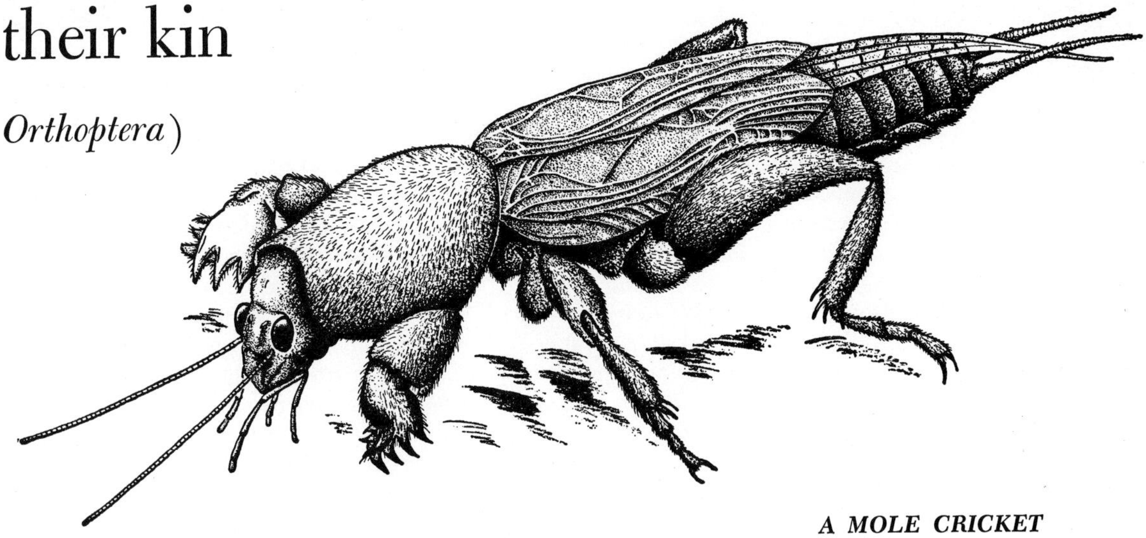

A MOLE CRICKET

THE Orthoptera are generally considered the most primitive of the winged insects (Pterygota), although many of them are quite specialized in their own ways. They include such well-known forms as the migratory locusts that have so often devastated man's crops, the curious praying mantids, the homely "cricket on the hearth," and the all too familiar roaches. The members of the order are all quite closely related, yet are sufficiently diverse for no single colloquial name to have been given to the group as a whole. It is a large order, containing perhaps twenty thousand species, and is nearly world-wide in distribution, only the Arctic and Antarctic lacking representation.

The mouthparts are of the primitive biting type, consisting of a labrum, a pair each of mandibles and of first and second maxillae, and a hypopharynx. The two second maxillae are fused together behind the mouth, thus forming a functional rear lip, the labium. This pattern, although primitive, is highly efficient for eating solid foods and has been retained in many more highly advanced orders.

The metamorphosis is incomplete (direct), the larva (or nymph) transforming directly to the adult at its last molt. In the majority of Orthoptera the larvae resemble the adults so closely in both appearance and habits that we have no difficulty in recognizing their relationship at a glance. A young grasshopper or mantis is unmistakably a grasshopper or mantis, despite the fact that its wings are

merely short, fleshy pads that do not attain full size or become functional until it transforms into the adult.

The great majority of the Orthoptera are winged; but in some sizable groups as well as in a scattering of members of others the wings have been lost or greatly reduced. We can feel sure that the wingless condition is not a primitive one, since those that lack wings are obviously very closely related to others that have the wings fully formed and functional; and also because in such groups it is not at all uncommon to find species with only partly degenerated wings. Moreover, we sometimes find that within a single species some individuals have long wings, others short ones and still others none at all. The front wings, which are called tegmina, are typically narrower and somewhat thicker and stronger than the hind ones. When not in use they are held back over the hind wings and the abdomen, for which they serve as more or less protective covers. They are often concealingly colored and patterned with greens and browns, closely resembling leaves or bark. The hind wings are much larger, with a great many small, strengthening cross veins, and when not in use are folded in pleats beneath the front ones. In many forms they are brightly colored with red, orange and yellow. Some members of the order, particularly the migratory phases of some of the locusts, are strong long-distance fliers; but the majority make only relatively short flights, if any,

[15

and are aided materially in the take-off by the thrust of the hind legs. The latter are notably long and strong, and in a great many forms are fitted for jumping.

The great majority are plant-eaters of a rather unspecialized type, feeding upon nearly any suitable plant material. However the members of one family, the mantids, have switched to animal food and are voracious predators upon other insects and small animals. A few very specialized forms live as guests or invaders in the nests of ants or termites. Most of the order are generally dwellers on the ground and among low vegetation, but some live in caves and dark, confined places and others have evolved strong front legs especially adapted for digging and live underground most of the time. A few are partially aquatic. The roaches are general scavengers and wood-eaters, the majority living outdoors; but a few have adapted to man's economy and are bothersome, although not serious, household pests. Some of the plant-eating species, especially of the locusts, occasionally form dense swarms that may completely devastate crops over large areas.

The Orthoptera are one of the two great musical, or at least noise-making, groups of the insects, the other being the cicadas. In both of these groups only the males sing, the females being condemned to perpetual silence. This might be regarded as one of the outstanding characteristics of these insects. The noises are produced in various ways, in some with the legs and in others with the wings, by rubbing together specialized rough structures. The vibration thus caused is amplified by the wing membranes,

A **Grasshopper** (*Apioscelis*), young nymph. It is believed the sticklike form enables it to escape the notice of many predatory enemies.

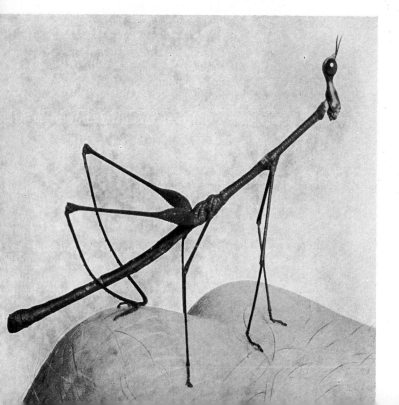

which are specially modified for this purpose. Undoubtedly the songs, which are often extremely distinctive for each species, play an important part in courtship. Organs of hearing are also usually present in both sexes; in some groups these are on the body, in others on the front legs.

ROACHES—Family Blattidae

A few species of these ancient insects have given the group a bad reputation as far as we are concerned by taking advantage of our domestic arrangements and moving into our houses as unwelcome guests (Plate 2). These are, however, only a small part of the family, since most of the thirty-five hundred or so species are wild-living and have as little to do with man as possible. The majority of the roaches are tropical, but a number of species occur naturally in the temperate regions, in addition to the domesticated species, chiefly tropical or subtropical in origin, which have followed man everywhere. The roaches are characterized by their long, slender legs, which have very large coxae and are well adapted for running; and by their very flattened body form, the prothorax in particular being extended out to the sides to form a flattened plate that quite covers the head from above. This shape enables them to penetrate cracks and crevices everywhere and to hide in very narrow spaces. Many of the wild species are brown like the domesticated ones; they live under dead bark and in decaying vegetation. Many others are quite brightly colored in shades of brown, green and yellow, and live among growing plants where their colors are highly concealing. One rather pretty little green roach, *Panchlora cubensis,* is often found in our northern cities, being commonly imported in bunches of bananas, and occasional individuals of some of the very large tropical species are similarly imported (e.g., the death's-head roach, *Blaberus craniifer,* which may attain a length of two or three inches). A few species live near water, and a few live in deserts. The wings are well developed in most of the roaches, but in some species those of the females are greatly reduced in size or altogether wanting. Many of even the large species fly well and at night in the tropics are often attracted to light in considerable numbers. We still retain the most vivid memories of one such roach in Brazil that was seized by one of the little house lizards scurrying across the ceiling, and of what happened when the struggling pair landed in a plate of soup.

The majority of roaches are naturally scavengers, perhaps feeding rather more on animal than plant matter, so that the transition for some of them to scavenging in our houses was a simple step. However, some feed upon fungi and others upon wood. The latter are particularly interesting since, although they eat wood, they are unable to digest it.

A Meadow Grasshopper (*Tettigonia viridissima*). The green color and leaflike wings render it inconspicuous among foliage.

This anomalous situation is made possible by the presence in their digestive tracts of thriving colonies of protozoa, microscopic one-celled animals, of species that occur only in roaches. The protozoa digest the wood that the roaches supply, and the roaches digest the surplus both of the digested wood and of the protozoa themselves. Such relationships of mutual dependence are known as symbioses or obligatory mutualisms. The large roach *Cryptocercus* of our southern woodlands is one such symbiotic, wood-eating species. The same phenomenon of dependence upon intestinal protozoa or bacteria is known in many other wood-eating insects, notably the termites.

Contrary to the general impression, roaches have not been incriminated as carriers or vectors of human disease except in the most casual way. Their continued presence in a house is, however, evidence of a lack of sanitation that may lead to the encouragement of genuine disease-carriers.

As in a number of other Orthoptera, the eggs of many of the roaches are enclosed in a sclerotized capsule, often flat and bean-shaped, the oötheca.

The females of some species carry this about protruding from the genital opening until the eggs hatch. Others merely deposit it somewhere, while a few species retain it within the body in a brood pouch, so that the young roaches are actually born alive. A very interesting group of parasites, the ensign wasps (Evaniidae), make a specialty of parasitizing roach oötheca.

As we mentioned earlier, the roaches are of ancient lineage, being very common among the fossil insects of the Carboniferous period. The fossil roaches show no great differences from the present-day ones, and doubtless lived much as their descendants do today, except that man and his kitchens were still several hundred million years in the future. The roaches early evolved a simple, secure and successful way of life and have stayed with it ever since, while other groups have attained great temporary success in more specialized ways and then have become extinct. The roaches are thus an excellent example of the rewards as well as the virtues of humility.

MANTIDS—Family Mantidae

Because of their characteristic form, resting position and habits of predatism, the mantids are one of the most distinctive and widely known groups of insects. Their front legs are greatly enlarged and powerful, and so constructed that the tibia can be snapped back against the femur; both are heavily armed with spines and teeth, which give a deadly grip on the mantid's prey. A resting mantis holds its head and very long prothorax up high and folds its front legs as though in an attitude of peaceful meditation or prayer; but it is always ready to lash out and seize any suitable victim that comes within reach. Because of this sanctimonious-appearing position the mantids have been regarded with curiosity, superstition or even reverence by various peoples from ancient times. This is evidenced by the name of the type genus, *Mantis* (that is, a soothsayer). Moslem peoples claim that the mantids always pray properly—facing toward Mecca. In the southern United States they are sometimes called "devil's coach horses" or "mule-killers," and are regarded with some fear by the superstitious.

The mantids are the sole family of the Orthoptera to have departed from the general plant-eating habit of the order and adopted a predatory life. The world over, in tropical and warm temperate regions, they feed voraciously on insects and other invertebrates (often on other mantids), and have even been known to catch small lizards, birds and frogs. The majority of the eighteen hundred species are colored and shaped to match their surroundings, enabling them to stalk or lie in wait for their prey without detection, as well as concealing them from other predators. Many are various shades of green, often with leaflike patterns on the front wings; others are extremely long and twiglike; still others have the wings and body flattened, irregularly shaped and colored with grays and browns so that they simulate lichens or bits of bark; and some, like the Asiatic rose mantis, *Gongylus,* are an exquisite match for the petals of the flowers in which they lie in ambush. Some species are quite large, attaining a length of four or five inches; others are less than an inch long.

The voracity of the mantids, especially of the females, is proverbial. It seems as though there is no end to their appetites, and even when stuffed with food they will still strike out at new prey. The female often eats the male after or even during mating, which seems a rather harsh way of making the bridegroom pay for the wedding breakfast.

The common European *Mantis religiosa,* a medium-sized species about three to four inches long, has been introduced into North America and is well established in central New York and New England. The much larger Chinese species, *Tenodera sinensis* and *angustipennis,* originally introduced into the New York City–Philadelphia area, have also spread widely and are quite common in some parts of the

A **Bark Mantis** (*Gonatista grisea*). Its shape and color blend remarkably with the bark on which it habitually settles.

East. The small native *Stagmomantis carolina* is common in the southern states, and other species are common in the western United States, especially in arid regions. In Arizona we have often seen large numbers of these, attracted by a bright light around which we were collecting insects, carrying on their business of catching and eating with great enthusiasm among the swarms of insects attracted to the light. Mantids are probably moderately beneficial to man since they undoubtedly kill many injurious insects, but their value is somewhat diluted by the fact that they also kill beneficial ones.

WALKING STICKS and LEAF INSECTS
—Family Phasmidae

Although these insects are largely Oriental, and although the majority of the two thousand species are tropical, some occur well northward in both Europe and North America. No other group of insects excels them in the profound modification of form and color that gives them their almost incredible protective resemblance to twigs and leaves. So attenuated are the heads and bodies, to say nothing of the appendages, of the stick insects (Plate 5) that one wonders how they can manage to move without breaking. Their twiglike appearance is heightened in many species by the complete loss of wings, and is still further enhanced by the peculiar attitudes that they assume. Many species are green when young and thus resemble the petioles and midribs of the leaves along which they stretch themselves. Some of the small species are green even when adult, and are thus almost impossible to detect in the grass in which they live. Some of the Asiatic stick insects, such as *Palophus titan,* are the longest of living insects, reaching a total length of a foot or more. Other tropical species are armed with sharp spines that not only resemble thorns of plant stems but can give a bird, lizard or human hand a nasty stab.

The famous leaf insects of Asia (*Phyllium,* etc.) have the wings, legs and sides of the body strongly and irregularly flattened; and this, with their leaf-green color (sometimes variegated with "dead" brown or yellow patches) and their very slow motions, makes them excellent mimics of the foliage among which they live. The females, which are considerably larger than the males, have lost the hind wings and are flightless, but retain the leaflike front wings. Large females may be more than four inches long.

Not only do some phasmids have various color forms but others show changes in color intensity as a result of changes in humidity, temperature or light. Sometimes these changes are rhythmic, as day turns to night and night to day.

The Phasmidae are all plant-eaters. Some species become abundant enough to defoliate large areas

Chinese Praying Mantids (*Tenodera sinensis*), shown hatching from the egg-mass, are now very common in the New York City–Philadelphia area.

of woodland. The eggs are laid singly, being simply dropped by the females. At times during heavy infestations of the common walking stick, *Diaphero-mera femorata,* of the eastern United States, the sound of the myriads of dropping eggs is as loud as that of rain falling upon the forest floor.

LOCUSTS and SHORT-HORNED GRASS-HOPPERS—Family Locustidae (*or Acrididae*)

This large, world-wide family (Plate 8) of over five thousand species contains the majority of the familiar grasshoppers of the countryside, as well as the notoriously destructive locusts. The antennae are relatively short and thick; the hind legs are long and strong and are used for jumping; and a hearing organ with a prominent, tightly stretched tympanic membrane is located on each side of the first abdominal segment. Some of the large bird-winged locusts of the tropics (*Schistocerca,* etc.) have a wing expanse up to six inches, while members of other groups such as the pigmy locusts (Tetriginae) are less than one-half inch long when mature.

Each of the major continents has one or more species of locust that at times builds up an enormous population that then migrates in incredible swarms. Despite a great deal of research, not all of the factors involved in this are known. A typical migratory species, such as the Old World *Locusta*

migratoria or *L. pardalina,* exists in two well-marked phases, a short-winged form that does not swarm and a long-winged one that does. The latter develops only in certain breeding areas under special environmental conditions that bring about much greater activity of the developing larvae. In many regions intermediate forms that do not swarm also develop. When conditions are just right a great swarm of the long-winged phase is produced, and this then sets off on a mass flight. The migrating individuals are not driven by hunger, since they do little feeding while en route, using instead the stored reserves in their fatty tissues. Eventually they cease migrating, and at that time feed voraciously and may do great damage to crops. One swarm that flew over the Red Sea was estimated to be two thousand miles in extent; and during a single infestation thirteen hundred tons of locust *eggs* were collected and destroyed on the island of Cyprus. The offspring of a migratory swarm are seldom if ever themselves migratory, but the next generation may be. The story of our North American migratory species, the Rocky Mountain locust, *Melanoplus spretus,* is similar; and many lesser migratory and nonmigratory species are also at times exceedingly destructive, especially in the Great Plains and prairie regions. Many people counter the damage done to their crops by feeding on the rich harvest of migratory locusts when these appear. Dried locusts, or meal made from them, is almost a staple with many primitive groups of man.

Many of the Locustidae are famous for their songs. In this family the sound is commonly produced by rubbing together a roughened ridge along the inner side of each hind femur and a hardened vein on the fore wing, causing the latter to vibrate and both produce and amplify the sound. In one subfamily (Oedipodinae) some of the males stridulate while flying, making a sharp crackling that can be heard some distance. Members of the other subfamilies stridulate while at rest.

The subfamily Tetriginae, the grouse and pigmy locusts, is often considered to be a separate family. Many of the species are extremely small, being no more than one-half inch long. The dorsal or upper part of the prothorax is produced posteriorly into a long, triangular piece that covers the whole back. The front wings are reduced to tiny scales, but the hind wings are large and are used in flight, being folded beneath the extension of the prothorax when not in use. A few members of this group are definitely aquatic. Some (*Hydropodeticus*) have the posterior legs modified for swimming.

Two pairs of short, strong, sharp appendages at the end of the abdomen of the female locust serve as ovipositors. With them a hole, sometimes large enough to receive the entire abdomen, may be dug in the earth or rotting wood. The eggs are then

A **Walking Stick** (*Pterinoxylus spinosus*). The slender, irregular form is almost impossible to detect when it is resting among twigs.

packed into this hole as the abdomen is withdrawn, and a waterproof covering is applied. Thirty to a hundred eggs may be packed in a single mass, and several masses may be deposited during a season by each female. Sometimes the male attends the female during her labors.

The large lubber locusts of the southern and western United States are well known for their size, clumsiness and occasional swarming. Their wings are considerably reduced in size, so that some fly awkwardly and for only short distances and others are unable to fly at all. Occasional large swarms of them have been seen walking across highways; and when these have been run over by a few automobiles the highway has been known to become so

slippery as to present something of a traffic hazard. When held in the hand a lubber locust makes a distinct hissing squeak by expelling air from the spiracles. It has a nauseating smell and taste, which is a much needed protection against predatory animals.

LONG-HORNED GRASSHOPPERS and CAVE CRICKETS—Family Tettigoniidae

Many of the members of this large, cosmopolitan family of over four thousand species are familiar insects, being the slender, usually green grasshoppers with extremely long, threadlike antennae, which abound in fields and meadows and among vegetation generally. The songs of many of the species, such as that of the well-known katydids (*Microcentrum*, etc.) are among the commonest sounds of the eastern American countryside in late summer. Many of the species have the front wings somewhat broadened and colored and patterned so as to resemble foliage closely; and among some of the very large tropical species (Plate 4) this resemblance is incredibly enhanced by irregular brown, yellow and transparent patches that simulate to perfection the damage done to a leaf by insects chewing. Some members of the family, especially the cone-headed grasshoppers that have the head produced to a point and have undershot, sharklike profiles, can give a nasty bite when seized; but most of the species are harmless plant-eaters that defend themselves only in the conventional grasshopper fashion of spitting up a bit of innocuous brown saliva.

The sound-producing (stridulating) apparatus consists of roughened areas at the overlapping bases of the front wings which, when rubbed together, set special resonant areas on the wings vibrating and produce astonishingly loud sounds. Many of the species have their distinctive "songs," differing in the number, pitch and sequence of the notes, so that they can be recognized by an experienced specialist as easily as though the specimen were in the hand. The song functions as a courtship performance or at least serves to bring the sexes of each species together. The hearing organ is located on the tibia of the front leg instead of on the side of the abdomen as in the locusts.

A number of quite diverse groups are members of this family. Common and widespread are the large, wingless, long-legged brown insects known as cave crickets and camel crickets (Rhaphidophorinae) that are found the world over in dark, cool places, where they scavenge on plant matter. One New Zealand species attains a length of twelve to fourteen inches, including the long antennae and hind legs. Here and in the subfamily Gryllacrinae belong a number of anomalous forms. The Carolina leaf-roller, *Camptonotus carolinensis,* is a small species that lives in a rolled leaf fastened together with silk, from which it sallies forth to hunt aphids. Similar are the large, clumsy Jerusalem crickets (Plate 3) or sand crickets (Stenopalmatinae) of western North America, which dig in sandy soil and wander awkwardly about in search of small game. The famous Mormon cricket, *Anabrus simplex,* of the Rocky Mountain region, which was threatening the vital first crops of the early Mormon settlers in Utah when a flock of sea gulls intervened, is still a serious pest to agriculture. Some of the related heavy-bodied "wetas" (*Deinacrida*) of New Zealand are the giants of the group, having a leg span of more than seven inches.

The females of a majority of the species have bladelike ovipositors that are sometimes longer than

Southern Lubber Grasshopper (*Rhomaleum micropterum*). A large, clumsy, almost flightless species of the southeastern United States.

the abdomen. With these some of them cut slits in plant stems in which to lay their eggs, and in times of abundance they may do considerable damage in this way.

CRICKETS and TREE CRICKETS
—Family Gryllidae

This large, world-wide family of over nine hundred species includes the familiar house and field crickets, noted for their chirping as well as for the occasional damage they do to starched fabrics and bookbindings when they invade our homes; the highly vocal tree crickets; the curiously specialized mole crickets that lead largely subterranean lives; and a number of lesser groups. The antennae are long and thin, like those of the long-horned grasshoppers; the ovipositor of the female is often long and slender, but is not flat and bladelike; and the wings, when present, are held flat over the back with the edges sharply bent down at the sides. Some forms lack the wings or have vestigial ones.

The stridulatory apparatus is most highly developed in the true crickets (Gryllinae) and tree crickets (Oecanthinae), a double file and scraper and a resonant sounding board being present on each front wing. A chirping cricket holds his wings over his back, slanting up at an angle of about 45 degrees, and rubs their bases together vigorously. Each species has its more or less characteristic note and sequence. Some of our pale, greenish white tree crickets of the genus *Oecanthus* are particularly sensitive to the temperature of the environment while chirping, speeding up as the temperature rises. So accurately are they adjusted that the temperature in degrees Fahrenheit can be calculated quite accurately by counting the number of chirps in fifteen seconds and adding 39. Or you may multiply the temperature by four and subtract 160 to predict the number of chirps per minute. Try it some summer evening—but make sure that you are listening to a tree cricket!

The mole crickets (Gryllotalpinae) are heavy-bodied, short-winged insects an inch and a half to two inches long that have the front legs marvelously enlarged and adapted for burrowing. Each of these tools is also equipped with very efficient shears for snipping rootlets. They make shallow tunnels for long distances just beneath the surface of the ground, feeding on tender roots as they go. There are more species in the tropics than in the temperate zones, but at least one *Gryllotalpa* is common in Europe and another, *G. hexadactyla,* in North America.

A particularly interesting group of Europe, Asia and North America is the subfamily Myrmecophilinae (meaning "ant-lovers"), which consists of a number of small, chunky, wingless species that live only in the nests of ants. They feed on the oily secretions of their hosts; but unlike so many other insects that live as ant guests they are not welcomed by the ants, which try to catch and kill them. They include the smallest of the true Orthoptera, measuring only three to five millimeters in length.

The classification of the Orthoptera has been greatly modified in recent years, often very differently by different authors. In general, what we have here treated as a single order has been split into three or four. Some authors place the walking sticks and leaf insects in a separate order, the Phasmida, and the roaches and mantids in another, the order Dictyoptera. Some authors split them still further.

The order Grylloblattodea, closely related to this Orthoptera complex, was established for one species, *Grylloblatta campodeiformis,* first discovered in the Canadian Rockies in 1914. This order now includes another genus from Japan and one from Russia.

Field Crickets (*Gryllus*). The wings of the male, the upper one of this pair, act as sounding boards that magnify his chirp.

They are extremely primitive insects of great phylogenetic interest, possibly representing, in some ways, the only living remnants of the ancestral stock from which all the Orthoptera evolved. *G. campodeiformis* occurs beneath stones at altitudes of 1500 to 6500 feet; it is apparently omnivorous and nocturnal, and is of very slow development, doing best at temperatures a little above freezing. Because of its great rarity, living specimens were brought to the Tenth International Congress of Entomology held in Montreal in 1956, where they served as the motif of the occasion and the symbolic insect of the congress.

22]

CHAPTER IV

Termites
(Order Isoptera)

THE reputation for destructiveness that many members of this order (Plate 7) have is fully merited, and has done much to obscure the fact that the termites are actually an exceedingly interesting group of animals. All of the seventeen hundred or more known species are truly social, forming communities that range from relatively small ones of only hundreds of individuals in some species, to enormous ones consisting of millions in others. Most of the species show a very high degree of social organization, marked by the presence of specialized castes of sexual individuals and sterile workers and soldiers, and the performance by these of various special tasks necessary for the maintenance of the society. In this the termites conform with relative unanimity to a single pattern of social organization, unlike the other great group of social insects, the ants, in which we see many peculiar types of societies and social behavior. The actual organization of a termite society is far from simple, except in comparison with what we may term the eccentricities of some of the ants; but it never fails to follow a pattern of practicality and efficiency. It is obvious that the termites evolved an efficient and stable pattern of social life early in their development and then settled down and refused to experiment further; while the ants, having quite independently evolved much the same pattern, continued their evolution to the point of developing scores of highly aberrant and sometimes degenerative societies.

Structurally the termites are relatively primitive, despite their high degree of social development. They are obviously related to some of the roaches; and it is worth noting that certain of these, such as the wood-eating *Cryptocercus,* appear to be in a very early stage of developing a communal life much like that of the termites. Termite mouthparts are of a decidedly primitive orthopterous biting type, although they are considerably degenerated and modified in some groups. Their metamorphosis is of the relatively primitive incomplete type, the larvae transforming gradually to the adult or fully grown condition. Except in the very primitive Australian *Mastotermes* (in which they are decidedly roach-like) the front and hind wings are quite similar to each other, and have the veins of the anterior part of each wing strong and those of the posterior part weak and degenerate. In most cases the wing membrane is more or less stiffened by an irregular sclero-tized network between the veins. Perhaps the most distinctive wing characteristic is the presence of a line of weakness across each wing near the base, the so-called humeral suture. It is along this line that the sexual forms break off their wings after a dispersal flight, in preparation for settling down, mating and forming a new colony, and spending the rest of their lives in tunnels, burrows and passageways. Compound eyes are present in the winged, sexual individuals; but they show some degeneration, or may be altogether absent, in other types. It is thus untrue, although widely believed, that all termites, or even all workers and soldiers, are blind.

The head capsule is usually more or less strongly sclerotized and dark, sometimes quite strongly so, but the general body integument of most forms is very light and pale, giving them a characteristic whitish appearance through which the dark intestinal contents may show plainly. This is responsible for the name "white ants" that is widely used for termites. The term is objectionable, since the termites and the ants have little more in common than the fact that they are both insects that form large societies of chiefly wingless individuals.

A distinctive feature of termites is the presence of a gland, the frontal gland, which when well developed opens to the exterior by a pore in the upper front part of the head. It is small and nonfunctional in many forms, but in the soldiers of many genera it is enormously developed, extending back internally to the rear of the abdomen. It secretes through the pore a liquid of great value both in nest-building and as a defensive weapon.

It is in the differentiation of various types of individuals and the organization of these into a complex society that the termites are most outstanding.

The winged reproductive individuals are the most nearly normal and conventional of all of the forms. They are periodically produced by a thriving society in enormous numbers, sometimes millions, when the right combination of internal and environmental conditions occurs. At this time they leave the home nest in a mass exodus, sometimes looking like a dense cloud of smoke as they fly upward.

The misnomer whereby these are called "mating swarms" arises from the mistaken idea that, like the honeybees and ants, the males and females mate during the swarming. Mating actually does not take place until considerably later; the chief function of the swarm is the dispersal of the sexual individuals for the founding of new colonies.

The flight of the termites is weak and fluttery because of their lack of adequate wing muscles and of any apparatus for coupling and coordinating the front and hind wings of each side; the sexual forms, however, are often carried for considerable distances by currents of air. At this time they are sorely beset by innumerable enemies, birds, bats, lizards and predatory insects gathering to take advantage of the opportunity. Many are trapped in spiders' webs. One observer watched dragonflies seizing termites in the air, daintily biting off and eating the abdomens (the choicest morsel) and dropping the still struggling remains. The swarming myriads are many times decimated, but so great are their numbers that thousands survive the first hazards of colonization.

Suddenly the termites cease to respond to the stimulus of light and the other factors that led them to fly out and upward from the home nest, and drop to the ground. Almost immediately they shed their wings, which have borne them perhaps for only a few moments of flight. This they do by arching their bodies strongly to press the wing tips back against the ground, or sometimes by twisting and rubbing against hard objects. Great windrows of discarded wings may mark the termination of a swarming.

It is now that the pairings begin, as the wingless males and females scurry actively about. Eventually, as the males find the females, which they follow closely, each couple turns its attention to homemaking. In the majority of species this begins with finding a suitable crevice in the soil or in damp, rotting wood; but in those species that prefer dry wood the pair, which we may call affianced but not yet wedded, laboriously evacuates a little cell in sound wood. Not until a proper cavity has been

found or prepared and they are safely immured in it, a matter perhaps of weeks, do they mate. With the phlegmatic termites there is no premature yielding to a careless rapture, as in the ants. Business comes first. It is all very practical and prosaic.

The male, be it noted, is an equal partner in all of this. In the Hymenoptera he passes out of the picture as soon as the female is fertilized, either dropping away and dying or else being killed by having his genital structures, which remain in the female, torn out bodily. The female ant or bee carries on alone, a true matriarch. But the termite male stays with his spouse, sharing the labor of getting the new colony started, and may live for many years —that is, as long as the female.

In a couple of weeks the female begins laying eggs, but only in very small batches. The small number of the first brood and the slow growth of a new termite colony are, in fact, most surprising in view of the great size that the colony may eventually attain. The eggs are assiduously licked clean and constantly cared for, a feature quite universal and most essential among termites, since neglected eggs quickly become moldy and die. Several weeks may be necessary for their hatching.

During their first stadium the tiny nymphs are fed upon liquid secretions of the parents. They may also browse a bit on fecal wastes in the nest cavity. In some two or three weeks they molt, shedding not only the exoskeleton proper but also the lining of the hind gut. If the nymph belongs to a species dependent upon micro-organisms for cellulose digestion, its intestine must now become infected or reinfected with the protozoa and/or bacteria without which it will be unable to utilize the cellulose of wood as food. Several more molts must take place and perhaps three to six months must elapse before

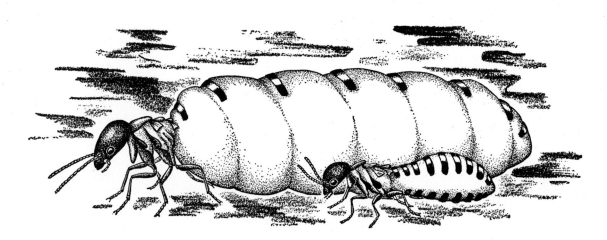

A TERMITE QUEEN AND KING AMONG THE NEST PASSAGES

the nymphs become fully grown. The first nymphs may show a somewhat accelerated growth and develop into undersized individuals in a considerably shorter period than their brothers and sisters who come along later, when the colony has become firmly established and prosperous.

For a long time to come, until the colony attains stability and a large population, the young can develop only into workers and soldiers. It will probably be many years before the society can afford the expense of producing a colonizing flight of winged, sexual males and females. The workers and soldiers cannot be said to be strictly sexless, since each is structurally recognizable as male or female; but they carry on no reproductive activities and are thus functionally neuters, whatever their inherited potentialities may have been. Only the original king and queen, and perhaps a few later developed, accessory individuals, can reproduce. The vast majority merely labor. The efficiency of the insect society is based upon sterilization of the proletariat.

For a long time, and in some termites for the duration of the colony's life, the original king and queen are the sole reproductive members. They may live for many years, perhaps a dozen or more. The fecundity of some queens is enormous, estimates having been made of productions of 30,000 eggs daily, although 8000 to 10,000 is probably a more representative figure. In many species additional reproductive individuals of both sexes may eventually appear, developing from worker nymphs. Sometimes these secondary reproductives appear while the primary ones are alive, but most commonly they appear only after the death of the primary king or queen or both. They never attain the stature of the original sexual forms and are wingless or have at most rudimentary wings. In this they resemble the immature stages, and are thus termed "neoteinic" kings and queens. In some species there may also develop a third type of reproductive individual, a sexually active soldier that lays eggs. There may thus be found various combinations: the primary king and queen, originally winged; neoteinic, wingless or short-winged replacement kings and queens; and soldier-like replacement queens. With such a reservoir of reproductive individuals to draw upon, it is no wonder that thriving termite colonies may consist of millions of individuals and endure for many years, perhaps for half a century or more.

The majority of the individuals in a mature colony are the workers and worker nymphs, which have short, broad mandibles with which they do most of the work. Even their head capsules are relatively pale, soft and unsclerotized. After the first stadium the worker nymphs begin to carry on various tasks, and they continue to toil for the rest of their lives. This is entirely unlike the situation in the social Hymenoptera, where the worker larvae are helpless grubs that must be fed and taken care of by mature individuals. Whatever we may think of child labor, the greater efficiency of the termite system is obvious. We may also note, in this respect, that among the termites, "male" individuals do their share of the work, while among the social Hymenoptera the males are at all times essentially parasitic upon the colony.

Certain other nonreproductive individuals develop into the so-called "soldiers," which may be distinguished from workers by their larger, broader, more heavily sclerotized heads, and often by their larger size. The common type has very large, powerful jaws, sometimes straight but often hooked or toothed, which may serve as defensive weapons, although in some cases this is open to question. The soldiers undoubtedly do congregate at points where a colony is attacked and may be effective in repelling enemies of small size. In some Kalotermitidae the hard heads of the soldiers are used as plugs to stop up the openings within and into the nest. A similar adaptation is found in the workers of some ants. In many termites the soldiers knock their heads against solid objects or snap their long jaws, producing clicks that are plainly audible even to a human ear. These serve as rallying signals when danger threatens a colony, although the termites certainly feel the vibrations rather than hear them.

In some species of the family Termitidae the fronts of the heads of many soldiers are produced to form a definite snout or beak, sometimes quite long. At the tip of this is the opening of the frontal gland. These individuals are called nasuti (that is, nosy ones). When an invader breaks into some part of the termite colony the nasuti quickly gather at the threatened point. From the orifice of its beak each one discharges a drop or fine stream of a sticky, perhaps repellent or somewhat toxic liquid. The spray thus produced does a great deal to repel or even to disable invaders, particularly other insects. The same liquid is also used by some species as a cement in constructing or repairing nests and runways. Most nasuti have the mandibles greatly reduced and thus, like the other soldiers, cannot eat for themselves and must be fed by nymphs and workers.

One of the most interesting problems to the biologist is that of the origin and control of these various castes in the societies of insects. To tell the truth we are still groping toward the answers. It is obvious that the organization of the members of the society into definite castes, each of which is specialized for certain tasks, is highly efficient and contributes greatly to the survival and success of the society. The mechanisms that control this must have evolved gradually during hundreds of millions of years, in accordance with the principle of natural selection of the more efficient and the elimination of the more inefficient. In the termites, sex is not involved in the caste problem, as it is in the matriarchal Hymenoptera where only potential females develop into workers. But in the termites as well as in the Hymenoptera the soldier or worker cannot reproduce because the sex organs fail to develop properly.

In bees and wasps the sterile workers develop because of some kind of underfeeding or improper feeding. It thus appears to be malnutrition that inhibits the full development of their sex. Every young female is a potential queen; but the vast majority never attain that status. In termites—and probably in ants—such differential feeding does not appear to be a factor, an idea confirmed by a good deal of experiment and observation. The underfed nymph will develop into an undersized individual, but it will undergo no qualitative change because of its nutritive handicap.

In order to understand what is believed to be the caste-determining mechanism in termites, we must first note that in any termite colony the individuals constantly indulge in an inordinate amount of mutual feeding and grooming. Hours are spent daily in feeding each other with regurgitated droplets and in licking the surfaces of each others' bodies. By means of this there is a constant oral passage about the colony of the various body secretions of any and all members. This, many students believe, is the mechanism for the transmission in the colony of specific substances that control the development of the nymphs. Such substances are analogous to the hormones, which, produced in one part of an animal's body, are carried in its blood to other parts where they exert specific controls. Familiar examples are the hormone produced by the human pituitary gland, which controls the development of the ovaries, and that produced by the thyroid, which regulates the rate of the body's metabolism.

We may term these postulated substances in the termite colony "social hormones." Passed about by the constant oral contact, they presumably act as inhibitors of growth and development. Those secreted by the primary reproductive individuals— the original king and queen—prevent the development of nymphs into secondary reproductive forms, so that few or none of these can develop while the primary king and queen survive. But should one or both of them die, the supply of inhibitory substance would vanish and at least some nymphs of the appropriate sex would be free to develop into sexually active individuals. We know that this actually happens. It is also apparent that when the secondary kings and queens have developed and begun functioning, they in turn secrete inhibitory substances that will prevent any more nymphs from developing sexual powers.

Similarly the presence of soldiers appears to inhibit the development of most of the nymphs beyond the worker stage, and thus to regulate the proportion of these useful but costly individuals. This is very necessary, since if there were no such regulation a colony could easily become top-heavy with soldiers; and inasmuch as the soldiers cannot feed themselves, they would constitute a dangerous drain on the economy.

We have gone into some detail about this, the most likely theory of the mechanism of caste determination and regulation in the termites, because of the interesting analogies that it offers with our own society. From time to time, for example, we hear much about a serious lack of trained chemists, physicists or engineers. Such a lack is publicized and this stimulates young people to seek training in these fields. In so doing they tend to avoid fields where there is less danger of an actual surplus. Of course the system, like all based on the so-called law of supply and demand, works very imperfectly, tending to bounce inefficiently from a condition of surplus to one of scarcity and then back again. In the termite society there are no lures and no rewards. The inhibitory social hormone mechanism prevents the development of any more individuals of a caste as soon as an adequate number has been produced, and thenceforth automatically continues to exercise its inhibitory control until, by the death of enough members of the caste, the inhibition is lessened or removed.

Needless to say there are great differences between various species of termites in the proportions or even presence of various castes and subcastes. In some there are no true workers, only a few soldiers and many developmentally arrested soldier nymphs occurring in addition to the sexual forms. In others there are few soldiers but many distinctive workers. Perhaps there is more than one inhibitory substance involved. In still others there are neither mature workers nor mature soldiers, all the work being done by nymphs and nymphlike individuals. In some species no secondary reproductive individuals develop; in others a few may be found but only on the fringes of very large colonies, far removed from the inhibitory source of the primary king and queen. In still other species a great many of the secondary reproductive individuals are found despite the presence of the primary ones. Such differences must have adaptive value, correlating with special features in the economies of the different species. But it will be many years before we will be sure of even the major details of the social mechanisms that control them.

Foods and Food Habits

The characteristic food of the termites, considered as a whole, is wood. Many species, however, seldom if ever eat wood but concentrate upon grass and general plant debris. And some species have evolved the same habit as the leaf-cutter ants (Attini) and tend fungus gardens, on the produce of which they nourish parts of the colony.

Curiously enough, the termites are unable to digest cellulose, although this substance composes the major part of the diet of the wood-eating forms, for they lack glands in their digestive tracts to secrete cellulase, the enzyme that digests cellulose. They have, however, evolved a relationship of mutual dependence (biologically a symbiosis) with many different species of bacteria and protozoa, the latter being the flagellated forms of the Hypermastiginae. These one-celled organisms, which are fundamentally aquatic, live and multiply within the termites' digestive tracts, sometimes in specially enlarged portions of the hind intestine. Since they are able to digest cellulose, with which the wood-eating termites constantly supply them, they produce in this way the foods that the termites actually utilize. Undoubtedly many surplus bacteria and protozoa are also used by the termites as food. If this appears to be a somewhat roundabout way of getting nourishment, a little reflection will show us that it is no more than what we ourselves often do as a matter of course. The dairy farmer cannot use as food the grass and hay he feeds to his cattle or goats, but he obtains food from these animals as a result of his having fed them. The fact that the termites' livestock live in their intestines is not without parallel in man, either; for as a matter of fact, we are probably dependent upon bacteria nourished in our intestines for at least some of the essential Vitamin K.

Many or perhaps all termites do not thrive on a diet of pure wood, despite the symbiotic bacteria and protozoa, and there is considerable evidence that at least some wood broken down by fungi is needed in every termite's diet. Usually this automatically becomes available, since termite burrows in even sound, clean wood are soon invaded by many fungi growing on the walls of the tunnels as well as on the termites' excreta. The food of many termites that do not harbor any of the intestinal symbionts is probably chiefly or entirely these wood-digesting fungi and bacteria and their products.

In Africa and Asia, but not in Australia or the New World, many termites gain a very important supplement to the diet of the colony by cultivating fungi. This is done in efficiently constructed chambers which are usually somewhat separate from the true nesting chambers. Within these the fungi are grown in masses of a shape that allows the maximum surface area for the crop. The termites' own excrement is used as the medium on which the fungi are cultivated, a very different technique from that of the Attine ants that cut green leaves and bring these to the nest as a culture medium. The termite fungi are harvested and used as food for the mature sexual individuals and the young nymphs, but not for the colony as a whole.

Some termites forage regularly in the open on the surface of the ground for grass and dead leaves and other plant debris and then carry these back to the nest. The workers and soldiers of such species (e.g. the Australian *Drepanotermes*), which have functional eyes, go out on their foraging expeditions chiefly at night, but often on cloudy days.

The great majority of termites, however, seldom if ever come out into the open air except for the emergence of the sexual forms during the colonization flights. Most of the soil-inhabiting species burrow underground to wood or other suitable foods that are in contact with the soil, and then tunnel into this. Many others construct tubular galleries on the surface of the ground, along which they pass without leaving shelter. These tubes are often built high up on the trunks of trees or over rocks or the stone, brick or cement foundations of buildings. It is through such tunnels that termites often gain access to wooden houses or other structures, even though an effort has been made to exclude them by constructing the house so that there is no wood in contact with the ground. Almost certainly termites are attracted to wood by its odor, which they are able to sense at some distance even through the soil.

Cannibalism is a constant and normal factor in the diet of many termites, although there is considerable controversy as to the amount that takes place in particular species. Wounded or crippled individuals are certain to be torn to pieces and eaten, and perhaps the same happens to the old. In some termite nests, however, accumulations of the heads of many individuals, as well as miscellaneous rubbish, are found walled off in special chambers.

Termites by no means confine their attentions to dead wood, but in many parts of the world attack and seriously damage or kill living trees. Very large trees are frequently invaded for the sake of the heartwood, which may be tunneled out for the entire length of the trunk. Sometimes the cavity thus formed is stoppered with earthen plugs. Considerable damage is thus done to eucalyptus in Australia. Fruit trees and vegetable and other crops are often destroyed or seriously damaged by the large Australian *Mastotermes*, as well as by other species in most tropical regions. One species in India does great damage in the tea plantations.

A curious habit of a number of species is that of damaging lead-sheathed telephone and other electric cables laid in the ground. There is no doubt that the termites actually chew the lead, thus admitting water to the contained wires, but the reasons for their doing this are not clear. Most likely they are attracted by the moisture that condenses on the metal.

The nests of the **Australian Compass Termite** (*Omitermes meridionalis*) are nearly always oriented along a north-south line.

Nests and Other Structures

A great many species of termites build nests or homes; these are called termitaria. They range all the way from objects no larger than a man's head and constructed of chewed wood pulp to giant earth-cement mounds that may be twelve feet in diameter at the base and twenty feet high. In all cases the materials used are cemented together with various mixtures of saliva, fecal matter and the secretions of the frontal glands of the soldiers.

The round or oval wood-pulp nests that are built in trees by some species are often a common feature of tropical forests. The most familiar types are fastened to the trunk, where they may be very prominent, but some apparently have no large central body but are diffuse and spread along the branches. The slender tubes through which the colony maintains its contact with the ground can be seen extending up the trunks. Some of these "carton" nests may be as much as three feet in diameter. Within them is a maze of perhaps dozens of layers and thousands of interconnecting passages. In Brazil we have sliced open many such nests in order to collect the termites; yet we never have failed to be surprised each time at the speed with which nasuti concentrated at the point of danger. The nests offer little defense against larger predators, such as arboreal anteaters and other animals that make a practice of feeding on termites; but they do offer a great deal of protection against the many other insect-eating animals that hunt entirely by sight. They also give the colony adequate safety from extremes of wetness and dryness; the first of these is a crucial matter in vast areas of the Amazon forest that are regularly flooded every year to a depth of several feet, making the maintenance of a purely terrestrial colony impossible.

The earthen termitaria are a familiar sight in the open landscapes of most semiarid and savannal regions of Africa and Asia, Australia and Central and South America. The techniques of construction differ greatly from species to species, and to some extent locally within species. In general, soil is cemented together with various secretions. So firmly constructed are some of the termitaria that it may be extremely difficult to break into one even with pick and shovel. They are certainly an efficient defense against many predators, although such powerful animals as the African aardvark and the big South American tamandua are able to break into them easily. Many other animals frequently take advantage of the shelter of the termitaria; one Australian parrot, for example, regularly excavates its nest cavities in them. Within an earthen termitarium the arrangement of galleries and passageways is quite consistent, surrounding and radiating from a deeply hidden chamber that contains the royal pair, the original king and queen. The tiny passageways that suffice for the movements of the nymphs, soldiers and workers are far too small to permit the queen to move about, even if she should still be able to drag her enormous abdomen, swollen many times with the incredible growth of her ovaries. She may thus be two to three inches long and an inch and a half in diameter. Attended by her faithful consort and assiduously fed, groomed and cared for by nymphs and workers, she is forever immured within the royal chamber, where she may continue for years her great output of eggs.

One of the most interesting of the above-ground termitaria is that built by the compass termite, *Omitermes meridionalis,* a species with a rather restricted range in the district about Darwin in northern Australia. The large mounds are relatively thin and raised on edge, so that a mound twelve feet high and ten feet long may be but three and a half feet thick. The long axis is invariably quite accurately oriented along a north-south line, so that the broad faces are toward east and west. Many suggestions have been made about the value of this remarkable consistency of orientation, ranging from adaptation to the force of the wind action to the effects of terrestrial magnetism. The answer probably hinges on orientation to the sun, with consequent temperature control in the galleries and chambers within.

The speed with which colonies repair their termitaria, and the difficulty of removing or leveling them, at times makes some of the mound-builders a serious problem on airfields. Structures large enough to endanger aircraft taking off or landing may be erected almost overnight.

Many other termites construct elaborate nests in the ground without any aboveground structures, adding underground tunnels that radiate out to great distances. Some of these subterranean nests are most exquisitely constructed, with multiple walls and perforated with millions of tiny holes for ventilation. Some species build vertical ventilation tubes extending upward through the soil and into the air for a considerable distance. In contrast, many other subterranean termites may hardly be said to build any regular nest at all, the colony living in an extensive meshwork of branching tunnels that may extend for great distances, turning frequently to reach some wooden object accessible from the earth. It is noticeable that in such species the queen may never attain great and unwieldy proportions, and may move freely about as the tunnels tap new sources of food. We may compare such termites with the army ants, which construct no definite abode and keep more or less constantly on the move.

As we mentioned above, the vast majority of termite societies, despite considerable differences from one another, follow with relative uniformity a pattern of efficiency and self-support, in contrast to the bees, wasps and ants, where many species have evolved various types of social parasitism. Among the rare exceptions are such species as *Termes fur,* which usurps space in the nests of *Constrictotermes* species and steals the hosts' food, and a few other species of *Termes* that make their nests in the termitaria of some of the fungus-growing species.

However, termite colonies are invaded by a great host of widely different insects which, by various devices, succeed in parasitizing them as a source of food and shelter. Many of these invaders have become highly specialized for the production of secretions that are greatly relished by the termites, and thus offer something to their hosts; many others, however, are outright thieves and parasites. Some of the guests are not merely tolerated but welcomed, fed and carried about by the termites. We shall have much more to say about such curious developments when we discuss the ants, which are perhaps even more imposed upon in this way than the termites.

Economic Importance

The wood-eating termites are among the most destructive of all insects as far as the works of man are concerned. It is fortunate that they have never really succeeded in penetrating the north temperate regions to an extent comparable with their occupation of the tropics. In vast tropical areas no wooden article is safe, especially if termites can gain direct access to it from the earth. The workers of the wood-eating species never break through the surface into the open air (except of course at the time of the colonization flight) even though the wood is in total darkness; they apparently are warned by minute changes in the humidity and perhaps in the tensions within the wood. But they will eat out a beam, sill or floor board, or an article of furniture to which they have gained access from a wooden floor, so that nothing but the merest shell remains. This will then collapse into dust and fragments at the slightest additional strain. Paper is perfectly good termite food, so that not the least of the dangers of an infestation is that to books and records. The powderpost termite, *Constrictotermes brevis,* which has been introduced from the tropics into the extreme southern United States, is particularly reprehensible in this respect.

The majority of the fifty-five species of termites in the United States and southern Canada are of relatively minor economic importance. The drywood termite, *Kalotermes minor* of the western United States from Washington south into Mexico and east into Texas, is a serious pest, doing great damage to houses, posts and lumber. It is especially difficult to control because it colonizes and feeds in wood that has no contact with the soil, and is therefore almost impossible to exclude short of drastic chemical treatment of nearly everything wooden. The very much larger damp-wood termites (*Zootermopsis*) of western North America are much less serious pests. They are the largest of North American termites, the soldiers being as much as three-quarters of an inch long and the winged forms having a wing expanse of more than two inches.

The most widespread and destructive of the North American termites are the species of *Reticulotermes* (Plate 7) at least one of which occurs practically everywhere northward into Canada. Damage done by these termites is seldom very extensive in the northern states (except in the exaggerated advertising of those eager to sell expensive protection and control to householders), but may be very serious in the southern states. They are rather small, soil-inhabiting species that make no very definite nests and lack the grotesquely swollen queens of so many of the tropical species. Wherever wood is in contact with the soil, burrowing pioneers are liable to discover the opportunity and lead an invasion that may result in damage to the object. Houses are seldom weakened seriously enough to collapse, as often happens in the tropics, but the total damage done by these insects in the United States runs to millions of dollars annually. We should note, however, that certain carpenter ants (*Camponotus*) are also destructive wood-borers and tunnelers, and that the termites are often blamed for the work of the ants. We recommend that everyone who has, or fears that he may have, a termite problem obtain the excellent United States Government booklets on the subject and study them before taking action.

We must not let the direct damage that termites do to man's economy blind us to the fact that in the economy of nature these insects play an extremely important, even an essential, part. Much of what they do is of direct value to man, and more is of even greater indirect benefit. The ground-dwelling species have an enormous effect in loosening, mixing and aerating the soil, to say nothing of fertilizing it. In vast areas they play as important a role as the much publicized earthworms do in other regions. Their tunnels also are important in making soil pervious to water, which can thus be absorbed quickly instead of running away over the surface, being lost to the area and causing erosion.

In breaking down immense quantities of dead wood, and in making still further enormous quantities of wood susceptible to quick decay by fungi, the termites are of great service to all forms of life. If

it were not for their eating of wood, a very large proportion of the organic matter formed by plants in the tropics would be locked for long periods of time in dead trees, instead of being made almost immediately available for the use of the next generation of plants and animals. In the boreal forests, where there are no termites, the dead wood of one or two hundred years ago may be found lying about on the ground, of little use to any living creatures. Think of the deadening effect on human economy of a law that completely froze every person's estate for even fifty years after his death! In the tropics there is little of this, thanks to termites. A dead tree, even a dead limb on a living tree, is quickly converted into termite substance and excreta and so, with what the businessman would call a very quick turnover, is made available for succeeding generations of life. Undoubtedly a large part of the luxuriance and abundance of plant and animal life in the tropics is thus due to the termites. Man must realize this and make intelligent use of it, while protecting himself, as necessary, against the termites' direct inroads.

Classification

The tendency in recent years has been to split the termites into more families than students a generation ago considered advisable. The actual study and classification is largely based on extremely technical structural characteristics, chiefly of the soldiers, and upon the organization of the colony.

Five families are recognized. Of these the Mastotermitidae, the most primitive, are found only in Australia, where so many other primitive relict animals occur. The others are world-wide. The Kalotermitidae are relatively primitive and chiefly wood-eaters, although a few live in the soil. They include many destructive species, such as our North American dry-wood termite *Kalotermes minor* and the powderpost termites. The widespread Hodotermitidae are also relatively primitive in structure, but have quite advanced foraging and nest-building habits. They include our damp-wood termites *Zootermopsis*. The Rhinotermitidae include many species with very pronounced nasuti, but others have merely normal soldiers like our *Reticulotermes*. They and the very large family Termitidae are almost world-wide. These two families are considered the most advanced of the termites and include the majority of the species with highly specialized societies and nest-building habits.

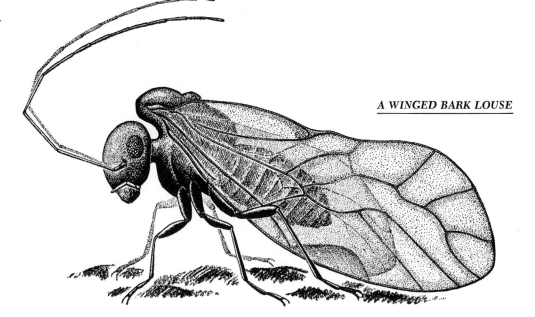

CHAPTER V

A WINGED BARK LOUSE

Earwigs, Thrips, Embiids and Booklice

WE include here a number of small orders, all of which have an incomplete metamorphosis. They have no other special resemblances or relationship to each other and are not necessarily primitive in other ways. Some of them, in fact, are not only quite advanced insects but are very narrowly specialized for their own ways of life. Some are of particular interest to the biologist and naturalist, and some are of considerable economic importance.

EARWIGS
—Order Dermaptera

The earwigs (Plate 6) are a small but cosmopolitan order consisting of about nine hundred species. They are common in Europe and most warm regions, but are, curiously enough, poorly represented in the northeastern United States and Canada. The maritime earwig, *Anisolabis maritima,* is locally abundant beneath loose debris along beaches of the eastern seaboard, occupying a rather narrow zone just at the high-tide mark; and a considerable number of native species occur in the southern, central and western states. The European earwig, *Forficula auricularia,* is sometimes a serious pest in greenhouses, where its secretive habits make it difficult to control.

Earwigs are somewhat flattened and rather slender, usually dark brown to black, with a shiny or leathery-looking integument. They have simple biting mouthparts. Some species are wingless. When wings are present the front ones are characteristically much shorter than the abdomen and leathery and, like the front wings of a short-winged beetle, meet in a straight line down the middle of the back. The pleated hind wings are tucked under the front wings when at rest, but when expanded they unfold like a fan into a wide-spreading membranous wing that, in some species, has a curious resemblance to a human ear. It is possible that this is how the proverbial name for the group had its origin, rather than from the superstition that they crawl into the ears of sleeping persons.

Earwigs range in size from species less than a quarter of an inch long to others an inch and a half in length. Their most outstanding characteristic is the pair of strong, sharp, forceps-like cerci that protrude from the rear end of the abdomen. These are elevated menacingly in defense, and are capable of giving a sharp pinch, although none but the largest species can draw blood from even the tenderest human finger. It is very doubtful that the forceps are ever used as an offensive weapon but they may serve some function in courtship, and seem to have a utilitarian place in replaiting the hind wings and tucking them beneath the front ones. At least a few of the species have a special gland on the abdomen that exudes a liquid with a creosote-like odor.

Earwigs are nocturnal and therefore seldom are seen unless one is looking for them under stones and dead bark or in loose debris, although they are sometimes encountered unexpectedly. In Europe they are proverbial inhabitants of old thatched roofs. The majority of the species are herbivorous; and it is some of these that may become serious pests on flower and vegetable plants, especially when introduced about seaports. Others are scavengers on dead animal matter, and still others are outright carnivores, preying chiefly on the eggs and small larvae of various insects.

An outstanding characteristic of some earwigs is the manner in which the female watches over her eggs until they hatch and after that broods and protects the larvae. Except in the highly specialized social forms, it is rare to find among insects any evidence of parental care for the eggs or young or, for that matter, even contact between parents and their offspring. Most insects merely deposit the eggs in a suitable place and leave them. This brief period of maternal care on the part of the earwigs represents, however, merely the first step toward social organization.

THRIPS
—Order Thysanoptera

Although a relatively small order consisting of perhaps fifteen hundred species, the thrips (Plate 18) exist in countless numbers; and since many of them feed upon cultivated plants they sometimes are of concern to the agriculturist. Most of the species are less than four or five millimeters in length, with long, slender bodies and very narrow heads. The mouthparts are extremely peculiar, forming a set of structures adapted for piercing and sucking, with an asymmetrical development of certain of the parts that has no counterpart in other insects. The wings are absent in many species; when present they are very slender and almost without venation, and bear fringes of long hairs. The tarsi of most of the species have at their tips a peculiar bladder-like organ, the use of which is not well understood. The metamorphosis is incomplete, the larvae resembling the adults strongly; but between the last active larval stage and the adult there are one or two inactive stages during which the insect hides, takes no food and acts like a pupa.

Thrips often infest the blossoms, buds, leaves and roots of plants in great numbers, sometimes doing considerable damage because of the sap they suck. They multiply very rapidly, especially in dry, hot weather. In the course of their reproduction, eggs frequently and sometimes consistently hatch without being fertilized. This phenomenon, known as parthenogenesis, is widespread as a normal way of reproduction in a great many groups of insects and other invertebrate animals, although almost unheard of among the vertebrates.

The suborder Terebrantia includes the common thrips of the family Thripidae, which lay their eggs in living plant tissues. The majority of the economically important species are all members of this family. Most of the species, such as the onion thrips, *Thrips tabaci,* and the wheat thrips, *Frankliniella tritici,* live in the flowers and foliage of a variety of plants; only a few are restricted to a single food plant. The greenhouse thrips, *Heliothrips haemorrhoidalis,* exudes minute reddish drops that turn black when left on foliage, seriously marring the appearance of the plant. The species that live in blossoms often injure the plant so that the leaves are stunted and the fruit scabby or scarred; and those on grasses cause a shriveling of the tops, called the silvertop condition, which effects growth and seed production. Even more serious may be the transmission of plant-diseases, both those caused by bacteria and those of fungus origin.

The suborder Tubulifera contains perhaps more species than the Terebrantia, but much less is heard about them since they are chiefly of no economic importance. The majority feed on dead leaves, fungi etc. Some cause the formation of plant galls, inside of which they live; and some are predatory, feeding upon other very small insects. One species in Florida is thus of considerable benefit by feeding on a destructive whitefly. This suborder also includes the largest of the thrips, such as the Australian giant thrips, *Idolothrips spectrum,* of which mature individuals may be a half inch long.

EMBIIDS
—Order Embioptera

The embiids are small, fragile insects that seldom exceed a quarter of an inch in length. Their wings are narrow and have few veins, so that they have very weak powers of flight. The thorax is unusually long and narrow, sometimes exceeding the abdomen in length. The mouthparts are for biting, and the metamorphosis is incomplete. Less than a hundred species are known.

Embiids are found chiefly in the tropics the world around, but include a few species of temperate regions. In North America they are known from only the southern and southeastern United States, where they feed chiefly on dead plant material. Occasionally they become established in greenhouses farther north but never present a serious problem.

[continued on page 49]

1. A **Silverfish** (*Lepisma saccharina* Although seldom seen, this primitiv insect is a frequent guest in our hous holds.

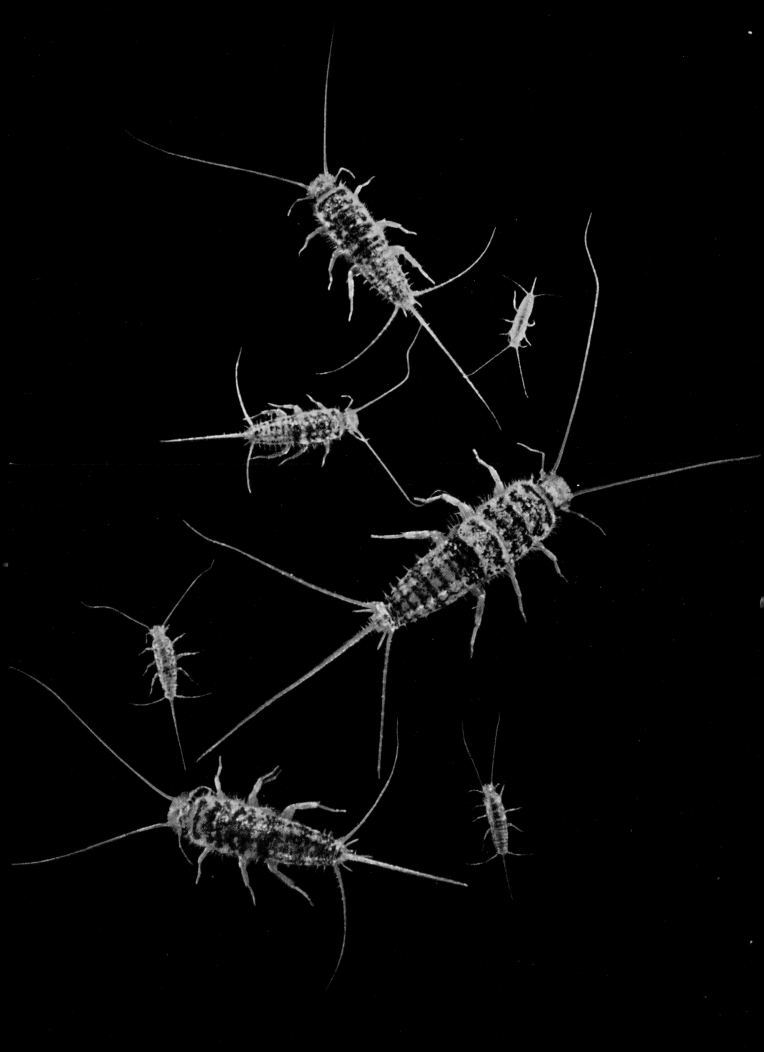

2. A **Cockroach** (*Periplaneta americana*). Member of the most ancient group of insects still in existence.

3. A **Jerusalem Cricket** (*Stenopalmatus fuscus*). A large, flightless Orthopteran common in Western North America and often injurious to young plants.

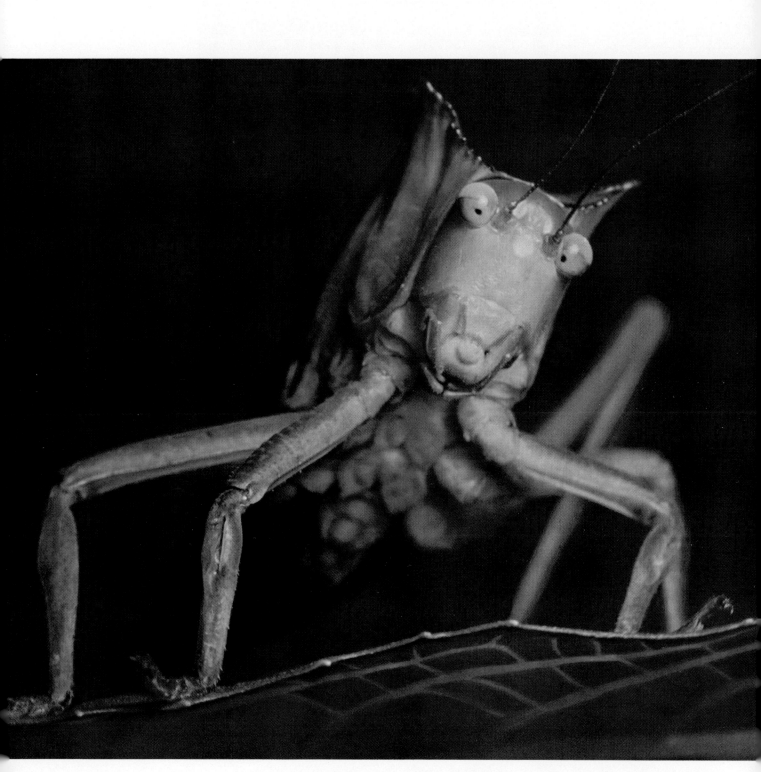

4. A South American **Katydid** (*Phyllolophus ponderosa*). The slitlike structure in its front tibia is a tympanum, or ear.

5. **A Walking Stick** (*Diapheromera femorata*). Common in eastern North America where at times it may be abundant enough to defoliate large areas of woodland.

6. **An Earwig** (Order Dermaptera). The forceps-like appendages at the rear of the abdomen are, despite their appearance, seldom used in offense.

7. **Termites** (Order Isoptera). Termite societies are among the largest and most complex known in the animal kingdom. Workers, such as these, are often very destructive to wood.

8. A Tropical **Lubber Grasshopper** (*Thrasyderes leprosus*). Many tropical members of this order are brilliantly colored. This one was collected in an Andean cloud forest, altitude 10,000 feet.

9 and 10. (Above) An **Ichneumon Wasp** (*Tetragonochora*) whose bold pattern and bright colors presumably serve as a warning to potential enemies. (Below) A Peruvian **Katydid** (*Aganacris*). This immature Long Horned Grasshopper is believed to obtain some protection from predatory enemies by mimicking the warning colors of the Ichneumon Wasp shown above.

11. A **Dragonfly** (Order Odonata). The enormous size of the eyes correlates with the extremely acute vision necessary for the capture of prey in mid-air.

12. A **Dragonfly** (*Sympetrum pedemontanum*). A common European species.

14. A Mayfly (*Hexagenia limbata*). This newly-emerged winged form is called a subimago and will have to undergo another transformation before it is fully adult.

3. **Stonefly** and **Mayfly** exuviae. The cast skins of aquatic nymphs, from which the adults have emerged, have been left clinging to plant stems near the water's edge. The lower one at the far left is a Mayfly skin.

15 and 16. (Left) Eggs of **Harlequin Cabbage Bug** (*Murgantia histrionica*) with a number of newly-hatched nymphs, and (above) a brightly colored adult.

17. **A Stink Bug** (*Edessa rufomarginata*). Members of this family usually suck plant juices and may do damage to fruits and vegetables.

18. **Thrips** (*Hoplothrips*), immature. Often abundant in rotting wood and fungi.

19. A **Plant Bug** (*Lygaeus kalmii*) common in North America.

20. An **Assassin Bug** (*Sinea*), member of a family that preys on other insects, sometimes including species much larger than itself.

21. A Coreid **Plant Bug** (*Pachylis pharaonia*) of a species found in Peru.

22. **Giant Water Bug** (*Belostoma*), showing the male carrying the eggs on his back.

23. A **Water Boatman** (Family Corixidae) swimming by means of its long, oarlike hind legs.

24. A Leafhopper (*Graphocephala coccinea*) that is abundant in eastern North America.

25. A Cicada (*Tibicen*). Its shrill songs resound in late summer.

27. A Cicada that has liv in the soil for seve years has just emerg from the nymphal sh which is shown clin ing to the bark.

26. A South American **La tern Fly** (*Lanternaria* which, despite its nam is not a fly and does n give off light.

28. A **Tree Hopper** (*Heteronotus*). Even in a group noted for the extraordinary shape and over-development of the prothorax, this species from tropical forests is unusual.

29. **Tree Hopper** (*Campylenchia lechia*). When immature these often line up on a twig like a row of spines.

[continued from page 32]

The females are wingless, but the males are either winged or wingless. An unusual characteristic of the order is the production of silk by glands located in the first segments of the tarsi, and its emission through a set of hollow bristles as a liquid that immediately hardens. This is a unique location of the silk apparatus among insects.

Our chief interest in the embiids lies in their social habits. The majority of the species are gregarious and may be found, sometimes in groups of several hundred, beneath stones and bark, where they run backward and forward with equal facility in silk-lined tunnels. Some western species are to be found beneath masses of dried cow manure. One species, *Embia major,* has been described as living gregariously in a nest composed of series of superimposed silken tunnels connected with one or two deep subterranean chambers. The tunnels serve not only as a retreat and protection against predatory insects but also as a means of maintaining the proper balance of moisture and temperature that seems to be an important factor for the survival of the embiids. The larvae as well as the adults of both sexes take part in forming the silken lining of the tunnels, scampering back and forth and exuding silk as they go.

BOOKLICE, PSOCIDS and OTHERS
—*Order Psocoptera*

The small and minute insects included in this order agree in having biting mouthparts, sometimes of a peculiar type, an incomplete metamorphosis and wings (when these are present) with a greatly reduced venation. They are quite diverse and have been classified in various combinations in two or more orders under several names. About one thousand species have been described.

The best known are the very small, wingless species commonly known as booklice or dustlice, which often infest houses in large numbers. They are especially likely to be abundant among old books and papers, where they feed on the paste, glue and sizing, as well as on fragments of animal and de-caying plant matter. Sometimes they feed upon our foods, and they not infrequently turn the tables on entomologists by destroying insect specimens in collections. The most familiar species is *Liposcelis* (*Troctes*) *divinatorius,* which has been called the "death watch" because of the attribution to it of the ability to produce regular ticking sounds. It is very likely, however, that this species does not tick, but has been receiving credit (or blame) for the sounds made by such other psocid species as *Clothilla pulsatoria.* The ticking is made by the females, supposedly as a mating call, by tapping a knob near the tip of the abdomen on the paper or other surface on which they are resting. Similar ticking sounds are also made by the "death watch" beetles of the family Anobiidae, which commonly bore into old beams and wood.

The winged psocids consist of a considerable number of species that live outdoors on bark, leaves, stone walls and fences, in birds' nests and so forth, where they feed on lichens, fungi and similar dry plant material. Some are rather specialized eaters of fungi and molds. Many live gregariously, and clusters of individuals of all ages may be found on bark under a canopy of fine silk. Sometimes they fly and drift through the air in swarms. They have little, if any, economic importance, although it has been suspected that some species may disseminate fungus spores.

The mouthparts of the forms described above are characterized by a special rasping structure on the first maxillae, which is used for chiseling and gouging dry plant matter. Those of the Zoraptera, which some authors regard as a separate order, lack this. They are minute insects, less than three millimeters long, that live gregariously under bark and in humus. Some forms lack wings, and others have wings but shed them by breaking them off at the bases. This and other characteristics point to a relationship between the Zoraptera and the termites. Only a few species are known, but all of the major continents except Europe have representatives. *Zorotypus hubbardi* of the southern United States is the best-known American species.

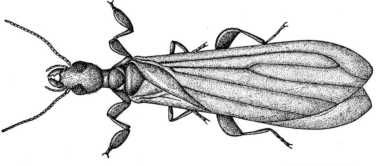

AN EMBIID

CHAPTER VI

Some Aquatic Insects

A MAYFLY NYMPH

WE have included here the mayflies, stoneflies and dragonflies, three of the four orders of insects which during their larval lives inhabit fresh water and breathe oxygen that they take directly from the water, but which as adults are airborne and breathe as normal terrestrial insects. These three are primitive in many ways, especially in having biting mouthparts and incomplete metamorphosis, but are not closely related to each other. The mayflies and dragonflies are known from lower Permian fossils, and so have existed as independent groups since relatively early in insect evolution. The stoneflies are not known from so early an era and seem to be more closely related to the Orthoptera. The fourth aquatic order, the caddisflies (Chapter IX) are more highly advanced, having a complete metamorphosis, and are obviously members of an entirely different group of orders. In addition to these four, individual species or families of several other orders have become adapted to the aquatic life, sometimes quite successfully. We thus find various members of the bugs (Hemiptera), beetles (Coleoptera), flies (Diptera), moths (Lepidoptera) and the Neuroptera, as well as a scattering of representatives of still other orders, more or less adapted to life in fresh waters. But these are all isolated groups within orders that are predominantly terrestrial. It is only in the mayflies, stoneflies, dragonflies and caddisflies that the aquatic life is the rule and not the exception.

The original arthropod ancestors of the insects were themselves aquatic. Undoubtedly they respired by means of gills, thin-walled sacs filled with blood,

through the walls of which took place the exchange of oxygen and carbon dioxide with the water. This is still the method of respiration of the Crustacea, which represent the great arthropod stock that remained in the water. But as the ancestors of the insects moved up onto the land and in time evolved into insects, the blood gills were abandoned, being highly unsuited for land life. Instead there developed the system of tracheae that the modern insects and their terrestrial relatives possess today. These are extremely thin-walled tubes with characteristically spiraled walls, which receive air through a set of paired spiracles and conduct it to all parts of the body. This is an unmistakable air-utilizing system that could have evolved only during a very long period of life on land.

It is significant that all of the truly aquatic insects have such a tracheal system, even in the larval stages during which they live in the water. Most of them have gills, to be sure, but these are not the same blood-filled gills that were possessed at an extremely remote time by their pre-insect ancestors, but are a new type that is a modification of the tracheal system. Such a tracheal gill contains a supply of air-filled tracheae into which oxygen diffuses from the water. Even when blood gills are present, as they are in a few insects, they are not at all of the original primitive type, nor is the chemistry of respiration the same as in the ancestral aquatic pre-insects. And of course the aquatic larvae are eventually transformed into adults that are relatively ordinary tracheate insects. All of the evidence, then, points to the conclusion that the aquatic insects went through a long ancestral period as terrestrial insects. After that they gradually moved into fresh waters and in time became adapted to life there, doubtless finding abundant opportunity and no great competition. There is no evidence that any of the aquatic insects are descended from ancestors that have always been aquatic.

The aquatic insects are almost completely limited to fresh water. A few odd species live in brackish water along the seacoasts, and a few of these are able to live in fully salty water. One small group of water striders (*Halobates*) lives on the surface of the ocean, and a few forms have become adapted to extremely salt or alkaline inland waters. It is surprising that more species have not taken advantage of the opportunities offered by a marine environment, for we would expect a group as dynamic as the insects to have succeeded in re-entering the oceans of the world as it has the fresh waters. Perhaps the Crustacea, which remained in salt water and attained a success there comparable to that of the insects on land, acted as a deterrent by presenting too much competition.

Within the limitations imposed by their small size, the insects have spread to every possible part of the fresh-water environment, where they are nearly everywhere the dominant invertebrates just as they are on land. We find them from the swiftest, coldest and most highly oxygenated streams and waterfalls to the warmest, most polluted and oxygen-deficient ponds. Only in very deep waters have they failed to prosper. Wherever they occur, we find forms exquisitely adapted to the specific environments. The majority of the stoneflies, mayflies and caddisflies are plant-eaters, feeding either on living green plants, the sole producers of food, or on plant debris. So, likewise, are many important groups of the orders that are only partially aquatic, especially various families of the bugs, beetles, moths and flies. All of these are primary consumers; they are the first link in the animal food chain, transforming basic plant material into animal matter. In turn they are fed upon by many other aquatic insects that have adopted lives of predatism, such as the entire order of dragonflies and many families of the partially aquatic orders. And all are fed upon by the larger vertebrates, especially by the fishes, for which they form a major food. We cannot calculate how many scores of thousands of tons of plant matter the aquatic insects annually transform into animal matter, making it available as food for the larger animals that form the upper links of the food chain. But we can be certain that without them there would be very few fresh-water fishes for man's food and recreation; and that there would be only fractional populations of many of our most characteristic fresh-water animals, from mergansers and ospreys to mink and otter.

MAYFLIES
—Order Ephemeroptera

Nowhere is the prodigality of nature more extravagantly displayed, nowhere are her timelessness and her seemingly purposeful direction of life activities towards the preservation and continuance of the species more strikingly demonstrated, than in the tremendous productivity and the unusual life cycle of the Ephemeroptera. The adults (Plate 14) emerge on summer evenings in such numbers that our windshields are spattered, our lake shores piled high with windrows of bodies and cast skins, and streets so littered that the morning chore of sweeping them is a major problem to many a lake-front and riverside town.

The life span of the adult is incredibly short, sometimes lasting for a few days but often for only a few hours; and in those few hours all activity is concentrated on the perpetuation of the species. The legs are weak or almost lacking; but no time is spent in walking. The wings are small, triangular in outline and usually very fragile; but strong powers of flight are not necessary. All that is required of the wings is to keep the body in the air for a few hours in the dancing nuptial flight and then to bear the female to a suitable place in which to lay her eggs. The mouthparts are degenerate and sometimes wanting; but the adult does not need to eat, since the nutrients required to give the energy for this day have been acquired in the one, two, three or even four years that, as an active nymph, it has spent in the waters beneath. Nor does the digestive system function as such, since no food is taken into it and no enzymes, those catalysts of the chemical activity that our appetites demand of us, are needed; it must only become filled with air, the stomach a balloon-like reservoir and the hind gut a complex valve, thus reducing the body's specific gravity.

Mayflies are probably best known for their so-called nuptial flights. The dancing mass composed of hundreds and sometimes thousands of individuals, mostly males, flying upward and then falling in endless repetition, is usually seen over or near water in late afternoon or early evening, although species of *Baetis* may swarm in the forenoon, those of *Tricorythodes* at midday, and a few other groups at almost any time throughout the day. Occasionally a female joins the throng and is promptly seized by a male, the two then leaving in a soaring, dancing course that permits them to mate in solitude. Although a few species do not swarm, the great majority do, and the enormous size of their hordes is proverbial. Woodsmen have reported their campfires being extinguished by the falling bodies of mayflies as clouds of them drifted overhead.

The eggs are usually laid just after sundown. The body of the female may be filled with them from one end to the other, even up into the rear of her head. She may scatter them a few at a time, as do species of the common *Heptagenia,* flying into the wind, upstream, in a series of up-and-down, zigzag flights. Dropping into the water, she is carried back downstream by the current, only to rise again upward and forward, and thus maintain a constant position in relation to the banks of the stream. When her task is completed she may fall to the water and with outspread wings drift on, out of sight. Others, such as the common *Isonychia* and *Ephemera,* may drop all of their eggs in a single mass; still others lay them under stones beneath the water, for which purpose the female may go below the surface, never to reappear. *Cloeon dipterum* of Europe, *Callibaetis vivipara* from Brazil and a closely related *Callibaetis* from New York have been found to give birth to living young, which emerge from eggs retained within the body of the female.

In many cases the eggs are marvelously contrived little structures with one or more skeins of fine yellow threads. These uncoil upon becoming wet, and thus anchor the egg either by entangling it with objects in the water or else by fastening down adhesive, button-like discs located at the ends of some of the threads. Some eggs hatch in ten days, others not for several months. A single female lays from several hundred up to several thousand, so that the security of the species is insured despite the hazards that now await the nymphs.

The young nymph that hatches from the egg is unusually well adapted to meet the requirements of some type of aquatic environment. Some species of *Ephemera* and *Hexagenia* burrow in mud and soft banks with their strong, fossorial front legs, tusked mandibles and narrowed heads. *Cloeon, Siphlonurus, Blasturus* and others swim actively among aquatic plants in quiet water; *Stenonema* and *Iron,* with their flattened bodies and flattened appendages, live where the water is fast-moving, perhaps even at the brink of a waterfall, clinging to the stones, sometimes half-concealed by the silt that settles in the crevices or is caught in algal growths on the surface of the stones. Many *Ephemerella* are completely hidden by silt and moss. Other groups live in decaying vegetation or under stones.

With but few exceptions mayfly nymphs (Plate 13) are herbivorous. They eat plant tissue that is in bits too small to be of interest to any but the tiniest of creatures, turning it into animal tissue as they themselves grow and molt and grow some more, this animal tissue all the while becoming of ever greater importance as food for young stoneflies, dragonflies and aquatic bugs, for fishes, amphibia, turtles and aquatic birds.

The nymphs usually have six or seven pairs of abdominal gills, the first pair vestigial and the others two-branched. Often one of the branches is broad and flat, protecting the delicate filamentous one beneath; and sometimes they are both turned upward toward the back of the insect so as not to be injured by rubbing against the stones or sand beneath. In one species of *Rithrogena* the flattened branches are expanded and overlapping, forming an oval ventral disc that acts as a sucker to help in holding the body to the stones in swift-moving water. A species of *Ephemerella* has attained the same result by a soft fringe of hair around the entire periphery of the abdomen. Sometimes the upper lamella of the first functional pair becomes so flattened and expanded as to conceal all of the gills behind; and these gills are then further protected by a fringe of hair that filters out silt and other foreign particles that might clog or injure them. And sometimes the gills are all protected by being located in a branchial chamber roofed over by an expanded carapace.

When fully grown and ready to transform, the nymph swims or crawls out of the water, sometimes transforming immediately as it comes to the surface, sometimes crawling a few feet up the shore or onto rocks, pilings or walls. The winged form that emerges can take flight at once and breathe through spiracles, but it is not yet an adult. It is an instar unique among insects, the subimago; and yet another molt is necessary before the glistening body, fully formed transparent wings and mature compound eyes of the true adult appear. When the adult is of a species that is short-lived, the subimaginal stage may last only a few minutes; in those species that live as adults a day or more, it may last several hours, sometimes as many as twenty-four, and fly conspicuously with the adults. The females of *Palingenia* and *Campsurus* never shed the subimaginal pellicle, and the males of *Oligoneura* do not shed the part over the wings. Most mayflies hibernate as nymphs and probably have only one brood a year, although it has been shown that they sometimes mature much faster.

Three world-wide families, the Ephemeridae, Baetidae and Heptageniidae, are divided into about seventeen subfamilies. Three of the subfamilies are not yet known from North America, while one, the Baetiscinae, with one genus *Baetisca,* is peculiar to North America. About one thousand species have been described.

Mayflies the world over are known to the fisherman, though he may call them shadflies, willowflies, cobflies, eelflies or dayflies; and so rich is the vocabulary of the follower of Izaak Walton that when these flies are simulated with a twist of silk and a hackle feather, and the resulting artifice tied to his line, he may refer to them as the dun, the drake, the spinner, the cocktail, the dotterel or the mackerel. What he calls them when they become caught out of reach in a tree, so that he is forced to break his leader, is not within our province.

STONEFLIES
—Order Plecoptera

Like the mayflies, this small order is of economic importance the world over because the immature stages serve as food for trout, bass and other game fish. Almost any stone picked from a clear mountain stream, from under a waterfall, or in a well-aerated lake will have clinging to the bottom one or more of the flat, elongated nymphs, their long antennae, long cerci and widespread legs holding them close to the stone for a moment until the capable legs take their stride and the creature scampers to the other side. Since they must have reasonably pure and well-aerated water and are sensitive to any reduction in the oxygen content, their presence is an indication of, at the most, but slight organic pollution; while conversely their absence from a seemingly suitable stream is often a sign of contamination (Plate 13).

The adults are structurally not unlike the Orthoptera except that the mouthparts are greatly reduced, the integument soft and the wings membranous. Although some species have biting mandibles, it is unlikely that many of the adults feed at all, though a few nibble on buds and leaves; and one species, *Taeniopteryx* (*Brachyptera*) *pacifica*, has been reported as a pest of fruit trees in the Northwest. This species, however, is doubly exceptional because stoneflies seldom wander far from the water where they grew to maturity. A few of the greenish species fly actively during the days of midsummer, but most species are weak and erratic fliers, have little directional control and are more commonly found resting on stones or tree trunks near the water's edge. When disturbed they run or slip away rather than take flight. The characteristic outline of the resting adult is elongate, flat and parallel-sided, with the long antennae sweeping forward and the long cerci protruding to the rear. The fore wings are held wrapped around each other, folded lengthwise along the back with the tips surpassing the end of the body and the large hind wings folded fanwise beneath them.

The eggs are dropped into the water in bundles held loosely together in a thin membranous packet which is often seen protruding from the abdomen of the female. The nymph is basically like the adult in structure except for its lack of wings and a few modifications that adapt it to its life in the water. Fringes of hair make the legs more efficient as swimming organs; and the tufts of tracheal gills, over which water is kept circulating by the more or less continual up-and-down motion of the legs, are located at the bases of the legs, and in some species under the head and the tip of the abdomen

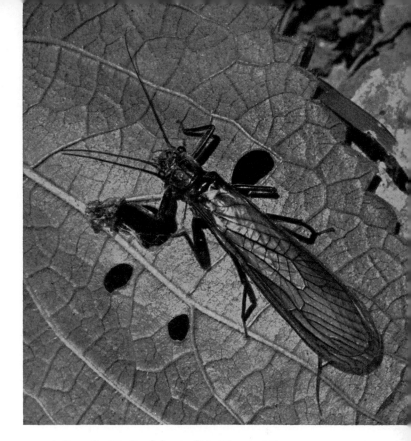

A **Stonefly** (*Perla abdominalis*). These are important as food for fish, especially in streams.

too. These gills are lacking in a few species, but in others may be persistent even into adult life.

Some of the smaller species transform into the adult in a single year, but larger ones spend three to four years as nymphs, undergoing as many as thirty-three molts. When ready to transform they crawl several feet from the water, fasten their toothed tarsi to a stone, tree trunk or other support, and split lengthwise down the back of the thorax.

Pteronarcys is one of the largest of the stoneflies. *P. californica* of the western United States is three and one-half inches long in the nymphal stage and is not only avidly eaten by fish but has been used by Indians as food. Other species, such as those of *Capnia*, are quite small, some never exceeding three-eighths of an inch in length.

In North Temperate regions adult stoneflies may be found nearly the year round. Species of *Capnia* emerge in the warm days of late winter and may even be seen resting on the snow; members of the family Nemouridae come out in early spring, followed by the Pteronarcidae and Perlidae; while in midsummer the greenish *Isoperla, Alloperla* and *Chloroperla* abound.

Many of the adults are quite beautiful, some of the Australian species strikingly so. One of these has a jet-black body with bright orange pronotum. Several have rich red hind wings tipped with purplish streaks on the borders. The nymphs of *Perla* and *Acroneuria* are handsomely patterned in brown

A Florida **Dragonfly** (*Libellula needhami*). It holds its long, spiny legs basketlike beneath its mouth as it swoops through the air.

or black and yellow. These two, incidentally, are voracious carnivores, having biting mouthparts, so can well afford to flaunt their colors.

The world fauna of stoneflies is not well known; about three thousand species have been described. There are at least five families in North America and Europe although some authors recognize as many as seventeen. One of these is common in Australia, where three additional families are recognized. Two families are peculiar to the New World.

DRAGONFLIES and DAMSELFLIES
—Order Odonata

Of all the insects it is the dragonfly of which the poet most frequently sings; it is the dragonfly that the sensitive Oriental artist depicts on silk and china or casts in silver and bronze; and it is the dragonfly that, as reflected in folklore and colloquialism, catches the small boy's fancy and at the same time frightens him with fearsome but groundless tales of having his ears or eyes sewed up by those darning needles, those horse-stingers, those snake doctors! We might add that of all insects these are the most sporting; and he who has ever prided himself on his wing shooting or his fly-casting should try his skill at netting a spirited, tantalizing Aeschnid.

Dragonflies (suborder Anisoptera) (Plate 12) and damselflies (suborder Zygoptera) are known the world over wherever there is permanent fresh water in which their eggs may hatch and their young grow to maturity. Most of the forty-five hundred

known species are beneficial. However, a few of the big *Aeschna* and *Anax* species are minor pests in fish hatcheries, where their nymphs attack young fish; and even the small *Leucorrhinia* has been reported in British Columbia as a pest in the salmon hatcheries. The adults of at least one species, *Coryphaeschna ingens,* cause some loss to commercial beekeepers in the southern states by destroying queen bees (hence its local name of bee-butcher). But these are exceptional, and the majority of species consume tremendous numbers of mosquitoes, flies and gnats in both their larval and adult stages. Odonate nymphs are thus an important link in the aquatic food chain, both as predators and as food for larger fish.

The Odonata have several strikingly characteristic features that admirably equip them for their role as skilled aerialists and rapacious predators. The head is hollowed out at the rear and loosely attached to the prothorax so that it rotates freely, enabling the insect to look in all directions by means of its enormous compound eyes (Plate 11). In the damselflies and in some of the Gomphid dragonflies the large projecting eyes are pushed apart by the widening of the head so that they become almost hemispherical, the head seeming to serve primarily as a pair of eyestalks. In the remaining dragonflies the eyes overspread the top of the head, where they often meet in a long, median eyeseam. The large, heavily sclerotized mandibles are toothed and ridged for cutting and grinding; the maxillae are bifid, one branch with five or six long, sharp tines for holding and turning the food, and the other platelike and sensory, aiding in holding the lacerated particles that escape the grip of the jaws. Both the mandibles and maxillae are concealed, except for their tips, by the large, flat, three-lobed labium, variously toothed and hooked, which in the Libellulidae has the median lobe so reduced that the lateral lobes meet to form the stem of a T-shaped slit. The prothorax is small and often largely covered by the head, but the fused meso- and meta-thorax form a large boxlike structure for the support of the powerful wing muscles, so tilted that the insertion of the wings is well backward and the base of the legs well forward. The legs are long and slender and extremely spiny. They are of little importance in locomotion save to enable the dragonfly to climb enough to orient itself for better concealment or observation, or for a better take-off. The position of the legs well forward on the thorax is of utilitarian importance during flight, when at least the first pair and possibly also the second are used as a basket for capturing insect prey on the wing. When at rest they are held beneath the mouth, with spines interlacing, to hold the victim or the half-chewed remnants and to stuff them into the mouth. The front legs are often swept over the large, prominent compound eyes in the seemingly endless grooming that goes on after a meal, the close-set spines of the front tibia doubtless serving as an eye brush. The wings are very long and membranous, nearly equal in size, with a remarkable bracing of the veins that gives both pliancy and strength, serving in some species as powerful organs of flight. The tremendously elongated abdomen usually is comparatively slender, in some damselflies being not much stouter than a coarse bristle, while in some of the Libelluline dragonflies it may be strongly depressed and thus quite broad.

Although many adults, especially of the damselflies, have a weak, fluttering flight and may sometimes even be caught between thumb and forefinger, the majority are noted for their swift, darting, soaring motions and for their power of strong, sustained flight. Their flight patterns are different and distinctive. The Gomphidae make short, seemingly purposeful loops and then alight, usually on the ground; the Cordulinae fly at considerable height, often near the tree tops; the Agrionid damselflies often flutter like butterflies or vibrate their wings like syrphid flies. The majority of the Libellulidae, however, especially the Trameini, are noted for their great soaring flights and most of the Aeschnidae for their agility and speed. The latter have earned for themselves such names as the Costa Rican "reyes" or "kings" and the Christmas Islander's "rajah." In tropical regions a flock of fifty or more Libellulidae may patrol a river's edge for two hours or longer at sunset. *Pantala flavescens,* a cosmopolitan species, although doubtless caught up and aided by the wind, has alighted on ships more than two hundred miles from shore. Measured flights of sixty miles an hour for short distances have been authenticated, although reputed speeds of ninety miles an hour are certainly exaggerated. Immense migrating swarms of *Libellula maculata* are frequently reported in Europe, and of *Hemicordulia tau* in Australia, but for the most part the migration instinct is not well developed.

It is in agility that the Odonata excel; in hovering at arm's length and then darting out of reach in the flick of an eye; in patrolling a "beat" with unfailing regularity, only to shoot instantly upward or

A **Damselfly** (*Calopteryx virgo*). One of the few damselflies with dark wings.

sideward at the slightest suggestion of interception; and in swooping down and up and back and forth as they scoop out of the air the mosquitoes, midges and other minute winged creatures on which they feed so voraciously. And it is for their seeming ability to outwit, as well as to madden and frustrate, the collector that they have become notorious in the eyes of the entomologist. Quietly perched on a rock or on a limb projecting over the water they sit sunning themselves for minutes at a time, now and then taking off to circle the pond or to scoop up a mouthful of midges, but returning to the exact same spot, to perch at the exact same angle, again and again. The collector, confident that the creature, too agile and too fast to be caught on the wing, can be netted when it returns to its favored perch, takes his stance near the spot and waits—and waits. The object of his desire does not return but alights, unperturbed, some ten feet away.

For the most part the Odonata are sun-loving and often disappear almost miraculously when the skies cloud over. There are exceptions to this, as there are to any rule, and *Aeschna umbrosa,* species of *Boyeria* and *Basiaeschna,* of *Somatochlora* and *Neurocordulia,* are crepuscular. In the tropics there are many more shade-loving forms of dragonflies such as *Gynacantha* (some of which get up into North America) and of such damselflies as *Hetaerina, Protonema* and *Palaemnema.* Most weird and exciting of all of these shade-loving forms are members of that extraordinary group, the Anormostigmatini. Known only from tropical America, they are recognized by the extreme length and excessive slenderness of the abdomen, and by the long, narrow, similar fore and hind wings with a large, many-celled, colored stigma. They include our largest known existing Odonata, *Megaloprepus coerulatus,* which is five inches long and has a wing-spread of seven inches. When it is flying in the dusk of the tropical forest, the body is scarcely discernible and only the colored tips of the wings can be seen weaving up and down. Some collectors say that the wings seem to rotate like the arms of a windmill. Many natives believe them to be human spirits that have but recently become disembodied, and insist that they be left undisturbed.

In some species mating occurs on the wing, in others when perched upon a twig or hanging from the foliage. In some it may last but a few minutes, in others for an hour or more.

The females of those species that have an ovipositor lay their eggs in mats of submerged vegetation, in reed stems along the shore, in overhanging leaves and even occasionally in woody stems. The delicate little tropical damselfly *Neoneura* has been seen ovipositing on floating nuts and seeds. Species of the damselflies *Agrion* and *Hetaerina* back down into the water, the body and wings encased in a silvery coat of air, to lay their eggs a foot or more beneath the surface, sometimes remaining submerged for as much as half an hour. A *Cordulegaster* lays them in sand, mud or gravel in shallow water or at the water's edge, penetrating the bottom with her stout, blunt-tipped ovipositor while her beating wings hold her poised above the surface. The Gomphidae and Libellulidae do not have an ovipositor but dip the tip of the abdomen into the water, thus washing the eggs in masses from the scoop-shaped genital plate. *Tetragoneuria* lays them in a gelatinous string which becomes entangled with submerged vegetation, and *Microthyria* attaches them directly to the undersides of floating leaves. In the process of egg-laying the female may be unattended or may be accompanied by the male, who grips her head and prothorax with his strong terminal appendages, just as he held her in copulation, so that the two ride tandem style. He may cling to her while she makes recurrent descents to lay her eggs or may fly with her to within a few feet of the water and then release her, marking time overhead while she drops to the surface, clasping her again as she rises, to circle off and away before repeating the performance.

The nymphs may hatch from the eggs in a few days or not for eight or nine months, depending upon the species or the season. They must then pass through a dozen or more molts. Most species reach maturity in one year but some require two, three or even more years.

The odonate nymph is one of the most grotesque of living creatures, as well as one of the most rapacious. The lower lip (labium) is enormously lengthened and has hinge joints at the base and across the middle. When not in use it is folded beneath the face like the snout of a gas mask. But it can be shot out forward with incredible speed to catch an unwary prey with the strong, movable hooks of the lateral lobes, and to draw it back to the mouth. The labium then serves as cup and saucer for holding bits that may fall from the jaws. Although the damselfly nymph respires by means of three gill plates at the end of the abdomen or by a series of small gill tufts along the sides, the dragonfly nymph has a unique mechanism that not only serves for respiration but provides nature's prototype of jet propulsion. The posterior end of the digestive tract is enlarged to hold longitudinal rows of minute flat gills. The expansion and contraction of this chamber sucks in fresh water, and therefore oxygen, for the insect's use; and this can be expelled with such force that the nymph is shot violently ahead through the water.

The nymphs have become adapted to many types of aquatic environment. The long, slender-bodied, delicate damselflies and the big, cylindrical Aeschnids, green or mottled in color, cling to reed stems and weeds or crawl in the vegetation, darting swiftly from one place of concealment to another. Greatly flattened, long-legged Libellulids sprawl on the bottom, their bodies often hairy and becoming covered with silt and slime, and occasionally overgrown with algae or bryozoa. And in the sandy bottoms the Gomphidae, with flat, wedge-shaped heads and strong, digging front legs, squirm and push their way into the sand, leaving the elongated, upturned terminal segments of the body protruding into the water. Individual species have their particular preferences: certain Aeschnids cling only to the blackish twigs and logs of woodland streams; *Thaumatoneura* of the Central American tropics is always in the splash of waterfalls, unless it has been swept downstream by the rushing torrent; and *Erythrodiplax berenice* often breeds in coastal lagoons where the water is very brackish.

Perhaps the most unusual location for aquatic nymphs is high in the trees of the tropical American rain forests. Here the large "air plants" or bromeliads grow, attached to the limbs and trunks of the giant trees. These epiphytic plants have unusual leaf bases which form a reservoir that may hold one or more quarts, or even gallons, of water. In this water *Mecistogaster* females lay their eggs, thrusting their long, bristle-thin abdomens deep between the leaves to do so; and here the nymphs develop, feeding on other aquatic insects that have also taken advantage of the unusual water supply.

And now a devastating anticlimax! and a reminder that nature's ways are unpredictable even though we insist on trying to rationalize them. A group of damselflies in Hawaii seem to have found terrestrial nymphal life more satisfactory than aquatic after all. Some species of *Megalagrion* live in streams and pools in the normal manner, although other aquatic insects are moderately rare; but *Megalagrion oceanicum,* although breeding in the water, crawls out on the banks or in wet, marshy places to seek terrestrial insects upon which to prey; and *M. oahuensis* has become truly terrestrial, laying the eggs in slits along the midribs of leaves of the lily *Astelia veratroides* and of *Freycinetia.* The nymphs of this species crawl about on the land, in the ground litter at the bases of dense clumps of ferns and in between and around the leaf bases of *Astelia;* they even seem to dislike the water that sometimes accumulates there and when caught in it are ungainly, ill at ease and unable to swim. Their short, thick caudal appendages are swollen and densely hairy and no longer function as gills.

Transformation of Odonata takes place on a twig, reed stem, bridge piling, bank or beach, usually only a few inches from the water but occasionally as much as twenty feet away. It occurs most successfully in the early morning before forag-ing birds have become too active, because the emerging teneral body is soft and helpless and highly vulnerable. The pulsating of the heart pumps the blood plasma into the short, broad abdomen and rumpled baglike wings, which thereby become elongated and stiffened. The pale greenish iridescence of the latter may remain until they have become thoroughly dried, the wing membranes in contact and the wing veins rigid; this may be a matter of a few hours or it may take days.

The adult Odonata are noted for their beauty, for the iridescence and brilliance of their color. Some have bright blood-red bodies with a splash of carmine or blotches of gold and black on the wings; others have the great swollen thorax a shocking chartreuse green combined with bright cerulean blue in a bold arrangement that few modern artists would dare attempt. Many of the damselflies are ultramarine blue or violet, marked with black; and some Oriental and Pacific island species have their delicate wings splotched with rectangular patches of iridescence that sparkle in the sun like stained-glass windows. The depth of the reflections of the many-hued eyes surpasses description. Unfortunately this color of the eyes disappears at death and most of the body colors fade shortly in preserved and dried specimens. Some species of dragonflies acquire a rich bluish white pruinescence when fully mature, as though becoming hoary with age; others may exhibit a slight bloom that serves to deepen their early adult coloration.

The dragonflies differ from the damselflies in having large compound eyes tending to overspread the top of the head, and the hind wings larger than the fore wings. They hold their wings outspread when at rest. The Petaluridae, an ancient family known from many fossil forms, are found as a few scattered, remnant species in Japan, Australia, New Zealand, Chile and the United States. The Cordulegasteridae, mostly large, hairy and striking in appearance, are cosmopolitan except for large areas in Africa. The quite inconspicuous and rather primitive Gomphidae are world-wide but tend to be large and robust in the north Orient. The Aeschnidae are the dominant family of today, most of them large, of brilliant blues, greens and browns and with many advanced specializations. The Libellulidae are also world-wide, have a characteristic specialization of wing venation, and include the most plastic and rapidly evolving forms.

The two main families of the damselflies, the Agrionidae and Coenagrionidae, are found the world over, but many of the subfamilies, of which there are some fifteen, are more localized in distribution.

A third suborder, the Anisozygoptera, has been established for the aberrant *Epiophlebia superstes,* known from Japan and India.

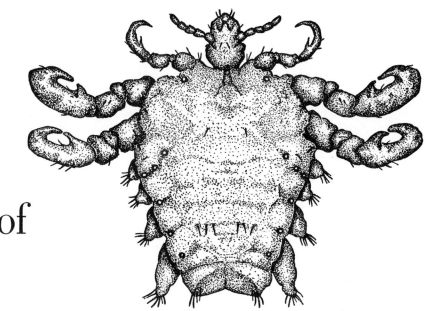

CHAPTER VII

A CRAB LOUSE

An Array of Parasites

PARASITISM is actually one of the commonest ways of life in the animal kingdom, as well as in such great groups of plants as the bacteria and the fungi. Although the idea may be emotionally abhorrent to some people, the truth is that perhaps a half of all animals are parasitic on other animals. In this respect the insects are quite representative, as might be expected in such a dynamic and opportunistic group, for a great many species of many orders live as parasites of other insects and invertebrate animals as well as of most of the land vertebrates.

In the true use of the term a parasite gains nourishment, and often shelter and other useful things, from its host without the use of obvious violence. By its own individual activities the well-adapted parasite disturbs its host but little, which is efficient; and provokes its defenses as little as possible, which is the better part of valor. It is almost a requisite, therefore, for successful parasitism that the parasite should be both smaller and weaker than its host. Many parasites, it is true, build up such populations upon a single host that they may enfeeble it and even cause its death. But this is merely evidence that they lack efficient means of controlling their own multiplication, and does not affect the essential parasitism of the individual.

The most competent parasites, therefore, are the ones that do the least damage to the hosts, thereby conserving them as a future source of supply for themselves and for their offspring. Regarded thus, two of the orders that we discuss below, the lice

and the fleas, are efficient and well-adapted parasites. They are, in fact, the most outstanding groups of parasitic insects, although various other groups scattered among a number of other orders are equally well adapted and perhaps, in some cases, even more advanced.

It does not detract in the least from the essential parasitism of these insects that many of them are more or less victimized by other organisms that use them as vectors or carriers. The rat flea is a perfectly normal parasite despite the fact that the organism of bubonic plague that it transmits causes the death of its host. The flea is, in fact, actually harmed by being exploited by the bubonic plague organism, since when its host dies it must find a new one. It is this secondary parasitism that gives us such an intense personal interest in these parasitic insects, since they are the carriers of some of the most serious epidemic diseases of man and his domestic animals. And it is this extremely vital involvement of ourselves that makes it advisable that we learn and understand the essential facts of parasitism.

True parasitism as a way of life is almost inevitably accompanied by certain changes of the adapting parasite that make it more efficient in its very narrow mode of existence. Structures that were necessary to the parasite's free-living ancestors, such as eyes and other sensory organs, and legs, wings and other locomotor structures, tend to degenerate and be lost. The parasite may, in fact, find such things an actual handicap once it has established itself on or in a host. It is true that sensory and locomotor structures may be helpful in finding the host; and many parasites still possess these organs, perhaps retaining them until they have become established on the host and then discarding them. Really advanced parasites, however, have lost some or all of such "free life" structures, and have substituted for them a greatly increased power of multiplication. By this means they effectively saturate the environment in which individuals of the host species occur, making it possible that the movements of these individuals themselves will bring them into contact with the parasite's offspring. Perhaps all but one or two of the offspring will fail to contact a host, and will therefore perish. This does not matter, for if only one or two do become established on hosts, the parasite has done its duty adequately by its species. Actually this merely represents a still higher type and a more intensive degree of parasitism; for the parasite is, in effect, using more of the host's substance to increase its own reproductive rate, and then is parasitizing the powers of locomotion of the host to get the next generation of parasites established.

Many invertebrate animals such as roundworms, tapeworms and flukes have evolved far more advanced types of parasitism than any of the insects, most of the latter being at best relatively primitive parasites. Nevertheless the parasitic insects have evolved many secure ways of solving the problems of existence and efficient distribution of their offspring to new hosts.

A very large number of insects, chiefly flies and wasps, are customarily referred to as parasitic because their methods of attacking the other insects upon which they feed resemble those of the true parasites. However, since their efforts invariably result in the death of their hosts, they are really predators with a parasite-like technique, and are more correctly called "parasitoids." We shall discuss them later at considerable length, since they are of enormous importance both biologically and economically.

THE LICE

—Order Anoplura

The lice consist of two quite different groups, which various authors have at one time or another considered as separate orders. None possesses wings at any time. The body is extremely flat, an adaptation that enables a louse to cling close to the skin of its host and avoid being scratched off. Correlated with this change of body form the spiracles, which normally occur in a row along each side of the body, have shifted to the upper surface where they have free access to the air. One of the two groups has sucking mouthparts and lives only on mammals,

feeding on blood which is obtained by puncturing the skin. The lice of the other group have mouthparts of a specialized biting type; they live chiefly on birds, although a small number are parasites on mammals.

BITING, BIRD or FEATHER LICE
—Suborder Mallophaga

Some twenty-six hundred species of these insects are known. With their biting mouthparts they feed almost entirely on feathers, hair and miscellaneous skin debris. Although they have been observed drinking blood from a wound, and will feed on dried blood, there is no evidence that they ever normally puncture the skin to get blood. Strictly speaking, they are scavengers rather than true parasites. They are not, therefore, directly harmful to their hosts. At times, however, they multiply in such numbers as to build up a heavy infestation on individual hosts; and when this occurs they may seriously damage the feathers or so weaken the bird by their continual irritation that it may then succumb readily to disease. This happens most frequently to birds kept in confined quarters in captivity. The dust baths that so many birds take at frequent intervals are without doubt of great service in getting rid of the lice.

The bird lice are so narrowly adapted for life on the hot, moist and oily bodies of birds that they can live for only a few days at most away from the host, or on its body after it has died. It is therefore extremely unlikely that very many of them get from one bird to another except when two birds are actually in bodily contact with one another. Some transferral of lice certainly must take place, however, in the nests.

The entire life cycle is passed on the body of the host, the eggs being cemented separately to feathers or hairs. The larvae resemble the adults very closely except in size and the lack of sexual maturity, and eat the same foods. They complete their growth after several molts and transform directly to the adult stage, the whole development taking but a few weeks.

The majority of the bird lice are specific in their host relationships, a given species occurring on only one or a number of closely related birds. Exceptions to this are most frequently found where the same louse occurs on predatory birds such as hawks as well as on the birds on which they prey. This host specificity is quite usual among parasites, and is of considerable interest since we often find a rather striking correspondence of degree of relationship between the different lice and the different groups of birds on which they occur. This has been used by students of the birds to draw inferences of relationship between apparently unrelated birds on the basis of the close kinship of their lice. The curious wingless bird *Apteryx* of the Australian region has always been something of a mystery. It was found, however, that its lice, of the genus *Aptericola,* were really very closely related to others of the genus *Rallicola* that were widely distributed parasites on rails. Encouragingly enough, independent research on the birds themselves confirmed the theory that *Apteryx* is more closely related to the rails than to other living birds.

The groups of these biting lice that are parasitic on mammals may be distinguished by the possession of only one claw at the end of the tarsus instead of the pair found in the bird-inhabiting groups. This correlates with the greater efficiency of the structure thus formed for grasping the base of a hair, an efficiency that reaches a much higher degree in the entirely mammal-inhabiting sucking lice. One small family, the Gyropidae, is confined to Central and South America, except for two or three species that occur on the guinea pig and have been carried along with it as it has spread to parts of the world far from its original South American habitat. The much larger family Trichodectidae contains many species parasitic on a large number of mammals, being known chiefly from domesticated ones such as horses, cattle, sheep, goats, dogs and cats, but also from wild species such as bears, porcupines, beaver and deer. The Australian kangaroo louse has shown rare adaptability and transferred its affections to the domestic dog, thus becoming widespread.

A number of the species on domesticated birds and mammals are of considerable economic importance because of the damage they do and the expense of controlling them. The most notorious is the abundant chicken louse, *Menopon pallidum,* which also infests such related birds as pheasant and guinea fowl. Poultry and pheasant raisers have to take constant precautions to prevent heavy infestations that will seriously handicap the growth of the birds and lower egg production. Ducks and geese are hosts to a number of species, turkeys to still others. The domestic pigeon suffers from the extremely elongate *Columbicola columbae.* Even the tiny hummingbirds have their more or less specific lice; and fittingly enough, the eagles have a gigantic species that is perhaps the largest of all. The species found on the elephant, a *Haematomyzus,* is not correspondingly large. It is, however, a most peculiar louse that was for a long time believed to be one of the sucking lice.

SUCKING LICE—Suborder Siphunculata

Although a much smaller group than the biting lice, numbering no more than two hundred or so species, these insects are far more widely known because of the abundance of the two species parasitic on man. Since some of them are carriers of dangerous diseases of man and domesticated animals, they have been extensively investigated by medical and veterinary entomologists. In general body form they differ little from the biting lice, being extremely flat. Their mouthparts are adapted for piercing the skin of the host and sucking blood. There is but a single claw at the tip of the tarsus, which is strong, curved, and activated by a very powerful muscle. This can be snapped tightly back against the last segment of the tarsus, which is hollowed out in such a way that the curve of the claw and the hollow of the last segment fit very closely around a single hair of the host, as the two concavities of the jaws of a pair of pliers fit around a tube or pipe. This forms a very efficient hair-grasping organ, especially since the concavities of the claw and segment are so closely correlated in some species that they exactly match the convex curvature of the particular host's hair. With its extremely flat body anchored securely by the grasp of six of these tarsi, a louse can weather a storm of even the most severe scratching and remain undamaged and unmoved.

Lice occur on a wide variety of mammals, one group even being characteristic on seals, sea lions and walruses, but the majority are on rodents, especially rats, mice and squirrels. One species, *Polyplax spinosus,* which parasitizes the common rat, transmits a trypanosome protozoan parasite from rat to rat. The trypanosomes are a group that include the species responsible for human sleeping sickness (transmitted by tsetse flies) but unfortunately this rat trypanosome does not appear to harm the rodents. The larger grazing mammals also have a number of characteristic lice, of which the short-nosed ox louse, *Haematopinus eurysternus,* is sometimes abundant enough to harm its host; the same is true of the hog louse, *Haematopinus suis.*

Man is the natural host of two lice: the crab or pubic louse, *Phthirius pubis,* and the body and head louse, *Pediculus humanus.* The crab louse, although a widespread and sometimes abundant pest, has never been incriminated as a carrier of disease despite very wide studies of the possibility. The body louse, on the other hand, is the carrier of extremely dangerous diseases. The life histories of these (and of nearly all other lice as well) are quite similar. As in the biting lice, the eggs are laid on the host, typically being fastened singly to hairs. The body louse departs from this to the extent of fastening the eggs to clothing, although its variety, the head louse, fastens them to hairs in the conventional way. The egg is oval and blunt-ended, with a little lid at one end that breaks away fairly easily. Within the egg the embryo develops into a small larva with its head at the lid end. When ready to hatch the larva swallows air and expels this from the anus at the bottom end, thus building up a pressure that eventually becomes strong enough to blow the larva forward and lift the lid. The larva is, in all important respects, a miniature adult, and it feeds on blood from the first. It reaches maturity about a month after the egg is laid and lives about three weeks longer. A female lays about three hundred eggs at the rate of eight to twelve a day, so that a very large population may be built up within the space of no more than three or four months.

The head louse was long considered to be a separate species, but has been shown to be no more than a minor variety of the body louse. It is distinguishable by only very slight structural differences and by its ability to live and breed on the head and to glue its eggs to the hair there. A number of other so-called species of the genus *Pediculus* that have been found on various apes and monkeys are now known to be likewise only subspecies of *P. humanus*, a matter of some interest as evidence (as though any more were needed) of the essentially close kinship of these animals with man.

Irritation from louse bites may be a source of insomnia, irritability and mental depression apparently disproportionate to the cause. The body louse is, however, chiefly important as a vector of the extremely serious diseases of typhus and relapsing fever, both of which often have fatal consequences. A third disease, trench fever, was of great importance during World War I but has practically disappeared since then. Serious epidemics of these diseases arise when conditions are such among human populations that personal sanitation becomes impracticable or impossible. The crowded masses of civilians, displaced from their homes and wandering about or herded together in camps and subject to exposure and malnutrition, that seem to accompany modern war on an unprecedented scale, furnish ideal conditions for large-scale breeding and transmission of lice from person to person. At such times epidemics have arisen that have caused scores of thousands of human deaths.

Endemic centers of typhus, where the disease continues to exist even during "normal" times, and from which it can spread to begin epidemics elsewhere, exist in Ireland, eastern Europe, most of Asia, North Africa, Mexico, Peru and northern Chile. Many peoples, it must be remembered, do not look upon personal infestation with lice with the distaste or horror that are automatic with most of us. In some regions, in fact, the support of a flourishing fauna of lice is considered a sign of manliness. Among many millions of people religious taboos prohibit killing a louse, although it is permissible to remove a specimen from one's own person

and deposit it unharmed on a neighbor. No better way of encouraging an epidemic can be imagined. The threat of louse-borne epidemics is always with us, awaiting only still further wars or social upheavals to be transformed into reality.

Typhus is transmitted from an infected louse to a human in one of three ways. The bite of the louse is infective. Lice crushed by scratching on the skin are very dangerous, their body fluids being rubbed into abrasions or feeding punctures. And the feces of the lice, abundantly deposited on the clothing and skin, also contain the virus of the disease; and these, too, can give an infection, often merely by being rubbed into the skin.

Fortunately for the human species, some modern insecticides such as DDT are excellent, cheap and practical means of controlling body lice. A dust containing 10 per cent DDT in a neutral powder can be blown under the clothing in wholesale, speedy treatments which, repeated at intervals, can almost or completely exterminate the lice. Without such insecticides and the techniques for their wholesale use, there would have been many more millions of deaths during World War II and the troubles that have followed it. Such work must, however, be continued even during peacetime, in the hope that the endemic centers where the virus of typhus lurks in waiting can be cleaned up before conditions again favor the outbreaks of epidemics.

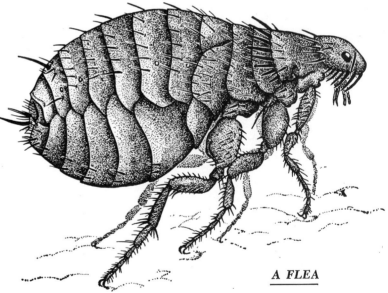

A FLEA

THE FLEAS
—Order Siphonaptera

Adult fleas, like lice, are external blood-sucking parasites of birds and mammals. There, however, resemblance between the two orders ceases, for they represent almost completely antithetical approaches to the same problems of life by two groups of insects of widely divergent ancestries, structures and habits. The lice are more or less related to the bugs (Hemiptera) and like them have an incomplete metamorphosis in which the larva is quite similar to the adult. The entire life cycle can therefore be passed on the host, the larvae and adults feeding side by side. The fleas, however, perhaps more closely related to the flies (Diptera), have a complete metamorphosis, a type of development in which the larvae and the adults are extremely different. The flea larva is a greatly reduced, legless, maggot-like creature that shares none of the parasitic habits of the adult. It lives as a scavenger among debris, though sometimes feeding in part on dried blood, usually in or near the nest of the host. Moreover, between the larval and adult stage some time must be passed in the inactive pupal stage that would have little chance of surviving if it were on the host, even though it is enclosed in a cocoon. With a few very rare exceptions it is, then, only the adult flea that visits or lives on the host.

While larval fleas are relatively simple, the adults are complex animals with many specializations for their parasitic lives. The piercing and sucking mouthparts enable them to take a blood meal in a matter of seconds. Their most obvious characteristics, however, concern their locomotion on the host and their way of escaping its biting and scratching defensive reactions to their presence. In these, also, they are as different from the lice as possible. Whereas both animals are strongly flattened, the body of a louse is depressed, or flattened from back to lower surface, so that it lies very close to the surface of its host. The flea, however, is compressed, or flattened from side to side, so that seen from the front it looks as though it were stood on edge. The strong, hair-grasping legs of the louse enable it to hold very fast to hairs, but not to move quickly. The flea, on the other hand, has long, slender legs with which it can run fast between the hairs of its host, a mode of progression for which its body form is highly adaptive; and when danger presses too close it can soar away in a leap many times its own length. The louse is adapted to anchor itself and weather the storm of its host's defensive reactions; the agile flea escapes them before they have more than barely begun. The body of the flea is covered with a much harder exoskeleton than that of a louse, as a result of which it can spend long periods away from the host in no danger of desiccation.

If number of species is any criterion, the fleas are a more successful group than the sucking lice, though not the biting lice, totaling more than a thousand known species, with many more as yet unknown. Their ability to live away from the host and feed on debris during larval life gives their food economy a much broader basis than that of the lice, since they thereby exploit two different sources of nutrition and are also kept from such complete and narrow dependence upon the host as is the case with lice. Adult fleas are quite long-lived, those of some species being able to survive for nearly two years. Considerable time may also be spent in the pupal stage in the cocoon. Certainly anyone who has ever camped in an abandoned cabin and been practically inundated by hordes of fleas that have been waiting in their cocoons for months for a good human blood meal can testify to their ability to live for long periods without a host. Under similar conditions lice would have either departed with the last host to leave the premises, or have died of desiccation and exposure within a few days. In every way, in fact, the fleas impress one as a far hardier and much less narrowly specialized group.

Usually each species of flea parasitizes only a single species of animal or a number of closely related species. But in the absence of the usual host the majority will feed from a completely different species of host. Dog and cat fleas thus readily attack man, and rat fleas will do the same, as well as feed on a large variety of rodents. The flea on a strange host, however, does not feed normally, but instead makes a series of feeding punctures rather than a single one, as though it were being partially repelled by the unaccustomed taste. In thus feeding from abnormal hosts the fleas show a much greater adaptability than most parasites. As a matter of fact it is this very adaptability that makes them dangerous to man as carriers of disease, since nearly all that transmit bubonic plague, the most important of the flea-borne diseases, are rodent fleas.

One of the most unusual fleas is the tropical species variously known as the jigger, chigoe or sand flea, *Tunga penetrans*. Originally a native of the New World, it has been widely disseminated in Africa and Asia. This is not the mite that is widely known in the central and southern United States as the "chigger" or "red bug" and that causes intensely itching, red spots on the skin. The jigger flea is the smallest species of the order, measuring only a millimeter long when mature. The adults often swarm in enormous numbers in dry dust and sand about human habitations. A fertilized female, gaining access to human skin, burrows beneath the surface and becomes encysted. The favorite areas are about the feet and ankles, particularly beneath the toenails. There the female's abdomen becomes swollen to the size of a small pea as she matures her eggs, which are extruded from the hole in the skin and drop to the ground. After this she dies. The burrowing in the skin causes intense itching and a great deal of pain; and the swellings often develop into large, infected sores. Deaths from the resultant gas gangrene or tetanus are common. The usual treatment is to pry out the flea before she becomes swollen, but this is a very delicate task since rupturing her will surely cause trouble.

One species, the human flea, *Pulex irritans,* is a normal parasite of man, occurring nearly everywhere in the world that man does. It will also attack many other animals, from badgers and skunks to squirrels and dogs, and is especially common around pigs. In North America it is particularly abundant in the Pacific Coast regions. The common cat and dog fleas, *Ctenocephalides felis* and *canis,* are similarly almost cosmopolitan, although the dog flea occurs more abundantly in cooler climates and the cat flea in warmer ones. Either will bite freely the primary host of the other, and both often attack man. They are, in fact, the species most commonly found in our houses, especially where dogs and cats are kept as house pets. They often breed abundantly in the cracks of upholstered furniture and will breed outdoors in spots frequented by dogs. The dog flea is an intermediate host of the common dog and cat tapeworm, *Dipylidium caninum,* dogs, cats and occasionally humans becoming infected by eating infected fleas. The human flea also serves as an intermediate host of this and other tapeworms.

The rat fleas are best known as the vectors of bubonic plague, one of the worst scourges of the human species. Perhaps the greatest epidemic was that known as the Black Death, which raged throughout Europe in the fourteenth century, killing at least one-fourth of the population. Other epidemics followed, of which the great plague of London in 1665 was one of the most dramatic. Nearly 70,000 people died out of a population of 460,000. No one who has ever read Defoe's *Journal of the Plague* or Samuel Pepys' *Diary* can ever forget the death carts rumbling through the London streets to the cry of "Bring out your dead," or the legend scrawled across nearly every door, "God have mercy upon us."

After that, the epidemics waned and almost ceased in Europe, for reasons that we do not understand. Certainly there was no shortage of rats. Then in 1896 the plague appeared in India and claimed ten million lives in the next twenty years; and it still takes its scores of thousands there. It has made sporadic appearances in nearly all of the tropical countries, killing perhaps one hundred thousand people in a single epidemic in Java. The disease is known to be endemic in a considerable area around San Francisco, California, from which at any time an epidemic may start. Cases have been traced as far east as Nebraska, carried by the fleas of such common rodents as prairie dogs and squirrels.

The actual cause of the plague is a bacterium known as *Bacillus pestis.* It kills rats as well as man,

the factor that, together with the willingness of the rat fleas to bite man, is responsible for the transmission of an epidemic to humans. As more and more rats die of plague, their fleas leave them and seek other hosts; and as rats become scarcer, more and more humans are bitten and infected and the epidemic waxes to a maximum. Even the human, the cat and the dog fleas may be carriers during an epidemic. The most important carriers, however, are the Indian rat flea, *Xenopsylla cheopis,* and the European rat flea, *Ceratophyllus fasciatus,* together with a dozen more fleas of rodents from Africa and Manchuria to California and Brazil.

Modern methods of quarantine and health inspection do much to prevent the spread of epidemics but are not wholly reliable. Fortunately the synthetic insecticides such as DDT, and the rodenticides such as warfarin, give us extremely effective means of controlling both rats, ground squirrels and the other small mammal hosts as well as their fleas. Despite all that can be done, numerous endemic centers of continual plague infection exist, some in every continent; and it is impossible to feel secure that the plague may not again become epidemic at any time.

The fleas are not limited to mammals, although only a small proportion of the order parasitize other animals. One species has been found on a snake. The most important of the bird species is the small sticktight flea, *Echidnophaga gallinacea,* often abundant in the southern and southwestern United States. At times it is a serious pest of domestic fowl, ducks and turkeys as well as dogs, cats, rabbits and, rarely, children. Unlike most other fleas, it does not

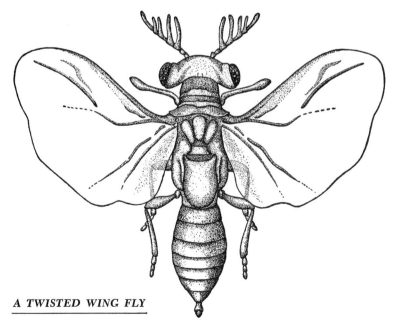

A TWISTED WING FLY

move about once it has become established in a favorable spot on a host, but remains for days or weeks with its mouthparts deeply and firmly embedded. Large clusters often form on the heads of poultry or in the ears of small mammals.

THE TWISTED-WINGED FLIES
—Order Strepsiptera

The twisted-winged flies, or stylopids as they are often called, are a most anomalous little order, chiefly of very peculiar parasitic forms. No more than two hundred species are known, although they occur in all of the continents. Because of their very small size and peculiar habits they are seldom seen, even by entomologists. Their relationships to other insects are obscure, although there is some evidence that they are perhaps more closely allied to the beetles (Coleoptera) than to any other order.

The tiny males, which in various species average from one and a half to four millimeters long, have the front wings reduced to small, clublike processes, but the hind wings are broad and fanlike, and folded when at rest. The antennae are large and branched and the compound eyes large and on short stalks. The mouthparts are of the biting type but greatly reduced. The female, on the other hand, is a wingless, legless, saclike creature who never leaves the body of the host in which she develops. The hosts of most of the known species are wasps and bees, and some Homoptera. Both males and females develop within the host's abdomen as larvae and pupate there, with one end projecting slightly between two segments of the abdomen. The males emerge from their pupae in a normal way, leave the host and set out in search of individuals of the host species in which females have developed. The females, however, never leave their pupal shells. Somehow they are fecundated by males through a slit in the upper part of the body. After this they die, but the fertilized eggs that pack their abdomens (there may be as many as two thousand) hatch there and the tiny larvae push out to the outer world through this slit. They are slender and bristly, with long legs, and so can run about and climb up to flowers and other places where an individual of the host insect may come along. If they are fortunate enough to contact a host they enter its body. Once inside, they molt and assume an entirely different form, that of a legless grub, and thenceforth live from the blood and fat body of the host. There are thus two larval forms, the first a tiny, active one and the second, legless and maggotlike. Such a development, which occurs in a few other groups of insects as well, is called a hypermetamorphosis. It is best known in the oil beetles (Meloidae).

Much of the interest attached to stylopids is due to the peculiar effects that they have on their hosts. Even when present in some numbers they seldom kill the host directly. They do, however, have a most drastic effect on its ovaries and testes and secondary sexual structures, which fail to develop or function properly. This failure may extend to such structures as the pollen-carrying legs of female bees and the stings of female bees and wasps, so that the host is not only castrated or sterilized but also rendered incapable of carrying on a normal existence in other ways. Sometimes other body characters of the host are also changed; and this has caused some confusion among entomologists, who have been known to describe such stylopized individuals as new species.

A few species of one family found in southern Europe are known to be free-living, the highly reduced females having been found beneath stones. It is not known on what they feed.

CHAPTER VIII

The Great Haustellate Groups

A LACE BUG

THE two large and extremely important orders that we consider here are so closely related to each other that they are often combined as a single order, the Hemiptera; the true bugs then being termed the Heteroptera, and the cicadas and their relatives the Homoptera. There is no satisfactory name for the group as a whole. The outstanding characteristic of these insects is the adaptation of their mouthparts for piercing and sucking. As with most other large groups of insects, so many species are probably not yet known that an estimate of their numbers in the world is at best only approximate; but there are probably more than fifty thousand species. The great majority feed on saps and other juices of plants, and include many of the insects most harmful to agriculture. In addition to their direct damage, some of these are carriers of plant diseases. A small number attack animals; and although most of these are predators on other insects, some attack vertebrates, including man.

The mouthparts are formed characteristically, the lower lip, or labium, being drawn out into an elongated, jointed beak that serves as a sheath for the long, slender, sharp mandibles and maxillae (or stylets). These, in addition to piercing, fit together so as to form a double tube, along which liq-

uids can be sucked in, while salivary fluids are being squirted out. The saliva not only facilitates the entry of the mouthparts into the tissues of the host plant or animal, but has a digestive and liquefying effect, breaking down the tissue and making it easier to ingest.

THE TRUE BUGS
—Order Heteroptera

The true bugs are in general characterized by the differentiation of the fore and hind wings. The latter are conventionally membranous and equipped with simple veins, but the former, called hemelytra, are thick in the basal portion but thin and membranous apically, and form something of a protection for the hind pair. The body is more or less flattened, sometimes extremely so; and the wings are carried flat over the abdomen. The beak is attached quite obviously to the front of the head, although it may lie, pointing backward, close to the under surface of the body. This, like the dissimilarity of wing texture, is an important point of distinction between the bugs and the cicadas in which the beak seems to arise from the rear part of the head or even between the legs.

The antennae are usually of very few segments;

[65

in the terrestrial groups they are usually quite long and prominent, but in most of the aquatic groups they are short and more or less concealed. The prothorax is very large and prominent; and the rear part of the mesothorax, the scutellum, is usually conspicuous, forming a characteristic triangular plate that points backward between the bases of the wings. In some groups this is very large, covering most or all of the wings and abdomen.

The metamorphosis is incomplete, the larvae (often called nymphs) resembling the adults quite closely in both form and habits. They lack functional wings, of course, but in the later stages of growth have prominent external wing pads. The eggs are often highly ornamented with sculpturing, spines or threadlike processes, and in some groups may be quite brightly colored or even metallic.

A number of the families have very effective stink glands that pour forth a nauseating secretion

A **Green Stink Bug** (*Loxa florida*). Noted for the nauseous taste and odor which protect it from predators.

on the lower surface of the body. Curiously enough this secretion, which is extremely unpleasant to humans, seems, in many instances at least, to have little deterrent effect on predators.

STINKBUGS—*Family Pentatomidae*

A number of closely related groups, sometimes classified as separate families, are included here. All have five-jointed antennae and a very prominent scutellum. They are the dominant family of the order (Plates 16, 17), including over five thousand species. As a group they are nearly cosmopolitan, although their numbers fall off rapidly toward the colder regions. Many people have, without recognizing it, been disgusted by the taste of their fetid secretions, for some of the species feed on fruit and berry juices and pollute the fruits while doing so. Despite their unpleasantness to most of us, some species in Mexico, India and Africa are relished by the inhabitants—to our mind one of the most painfully acquired tastes.

Most of the forms are quite broad and convex, with the head and thorax forming a forward-pointing triangle; but some are slender. The majority are brown, but others are green or brightly variegated or metallic. The brown and gray members of the genus *Brochymena* are often cryptically patterned with scrawls, dots and patches of dark and light; and this, combined with their flat shapes and rough surfaces, makes them extraordinarily difficult to detect when they are resting on bark. Many of the green forms are excellent matches for the foliage among which they sit.

Most species are from one-quarter to one-half inch long, although *Oncomeris flavicornis,* a striking red, black, orange and blue species from Australia, measures two inches in length. Several species have sound-producing organs; in fact *Tessaratoma javanica* from the South Pacific makes a really startling amount of noise if seized; and its relative, *T. papillosa,* which feeds on the logan and lichee trees in the Orient, not only makes a loud noise but can eject its noxious secretions for a distance of six to twelve inches. Difference between the sexes (sexual dimorphism) is fairly common and in some species is quite striking, as in the genus *Ceratocoris,* the males of which have the head between the eyes drawn out into a long, hornlike protuberance. A suggestion of maternal instinct has been noted in quite a few species in which the female broods over her eggs and stays for a while with the newly hatched larvae. The barrel-shaped eggs are usually sculptured and ornamented (Plate 15) and laid in groups. They have a tight-fitting hinged cover that is pushed off by the emerging larva.

A few species are predatory, and some of these are beneficial to man, like *Podisus* that destroys many Colorado potato beetles, and *Zicrona caerulea* in China that feeds on beetles in both the larval and adult stages. Many, however, are more or less injurious to fruits, vegetables and plants in general. The world-wide *Nezara viridula,* for example, does great damage to beans, berries of various kinds and tomatoes. The best known of the North American species is *Murgantia histrionica* (Plate 16). Introduced from Mexico and Central America, it was first found in the United States in 1864 in Texas. As it spread rapidly through the southern states its presence was blamed on the Yankee soldiers. The number of names that it has been given speaks for the attention that it has attracted: harlequin cabbage bug, terrapin bug and fire bug are but a few of many. It is now very destructive all over the southern states and on the Pacific coast, and is common north to New England and Washington wherever plants of the cabbage and mustard family (Cruciferae) grow. It is most bizarre in appearance, having red, orange or yellow bands, stripes and margins on a black or dark blue ground color. Its eggs, which are laid twelve at a time in two neat parallel rows on the lower surfaces of young leaves, look like miniature white kegs with dark hoops and bung holes.

The shield bugs of the family Scutellaridae are shorter, broader and more convex than the true stink bugs, usually being somewhat tortoise-shaped. They are all vegetarians, often preferring plants that grow near water. Many are metallic green, blue or purple, reaching their greatest brilliance and size in the islands of the Pacific. *Calliphara imperialis* of Australia is an inch long and brilliant red, and *Tectocoris lineola,* which ranges from Australia to China, is bright orange with variable markings that look like Chinese characters.

The burrower bugs, or Cydnidae, are a group of small, convexly rounded bugs with broad, shiny tibiae. They usually burrow under stone and boards, or in sand or mold. Some are occasionally found in ant nests.

The negro bugs, or Corymelanidae, are also very convex, almost hemispherical. They are so black and shiny that they are often mistaken for beetles. Some are sporadic pests on celery and related crops, and often around berries, leaving their disagreeable bedbug-like odor wherever they crawl.

SQUASH BUGS—Family Coreidae

The name "squash bug" is appropriate enough for this group in America, where by far the best-known member of the family is the too familiar pest on squash and related plants. In other parts of the world, however, prominent species are called gum-tree bugs and crusader bugs, the latter name arising from the pale St. Andrew's cross on the wings of *Mictis profana* of Australia.

The family (Plate 21) includes more than two thousand species. They are in general more elongate than the stink bugs, and show considerable variety of form. As a rule the margins of the abdomen are turned upward so that the wings lie in a depression on the back. Many genera show extraordinary dilatations of the antennae and of the tibiae; *Leptoglossus membranaceus* of Australia and *L. phyllopus* of North America are consequently known as leaf-footed bugs, so thin and leaflike are these enlargements. The very large *Acanthocephala femorata,* a cotton bug of the southeastern United States, has the femora of all its legs and the tibiae of the hind pair most strikingly enlarged, flattened and deeply notched.

The members of the family show widely differing habits, since many are carnivorous, a few feed on both plants and other insects, and many more are strictly vegetarian. Of the last, quite a few species are destructive pests, such as *Leptocorisa varicornis* of the Orient, which does great damage to rice and millet.

The squash bug, *Anasa tristis,* widespread from Mexico to Canada, is ocher yellow in ground color, with so many minute black punctures as to appear blackish in over-all color. The yellow spots on the head and on the margins of the thorax and abdomen are merely areas that are not thus pitted. The black-legged, whitish larvae will feed on beans, peas and corn as well as squash. Since this species produces several generations a year the devastation it causes is serious. Control is difficult because the larvae often work underground and the adults often seem to attack the plants in places untouched by insecticides. The small boy who picks these bugs and their egg masses by hand has not yet been replaced by modern science, although a Tachinid fly that parasitizes both larvae and adults is of some help.

PLANT BUGS—Family Lygaeidae

This large family (Plate 19) comprises over fifteen hundred species, some of which cause losses of millions of dollars a year by their depredations on grains and grasses. Many of the species resemble the Coreidae but are smaller, with a softer integument and often with brighter colors. They are all plant-feeders, living in moss, on rubbish or under stones and low bushes.

Oxycarenus hyalinipennis, known as the Egyptian cotton-stainer, and *Nysius vinitor,* a very destructive pest of fruit trees in Australia, are only two of the many harmful species. Best known in North America is the chinch bug, *Blissus leucopterus.* (Bedbugs are sometimes called "chinches" in the South.) A native of tropical America, it has now extended its range to cover all of the United States. Less than one-sixth of an inch long, blackish, with white wings marked with black, red legs and a red spot at the base of each antenna, it is

Milkweed Bug (*Oncopeltus fasciatus*). This Lygaeid has bright black and orange colors that warn potential attackers of its inedibility.

striking in appearance; and since it is energetic as well, it is altogether unforgettable once one has made its acquaintance. An account of its activities might well be entitled "The Insect That Goes for a Walk," because at the critical moment of its life cycle it walks forth searching, quite literally, for new fields to conquer. The females lay about five hundred eggs apiece on the roots and stems of grain close to the ground. The newly emerged larvae feed on these before climbing the stalks to continue the foraging, which must go on for forty to fifty days before they become full grown. There are two generations a year; and the fall brood may have to be raised not on the crop that was home to its parents, but in another grainfield that is still succulent and full of nourishment. To this fresh field the bugs migrate, walking over fields, stubble and hedgerows, and even at times across roads, to the new stand, there laying the eggs where the new brood will grow to maturity. There also the new brood will hibernate, sometimes in aggregations of as many as thirty thousand bugs in one clump of grass. A study of these habits has resulted in various devices for control based opportunely on their life history. Rubbish in which the adults hibernate may be burned; ditches are dug around the fields in which the first generation develops so that the migrating adults may be trapped and destroyed; decoy plots of grain are planted to which they may wend their way, only to be ploughed under and tamped down. Artificial dissemination of a fungus that attacks them may also help. But of all controls the most efficacious is that practiced by Nature herself, who occasionally sends wet years or long wet springs that are unfavorable to the development of chinch bugs.

FLAT BUGS—*Family Aradidae*

Their extreme flatness adapts these bugs for thei life in cracks and under the bark of decaying trees. They are dull brownish or blackish, sometimes with red markings; as a result they are often mistaken

for bedbugs, from which, however, they can be distinguished quite easily by the prolongation of the head between the antennae. They feed on fungi and the juices of decaying wood and bark. *Aradus* is a world-wide genus.

LACE BUGS—*Family Tingitidae*

This small, easily recognized family contains species that are beautiful indeed under a microscope but too small to be appreciated with the naked eye. They are only two to five millimeters or so in length but often occur in great numbers on the underside of leaves, where they suck the juices to such an extent as to cause browning or stippling of the foliage. The gauzelike hemelytra are finely reticulated, often extending well beyond the sides of the abdomen to match flat outgrowths of the pronotum that are similarly lacelike. The whole often bears fringes of tiny spines. The pronotum, which is often inflated like a small balloon, usually covers the scutellum.

The eggs are inserted upright in the leaf tissues and then covered with a brown viscous secretion that hardens to form a conelike elevation. The emerging nymphs are very spiny and leave a sticky trail on the underside of leaves, to which their cast skins often adhere. A hundred or more nymphs of various sizes may be found clustered with the adults on a single oak leaf.

The sycamore lace bug, *Corythucha ciliata*, is common in the United States and Canada. *Stephanitis pyri* attacks pear and apple in Europe, and several species attack fruit and olive trees in Australia. About seven hundred species have been described.

RED BUGS—*Family Pyrrhocoridae*

These stout, heavily built, red-and-black bugs are large and conspicuous. The family is only moderately large and the species mostly occur in the tropics and subtropics. They are not to be confused with certain species of mites (class Acarina) and of plant bugs (Miridae) that are also called red bugs.

Many of the members of this family are called cotton-stainers because they pierce cotton bolls and stain the fibers. Species of *Dysdercus* are bad pests in this way in both India and America; they also puncture oranges, causing the fruit to decay. Since these same species feed on hibiscus and Spanish cocklebur, the eradication of these plants limits their breeding. At one time it was customary to leave little piles of sugar cane between the rows of cotton plants and orange trees to attract the bugs, which could then be picked up in numbers and destroyed.

Dimorphism sometimes occurs; the widespread *Pyrrhocoris apterus* may be winged or wingless; and the Oriental *Lohita grandis,* a handsome species over two inches long, exhibits a sexual dimorphism in that the male has greatly enlarged antennae and a swollen abdomen.

Some species are very antlike in appearance, perhaps gaining thereby a certain protection against predators. A few species have completely departed from the plant-eating habits of most of the family and become predaceous; *Dyndymus sanguineus* of India, for example, feeds on flies as an adult and on termites when a larva.

AMBUSH BUGS—Family Phymatidae

These bugs, of which there are only about one hundred species, are primarily tropical and poorly represented in Europe and North America. They are unusual little creatures with the body laterally extended to form rounded projections or, as in the species of the oriental *Carcinocoris*, fine spines. The forelegs are developed in a remarkable manner for grasping and holding their prey; the coxa is greatly elongated, the femur thickened so that it is two-thirds as broad as long, and the tibia sickle-shaped and armed with close-set teeth, which mesh with similar teeth located on the femur.

Phymata erosa, the common North American species, is yellowish and marked with a broad black band across the expanded portion of the abdomen. It rests inconspicuously in flowers, where it awaits the coming of some insect that it can grasp with its raptorial front legs. It is able to master quite large insects, sometimes catching cabbage butterflies, fritillaries, honeybees and even large wasps, although it is less than half an inch long itself.

FLOWER BUGS—Family Anthocoridae

The members of this family are comparatively few in number but are of some importance as predators. They live inconspicuously in woodlands and hedgerows, preying primarily on aphids and their eggs but occasionally eating other small insects. About three hundred species are known.

Orius (*Triphleps*) *insidiosus*, the insidious flower bug, is a small black-and-white species common in flowers in the United States, preying on the grape phylloxera and on the common chinch bug. The cosmopolitan *Lectocoris campestris* and the Sudanese *Anthocoris kingi* suck human blood.

ASSASSIN BUGS—Family Reduviidae

This is a large, world-wide family (Plate 20) of nearly four thousand species. Some are very small and others more than an inch in length; but all possess a short, powerful beak that is used for sucking the blood of other insects, larger animals and even man. In attacking man they not only cause annoyance or even considerable pain, but may also transmit pathogenic organisms that sometimes prove fatal. They can usually be recognized by the neck-

Ambush Bugs (*Phymata erosa*), mating pair. The grotesque form and color make them inconspicuous among the flowers where they await their prey.

like narrowing of the head behind the eyes. Many have strong, raptorial front legs with which they grasp and hold their prey.

The masked hunter, *Reduvius personatus*, a Central European species that was introduced into New York and then spread southward, is now common in the southern states, where it often enters houses to feed on bedbugs and other small insects. It oc-

Wheel Bug (*Arilus cristatus*). An unusually large and powerful Assassin Bug which preys on other insects.

Bedbug (*Cimex lectularis*), shown feeding from the human skin, is a major pest of man but is not a carrier of disease.

casionally feeds on man, inflicting a painful bite. It is not born masked; the larva acquires a coating of dust on the adhesive hairs that cover its body and thereafter crawls about looking like a bit of lint. Another species, the cone-nosed bug, Mexican bedbug or big bedbug, *Triatoma sanguisuga,* of the southern and western states, also enters houses in search of warm human blood. Its bite is so toxic to some people that it may prove as dangerous as a poisonous snake bite: general swelling, often faintness, vomiting and other bad effects that may last for several months. When out of doors it is satisfied for the most part to feed on other insects. Its relative *T. megista* is one of the important carriers of the protozoan *Trypanosoma cruzi,* the cause of a fatal human disease in South America. *Triatoma rubrofasciata* of Madagascar and southern Asia lives as a nymph in the debris on the floor of native huts and may carry the organism that causes the fatal disease known as Kala-azar.

The best-known kissing bug is *Melanolestes picipes.* It is little more than half an inch long, black, with a well-drawn-out head and a bell-shaped, bilobed prothorax. Its preference for biting on or about the face and mouth explains its common name. It is normally found under stones and bark, feeding on grasshoppers and white grubs, especially those of the June beetle; but sometimes it enters houses at night and bites sleeping humans.

Pristhesancus papuensis, which ranges from Papua to northern New South Wales, is known as the bee-killer because it lies in wait on flowers to seize honeybees, as well as other flower-visiting insects, and to suck their body juices. Another remarkable Oriental species is *Ptilocerus ochraceus* from Java, which also waits in ambush instead of seeking its prey. It frequently lives in large numbers in the bamboo rafters of houses. Ants of the species *Dolichoderus bituberculatus* seek out the bugs for the purpose of licking the peculiar glandular hairs, or trichomes, on the front of their bodies. They pull on these hairs much as in milking and seem to rel-

ish the secretion greatly; but they soon become paralyzed by its toxic effect and are then seized by the bug and sucked dry. This is certainly one of the most unusual adaptations for luring its prey shown by any predator, exceeding even that of the angler fish that dangles an imitation worm in front of its mouth.

BEDBUGS—*Family Cimicidae*

These loathed creatures make up a small but cosmopolitan family of not over thirty species, of which eight have been recorded in North America. They are easily distinguished by their structure and their habits. All are greatly flattened dorso-ventrally and are without wings, although they may have vestigial elytra; and all are ectoparasites upon birds or mammals, since they require warm blood on which to feed.

The chief bedbug that attacks man, *Cimex lectularis,* is widespread in Europe and North America and in fact is world-wide in temperate regions, having undoubtedly been carried everywhere by man. The eggs, which are laid in crevices in baseboards, behind loose wallpaper and picture frames or in the cracks of bedsteads, hatch in about seven days. The life cycle may be completed in seven or eight weeks, but if conditions are unfavorable it may stretch out over six months or more. Individuals can live a year without a meal, but if no human is available they may find mice, rats, poultry or even cattle and horses on which to feed. The adults are nocturnal, hiding by day in cracks; but their presence can often be detected by the characteristic odor of the oily secretion that comes from a pair of glands opening on the underside of the third thoracic segment. They are active migrants, since they can be transported easily in clothing and luggage and can travel from apartment to apartment and even from house to house on utility pipes and wires. However, they often are extremely conservative about moving around; for cases have been known of a heavy infestation limiting itself to a single room for months and never spreading to other parts of the house. But many a human traveler has been dismayed to discover that the lodgings he found clean and attractive in June had become pest-ridden by August. Such conditions are no longer necessary, for with our modern insecticides bedbugs can be controlled easily and cheaply.

Cimex hemipterus, also parasitic upon humans, is a tropical form abundant in Asia and Africa. *C. pilosellus* lives only on bats; species of *Œciacus* are found only on swallows and martins; and *Cimexopsis nyctalis* on chimney swifts. *Haematosiphon inodora* of North and Central America lives usually on poultry but is not reluctant about feeding on man; it differs from most other species in having a greatly prolonged beak.

Bedbugs are often accused of carrying diseases such as European relapsing fever, Kala-azar, bubonic plague and leprosy; but they never have been proven guilty and probably are not, any transmission of disease for which they have been blamed having likely been due to other means. But they do inflict a bite that may be a source of great irritation and inflammation to some people, although scarcely noticed by others. We once heard of a young man who suffered severe anemia from a continued loss of blood to bedbugs of whose presence and of whose biting he was unaware.

PLANT BUGS—Family Miridae

This universally abundant family of about five thousand species is made up of very small, fragile, soft-bodied bugs, only a few of which are over one-fifth of an inch in length. They are usually elongate in form, although a few are ovoid and resemble stink bugs in miniature. A few species are predaceous, but for the most part they feed on plant juices, frequently changing over from wild plants to cultivated ones when the latter offer a more abundant and easily obtainable food supply.

The tarnished plant bug, *Lygus pratensis,* is a cosmopolitan species that feeds on more than fifty species of plants, ranging from strawberries to fruit trees, cereals and grasses, and flowering plants such as chrysanthemums, asters, dahlias and peonies, the beautiful flowerheads of which it pierces and "buttons," causing great damage. *L. pabulinus* feeds on potatoes.

In the United States the garden flea hopper, *Halticus bractatus,* is a common species on corn, beans, cucumbers and tomatoes; and the four-lined leaf bug, *Poecilocapsus lineatus,* occurs on a wide variety of plants. In the Orient *Helopeltis theivora,* common and destructive on tea plants, has a curious erect pin rising from the scutellum.

A few species carry disease from plant to plant. Still others are beneficial in that they are predaceous on plant lice and other small, harmful insects. The Australian *Cyrtorhynus mundulus* feeds on the eggs of the sugar cane leaf hopper and has been introduced into Hawaii and other places as a control for that pest.

MARSH TREADERS or WATER MEASURERS —Family Hydrometridae

The marsh treaders are few in number of species, only about seventy having been described, but the genus *Hydrometra* is world-wide in distribution. Where cattails grow and algae flourish, where mosquito larvae hang suspended from the surface film and dead insects float on the quiet water, these slender, fragile-looking bugs can be seen crawling slowly about over the vegetation at the edge of shallow

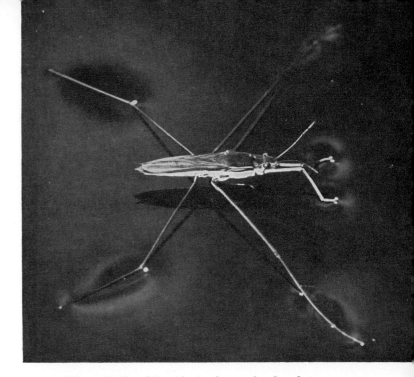

A **Water Strider** (*Gerris*). Its feet make dimples on the surface film.

pools and even out onto the surface film. The adults, which are less than an inch long, can be identified by the attenuated head that is fully as long as the entire thorax, by the long, elbowed antennae that reach out in front like another pair of legs, and by the long, threadlike legs. When at rest they cling to a plant stem with a single claw. They feed on crustacea or aquatic insect larvae, especially mosquitoes, which they skillfully spear with their long beaks. The ventral surface of the body is clothed with a fine pubescence that keeps the body from becoming wet. Their deliberate movements have inspired the name "water measurer" because of the manner in which they seem to pace their length upon the reeds.

The beautifully sculptured eggs are nearly one-fourth as long as the female who lays them and are glued singly to cattail leaves or other aquatic plants just above the water line.

WATER STRIDERS or WATER SKATERS —Family Gerridae

Drifting on the surface film of quiet pond waters, the members of this small family may often be found in large numbers, for they are gregarious and tend to gather in schools along the shady margins. When startled they scatter in all directions but soon reassemble. A few specialized forms prefer swift-moving waters. Water striders are characterized by long, slender legs, especially the last two pairs, which may be two or more times as long as the entire body and are considerably separated from the shorter, grasping forelegs. The hind legs are used primarily for steering while the middle legs propel the body as it skims over the surface film, making little dimples that cast a shadow on the bottom, showing that only the feet touch the water and that even these do not break through the surface film. They feed on dead insects or whatever live ones they can capture as they drift, skate and leap about; when overcrowded they may even seize one of their own kind. They winter as adults and may often be seen running about on warm winter days.

Gerris is a cosmopolitan genus, some of whose species are wingless. One of these is *G. remigis,* which extends from Labrador to Mexico. *Halo-*

A **Giant Water Bug** (*Benacus griseus*), nearly two inches long, sucking the blood from a captured Newt.

bates, also wingless, lives on the tropical and subtropical oceans, often hundreds of miles from land, where it runs about on the surface of the sea, feeding on dead, floating marine animals. It has been claimed on good authority that even a single drop of water landing on the back of a *Halobates* will wet it so that it drowns. This poses the interesting question of how they survive when a storm or a rain squall catches them. So far, nobody knows.

The cosmopolitan *Microvelia* and *Rhagovelia* and the Palearctic *Velia,* known as broad-shouldered water striders, are sometimes placed in a separate family, the Veliidae. *Rhagovelia* is often found running against the current in rather swift streams, aided by a special fanlike arrangement of bristles on the middle pair of legs.

The Gerridae and Veliidae each include about two hundred species. A third closely related family, the Mesoveliidae, has twenty species, one of which, *Phrynovelia papua* of New Guinea, is terrestrial, living among the leaves of the forest floor.

GIANT WATER BUGS
—Family Belostomatidae

Some of the largest known insects and certainly the largest bugs belong to this family (Plate 22). Although found in most tropical and temperate regions, there are probably fewer than two hundred species in all, less than a dozen of which are found in the United States. *Lethocerus grandis* of South America and *L. indicus,* which ranges from India to Australia, are both over four inches in length; but our largest North American species, *L. americanus,* seldom exceeds an inch and a half.

Although these bugs fly strongly, sometimes for great distances, and often come in to light at night (whence their common name, electric light bugs) they are especially adapted for life in the waters of ponds and lakes, where their wide, flat bodies may be seen resting suspended head downward from the surface film, with the tip of the abdomen protruding. The femur of the front legs is wide and flat and sometimes has a groove for the reception of the sharp cutting edge of the tibia that folds down onto it, the whole making a powerful organ for the capture of other insects, tadpoles and even of fish as much as three and a half inches long. The other legs are flattened and oarlike and thus adapted for swimming. The strong, sharp beak can inflict a painful sting.

The common American *Belostoma flumineum,* which is about an inch in length, spends most of its time lurking in the weeds on muddy bottoms. When it comes up for air, as it does occasionally, it pinches the surface film with the retractile appendages located at the apex of the abdomen; these conduct air to the abdominal spiracles. The female forcibly lays her eggs on the back of the male. Approaching him while he is suspended from the surface film, she wraps her legs around him, secretes a waterproof glue over his back and attaches one hundred or more eggs, which he then has to carry for about ten days, or until they hatch. Not even the most militant suffragette ever carried feminism this far! Females of the widespread *Abedus* and the Austro-Asian *Sphaeroderma* have also adopted this custom, but the widely distributed *Benacus* and *Lethocerus* conservatively lay their eggs in masses on plants.

Some species have a curious death-feigning habit, assuming a characteristic rigid position when removed from the water or upon contact, which they may hold for as much as fifteen minutes. When disturbed, others forcefully eject an odorous fluid from the anus, while a few have been known to make a wheezing or soft chirping noise.

Lethocerus indicus is commonly eaten in parts of Asia and may be purchased in food shops in many local "Chinatowns."

WATER SCORPIONS—*Family Nepidae*

The members of this small aquatic family walk sluggishly around on the bottom of quiet waters or rest in the vegetation, sometimes remaining motionless for hours. In Australia they are called toe-biters or needle bugs because of their habit of stabbing bathers. Their sting is painful but has no lasting effects. They can be identified by the slender respiratory tube at the rear end of the abdomen. This tube may be nearly as long as the rest of the body. Water scorpions may be said to have evolved the snorkel long before man invented it. The strongly prehensile front legs speak for the carnivorous habits of these bugs in the way the tibiae and tarsi close down into the groove of the femur, like a knife blade into a jackknife handle. Their unspecialized middle and hind legs are suitable only for walking, so that although they are voracious feeders on small aquatic larvae and crustacea, they do not particularly pursue their prey.

Water scorpions may often be seen hanging from the surface film with the respiratory tube projecting into the air; or they may be observed awkwardly backing up a submerged stem to find a resting place that will enable them to draw down air from above. The tube, which is not fully developed until the adult stage, is formed by two grooved filaments that lie side by side and are hooked together by interlocking bristles. Air is conducted through it to spiracles at the tip of the abdomen. Three pairs of false spiracles on the middle abdominal segments are covered by a sievelike membrane through which oxygen may pass directly into the body fluids; they seem to have no connection with the tracheal system.

The two cosmopolitan genera, *Nepa* and *Rana-tra,* are very different from each other. *Nepa* is broad and flat and about half an inch long; *Rana-tra,* on the other hand, is very thin and sticklike and nearly two inches long, being quite as remarkably slender as the terrestrial walking sticks. The females of *Nepa* lay their eggs in such a way that they adhere in chains by means of long filaments, seven to an egg; *Ranatra* females have a pointed toothed ovipositor and lay their bifilamentous eggs in notches cut into plant stems. Both are inconspicuously colored, although *Nepa* has some reddish on the top of the abdomen, which seldom shows since the wings are scarcely ever spread.

Water scorpions rarely fly; but if the water in which they breed dries up they may fly considerable distances, if necessary, to find more.

WATER BOATMEN—*Family Corixidae*

This is the dominant family of water bugs (Plate 23). They are often abundant in fresh-water ponds and lakes and occasionally in streams and even in brackish pools just above high-tide mark along the shore. They are found below sea level in Death Valley and at an altitude of fifteen thousand feet in the Himalayas.

Most of the two hundred species are darkish in color, sometimes mottled with black. The dorsal surface of the body is faintly crosslined, strongly flattened and even slightly concave. Within this concavity beneath the wings a reservoir of air may be retained, which, with the silvery coating of air that covers the body during submergence, supplies the water boatmen with oxygen during the long periods they spend beneath the surface. Since their soft beaks are quite useless for piercing, they differ from other members of the order in their food habits, scooping up ooze and algae with their spoon-shaped, fringed front legs. They are seldom eaten by fish or disturbed by other predators, so they often rest quietly, clinging to vegetation or debris on the bottom by means of the two terminal claws of one of their long, slender, middle legs, and thus anchored, float out horizontally with hind legs outstretched at right angles to the body. Since the body is lighter than water, they rise to the surface once they let go their hold. The hind legs are flattened and oarlike and are used to propel the body as they swim jerkily along. Water boatmen occasionally come out of the water at night, leaping into the air to take flight and frequently flying in to light in large numbers.

The eggs are usually glued to submerged stems and leaves. Those of one species, *Ramphocorixa acuminata,* however, are attached to the bodies of crayfish, a most unusual way of insuring dispersal of the young.

Some species are so abundant at times that they have been used by man as food. *Corixa femorata* in Egypt and *Corisella mercenaria* in Mexico have been cultivated on bundles of sedges placed in the water by the natives; the adults and the eggs are then gathered and eaten directly or ground into flour. Tons of *C. mercenaria* were at one time imported into England for feeding insectivorous birds. They are sold in cellophane packages in pet shops in the United States.

BACKSWIMMERS—*Family Notonectidae*

The backswimmers, unlike the Corixidae which they otherwise resemble in size and shape, are convex and keeled on the dorsal surface. The sides of the back slope much like those of a boat and usually are lighter in color than the rest of the body, thus exemplifying the principles of countershading when the creature is swimming or floating on its back, as is its custom. Why the members of this family evolved this curious habit of swimming upside down is a mystery. Like the water boatmen these bugs are lighter than water and so must fasten themselves to something if they are to remain submerged. When thus anchored they assume a characteristic pose with their long, fringed hind legs stretched forward. When at the surface they can leap out of the water and take flight or, with air supply replenished, may dive rapidly after the crustaceans, insects and small fish on which they feed. Most species can inflict a painful puncture when handled, which no doubt explains how they are able to capture and kill insects and fish larger than themselves.

The genus *Notonecta* is world-wide and may at times be quite destructive to young fish and tadpoles. The North American *N. undulata* is a beautiful black-and-white, extremely active, voracious species. Its keeled abdomen has a long row of outwardly pointing hairs on either side that meet a similar series projecting inward from the lateral margins, thus making two channels that hold a reservoir of air. Some species lay their eggs on stems; others possess an ovipositor and lay them within the stem tissues. Most species winter as adults and may sometimes be seen walking beneath the ice in midwinter.

Buenoa, a Western Hemisphere and Hawaiian genus, as well as the old world *Anisops,* show a considerable amount of red through the thin body wall because of the large amount of haemoglobin that fills certain large cells clustered around the tracheae. *B. margaritacea,* one of the American species, is one-fourth of an inch long, with white wings and a lovely blush of pink on the back of the thorax, turning to deep red beneath the abdomen. The long bristles of the first and second pair of legs intermesh to form a cage in which to hold the crustacea and small insects on which it dines. *Plea,* a widespread genus sometimes placed in a separate family, is only about one-eighth of an inch long.

THE CICADAS, HOPPERS, SCALE INSECTS, APHIDS etc.
—*Order Homoptera*

An indication of the great diversity of size, form and habits of the members of this order is the fact that there is no inclusive name for all of them. They differ from the true bugs in having the beak attached to the very rear of the head, sometimes even apparently between the front legs; and in having both pairs of wings uniformly membranous in texture. The wings are held slanting and rooflike over the body, with the inner margins overlapping. Many have seemingly complex and varied life histories. They may reproduce sexually or by the development of unfertilized eggs; they may lay eggs or give birth to living young; they may have winged forms or wingless forms; and they may alternate between very different food plants at different stages in their life cycle.

In some forms the mouthparts are vestigial or even entirely lacking in the adults, although they are always functional in the nymphs. Fundamentally they are like those of the bugs. In many the stylets are so greatly enlarged that they exceed the body in length and are looped or coiled upon themselves or withdrawn into a backward-directed pocket on the lower side of the body. All are plant-feeders, exhibiting in this respect a homogeneity unknown in any other order of insects.

The prothorax tends to be proportionately smaller than in the bugs, except in the family of treehoppers, the Membracidae, where it is extravagantly enlarged and often produced into horns, tubercles and grotesque elaborations. The mesothorax, on the other hand, is relatively larger.

As in the Heteroptera, many members of the Homoptera are serious pests to agriculture. A very important factor in this is their tremendous fecundity. It has been estimated that the progeny of a single female leafhopper would, if allowed to reproduce unchecked for a year, number 500 million individuals; or that those of one aphid would be represented after three hundred days by the number 210 to the fifteenth power. Such a reproductive potential, although never by any means completely realized, makes possible sudden outbreaks that can, by sheer force of numbers, do enormous damage to plants before they can be brought under control, either by man directly or by natural enemies.

On the other side of the picture, a few Homoptera are directly useful to man because of the usefulness of their products, although decreasingly so as man-made substitutes are developed. Shellac, still an important commercial substance, is one of these products; and so is cochineal, at one time one of the most important dyes. The waxy secretions of some are still used locally for making candles, and the sweet honeydew secreted by certain species is occasionally collected and eaten by man. These benefits are, however, comparatively small when weighed against the total damage done by many members of this order.

CICADAS—Family Cicadidae

There are more than fifteen hundred species of these insects in the world, of which about seventy-five occur in North America and only one, *Cicadetta montana,* in Britain. Though they vary in size, most of them are large; two Australian species of *Tettigarcta* and *Abricta,* the floury millers, are respectively three and four inches in wing expanse. The membranous wings, of which the front pair is the longer, are held slanted back and rooflike over the abdomen, exceeding it in length. The head is wide and blunt (Plate 25), with prominent compound eyes capping the outer corners and three beadlike ocelli forming a triangle between.

Cicadas are reputed to be the noisiest of all insects. Their voice is due to a unique apparatus that is one of the most complicated sound-producing mechanisms in the entire animal kingdom, although the sound it produces is a simple one, differing in each species sufficiently to make it of use in identification. It has been compared to the sound of a knife-grinder, a scissors-grinder, a railway whistle and even, as in the case of the Japanese oil cicada, of fat spitting on an overheated pan. But it makes up in volume for what it lacks in delicacy and melodiousness, and at time is deafening and wearyingly monotonous.

As a rule the female is mute, possessing mere vestiges of a sound-producing apparatus, but in a few species she is nearly as voluble as the male. Typically the apparatus is formed around four small cavities located on the lower surface of the body. These are covered by a pair of earlike flaps, which are projections of the rear margin of the thorax, each one covering two cavities. The contraction and expansion of a large muscle in the second abdominal segment vibrates a membrane, the timbril, in the inner wall of each lateral cavity. These vibrations are transmitted by a large air chamber within the body to the folded membrane that lies on the anterior wall of each ventral chamber and to the iridescent mirror membrane that is located in the posterior wall of the same chamber. Acting as resonators, these greatly increase the sound; and the opening and closing of the ear flaps give a rhythmic increase and decrease to the loudness.

In the United States the often abundant dog-day cicadas, or harvester flies, of the genus *Tibicen,* of which there are several species, sing loudly in the latter part of summer. They vary in size and color but usually are about two inches in length and are blackish green, powdered with white beneath.

A **Periodical Cicada** (*Cicada hieroglyphica*). Cicadas are noted for their loud, shrill voices and their long lives as nymphs underground.

Their life cycle is similar to that of the periodical cicada but usually is completed in two years. The widely publicized periodical cicada, or seventeen-year locust, *Magicicada septendecim,* was mistakenly called a locust by the early settlers, who saw in its periodical appearance in great numbers a resemblance to the migratory locust of the old world. The females lay their eggs in twigs of forest and fruit trees, usually making a slit in the bark for their insertion, a habit that at times results in considerable damage. The nymphs (Plate 27) hatch in about six weeks, drop to the ground and dig their way into the soil by means of their enormously expanded, powerful front legs. They then suck the juices of roots, remaining underground until the seventeenth spring following their hatching, whereupon they dig their way to the surface, climb up the bark of a tree or up palings, and emerge, leaving their cast skins in great array. In a few weeks the adults will have mated, laid their eggs and disappeared. A score or more of broods have been identified in the United States, so that one or more appear somewhere in the states each year. As many as seven different broods have been located in one locality, which means that the residents of that area do not have to wait many years between emergences. The southern broods have a shorter cycle, a single brood apparently maturing in thirteen years instead of seventeen.

Sometimes the nymph constructs an earthen cone or chimney about four inches in height, in which it remains for several weeks before coming out into the open to transform. There seems to be some correlation between the construction of these chimneys and high temperatures, so that the explanation may lie in the premature attraction of the nymph to the surface before it is ready for transformation. The

[75

construction of the external chamber gives it a waiting room for the final touches before its debut.

The great swarms of adult cicadas are exceedingly attractive to gulls, terns, grackles and many other birds, which feast avidly on the emerging hordes. In Borneo and Malaya and many other regions of the South Pacific the large species are used for human food. One species that extends from Japan and China down through southern Asia is used as a vesicative because of the peculiar blistering effect of its secretions.

LEAFHOPPERS—Family Cicadellidae (Jassidae)

This is a large family of great economic importance and, except for the aphids, the most abundant of the Homoptera. There are well over one thousand species in the United States alone. They are small or medium-sized insects, a few in the South Pacific region getting to be as much as half an inch in length, but the majority very much less. They are usually elongate and slender, often spindle-shaped, with the front margin of the head triangular or broadly rounded. The small hairlike antennae lie in front of and below the low-placed eyes. Most characteristic are the long hind femora, which are armed with a double row of spines. Most of the species are powerful jumpers. Often, however, when disturbed they run around to the other side of the twig of leaf, then perhaps return quickly to see if danger is still present, only to retreat once more, thus earning their common name of dodgers. They are also called sharpshooters from their habit, while eating, of forcibly expelling tiny drops of clear liquid from the tip of the abdomen. These drops, which shoot out with regularity, often one every second for a period of as much as two minutes at a time, are mostly plant juices that are being imbibed with such speed as to flow in an almost uninterrupted stream through the digestive tract, becoming only slightly mixed with the body wastes. Sweet to the taste, these liquids are attractive to flies, bees, wasps and ants. In fact many species, such as those of the large, handsome *Eurymela* group of Australia, which live in colonies on the eucalyptus trees, are generally attended by ants.

The eggs are placed in longitudinal rows on stems or leaves by the sharp female ovipositor. The young nymphs, though at first restricted in their diet to one food plant, may later become quite indiscriminate. *Empoasca fabae,* for example, is widely known as either the apple leafhopper or the potato leafhopper; but it could just as well be called the currant, gooseberry, beet, bean, celery, grain, grass, shade tree or weed leafhopper.

The group contains some of the most serious pests in the garden, orchard and vineyard, the pasture and grainfield. The rice leafhopper, *Nephotettix,* has caused millions of dollars of damage annually in one small area of India. *Eutettix tenellus* attacks more than a hundred species of plants but is particularly harmful in causing a condition of beets known as curly top, as a result of its introduction of a virus into the plant tissue when it inserts its slender mouthparts. The damages done by other members of this family consist of wilting and discoloring resulting from loss of plant juices; stunting of growth by blocking the conductile tissues of the plant; direct damage to plant cells by the insertion of the beak; or disease caused by viruses, fungi or bacteria introduced by the hoppers.

One relatively large and strikingly colored species is the common American *Graphocephala coccinea* (Plate 24), which has red wings striped with bright green. The adults, as well as the bright yellow larvae, are often seen on forsythia and other ornamental shrubs, which, however, they seldom damage seriously.

JUMPING PLANT LICE—Family Chermidae

None of these small insects is more than five millimeters long and the majority are much smaller. They resemble tiny cicadas, but have proportionately much longer antennae and weaker, fewer-veined wings. They are active jumpers, but fly only feebly. Despite the small size of the individuals many of the species are of considerable economic importance, having the great reproductive powers characteristic of the Homoptera.

One of the best-known species is the apple-sucker, *Psylla mali,* originally European but imported and now widespread in the United States and Canada. In addition to the direct damage done by the sap-sucking of both larvae and adults, further harm results from the smearing of the plants with the abundant honeydew secreted by the larvae. Not only does this handicap the plant tissues by its exclusion of the air; it also encourages the growth of molds, which may form thick, impervious coatings. The pear psylla, *Psylla pyricola,* similarly imported, is harmful in much the same way. A western species, *Paratrioza cockerelli,* is a bad pest on potato plants. The direct damage done by the insects is relatively slight, but a virus disease transmitted by them is extremely serious. We have seen a half-mile square near Durango, Colorado, where some of the finest seed potatoes are grown, that contained nothing but wilted, yellowed plants although no more than half a dozen psyllids could be found on each plant.

Some species stimulate the formation of plant galls, and others cause malformations of stems. In Australia, where the psyllids are known as lerp insects, many species are very abundant on eucalyptus and wattle trees. The aborigines collect and eat the honeydew of several species, particularly of the sugar lerp insect, *Spondyliaspis eucalypti.*

FROGHOPPERS *or* SPITTLE BUGS
—Family Cercopidae

What child has not kicked his way through the tall timothy on an early summer's day and wondered at the "spittle" or "cuckoo spit" in white, frothy masses on the grass stems! But how many have stopped to examine these masses and been rewarded with a glimpse of the one or two small, semi-helpless, immature insects resting within? The little froghopper larvae sit there in a whipped-cream world, sucking juices from the grass stem, probably protected from many predaceous enemies and certainly safeguarded from the desiccating effect of the hot summer's sun. Later when they emerge as adults they become active, hopping and leaping about and feeding on the shrubs or plants characteristic of their species.

The adults of this moderate-sized family (Plates 30–32), of which some thirty species are known from the United States, are small in size, rarely over half an inch long, with rather large heads. They are brown or greenish in color, indistinctly patterned in such a way as to bear a faint resemblance to tiny tree frogs. In Britain, *Cercopis vulnerata* is exceptionally brightly colored for a froghopper; it is black and red and, like most strikingly colored insects, displays itself quite openly on the sallows and alders on which it feeds. Its larva, too, is unusual in that, although it lives in a ball of spittle, it attaches itself to grass stems or roots some six inches below the surface of the ground.

Cercopid eggs are laid in the early spring or summer on grasses but do not hatch until the following spring. Not all the species have larvae that make spittle, but those that do usually place themselves head down on a plant, causing the substance which flows from the anus to become mixed with a mucilaginous excretion of glands on the seventh and eighth abdominal segments, and then to be blown up into a froth by means of air expelled from between the recurving side of the abdomen and its inner surface. The whole foamy mass then flows down over the little creature, providing it with a moist environment that lasts for some time, even through heavy rainstorms. In Madagascar, *Ptyelus goudoti* discharges a clear liquid, instead of a foam, which may fall to the ground like rain. One observer collected a quart of this liquid in one and a half hours from an aggregation of seventy of the larvae. In Australia and India the larvae of several genera form delicate tubes, ten to twelve millimeters long, which they attach along the sides of twigs, often of the eucalyptus tree, and which they inhabit after having filled them with spittle.

Species of *Philaenus* are common in Europe and North America; one, *P. leucophthalmus,* may cause severe stunting of the heads of clover. *Aphrophora parallela* and *A. saratogensis* are pests on pine in many parts of North America. And everywhere, the larvae, sucking the juices from grasses, cause withering of the heads above.

PLANTHOPPERS—*Family Fulgoridae*

For simplicity's sake we are treating this group of over five thousand species in the still more or less conventional fashion, that is, as a single family. Recent entomologists, however, have quite justifiably split it up into as many as eighteen families, treating the whole as a superfamily. The differences are quite technical and not correlated with any outstanding characteristics of habit or behavior. The group as a whole has long been referred to as "lantern flies" (Plate 26) because in the early days a widely read author named a South American species *Lantenaria phosphorea* and described it as being luminous. We now know that this was all a mistake, and that no members of the family appear to have any luminosity at all; yet many authors still use the misleading and inappropriate name.

Many have the head enlarged and protruding between the eyes, sometimes enormously and grotesquely so. Nearly all are accomplished hoppers. A great many of them have bright colors; and many others are covered with a waxy white secretion that may hang in woolly strands or clothe the insect in a thick, powdery coat. A few other insects, notably the larvae of a small family of small moths, the Epipyropidae, live on the bodies of such Fulgorids and feed on this secretion.

The Flatinae contain many beautiful mothlike forms, often delicately or brilliantly pigmented, which are found chiefly in the tropics. The larvae and adults often live together gregariously. In an African species of *Flata* two distinct color forms of the adult occur, bright green and bright red individuals living together in considerable numbers. They have been recorded as tending to cluster together on a stem with the green individuals above and the red ones beneath, so that the group bears a striking resemblance to a spike of red flowers with a mass of green, unopened buds at the tip.

The Delpharinae all have a large, mobile spur at the tip of each hind tibia. To this subfamily belongs the notorious sugar-cane leafhopper, *Perkinsiella saccharicida,* of Australia. Accidentally introduced into Hawaii, it caused great damage until it was brought under control by the introduction of a predaceous bug of the family Miridae.

The main subfamily, the Fulgorinae, chiefly tropical, is characterized by a marked frontal prolongation of the head in many of the groups. The original "lantern fly," *Lantenaria,* has a wing expanse of six inches. Its enormously expanded head resembles a big peanut in configuration. *Pyrops nobilis* of Africa, India and Ceylon has a similarly large head covered with spikes and spines. The Chinese candle fly, *Fulgora candelaria,* also said to be luminous (of course there *may* be some fire where there is so much reputed light), also has a strikingly overdeveloped head. The common species of *Scolops* of North America, although no more than one-quarter of an inch long, have the head very slender and lengthened out to account for half the total length. The various species of the widespread American *Ormenis,* however, have practically no special development of the head, but have very broad, mothlike wings that are often of delicate shades of yellowish green or pale aquamarine. Although at least some of the species feed on grapevines, they are not abundant enough to be noticeably harmful.

TREEHOPPERS—*Family Membracidae*

A relatively large family of world-wide distribution containing many thousands of species, the treehoppers lead much the same sort of lives as the leafhoppers, feeding on plant juices in both larval and adult stages and often jumping vigorously when disturbed. They are characterized by the great development of the pronotum, the upper part of the skeleton of the prothorax. This is greatly lengthened backward, extending far behind the thorax and usually covering the abdomen and the folded wings. In many forms the pronotum is merely rounded and slightly expanded; but in others it is greatly enlarged in a multiplicity of grotesque shapes, some of which beggar description. In some it forms a sharp, projecting spine or pair of spines which are definitely of protective value, making the insect look like a thorn (Plate 29) as it rests along a twig. The resemblance is very close in species that habitually rest on thorny plants. In others, particularly in many species of the New World tropics, the development of the pronotum has exceeded any possible value to the insects (Plate 28), and appears to be an instance of evolution running wild and out of control. In one it forms a great crescent with arms rising forward and backward to two or three times the height of the rest of the hopper. In another the arms of the crescent meet to form a complete circular arch. In still another (our favorite) a process rises and curves forward over the head, bearing at its tip a slender stalk from which spring three perfect balls arranged in an isosceles triangle—a pawnbroker's sign flaunted aloft! Many others are almost equally bizarre, completely overshadowing the insect beneath. It is impossible that such structures cannot seriously handicap their possessors in moving freely about; and except for the possibility that they are of some value as a disguise against predatory enemies, it is difficult to see that they can be of

A **Treehopper** (*Umbonia crassicornis*). Many members of this family are called Thorn Bugs because of their resemblance to thorns.

any use. Proponents of the school of evolutionary thought who claim that every plant and animal structure must be of some definite benefit will have a hard time explaining these treehoppers.

The females lay their eggs in two parallel slits, sometimes curved and looking like a pair of parentheses, which they cut in the bark of twigs. In some species they appear to exhibit some degree of maternal solicitude for the eggs. The larvae seldom show the developments of the pronotum that they will wear as adults, but are often armed with rows of spines or filaments. They often are more or less gregarious, resting side by side in rows. When disturbed they tend to dodge rather than to hop immediately.

Few species are abundant enough to be serious pests. One of the commonest in North America is the buffalo treehopper, *Ceresa bubalis,* light green and triangular with a short, pointed, projecting pronotum. The adults sometimes injure fruit trees by the egg punctures, while the larvae feed on grasses, corn and legumes.

WHITEFLIES—*Family Aleyrodidae*

The exceedingly minute adults of these curious insects, which seldom exceed two or three millimeters in length, resemble tiny moths with a covering of white powder. The majority of the species are tropical and a few are more or less injurious to citrus or greenhouse plants. Although undoubtedly members of the Homoptera, an order in which most forms have a normal incomplete metamorphosis, the last (preadult) stage of these insects is a quiescent one, encased in the skin of the previous stage. During this period the wings, which have previously developed internally (another feature characteristic of complete metamorphosis) evert and become external, and the other changes to the adult stage are accomplished. We may say, then, that the members of this family, as well as some scale insects, seem to be developing a complete metamorphosis similar to that of the more advanced insect orders.

The greenhouse whitefly, *Trialeurodes vaporariorum,* has been introduced into nearly every part of the world, having originated in some warm region, probably Brazil. It may become a pest on almost anything that grows under glass and occasionally on tomatoes and related plants outside. In the tropics several species assume importance, at times, on citrus fruits. They not only injure their host by sucking sap from the leaves, but in addition secrete a honeydew that contains the essential ingredients for the nourishment of a fungus, the sooty mold *Meliola camelliae.* Since this discolors the fruit badly, as well as the plant, it is necessary to wash the fruit before it can be marketed.

SCALE INSECTS and MEALY BUGS
—Family Coccidae

Because of the ease with which they can be transported, many of the species of this family have become practically cosmopolitan. Although the individuals are small they occur in such enormous assemblages, encrusting the leaves, twigs and bark, that they are a familiar sight; and many are among the most serious of all agricultural insect pests. Some species are general feeders, attacking hundreds of different plants; others are restricted to a single host.

The females are often wingless, legless and eyeless and are generally degenerate in form, although all degrees of reduction of parts occur. Thus lacking powers of locomotion, they must remain on the plant, sessile and immobile. They are always clothed in a vestiture or protective coating of their own secretion. This covering may be of a mealy nature; it may be a cell of resin; it may be in the form of waxy plates or a simple waxy cuticle; or it may be a definite scale which, though secreted by the body, is separate from it.

The males lack mouthparts and do not assemble in such large aggregations on the food plants. Although some are wingless, the majority have the front pair functional for flight, the second pair being replaced by two tiny, slender structures, known as halteres, that are equipped with one or two hooks for fastening onto the rear margin of the front wings. Sometimes the males show an alternation of generations, a wingless form followed by a winged. In most species the males are seldom seen. In some species that alternate between different host plants the males may be moderately common in the generation on one plant but unknown in the generation on the other. Parthenogenesis, or agamic development from an unfertilized egg, is common, thus dispensing with the male sex for many generations.

The eggs are never deposited in the open. They may remain beneath the body of the sessile female or, if she is armored, beneath her scale; they may be covered by a white cottony or felted mass of secretion; they may be carried about in plates of wax hanging from the female abdomen; or they may even be covered over for the winter by the dead body of the female who laid them. Some species are ovoviviparous as well as oviparous; that is, they retain the eggs within the body until they hatch and thus give birth to living young. The flat, oval larvae crawl about quite actively at first, but soon lose their legs and cover themselves with their characteristic secretions.

The giant coccids belonging to the subfamily Margarodinae are few in number of species but world-wide in distribution. They are the largest members of the family, *Llaveia* and *Callipappus* reaching an inch in length. *Llaveia auxin* was long used by the natives of Mexico, who made varnish from its waxy secretions. Species of *Margarodes* in South Africa and the Bahamas live on the roots of plants. Each female surrounds herself with a wax cyst of a beautiful metallic bronze or gold color; these are used for beads and are called ground pearls. To this group belongs the cottony cushion scale, *Icerya purchasi,* the chief citrus pest of the western United States. Introduced into California from Australia and New Zealand in 1868, the scale had killed hundreds of thousands of trees by 1890, threatening to wipe out the orange groves of the state. It was for the control of this scale that the Australian ladybeetle was introduced (see p. 121).

The ensign coccids, belonging to the subfamily Ortheziinae, also live underground on roots. The females are covered with a large number of white waxy plates, and may have a waxy egg scale attached to the end of the abdomen. *Orthezia insignis* is a native of the tropics but is now widely distributed, living on a wide variety of ornamental shrubs and plants.

The females of the subfamily Lacciferinae cover themselves with a layer of resin that hardens upon contact with the air. When a large number of the females are crowded together, the little cells of resin form a very sizable mass, known as stick lac, that may occur in layers one-fourth to one-half an inch thick. Since at least as early as 1590 this has been gathered for use in making varnishes. In 1709 the insect was described by Father Tachard and for a long time bore the name *Tachardia lacca,* but it has now been placed in the genus *Laccifera.* It lives in the fig, banyan and other forest trees of India and Burma, north to Formosa and the Philippines, usually uncultivated, but growing in such numbers that up to ninety million pounds of stick lac may be collected yearly. This is cleaned and treated to make flakes which, when dissolved in alcohol, form the shellac with which we are familiar. It has been estimated that it takes the resinous products of about 150,000 lac insects to make a pound of lac. Its use is far more extensive than most of us realize, for in addition to its functions in shellacs, varnishes and polishes it is used in stiffening hats, for lithographic ink, sealing wax, electrical insulations, phonograph records, airplanes, linoleum, buttons, pottery, toys, imitation flowers and many other articles. It is, however, being increasingly replaced by synthetic plastics.

In Madagascar species of *Gascardia* are dried and melted down in making a somewhat inferior lac known as gum lac. In the southwestern United States the Mohave Indians used to gather species of *Tachardiella* living on cacti, making from their secretions a substance with which to waterproof their closely woven baskets.

The gall-like coccids, or pseudogalls, of the family Kerminae (Plate 35), are of considerable interest historically. *Trabutina mannipara,* which feeds on the tamarix of Palestine, secretes enormous quantities of sweet honeydew which solidifies on the leaves of the trees and the ground beneath. We read in the sixteenth chapter of Exodus that "upon the face of the wilderness there lay a small round thing, as small as the hoar frost on the ground. . . . And the house of Israel called the name thereof Manna: and it was like coriander seed, white; and the taste of it was like wafers made with honey. . . . And the children of Israel did eat manna forty years." Females of the genus *Kermes* look like small spherical galls as they rest on the twigs and branches of oaks; and like some true galls, their outer coatings contain substances that are used in making dyes. The bodies of *K. ilicis* in particular are dried and sold as "Kermes" or *granum tinctorum.* The space beneath the scale of a female may be tightly packed with the great masses of eggs into which practically all of her substance is transformed.

Another scale insect of tremendous importance in the past, but no longer used as extensively, is *Coccus cacti* of the subfamily Dactylopiinae, the source of the red dye, cochineal. Known to the Aztecs long before Europeans discovered America, it is cultivated in Honduras and the Canary Islands and to some extent in such widely separated places as Mexico and Peru, Algiers and Spain. The insect lives on one of the prickly pear cacti and may be brought indoors in the winter on little branches of the cactus that may then be set out again in the spring. When the females are fully mature they are brushed off into bags, killed, dried and pulverized. From these cochineal is obtained, a pound of it requiring the bodies of about 70,000 insects. Cochineal was formerly used extensively in cosmetics, medicines and beverages to give permanent color, and also as a palliative in whooping cough and neuralgia. It is little used nowadays, having been replaced by synthetic dyes.

The mealy bugs, or Pseudococcinae, are so named because of their mealy or waxy secretions. There are many species, most of which, like the citrus mealy bug, *Pseudococcus citri,* are minor pests on citrus fruits and greenhouse plants. The elm scale of Europe and North America, *Eriococcus spurius,* weakens and kills elm trees by sucking sap from the undersides of the limbs, making sticky and sooty everything that lies beneath. In England the heaths are similarly harmed and deformed by the gall-like formations of *E. devoniensis.*

The pit scales, or Asterolecaniinae, covered with a tough, waxy film, are best known for *Cerococcus quercus,* which lives on oaks in California and was formerly collected by the Indians for making an equivalent of chewing gum. The soft scales, or Coccinae, contain a number of injurious species. They are sometimes called wax scales or tortoise scales but the name "soft scale" is more descriptive because their protective shell is not formed of wax but of the bare chitinous wall. The females, which retain their legs and move about while feeding, often become pests in greenhouses in temperate regions, and outdoors in the tropics. The Chinese wax scale, *Ericerus pe-la,* a member of this group, has long been collected in the Orient for the pure white wax that is secreted by the males and can be used for making candles. Another species, *Ceroplastes ceriferus* of India, provides a different wax that is used locally in medicines.

The hard or armored scales (Plate 34) make up the largest and most degenerate of the subfamilies, the Diaspidinae. The soft-bodied female is protected by a scale formed from her waxy secretions mixed with the dead cast skins of her earlier larval stages, which is quite free from her body. These scales differ greatly in color, shape and surface texture from species to species. Many of the species are serious pests. The San José scale, *Quadraspidiotus perniciosus,* received its name from San José, California, where it was first found in the ground of a large estate on plants that had been brought from China in 1870. In the year 1922 more than a thousand acres of apple trees in southern Illinois were killed by the scale, which now does serious

[continued on page 97]

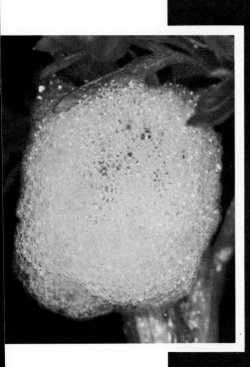

30–32. **Spittle Bug** (Family Cercopidae) sequence showing (above and below) the frothy substance secreted for protection by newly-hatched nymph and (at right) the adult bug emerging.

33. **Aphids** (Family Aphididae). The larger ones are wingless females that give birth to living young.

34. **Oyster Shell Scales** (*Lepidosaphes*). Beneath each scale the insect lives and sucks sap from this willow stem.

35. **Oak Scales** (*Eulecanium quercifer*). One has been torn loose from the stem to show the thousands of eggs produced by a single female.

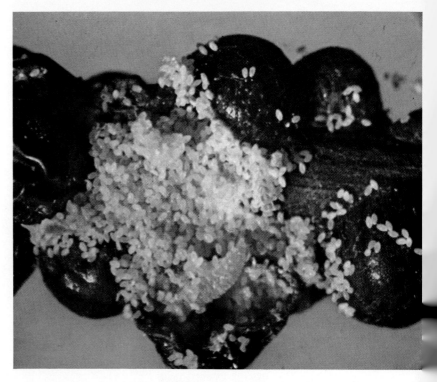

36. A **Diving Beetle** (Family Dytiscidae). A voracious fresh-water insect that may catch small fish and tadpoles.

37. **The Searcher** (*Calosoma scrutator*). A ground beetle that kills many harmful insects, it is often called the Caterpillar Hunter.

38. A **Firefly** (*Photinus pyralis*). The source of a far more efficient light than any produced by man.

39. **Burying Beetles** (*Necrophorus*). and a dead mole. They will completely bury such an animal in a few hours and then feed on it underground.

40. An **Oil Beetle** (*Meloë*). One of a worldwide group noted for their distasteful, burning secretion and for their complex development.

41. **Ladybird Beetles** (*Hippodamia californica*) forming a summer swarm. In the autumn such beetles gather in similar groups to hibernate.

42. **A Ladybird Beetle** of a species that feeds on aphids.

⟶

45. Luminous larvae of a South American beetle, locally called "Railroad Worms," photographed by their own light. The inset (upper right) shows one of the larvae.

43. A metallic **Flat-headed Wood Boring Beetle** (*Buprestis curulenta*). The larvae are among the most destructive of timber pests.

44. **A Click Beetle** (*Tomicephalus sanguinicollis*). When on its back it is able to snap itself up into the air by means of the hinged joint behind the prothorax.

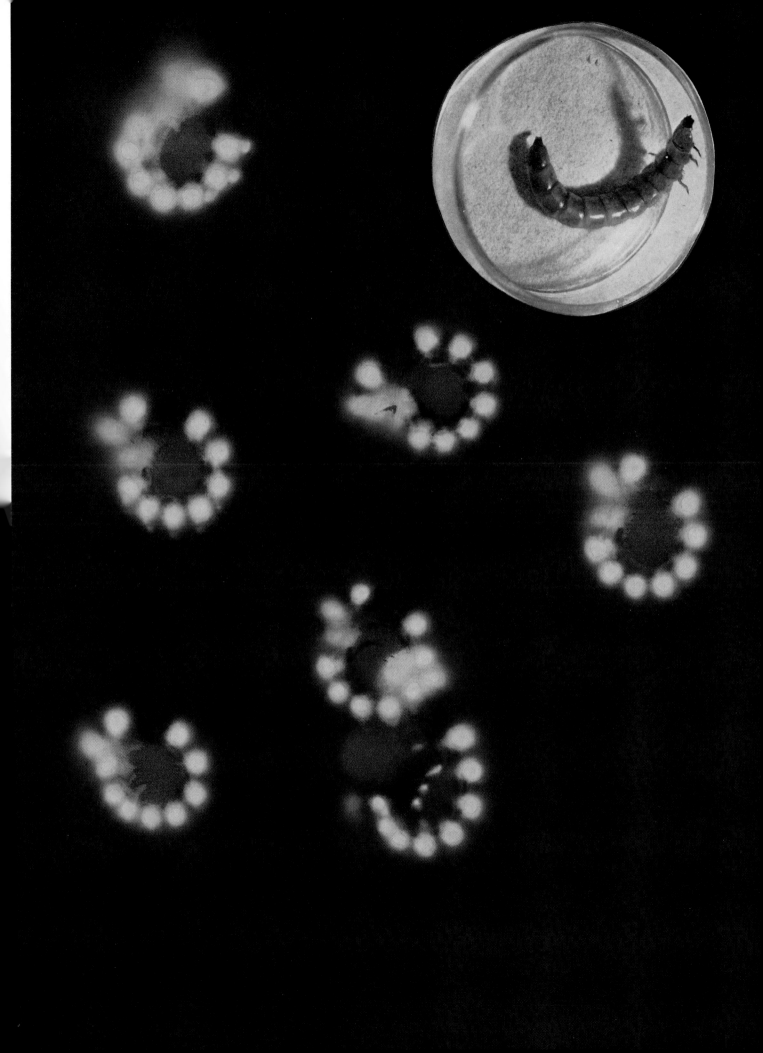

46. A **Tumble Bug** (*Pinotus carolinus*) rolling a ball of dung—provender for its prospective young.

47. A Cetoniid **Scarab** (*Cotinus mutabilis*) found in the southeastern United States.

48. **Rhinoceros Dung Beetle** (*Phanaeus vindex*). A species common in the southern and central United States.

49. **Striped Chafer** (*Polyphylla decemlineata*). A Scarabeaeid beetle of the arid regions of North America.

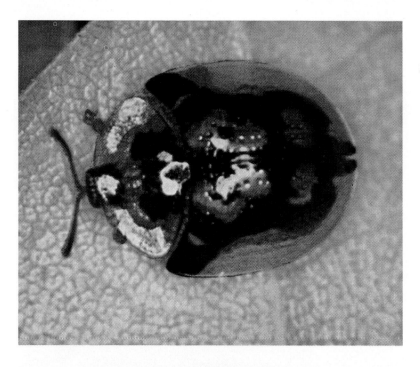

50. A **Tortoise Beetle** (Cassidini) whose metallic, structural colors disappear soon after death with the shrinking of the integument.

51. **Locust Borer** (*Cyllene robiniae*). A Longicorn beetle with the coloring and pattern of a wasp.

52. **Japanese Beetles** (*Popillia japonica*). Introduced into the United States from Asia, they have proved to be among the worst of all insect pests.

53. **Four-eyed Milkweed Beetle** (*Tetraopes tetraophthalmus*). Each compound eye is divided into two separate parts.

54. A South American **Darkling Beetle** (Family Tenebrionidae). In the Temperate Zones most members of this family are dark and plain colored.

55. **Milkweed Leaf Beetle** (*Labidomera clivicollis*). The bright colors warn potential attackers that it is highly inedible.

56. **Dogbane Leaf Beetles** (*Chrysochus auratus*). Often abundant in eastern North America.

57. A pair of mating **Leaf Beetles** (*Doryphora*) from Peru.

58. A **Golden-eyed Lace Wing** (*Chrysopa*). Its larva is extremely beneficial, feeding on such small insect pests as aphids.

59. A **Caddis Fly** (*Hesperophylax incisus*). The aquatic larvae of these mothlike insects are an important food source for fresh-water fish.

60. **Dobson Fly** (*Corydalis cornutus*), female. The jaws of the male are many times longer.

61. A **Scorpion Fly** (*Panorpa*). Its curious head has tiny jaws at the end of a long beak.

[continued from page 80]

damage all the way to the Atlantic coast. The reproductive rate is high; one female could have 30,000,000 progeny in a single year, since there may be as many as six generations annually. They may be carried from orchard to orchard by birds or by wind as well as by human transportation of plant stock. The scale can withstand temperatures of ten degrees above zero, so securely is it fastened down to the bark of the tree and protected by its hardened waxen armor. Another of the many harmful species is the oyster shell scale, *Lepidosaphes ulmi,* which attacks many shade trees and shrubs. Others may attack the needles of evergreen trees, such species as the pine leaf scale, *Chionaspis pinifoliae,* sometimes almost completely covering the needles of the hard pines and seriously stunting the growth of the trees.

APHIDS, GREEN FLIES or PLANT LICE
—Family Aphididae

Tiny, but mighty through sheer force of numbers, the aphids are unquestionably one of the dominant groups of insects (Plate 33); yet relatively few people other than agriculturists and gardeners give them more than a passing thought. Practically all are less than one-quarter of an inch long, and all are soft, weak and well-nigh defenseless; yet by their secretion of copious honeydew many species have gained ardent defenders in the ants (Plate 142), who exploit them but attack their molestors, build shelters around them, carry them to fresh pastures and even take them into their own nests during inclement weather. The winged forms are feeble fliers, but with the aid of air currents they manage to cover great distances through the air. All such specializations, however, are trivial compared with their unexcelled powers of reproduction, and the accuracy with which their extremely complicated life histories are adjusted to the food plants and other factors of the environment. Needless to say their great numbers and the variety of the plants upon which they feed make them of primary economic importance to man.

A typical aphid has a very small head and thorax but a relatively large pear-shaped abdomen. From the rear end of this project two slender tubes, the cornicles. The antennae and the beak are long and slender. If wings are present, they are weak and lightly veined. Few species have decided color patterns, most being green, red or brown. The legs are thin and useful only for slow walking about. The whole insect looks as unimpressive, defenseless and unlikely to lead a successful life as any we can imagine.

Many species secrete waxy substances from the cornicles, sometimes as long, curling strands that may form a dense investing mass. Such "woolly" aphids, like that of apple, *Eriosoma lanigera,* or of alder and maple, *Prociphalus tesselatus,* may form dense, flocculent colonies visible from many yards away. The covering doubtless has considerable protective value against rain and cold, and possibly against predators and parasites.

It is in their secretion of honeydew, however, that aphids excel. This is simply the sap that is sucked in through the beak and, only partially digested and with its sweet contents concentrated, is given off from the anus. So great is the flow that the ground and everything else beneath a thriving colony may be completely wetted by the sweet rain, which dries to a shiny glaze. Entirely aside from the damage done to a plant by the withdrawal of so much of its sap, the clogging and shading of the surfaces of leaves by the dried coating and by the thick layers of molds and fungi that grow on this may be a serious handicap. All leaves beneath an aphid colony may be blackened by such molds, which are sometimes of species that grow nowhere else.

One of the most characteristic types of damage done by aphids is the curling of leaves. This occurs when a colony withdraws sap from the lower surface of a leaf, scarring and drying it. The leaf then curls downward, forming a protective enclosure for the aphids but being of little further use to the plant and having an unsightly appearance. The growth of the stem is often seriously aborted by such continual attacks on the tender, developing terminal leaves.

Many species of aphids cause the formation of galls by their host plants, some secretion of the aphids stimulating the growing plant tissue in a very specific way. Such galls are characteristic in size and shape, being often much more easily recognizable than the aphid that causes them. The sharp cone galls on the leaves of witch hazel are familiar wherever that plant grows, being caused by the aphid *Hormaphis hamamelidis.* So is the cockscomb gall on the leaves of elm, caused by *Colopha ulmicola.* Clusters of the aphids live inside the hollow galls, which have a small opening communicating with the exterior. Stem, petiole and root galls are caused by other species.

Many aphids live underground, sucking the sap from roots. In some cases, as with the corn root aphis, *Anuraphis maidi-radicis,* the aphids are dependent upon ants, chiefly of the genera *Lasius* and *Acanthomyops* (see page 285), which carry them through tunnels in the soil and set them out on fresh roots if necessary. In other instances the aphids apparently have to gain access to the roots by themselves.

A characteristic of many aphids is a regular alternation of host plants, typically synchronized with alternation of the structure of the aphids themselves and of their methods of reproduction. Needless to say this produces some extraordinarily complex puzzles for the entomologist who studies these insects, since a population of aphids living in a peculiar way on one plant may actually be no more than the offspring of a very different-looking population that lived in another way on a different plant. After a period of reproduction and increase on one of the hosts, the aphid moves to another, and after a while moves back to the original host.

A typical life cycle of this sort might start on one tree, such as elm, as is the case with the woolly aphis mentioned above. In the autumn each female has laid a single egg on the bark and then died. In the spring the eggs hatch, and the young aphids feed on the tender leaves. They all mature into wingless females that give birth without fertilization (whence they are called "agamic," i.e. without marriage) to individuals that develop into a second generation like their mothers. This generation, however, gives birth to a third agamic generation that, although all females, have wings. These fly to apple and there produce on the twigs and leaves a fourth generation of wingless agamic females. Many of these migrate to the roots, where their descendents may remain for years, producing gall-like growths. Those that remain above ground give birth to a largely winged generation, most of which migrate back to the elm. Having done so, they give birth to a wingless generation that consists of both males and females. The males cannot feed when mature, existing only long enough to fertilize the females. These, the last generation of the year, lay the eggs that will overwinter and hatch the next spring.

The subfamily Phylloxerinae consists of aphids lacking the wax-producing cornicles, whose agamically reproducing females lay eggs instead of producing the young alive. The life cycles of many are just as complex as the one described above. An important and widespread species that shows some peculiarities is the spruce gall aphid, *Adelges abietis*. It is abundant in both Europe and North America; but the European populations alternate the life cycle between spruce and larch, while in North America the species stays on spruce (including the imported Norway spruce) even when European larch is available. Moreover no males have been found in America, all reproduction being agamic. Perhaps there are two or more different species now passing as one. The aphids cause a stunting of the new growth at the tips of twigs, forming a gall-like structure that looks like a small, shaggy cone. In very heavy infestations practically every tip may be thus infected, seriously damaging the growth of the tree and giving it a most unsightly, ragged appearance. Many of our finest ornamental conifers are spruces susceptible to such attacks.

The most internationally infamous of aphids, however, is the phylloxera of the grape, *Phylloxera vitifoliae*. Its life history is exceedingly complex, involving generations spent in galls on the leaves of grapes and others in galls on the roots, with the usual aphid complications of sexual and asexual and winged and wingless generations. Different varieties of grape show very different degrees of resistance to the aphids, the European *vinifera* or wine grapes being most greatly injured. The insect is a native of North America; and the North American grapes are most resistant to it. Imported into Europe about the middle of the last century, the phylloxera threatened for a time to wipe out grape culture in some of the most magnificent vineyard regions of France from which come many famous vintages. The problem was at last partially solved by importing North American grape varieties and from these growing rootstocks that carried the resistance. On these were grafted the French *vinifera* plants, which therefore form the aboveground plants and, of course, determine the type of fruit produced. The grapes in many European vineyards are now, therefore, growing on plants supported by American rooting systems. Whether or not this caused a deterioration of the quality of the grapes and wine, as many connoisseurs claim, is debatable. Without it, however, many of the most famous wine-producing regions might be unable to produce any vintage wines at all.

CHAPTER IX

Scorpion Flies, Lacewings and other small Orders

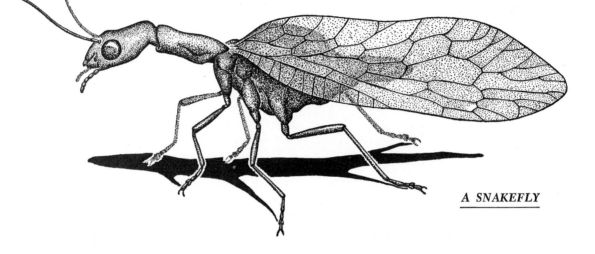

A SNAKEFLY

WE group together here three of the smaller orders, which have a complete metamorphosis and biting mouthparts. All are actually more or less related to each other as well as to the Lepidoptera, Diptera and Siphonaptera, forming with these an ancestrally connected group known as the Panorpoid complex. All are world-wide, and each contains common insects that may be encountered anywhere.

THE SCORPION FLIES
—Order Mecoptera

Although a relatively small order containing less than three hundred species, the Mecoptera (Plate 61) are of extremely ancient lineage, since the earliest Endopterygote fossils known are true Mecoptera allied to the present-day Australian Choristidae. These curious insects received their common name from the appearance of the genital structures of the males of one of the most familiar groups. Located at the tip of the abdomen, these are turned upward and forward so as to look almost exactly like the stinging apparatus of a scorpion. They are actually harmless.

The order is composed of six families, of which two are known to be world-wide, two are restricted to the Australian region, one occurs in Europe and North America, and one is limited to the New World. Few of the species are more than an inch long, although the extremely long legs of some make

them look larger. The most distinctive characteristic is the prominent downward-pointing beak, which is formed by the elongation of the front part of the head. The biting mouthparts are located at the end of the beak. All four of the wings are of approximately the same size and shape, being slender with rounded ends. In many species they are blackish or blue-black with white patches, or yellowish with prominent dark spots, but in many others they are uncolored and transparent.

The larvae of nearly all species live and pupate in loose soil or debris. Some are predatory on small insects, as are their adults; still others, however, either feed on dead animal matter or on plant debris. The order, as a whole, is considered somewhat beneficial because of the predatory habits of so many of its members.

The family Panorpidae includes the commonest species of our damp, shady woodlands, where the adults, many of which have dark-spotted wings, may be seen flying about and resting in low vegetation. They are the ones whose characteristic male appendages are responsible for the ordinal name. They feed chiefly on dead and injured insects, as well as upon sap and fruit juices.

Members of the genus *Bittacus* of the family Bittacidae resemble large craneflies, for which they are often mistaken because of their attenuate bodies and extremely long, slender legs. They may be

[99

GORDON M. NISHIDA

A Slender Scorpion Fly (*Bittacus*) hanging by two feet and ready to seize with its hind feet any small insects that fly near.

distinguished easily by their two pairs of wings, since craneflies have only a single pair. These scorpion flies are adapted for the lives of consistent predatism that they lead by having the last joint of the tarsus free to snap back against the next joint, forming an efficient, although not very strong, prehensile organ. They use these to hang from a leaf or twig, perhaps holding on with but one or two feet while the other legs sprawl widely in the air, ready to seize any small prey that comes in reach.

Boreus of the family Boreidae, known only from Europe and North America, is only two and a half millimeters long. Since its wings are vestigial or entirely lacking, it greatly resembles a grasshopper nymph as it crawls about on logs or stones seeking the plant debris on which it feeds. It may always be recognized by the characteristic beaklike mouthparts. It is often found in great numbers on the snow in winter or early spring, and because of this shares the name "snow flea" with such other hardy insects as the collembolan *Achorutes* and the stonefly *Capnia.*

The larvae of the Australian Nannochoristidae, all of the species of which are quite small, are almost certainly aquatic. One species of the similarly Australian Choristidae, *Taeniochorista pallida,* is particularly known for its courtship. During pairing the male embraces the mouth of the female with his greatly enlarged mouthparts and exudes a sweet, sticky secretion upon which she eagerly feeds.

LACEWINGS, ANT LIONS, DOBSON FLIES etc.
—Order Neuroptera

Although the Neuroptera are a relatively small order, consisting of about 4300 species, they are extremely diverse in both habitats and appearance. Some are aquatic as larvae, while others are found only in exceedingly arid desert regions. In appearance the adults range from the very large, enormous-jawed dobsonflies to the slender, fragile ant lions and the tiny spongilla flies which live as larvae in the bodies of fresh-water sponges. All are predatory as larvae, using their strong, often extremely long jaws to capture other insects and feed upon them in a diversity of ways. Some are extremely beneficial, feeding upon groups of insects that are highly injurious to agriculture. The metamorphosis is complete, the pupa being of the type known as exarate, which has the appendages free from the body, even though they cannot be used.

The order separates into two quite natural groups, which have been treated as two orders by some authors. The first, the Megaloptera, contains the families Corydalidae, the dobsonflies; Sialidae, the fish flies or alderflies; and Raphidiidae, the snakeflies. The other group, or Plannipennia, the conventional Neuroptera, contains a considerable number of families.

The dobsonflies (Plate 60) and alderflies both have the anal area of the hind wing folded fanwise. Both are aquatic as larvae, living under stones, sometimes in fast-running water, or among the trash and debris of the bottom. The larvae have strong biting jaws, are predaceous and respire by means of several pairs of threadlike gills on the abdomen. The large larvae of the dobsonfly *Corydalis cornutus,* which may attain a length of three inches or more, are particularly common in shallow, fast-running water beneath stones. Here they are actively sought by anglers, since under the name of hellgramites they are used as one of the favorite bass baits. Although they have strong jaws, the adults of these insects probably feed little if at all. The jaws of the male dobsonfly are enormous, out of all proportion to the rest of the head, being, in fact, so long that they are extremely inefficient levers and can do no more than give a firm pinch. They are presumably used to hold the female during mating. The much shorter and less imposing jaws of the female and of the alderflies are really much more efficient weapons.

Entirely aside from their use by humans as bait, the larvae of the dobsonflies and alderflies are of considerable importance in the ecology of stream animals. They produce nothing, of course, for only the green plants do that; nor do they play the part of primary consumers, for that is done by the plant-eating animals that transform plant matter into animal matter. They are secondary consumers, the third step in the food chain. By feeding upon small animals they increase the size of the animal food units available and then serve as food for the still larger animals, such as trout and bass, for which direct feeding on much smaller animals would be uneconomical. They are thus, so to speak, important middlemen—jobbers and distributors—in the food chain leading from the plants to the fish.

The Raphidiidae, or snakeflies, are grouped with the preceding families because of similarities of the wing venation and the fact that as larvae they have normal biting mouthparts. They are easily distinguished by their exceedingly long, slender "necks" —actually the greatly lengthened prothorax and back of the head—and small heads. They are often attracted to light, especially in arid and desert regions. Although weak fliers, the adults are rapid runners. The larvae, unlike those of the dobsonflies and alderflies, are terrestrial, scampering actively about beneath loose bark, especially of conifers, but often in orchards, where they are highly beneficial because of their predaceous habits. They occur in all continents except Australia. In North America they occur only in the West, being especially common under the bark of eucalyptus in California.

In the true Neuroptera or Plannipennia a number of families are recognized, nearly all of which are terrestrial and differ considerably in the appearance of the adults, but on the whole are quite closely interrelated. All are predatory as larvae, but eat relatively little, if anything, as adults. The mouthparts of the larvae are very characteristic and represent a most efficient adaptation for preying on other insects. The mandibles are long and sharp, often bearing teeth; they are usually extremely slender and hooked inward, serving excellently for gripping, holding and piercing the prey. Each mandible is also so constructed that the maxilla of its side coordinates with it to form a channel along which the blood of the prey can flow. Some forms merely insert the mandibles and then hold the prey up in the air, letting the blood run down the channels into the mouth; others have more or less of a sucking apparatus. Structurally, then, the mouthparts are of the unmistakable biting type; but functionally they serve for feeding on liquids only.

THE MANTISFLIES—*Family Mantispidae*

The front legs of these insects are extremely distinctive, being proportionately very large and powerful and formed, like those of the mantids, with a tibia that can be snapped back against the femur to hold prey. It would be very easy, in fact, to mistake a mantisfly at first glance for a small mantis one-half or three-quarters of an inch long. The front wings, however, being normal wings with a distinct venation like that of the hind wings, are nothing like the more or less thickened front wings that cover the pleated hind wings of a mantis. The strong resemblance between the mantisflies and the mantids is, therefore, convergent; starting from widely different ancestries, the two groups have come to resemble each other merely because both, quite independently, have become adapted to the same way of life.

The mantisflies are quite rare insects found chiefly in tropical and subtropical regions. We have caught one in Connecticut, but this represents an abnormally northern record. The rose-red eggs of the European *Mantispa styriaca,* like those of many other Neuroptera, are laid on long, slender stalks. The agile larvae feed on the eggs in the sacs of the big *Lycosa* spiders. The metamorphosis goes considerably beyond being merely complete, for there are two extremely distinct stages during larval development and two stages of pupae, the second of which is an active one outside the cocoon. This type of complicated metamorphosis, which is known in a few groups of insects, is called hypermetamorphosis. We will describe it more in detail under the oil beetles (Meloidae) which represent a classic example of it. A Brazilian mantisfly, *Symphasis varia,* has a similar hypermetamorphosis, but its larvae live as parasites in the nests of wasps, pupating in the nest.

SPONGILLA FLIES—*Family Sisyridae*

The small, smoky brown spongilla flies are known from many parts of the world, wherever they have access to the fresh-water sponges upon which they live parasitically in the larval stage. Since sponges are animals, this is technically genuine parasitism, although the immobility and plantlike growth of the sponge makes it unusual. The larvae respire by means of tracheal gills, and penetrate the openings in the body of the sponge with the long, slender mandibles plus maxillae. When full grown they leave the water and spin double-walled lacelike cocoons within which they pupate. The adults lay their eggs in clusters under a silken web spun on objects close to the water's edge, sometimes actually in the water. The way in which this little group of small, terrestrial insects has become adapted to such an unusual way of life and source of food is an excellent example of the dynamic evolution of the insects. Wherever a source of food exists, no matter how far removed from conventional habitats, there we are very likely to find some insect thriving in its exploitation.

GOLDEN-EYED LACEWINGS
—Family Chrysopidae

In nearly every part of the world there are at least some common, often abundant, species of this family (Plate 58). They are delicate, pale green insects about half an inch long, with long, threadlike antennae and bright golden or brassy yellow eyes. They are often seen fluttering about, quite clumsily, among vegetation. They have a characteristic strong odor with a touch of garlic about it which some people find very unpleasant; birds and other predators do not like it either, so that adult lacewings are quite free from such enemies (although we have seen many of them caught in spiders' webs). The European species have a much stronger odor than those of North America.

The larvae are flattened, with rather stout abdomens. They crawl on the foliage, hunting for small, soft-bodied insects which they pierce with their long mandibles. The larvae of many species cover themselves with the dried remains of their victims, so that each one looks like a tiny mass of debris rather than a living insect, an illusion that is destroyed when the bit of fluff starts crawling about. The voracious appetites of the larvae are of enormous benefit to man, since the insects upon which they chiefly feed, aphids and scale insects, include many of the most injurious species of the world, from man's point of view. The lacewings, ladybirds and flower flies are, in fact, our chief allies in controlling such extremely harmful pests.

The eggs of the lacewings, like those of related Neuroptera, are laid separately, although often in small groups, and each egg is placed at the end of an extremely long, hairlike stalk. It has been suggested that this is of adaptive value, since otherwise the first larvae to hatch would eat the rest of the eggs or the late hatchers. This seems plausible, but one wonders if the larvae actually would be cannibalistic if given the opportunity. However, we are highly in favor of anything that will increase the numbers of lacewings.

BROWN LACEWINGS—Family Hemerobiidae

Most of these insects are rather smaller than the Chrysopidae. The adults typically have brownish, often spotted wings. The larvae live much as do the

Lacewing eggs (*Chrysopa*), each at the tip of a delicate, hairlike stalk.

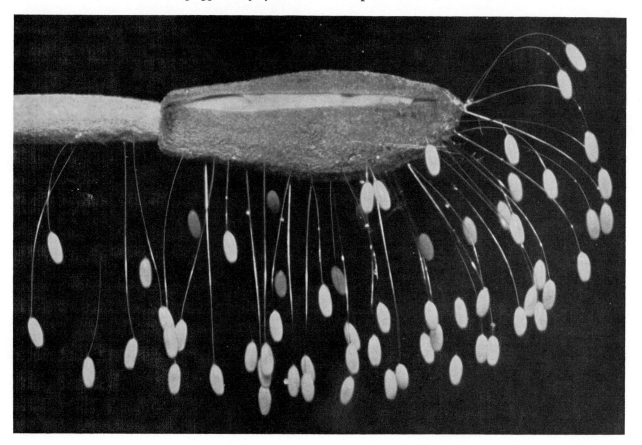

Chrysopidae and are equally beneficial. In some regions, in fact, they are the dominant lacewings.

ANT LIONS—Family Myrmeleontidae

The adults look very much like dragonflies, having long, slender bodies and four long, slender wings about equal in size, which have a great many small, branching veins and cross veins. Their flight, however, is much weaker and very fluttery, their heads are much smaller, and their antennae, although short, are threadlike and knobbed at the end. Some species are three or more inches long, and some have the wings adorned with black spots and patches.

The larvae of the best-known genera and species are the ant lions or doodle bugs, which dig large, conical pits and there lie in wait. They are flattened, obese-bodied creatures, nearly an inch long in the largest species, with the usual long, wide-spreading jaws of the whole group. Placed on loose, fine sand or dust, a larva shuffles itself down under the surface with a few backward steps. In digging a pit it simply keeps going around and around backward in small circles, with constant upward jerks of the head. Each such jerk tosses away the sand that has accumulated on top of the head. A conical pit results, which is surprisingly wide and deep. We have found such pits nearly three inches in diameter and two inches deep that had been dug by a larva only a fraction over one-quarter of an inch long. The steepness of the sides of the pit depends, of course, on what an engineer would call the "angle of rest" of the medium in which it is dug. At the bottom of the pit the larva lies shallowly buried with its jaws spread wide, ready to seize any ant or other insect that may crawl or fall in. It is often possible to see just the slender jaws exposed at the bottom of the pit. If the prey is not caught at once the larva excitedly hurls "headloads" of sand, and these, together with the sliding sand of the steep walls, bring the prey tumbling down to the bottom again, and possibly again, until eventually it is seized. Imagine yourself trying to run up a very steep bank of loose sand while bushels more of sand were being hurled at you. Once seized, the prey is soon perforated and drained dry and its empty shell is discarded; after which the larva repairs the damage to the pit and awaits another victim.

In very arid regions the pits are frequently dug anywhere that loose, fine, dry sand or dust is available. In more rainy regions they are usually under the shelter of some overhang where raindrops will not flatten them out. We look for them under bridges or wide eaves, or beneath rocky ledges and in caves. We once found a fine colony in the thick layer of wood dust that had accumulated beneath the overhang of a large dead log lying on the ground, the debris resulting from the boring within the log

An **Ant Lion** (*Euroleon europaeus*), adult. The larvae dig pits in loose sand or dust and prey on small insects that tumble in.

of carpenter ants and wood-boring beetles.

The larvae of many Myrmeleontids do not dig pits but merely shuffle about under loose debris to lie in wait, shallowly buried with their wide-spreading jaws extended to seize anything coming within reach.

ASCALAPHIDS—Family Ascalaphidae

These are chiefly tropical insects of world-wide distribution, but a few species occur northward in Europe and the United States. We have taken them in New York. The adults are much like those of the ant lions, but usually fly during the daytime, and have very long, strongly knobbed antennae. When at rest they hold the wings pressed down below the body at the sides, the antennae outstretched in front and the abdomen curved upward. They are fast fliers. The larvae resemble those of the ant lions but do not excavate pits; they are very rapacious and, at times, cannibalistic.

THE SPOON-WINGED and THREAD-WINGED LACEWINGS—Family Nemopteridae

Members of this family are found from southern Europe and Africa to Australia. The adults are noteworthy for the forward prolongation of the head to form a beak and for the unusual shape of the hind wings. These are very long and narrow, either ribbon-like or else very narrow at the base and then abruptly broadened and spoon-shaped, and twisted where they broaden. The larvae, too, are unusual. When we first held in our hands a living larva of *Pterocroce storeyi*, a species found in caves in Egypt and Palestine, we could not believe our eyes. The large flat head, with incurved, toothed mandibles that were longer than the head itself, was balanced at the end of an incredibly attenuated, thread-like neck that was longer than the rest of the body. When we put this believe-it-or-not back on the sand, it sprawled with its long legs outstretched for a second; then, before we could say "It matches the sand in color," it had disappeared beneath the surface with a flick too fast for the eye to follow.

[103

About ten other families of Neuroptera are known, of which the great majority are from Australia, where the Plannipennia are best represented. The Psychopsidae have broad, brightly colored and patterned wings; they are often known as silky lacewings because of the long, silky hairs on the wing veins. The larvae of some of the Australian Myiodactylidae are extraordinarily flattened, disc-shaped and bright green; they hide on the underside of leaves, which they just match in color, and snap at any insect that comes within reach. The Coniopterygidae are tiny insects, mostly from three to five millimeters in wing expanse, with the wings covered with a whitish powder. A number of species occur in North America and Europe and still others in tropical regions. The larvae of all are predatory upon small insects, chiefly of groups injurious to man. The Neuroptera are the most consistently beneficial order of predatory insects.

THE CADDISFLIES
—Order Trichoptera

In spite of the relatively small size of the order, which consists of about three thousand species, the caddisflies are of great interest as well as ecologic and economic importance. They make up one of the four orders that have become wholly or almost wholly aquatic during their early stages, exploiting the abundant food supply of the fresh waters and thus playing a major part in the ecology of our lakes, ponds and streams. They are the only one of these orders that has complete metamorphosis. One of their chief interests to us lies in the great diversity

An **Ascalaphid** (*Ascalaphus macaronius*). Very long, knobbed antennae characterize members of this worldwide group.

of the cases that the larvae construct and in which they live, some of these being as technically remarkable as any examples of insect architecture known.

The caddisflies (Plate 59) are closely related to the moths; in fact, certain species of insects that are now generally regarded as primitive moths were formerly classified with the caddisflies, from which they cannot be distinguished by any major characteristics. Some authors have combined the two orders, in spite of the fact that this tends to minimize the essential unity of the caddisflies as a group that has abandoned the land for all activities except reproduction, while the moths and butterflies have most decidedly done nothing of the sort.

Adults are rather mothlike in general appearance, the wings being characteristically covered, sometimes very thickly, with hairs. This feature alone, of course, will differentiate them from any similar moths, which have the wings covered with tiny flat scales that rub off easily, while the hairs of the caddisflies do not. They are seldom brightly colored, most of the species being gray or brown, but some have quite bright patterns of browns, yellows and black. In size they range from very small species no more than one and one-half millimeters long to others with a wing expanse of two or more inches. The antennae, which are long and threadlike and in some species several times the total length of the head and body, are usually held close together and extended forward when the caddisfly is at rest. The wings are usually held back, covering the abdomen and slanting down rooflike at the sides. The adults fly chiefly at night and are seldom seen during the day, when most of them hide among the vegetation near the water or under ledges, in caves or boathouses and even, at high altitudes where there is no other shelter, under stones. They come to bright lights at night in large numbers, often long distances from water. This is one of the best methods of collecting them.

The eggs are laid in strings or masses attached to rocks, logs and plants near the water, occasionally beneath the surface, and are covered with a mucilage that swells and softens when wet. The larvae are all aquatic, except for those of the European *Enoicyla,* which live in moss at the bases of tree trunks in damp woods. They are of never ending interest because of the seemingly infinite variety of the cases that they construct and inhabit during their larval and pupal lives. The members of each species make uniform cases, which are often a far more reliable means of identification than the larvae themselves. Many of the species that live in ponds and slow streams take very kindly to life in an aquarium (providing no fishes or predatory insects are included) and so can be watched building and enlarging their cases.

The larvae are elongate, with a heavily sclerotized head, a short thorax, and long legs that are directed forward. They can thus extend the head, thorax and legs from the case and drag themselves along as they feed. The abdomen is long and slender and slightly sclerotized, with numerous projecting threadlike tracheal gills by means of which oxygen is obtained from the water. At the posterior end is a pair of strong hooks that act as holdfasts inside the case. Movements of the body cause an almost continual flow of water from the rear end of the case to the front, this irrigation serving the purpose that ventilation does in an air-filled chamber.

The great majority of larvae feed upon living plants and plant debris, acting as primary consumers along with mayflies, stoneflies and the other plant-eating aquatic animals, and are thus essential links in the food chain of the fresh-water animals. A few species are predaceous.

There are twenty or more families of true case-bearers, which start their case by constructing a basic silken tube. In this are then embedded pieces of sticks, leaves, stones, shells or sand with skillful precision and specific uniformity. The Phryganeidae, a family that includes some of the largest species, use bits of leaves. Some species cut these into rectangular pieces and fit them together around the tube; others arrange thin strips side by side to form a narrow ribbon coiled spirally around the case. The Molannidae make a tube of small stones that has a broad, flat flange along each side. Some Leptoceridae and Odontoceridae use fine grains of sand to make curved, cylindrical tubes, which may increase so regularly in diameter from the rear to the front as to look like horns or trumpets. The Limnophilidae build as though with imagination, sometimes using relatively large sticks that may be placed lengthwise or crosswise in log-cabin style, or sometimes pebbles, large or small, or even snail shells. But we like best of all the cases of two of the Sericostomatidae: the spiral case of *Helicopsyche,* made of fine grains of sand, in an almost perfect duplication of the form of a snail shell; and the tapered tube of *Brachycentrus nigrisoma,* which is an exact square in cross section and is made from bits of twigs and roots cut neatly and accurately to the proper size. Every available material is used by one or another of these builders to form the distinctive case of its species. Stones and sand may seem like too heavy material for a case that must be carried everywhere; but a bubble or two of air inside the case counteracts this and actually makes it weightless or lighter than water.

By no means all of the caddisflies make portable cases, nor are all of them plant-eaters. Members of several families make silken tubes or nets that are permanently affixed to stones, and it is among these that we find the predaceous species. The Polycentropidae make fixed tubes, sometimes single and sometimes multiple, that may be nearly four inches long and branched, and are shallowly buried in the bottom of a stream with one end projecting up into the water. Some species build the tubes on the undersides of stones, to which they are fastened for their entire length, with a tangled mass of silk threads floating above them that soon becomes filled with silt. The Philopotamidae spin funnel-shaped tubes with the wider end fastened and the smaller end floating downstream. The species of *Hydropsyche* of the family Hydropsychidae live in rapid streams or where the current beats against the shore. Here they build a tube of silk and debris in which to live, and a most beautifully made silk "fishing" net that compares favorably with the best product of any spider, stretched between two stones or on a horizontal surface at the brink of a waterfall. In all of these groups the silken tubes, funnels and nets serve to catch whatever is floating along in the water. Much of this is merely dead plant and animal matter; much consists of living plants; but much else is composed of small animals ranging from crustacea to other aquatic insects. Upon this game the caddisfly larvae feed, making regular trips to clean out the accumulation and to repair the nets. Needless to say this type of food-getting, which the ecologist calls "filter feeding," is efficient only where there is a consistent current in the water to bring food to the nets; and so it is that we find the majority of the net-making caddisflies in streams, sometimes in extremely swift and rocky ones.

The smallest of the caddisflies are members of the family Hydroptilidae. The adults, which may be no more than two or three millimeters in length, have relatively short antennae and wings thickly covered with hairs. They are easily mistaken for small, primitive moths. Their larvae decorate their silken tubes with tiny grains of sand or small bits of plant material. One species regularly uses the filaments of the beautiful alga *Spirogyra,* which has prominent spiraled green chloroplasts.

Caddisfly larvae typically transform to the pupal stage in the tube or case, which at this time is sealed at the ends except for small irrigation openings. When the pupa is ready to transform to the adult it cuts itself free from the case with its mandibles, rises to the surface by means of its gaseous buoyancy and splits as it reaches the air. The adult emerges, spreads its wings and takes flight almost immediately, avoiding wetting its wings by its speed and by the water-repellent quality of its hairy covering.

The adults have biting mouthparts but eat little, if anything. Some species definitely lick sweet liquids, but the majority live, mate and carry on reproduction on the basis of the foods that they consumed as larvae.

CHAPTER X

Beetles
(*Order Coleoptera*)

ANT-GUEST BEETLE AND ITS ANT HOST

IT is difficult to avoid the constant use of superlatives when talking about beetles, for they are unquestionably the outstanding order of insects. There are so many species that even the best estimates vary widely, ranging from 100,000 to 250,000. Many of the described species are probably synonomous with others, but the study of some of the large families of the smaller beetles of the tropics has hardly been begun and will undoubtedly show that there are many more than the present top estimate of a quarter of a million species. This means that there are nearly five times as many species of beetles as there are of all vertebrate animals.

Such numbers signify unparalleled success in life; and it is natural and logical that one should inquire what it is about the lives of beetles that can explain this, or what combinations of characteristics they possess that may account for such success. They have a complete metamorphosis that permits a high degree of specialization of the adult stage and also allows the larvae and the adults to exploit different environments. So, be it noted, do the other three largest orders of insects. The beetles have one distinctive characteristic, however, in the transformation of the front wings into hard or tough, impermeable covers, known as elytra, that protect not only the delicate hind wings but usually the abdomen as well. With the hind wings folded beneath these elytra, a beetle can burrow, creep into cracks and crevices or withstand hard knocks without impairing its ability to fly. Although the hind wings are folded in intricate patterns, both crosswise and lengthwise, they can be spread out very quickly to the sides and used to drive the beetle in a flight that, although lacking the speed, grace and control

shown in the air by many insects, is at least adequate transportation. Few beetles fly fast; compared with dragonflies, hawk moths and bee flies they look like airborne trucks in low gear, yet they can fly well enough for all practical purposes of mating and of distributing eggs. The combination of the elytra and a much more durable skeleton than most other insects have affords them a protection that provides considerable safety from enemies and does a great deal to prevent desiccation in very dry environments.

The beetles have retained the primitive chewing mouthparts that are a necessity in feeding on all kinds of solid food. In this they have lagged behind the orders that have evolved sucking mouthparts, but perhaps this is another reason for their success. There is never any lack of solid foods, but the supply of liquids may often be limited, so that being restricted to a liquid diet may have its disadvantages. The beetle of course can drink liquids, although it does so only secondarily. There are a few that include sap, nectar and other juices as an important item in their diet, but the majority are primarily chewers of solid food.

Beyond this there is little that is distinctive about the beetles as a group. They have shown a striking ability to penetrate to every part of the land environment where an insect can live, and to adapt to every means of exploiting the food resources available. Several families have entered the fresh waters, where they live, as adults as well as larvae, in all possible places from the swiftest streams and waterfalls to the muddiest ponds. On land and in the water we find beetles with nearly every type of food habit: living on and in plants, scavenging on plants and on animal remains and preying on other insects and small animals. Relatively few are parasites, but even here some families have evolved a high degree of specialization and success. Only a few have developed any sort of social life, and that of the most rudimentary kind. With these exceptions, however, a list of the ways that various beetles make their living would include practically everything done by any insect.

Although the majority of beetles are relatively plain and humdrum looking, some have brilliant colors, often metallic or iridescent, that vie with those of any other animals, even of the brightest of the birds and butterflies. The hercules and goliath beetles are the most massive of all insects, and they and their relatives are justly noted for the incredible and more or less inexplicable horns of the males. The lure of the beautiful and the curious, together with the great abundance of beetles, has made them a favorite group with amateur collectors, more of whom are interested in these insects than in any other group except the butterflies and moths.

Needless to say, the classification of such an enormous order is a complex matter. It is not rendered any simpler by entomologists who constantly shuffle the families about and split them to make many little ones out of the big ones. More than two hundred families have thus been named. Since a great many of these are small and of little interest except to the specialist, we shall omit the majority and concern ourselves only with those of importance or general interest. The order is divided into two suborders, the Adephaga and the Polyphaga, differentiated chiefly by the method of attachment of the hind legs to the body. The former includes only a dozen or so families, but some are of major importance; the latter is divided into a number of smaller groups, each containing many families.

TIGER BEETLES—Family Cicindelidae

The tiger beetles are familiar insects nearly the world over. The adults are slender, mostly from half an inch to an inch long, with long, thin legs, bulging eyes and very long, sharp, saber-like jaws. Many are iridescently colored with blue, green, purple, orange or scarlet, sometimes brilliantly; but most species are dull brown or black. Nearly all of the common species of *Cicindela* have zigzag or scroll-like marks across the elytra, usually light on a dark ground but occasionally the reverse. Species that live on sandy beaches and dunes and in deserts are often very light colored, almost perfectly matching their environment. The majority of the two thousand species are tropical or subtropical.

The adults are most frequently seen where there is bare dirt or sand, along roads and paths, on beaches or in arid regions. They run about on the ground, hunting other insects, especially caterpil-

A **Tiger Beetle** (*Cicindela formosa*). Noted for its rapid movements and strong, sharp jaws.

lars, which they kill with great efficiency. When disturbed they take flight, sometimes with a very fast take-off, and fly ahead fifteen to fifty feet, alighting again with head directed toward the source of the disturbance. Although the flight is not fast or well controlled, they get off to such a quick start that they are not easy to catch and their capture thus becomes a decidedly sporting proposition. Because of this, and the great variety of colors and patterns found in some of the species, they are great favorites. Each species has its particular type of habitat that must be learned by the collector; many, especially in the desert regions, are nocturnal and are best collected by being attracted to trap lights.

The eggs are laid singly in the soil in burrows excavated by the female. The larvae, which share with the larvae of the ant lions the name "doodle bugs," live in short, cylindrical burrows perhaps three-sixteenths of an inch in diameter. The awkward-looking creature waits at the mouth of the burrow with the top of its dirty brown head bent at right angles to the body and held so as to plug the opening neatly. The head with its long, sharp jaws, and even the fore part of the body, will shoot out in a flash to grasp a passing insect. On the fifth abdominal segment is a pair of curved hooks that catch in the wall of the burrow, anchoring the larva and preventing it from being dragged out by the struggles of the victim.

The genus *Cicindela,* which is found in every continent, includes most of the familiar species seen during the daytime. The species are small to medium in size, often brilliantly metallic. The emerald green *C. sexguttata* is a familiar species of North America. Many species, however, especially the forest-trail ones, are dark, though often metallic beneath; while others, such as the sand-dune and beach species, *C. formosa* (sand dunes) and *C. dorsalis* (beaches), are largely white with dark markings. The species of *Tetracha* (or *Megalocephala*) are larger, an inch or so long, metallic green and nocturnal. *T. carolina* is a common species of the southeastern United States. In the southwestern states occurs the genus *Amblycheila*, dull brown beetles an inch to an inch and a half long, with heavy body and slow motions. They are now known to be nocturnal and obtainable in numbers if one goes out to the right places at night with a flashlight. At one time, however, only a very few specimens of the large *A. cylindriformis* were known, and these commanded prices of fifteen to twenty dollars a specimen among collectors.

In the far Pacific world of southern Asia and Australia the species of *Tricondyla* run about on the floor of the jungle, the larvae burrowing in humus and the adults avoiding bright light. Many strongly resemble ants. One species, *T. aptera,* large and blue, with long, reddish legs, is wingless.

Throughout the East Indies considerable damage is done in the cacao, coffee and tea plantations by *Collyris emarginata,* a small blue tiger beetle with red legs, whose larvae live in burrows excavated by the parents in the pithy branches of trees and shrubs. This arboreal habit likewise characterizes *Distypsidera,* the species of which live in tree trunks in warmer parts of Australia. Since the majority of tiger beetles are more or less beneficial as far as man is concerned because of the harmful insects that they eat, it is unusual to find one that is itself harmful even in an indirect way.

The bright colors of tiger beetles very likely are of a warning, or aposematic, nature, serving to let predators know that here is an insect that can fight back. Many are involved in mimicry groups with the warningly colored wasps and bees. It is interesting that in Borneo there is a locust, a perfectly edible, quite defenseless insect, that mimics not one but three tiger beetles. When very young it resembles a very small tiger beetle, *Collyris sarawakensis;* when partly grown it mimics the somewhat larger *Tricondyla gibba;* and when fully grown it matches a large species, *Tricondyla cyanea wallacei.* The resemblance is so close that the first specimens of the locust to be recognized by an entomologist were found, not in Borneo, but in a museum collection where they had been identified as tiger beetles.

GROUND BEETLES—Family Carabidae

More than 24,000 species are known of this enormous world-wide group, the third largest family of beetles; undoubtedly many thousand more are yet to be discovered and classified. Although some species occur in the subarctic and many in the tropics, they reach their greatest development in the temperate regions. Here they are primarily terrestrial, running swiftly with their long, strong legs over the ground and among vegetation. They prefer cool, moist areas such as open woods, rocky hillsides and the edges of streams, tending to seek concealment during the daytime but at night foraging actively for insects, earthworms, snails etc., on which they prey. They are proportionately flatter, broader and more heavy-bodied than tiger beetles, with shorter legs and antennae and less prominent eyes. The majority are black or brown, but a few are metallic, iridescent or brightly pigmented. The elytra are more or less firmly fused together along the midline of the back, forming a firm protection for the abdomen. The hind wings are usually reduced and often entirely absent, although in the tropical forests, where the species are likely to be arboreal, many of the species have the wings well developed and are able to fly.

The active larvae are mostly carnivorous, although a few feed on cereals and seeds. They are usually long and slender, and have sharp, projecting mandibles, bristle-like terminal appendages and sharp tarsal claws that facilitate their crawling under stones, logs, bark and debris. The adults of some of the larger species have been known to live for several years.

Among the larger species the searcher, *Calosoma scrutator* (Plate 37), is a handsome beetle marked with violet, blue, green, gold and coppery iridescence. It and many of its relatives often climb high trees in search of the caterpillars that they devour in great numbers. Like many other carabids this group secretes fiery, burning acids that will blister the human skin, and effectively protect them from many of their enemies. The similar *Calosoma sycophanta,* an inch and a quarter long and iridescent green, was introduced from its native home in Europe into North America to aid in the control of the likewise introduced gypsy and brown-tail moth caterpillars. It has been of some service but has failed to establish itself in the numbers hoped for. The even larger *Coptolabrus lafossei,* which is common in the South Pacific area, is two inches long with bright green head and thorax and coppery-margined elytra on which are seven rows of purplish elevations, and has bright purple legs.

One of the specialized groups consists of the snail-hunters of the genus *Scaphinotus* and its relatives, whose bodies tend to be more spherical than those of most ground beetles and are often tinted with violet. The mandibles are peculiarly elongated and hooked in what at first looks like a most awkward and useless fashion. They and the spoonlike palpi are actually beautifully adapted for reaching deep into a spiraled snail shell and extracting the luckless owner. Some of these beetles may be pests where edible snails are being reared for human consumption. Just the opposite of the snail-hunters in form are the giraffe beetles such as *Casnonia,* which have the prothorax extremely long and slender, looking like an elongated neck with the small head on top.

The small blue-gray and orange bombardier beetles of the genus *Brachinus* and its relatives have evolved a most efficient means of chemical defense. Sacs at the posterior end of the abdomen contain a pungent fluid that volatizes explosively on contact with the air to form a smokelike gas. The fluid can be ejected in a series of four or five shots, each with a distinct "pop," and may form quite enough of a gas cloud to enable the beetle to escape an attacker. In some species the fluid has the acid odor of iodine and is quite irritating to the eyes. A similar group, *Pherosophus,* contains many species of bombardier beetles in Africa, Asia and the East Indies.

The genus *Mormolyce* contains four species that live in Borneo, Java and Sumatra and are known as Malayan leaf beetles or fiddle beetles. They are so unusual that in the early part of the century, when they were believed to be very rare, a large museum in Paris paid a thousand francs for a single specimen. They are about four inches long and incredibly flat, with antennae as long again as the body. The head and thorax are very slender, but the elytra extend out to each side more than the width of the abdomen, giving the beetle the general outline of a violin. The horny expansions of the elytra are so thin and transparent that print can be read through them. With the elongate head and thorax the beetles, despite the great width of the elytra, can probe into small crannies for food; and because of the extreme flatness of their large bodies they may hide in the narrow crevices under bark or between the tree trunks and the large polyporous fungi on which they are often seen resting and in which their larvae tunnel. They exemplify the statement that nature never leaves a crevice without creating some creature that can fit into it.

Various other carabids show additional interesting modifications. In many caves have been found species such as those of the European genus *Anophthalmus,* in which the eyes have totally or almost entirely degenerated, as in so many other groups of cave-inhabiting animals. The famous Postumia caves of Italy are among those noted for the presence of blind cave beetles. In ant nests there are small beetles that are among the most extraordinary of all of the insects that have established permanent relationships with ants (see page 289). Chiefly of the Old World tropics, they are sometimes regarded as Carabidae and sometimes placed in a separate family, the Paussidae.

The great majority of the ground beetles are, however, relatively normal predators, living in trees and other vegetation as well as on the ground. As such they are without doubt of great value to man since they destroy incalculable numbers of harmful insects annually, kill far fewer beneficial ones and themselves do negligible damage.

TRUE WATER BEETLES or DIVING BEETLES—Family Dytiscidae

Both the larval and adult stages of these beetles (Plate 36) are spent in fresh waters, where they are very much at home and have become highly evolved for successful lives of predatism. They are closely related to the tiger and ground beetles and are, like them, dependent upon breathing air taken in through the spiracles. To do this they must come to the surface at intervals, or else they will drown as surely as any land animal. They can live out of water for a long time, but, because their legs are adapted for swimming, they are awkward in their movements on land. Some species have wingless forms and others, having wings, cannot fly because of atrophy of the flight muscles; but most species have strong powers of flight and pass freely from one body of water to another and frequently come in to lights at night. But their life is in the water, and they have evolved various special devices for coping with it successfully. There are about four thousand species.

Approaching a quiet pool or lake some summer's day, with due care not to cause any disturbance, you may see suspended just below the surface the flattened, smooth, streamlined bodies of water beetles, head down, with just the tip of the abdomen coming up through the surface film. Perhaps a big *Dytiscus,* an inch and a half long, will be visible, or smaller members of the family ranging down to less than two millimeters in length. The last two spiracles of the abdomen are larger than the others and are now exposed to the air, thereby replenishing the body's store. The elytra are elevated slightly, allowing fresh air to flow beneath them to be held among the felted hairs that cover the top of the abdomen.

A **Water Tiger,** the larva of a **Diving Beetle** (*Dytiscus marginalis*), with a captured **Stickleback** (*Gasterosteus*).

Here a large reserve supply can be carried when the beetle dives beneath the surface.

The beetles are beautifully streamlined, offering little resistance as they cut swiftly through the water. The females are so smooth and slippery that the males may have trouble holding fast to them during mating. Thus in many species the front feet of the males are modified to form adhesive cups that cling tightly to the female during this time. The hind legs are widely separated from each other, forming a pair of oarlike structures that project on each side. Like oars also, they are considerably flattened, as well as being furnished with fringes of hairs along the edges that greatly increase the area of the surface used for the swimming stroke.

The adults are exclusively carnivorous and extremely voracious, preying on any suitable animals that they can master. They frequently feed on snails and pollywogs, in addition to other insects, and on small fish considerably larger than themselves. It is disastrous to introduce one into an aquarium, for nothing else will survive. They can be kept quite well on a diet of raw meat or fish if no suitable prey is available. Occasionally they may be heard making grating sounds by rubbing the elytra or the hind legs against the abdomen.

The long, slender larvae, which are commonly known as water tigers, are as rapacious as the adults. They lurk or crawl about on vegetation or swim actively by means of serpentine movements of the body. They have long, sickle-shaped mandibles, perforated at the tip and traversed by a canal that communicates with the pharynx. When a victim is seized and impaled on the mandibles, digestive juices from the mid-gut are pumped out through this canal and into the victim. After a time the tissues of the prey, digested and liquefied, are sucked in and its empty shell is discarded. Like the adults, the larvae of most species must come to the surface for air, drawing it into the tracheal system through the last two spiracles; these are surrounded by water-repellent hairs that perforate the surface film and suspend the larva head downward. Some species have filamentous abdominal appendages and therefore do not need to come to the surface for air, the appendages serving as gills. When ready to transform the larvae leave the water and pupate in moist ground.

The large species of diving beetles are somewhat harmful to man's interests, since they prey on and compete with fish and are not particularly suitable or abundant food for fish themselves. The very large genus *Cybister* is almost world-wide in distribution. It and the genus *Dytiscus* include most of the large species, some of which may be more than an inch and a half long. In the Orient these large beetles are reared commercially for human food; children munch on them as prized tidbits. Many smaller species abound in both quiet and running water, and some occur in brackish tide pools. In France an interesting eyeless genus, *Siettitia,* lives in deep wells that are fed by subterranean springs, a striking analogy to the blind Carabid beetles found in dark caves.

WHIRLIGIG BEETLES—Family Gyrinidae

The members of this small family of about four hundred species, many of which are cosmopolitan, are found chiefly in quiet, shady pools and in the sheltered coves of lakes or the backwaters of streams, where they are most commonly seen in gyrating groups, spinning about on the surface, now this way, now that. They seldom dive unless attacked, but may whirl out of the spinning group, round and round on the surface, or may take flight. They are easily recognized by their smooth, oval, flattened bodies, typically blue-black or dark bronze. Since they are extremely smooth and slippery they easily escape the grasp if captured. The first pair of legs is long and slender and held out in front; the other two pairs are shorter and flattened for sculling. Each of the compound eyes, located at the edge of the flattened head, is completely divided in two, one part above and one part below, so that the beetle has separate vision for what is above the water and what is beneath. Many species exude a milky fluid that is doubtless somewhat protective; it usually has a disagreeable odor, although that of the common *Dineutes americanus* is like apples.

As far as is known, the adults are chiefly carnivorous, feeding on small insects and other animals that fall on the surface of the water, or doing some scavenging. The pale, slender larvae, which have long, flattened bodies, swim wrigglingly through the water or crawl about the debris on the bottom. They look curiously like centipedes since, although they have only three pairs of true legs, they have a pair of long, fringed gills on each abdominal segment. At the posterior end of the larva's abdomen are four long, sharp hooks that are used as a holdfast when capturing young mayfly or dragonfly nymphs that resist being victimized. At the time of pupation the larva crawls out onto the bank and hangs itself head downward by these hooks, from which position it scoops up mouthfuls of dirt which, mixed with saliva, are used to form the pupal case.

WATER SCAVENGER BEETLES
—Family Hydrophilidae

Many of the beetles of this large, world-wide family look extremely like the Dytiscid water beetles, being dark brown or black, oval and smooth. In general, however, they are somewhat stouter and not so flat, and differ almost completely in habits and behavior. They are most abundant in the warmer regions of the world, being commonest in marshy places or shallow, weedy ponds, although a few live in brackish water and a few in running water that is especially rich in algae. Whereas the water beetles are voracious predators, these beetles are primarily scavengers, feeding on algae or decaying organic matter. Only a few are predators, but many are themselves preyed upon, serving as an important source of food for birds, fish, frogs and toads.

When coming to the surface a Hydrophilid projects its short, hairy, club-shaped antennae up through the surface film and hangs thus suspended. The unwettable antennae, by their contact with the surface film, make a funnel of air that extends from the surface to the silvery coating of the underside of the body and the reservoir of air that lies in the hairy tracts beneath the elytra. When the antennae are folded back against the body a pumping action of the abdominal segments forces out the old supply of air and draws in a new one. Sometimes the buoyancy provided by all of this air makes swimming difficult, and it is then easy to observe the pacing action of the beetle as it uses first the middle and hind legs of one side and then those of the other. The first pair of legs is not adapted for swimming.

The adults fly well and often participate in dispersal flights in early spring and again in the fall.

The eggs are laid in silken cases or cocoons, usually in batches of a hundred or more. The female may fasten them to the underside of a leaf or simply launch them to float at will; in a few species she carries them between her hind legs. The young larvae have enormous heads and very long mandibles; they are predatory on other small aquatic insects as well as being markedly cannibalistic. Many species have to come to the surface for air despite being able to carry on a certain amount of subsurface respiration through the wall and filaments of the abdomen, but *Berosus* is able to use the abdominal filaments more efficiently and lives in deep water somewhat farther from shore.

Hydrophilus and *Tropisternus* are two common genera with many large species, some of which are as large as the big Dytiscids. *Sphaeridium,* which was introduced into North America from Europe and is now widely distributed and common, is not aquatic, its larva living in dung and feeding on fly maggots. At least one of the Oriental species has been found useful in the biological control of beetle larvae in sugar cane and banana stems. There are probably about two thousand species in all.

OTHER AQUATIC BEETLES
—Families Haliplidae and Psephenidae

The crawling water beetles of the family Haliplidae are small, usually no more than one-eigth of an inch long and characteristically spotted with dark and light. Their bodies are quite stocky, being little or not at all streamlined, nor are their legs adapted for swimming. Nevertheless they abound in both running and standing water, where they and their larvae feed primarily on algae. Adults come to the surface for air, breaking through the surface film with the tip of the abdomen to obtain the supply that they carry beneath the elytra and in the coxal cavities. They pupate on shore in a chamber beneath logs and stones.

The "water pennies" of swift streams are the larvae of the Psephenidae. These larvae are extremely flat and almost circular, having the edges of the body widely expanded out to the sides and forward. The whole body appears to act as a single suction cup that holds the larva flat to the surface of the rock in even the swiftest water. Some species are found at the edge of Niagara Falls, others in the rapids of dashing Himalayan streams. The pupae are similarly shaped and are cemented fast to the rocks in the same environment, although usually just above the water line. Their remarkable specialization is all the more unusual because the adults are conventional-looking little beetles that show no particular adaptations for swimming or for aquatic life.

CARRION BEETLES—Family Silphidae

The beetles of this small family, which occurs chiefly in the north temperate regions, show great diversity of form, coloration and habit, as well as size. The majority are scavengers, feeding on dung, dead animals, fungi or decaying plant material. Some are predaceous on snails, other insects and, when hard pressed, on their own kind. A few specialized forms live in ant nests, chiefly as scavengers; and a few eyeless forms live in caves, again as scavengers, sometimes on the leavings of bats.

Among the best known are the carrion beetles of the genus *Silpha* and its relatives. The adult beetles are extremely flat and very broad in proportion to their length, with leathery, flexible bodies and elytra, the latter often covered with fine wrinkles. They are primarily scavengers, although they do show some diversification of food habits, and as carrion-feeders play an important role in the economy of nature. A few species are plant-eaters, sometimes attacking crops. The larvae are most unusual looking, being exceedingly flat, yet long and tapering, with triangular points projecting at the sides of each segment. They thus bear a curious resemblance to crustaceans or to fossil trilobites.

Some of the species of the burying or sexton beetles of the genus *Necrophorus* (Plate 39) attain a length of an inch and a half. They are not flattened like *Silpha* and have the elytra much shorter than the abdomen. Some are all black, others conspicuously black and orange. This is possibly an example of warning coloration, since these beetles seem to intensify within themselves the odors of putrefaction and decay that arise from their food, and are very likely shunned by at least many normally insect-eating animals. The burying beetles are famous for their ability to inter the body of some small animal that they have found dead. This is done by digging away the soil beneath the corpse and pushing it out and up to the sides. In fairly loose ground a couple of beetles will thus completely conceal the body of a mouse in only a few minutes. There are records of two beetles, working together, actually managing to move the body of a rat for some inches to where the ground was softer and more suitable for digging. This is, of course, the sort of thing that has been grossly exaggerated by the type of naturalist who tends to endow animals with human mentality and powers of reason. What really happens is that the beetles perform a simple set of digging activities in a random manner, while remaining close to the carrion that attracts them by its odor. Eventually the activities result in the body being buried. But it is a grave error to attribute consciousness, forethought or purpose to these or any other insects.

When the body has been entombed the beetles feast upon it in seclusion, relatively free from the competition of maggots and other carrion-feeders. The females lay their eggs in such carrion as well as in larger bodies too sizable for burial, and the larvae grow and feed in the same food. Repulsive as we may find these insects, there is no denying that they are of primary importance in greatly speeding up the utilization of many bodies and the subsequent return of their substance to circulation in the world of life. Without them and other carrion-feeders, such as many of the flies, great quantities of dead animal matter would simply desiccate and then take years to decay.

Often associated with the carrion beetles around dead animals may be found many of the small beetles of the family Histeridae. The elytra cover only the basal part of the abdomen, as in the burying beetles, but the end of the abdomen is characteristically cut off square and the whole beetle often looks extremely hard, smooth and polished. The antennae are peculiarly elbowed and clubbed. Many species occur under bark and in the tunnels of wood-boring insects, and many others are regular guests in termite and ant nests. The adult beetles usually feign death when alarmed, drawing all of the appendages close to the body and lying perfectly motionless. When they do this they look like shiny seeds. As far as is known the species are all carnivorous, those found in carrion being there to prey on the carrion-feeding beetles and flies.

ROVE BEETLES—Family Staphylinidae

More than twenty thousand species of this large family are known, many occurring in every continent. The majority are relatively long and slender, with the elytra very short. Often the abdomen is curled upward beyond the end of the elytra, especially when the beetle is alarmed. Despite the short elytra, the wings of the great majority of species are large and capable of sustaining the beetles in powerful flight. They can be unfurled very rapidly, but refolding them into tight packages beneath the short elytra is a complex task that requires the aid of the tip of the abdomen and sometimes of the hind legs as well. A great many species are consistently found associated with dung and carrion, but probably because they feed on the carrion-eating insects and not because they themselves are scavengers. The majority have characteristically foul odors.

While the greater part of the species are small or even minute, some are quite large and conspicuous and may have bright black and yellow colors. It is very possible that these are warning colors which, with the peculiar actions, make some of the species resemble wasps. The Australian devil's coach horse (a name also used for Staphylinids in other countries), *Creophilus erythrocephalus,* is a broad, black species with a large red head. The related *C. maxillosus* is more than an inch long and shining black, with conspicuous patches and bands of gray hair on the body and elytra.

Minute members of one small subfamily frequent rocks below the high-tide mark or crawl about the bottom of the tide pools, remaining beneath the surface for two or three hours. Some of the European species of *Bledius* have extraordinarily restricted ranges; one, for example, lives on muddy beaches on coastal islands within a narrow strip only a few inches wide. Here, above high-tide level, it burrows in the wet beach.

The most interesting of Staphylinid beetles are the species that have become adapted for life in ant and termite nests, where they are among the most numerous of many guests. Most of them have evolved unusual body form, structures and activities that enable them to be, in many cases, welcome and even highly cherished members of the ant and termite societies. The European *Lomechusa* and *Atameles* and the North American *Xenodusa,* for example, have special glands that secrete a liquid greatly relished by the ants, which feed the beetles in return (page 289). There are even some that live with the colonies of army ants that have no nest but keep moving about; these beetles mimic the appearance and behavior of the ants. Among the termite guests are some that give birth to live young.

The small beetles of the related family Pselaphidae are also very largely specialized as ant guests, although there are quite a few that lead independent lives. The ant guest species have glands opening at tufts of yellow hairs which, as in the rove beetles, secrete substances much relished by the ants.

A single very small beetle makes up the family Platypsyllidae, yet it is well worth our attention because of its unusual and restricted habitat. The beaver beetle, *Platypsyllus castoris,* is found only in the fur of beavers, in both Europe and North America. A minute wingless insect with very short elytra, it has even been considered by some authors as a distinctive order. Its eyes are wanting and its mandibles vestigial. The larva, however, is undoubtedly that of a beetle. It is not even known upon what they and the adults feed, whether on the skin products of the beaver or on parasites that likewise live in the fur. The problem of respiration when the beaver is under water is not so serious as might be supposed, since the thick fur repels water and entraps a great deal of air, but the extreme oiliness of the beaver's coat must present difficulties.

FLAT BARK BEETLES and GRAIN BEETLES—Family Cucujidae

Nearly five hundred species of these small and minute beetles are known, well distributed around the world. Most of them are very flat, sometimes bright red but more often dull brown. Typically they live beneath slightly loosened bark. In at least the larval stage many of them are predaceous on wood-boring and wood-eating insects. Two very interesting species of British Guiana live, along with their broods, in the hollow petioles of certain leaves. With them lives a species of scale insect (*Pseudococcus*) that secretes a sweet honeydew upon which the beetles and their larvae feed.

Several species that feed upon grains and similar stored products have become widely distributed around the world and are rather bad pests. Most harmful is the saw-toothed grain beetle, *Oryzaephilus surinamensis,* a slender, reddish species about a tenth of an inch long. On either side of its prothorax are six prominent saw teeth. It is one of the commonest insects of warehouses and stores where food is kept or processed, and undoubtedly appears very frequently on our tables, although fortunately for our susceptibilities usually in unrecognizable form. Despite their tiny size, which we often (quite incorrectly) associate with short lives, adults of this beetle have been kept alive for as long as three years. They infest nearly any plant material from grain products and candy to tobacco and snuff.

PLEASING FUNGUS BEETLES —Family Erotylidae

There are more than two thousand species of these beetles, widely distributed but chiefly tropical. As the common name of the family implies, they are essentially fungus-eaters, although quite a few are borers in the stems of plants or in wood. The "pleasing" part of the name refers to the bright colors that are especially predominant in many of the large tropical forms. They are one of the most attractive families of beetles to collectors, many of the South American species being particularly noteworthy.

The Languriidae are sometimes recognized as a separate family, sometimes regarded as merely a subfamily of the Erotyliids. They are primarily borers in the stems of herbaceous plants, some species such as the red and black clover stem borer, *Languria mozardi,* of the eastern United States, being minor pests. Many of the species have a well-developed stridulatory organ on the head by means of which they are able to make squeaking sounds.

FEATHER-WINGED BEETLES —Family Trichopterygidae (Ptilidae)

The beetles of this small but widely distributed family are noted for their exceedingly minute size. The tiny *Nanosella fungi* of the New World tropics is about a quarter of a millimeter (one one-hundredth of an inch) long and is the smallest known beetle. Other species may range up to two millimeters in length. They are characterized, among other features, by the extremely long fringes of hair on the edges of the hind wings, although a few species are wingless. Many live in rotting wood, manure, fungi or under bark, and some live in ant nests. Some of the Australian species are blind.

FIREFLIES and GLOW WORMS —Family Lampyridae

Commonplace and prosaic beetles and grubs by day but friendly torchbearers by night, the fireflies illuminate the darkness of summer evenings with their rhythmic flashings. The adult beetles (Plate 38) seldom fly during the day but when found on vegetation may be recognized by their elongate, flattened bodies and by the soft elytra that fit very loosely over the sides of the abdomen. The broadly expanded, thin prothorax projects at the sides and nearly covers the head from above; in many species it is conspicuously colored with yellow or orange, perhaps with a couple of dark spots. The edges of the elytra may likewise be of the same colors, the remainder of the beetle being largely brown or black. In a large proportion of the species the females have the wings greatly reduced or absent, and in such cases strongly resemble the flat larvae.

At night both males and females alike glow with a cold, greenish light, sometimes steadily and sometimes intermittently, depending on the sex, species and conditions of the environment. The luminous organs are located on the abdomen, in some species in several segments, in others only in the sixth and seventh and in some females only in the seventh. They are complex masses of cells that act as glands to secrete and store the substances known as luciferin and luciferase, the latter an enzyme or, chemically speaking, an organic catalyst. When luciferin and oxygen are brought together they combine to form oxyluciferin; and when luciferase is also present this gives off light. The light itself is cold, very little heat being produced, a feature that has made the details of this activity of major interest; for man never has succeeded in devising any means of producing light so efficiently and so unaccompanied by heat. Some day the secrets of the fireflies' production of these substances may be understood and perhaps duplicated cheaply, a discovery that will revolutionize our present methods of lighting. The light is at least 98 per cent efficient and qualitatively is in the zone of visible light to which the human eye is most sensitive, occupying a very narrow belt of 5180 to 6560 Ångstrom units, that is, from a yellow-green to an orange-red.

It is possible for anyone to perform interesting experiments to demonstrate many of the important features of the fireflies' light. A number of the insects can be ground up, and the product will continue to glow. If, however, part of this is treated with hot water, which destroys the luciferase, it will cease to glow. The addition to this of some of the untreated material, still containing luciferase, will cause it to glow again. Similar work shows that it is apparently the presence of different types of luciferin that causes differences in the quality of the light, from greenish yellow to reddish. That the luciferin does not become all used up during a long night of glowing is probably due to the intermittency of the light, permitting it to become deoxidized and then used over again.

A feature of the luminescence of some fireflies that has attracted much attention is the tendency of large groups of males to flash on and off in unison. Some very startling observations have been made, particularly in South America, of all the individuals on one bank of a river flashing together while those on the other bank follow a different rhythm. Nobody has figured out a plausible explanation of the coordinating mechanism.

All evidence shows that the light serves an important function in bringing together the males and females. There are, however, many nonluminous species that are just as abundant as the luminous ones. In one luminous species it was shown that the time interval of 2.1 seconds between the flash from the male and an answering female was the important factor in attracting the male to the female. A dilatory or too eager female would thus attract no male; and a male answering a flash after such an interval would be liable to be mistaken for a female. It is doubtful whether the luminosity has any protective value, although some predators seem to find fireflies distasteful. Frogs, however, often eat large numbers and in fact may glow themselves from the light that emanates from a stomachful of luminous fare.

The beetles of this family are by no means the only luminescent insects, since springtails, fungus gnats and members of other beetle families also produce light. The related Phengodidae contain some brightly luminescent forms, the wingless females sometimes showing a line of lights along the sides of the abdomen that makes one of them look like a ship with a row of brightly lit portholes. The most luminescent of all insects are the large click beetles of the tropics of the genus *Pyrophorus,* some of which are two inches or more long. These are often tied in little gauze bags and used as glowing hair ornaments, a most charming and effective custom. In one species there are two bright, whitish spots of luminescence near the front end and a single reddish one at the rear end. The resemblance to a miniature automobile with headlights and tail light is startling and accounts for these beetles in parts of Central America being called "Ford bugs."

The adults of many fireflies never eat, but those of many others feed to some degree on products of flowers such as nectar and pollen. The larvae are predatory, feeding especially on slugs and snails. Piercing their victims' bodies with their long, hollow mandibles, they inject a dark secretion that liquefies and partially digests the prey. The fluid is then sucked in, the mouth being surrounded by a fringe of fine hairs that prevents the entrance of any but the tiniest solid particles. Some larvae are luminous even before hatching from the egg.

SOLDIER BEETLES—Family Cantharidae

Due to an unfortunate scientific mix-up in the past, a group of beetles now known as the Meloidae, an entirely different and unrelated family, was for long known as Cantharidae; and this name, applied to them, even had wide use in medicine. The beetles now correctly called the Cantharidae are a relatively small although widely distributed family with elongate bodies and soft, almost parchment-like elytra. Many are called soldier beetles because of their bright colors and trim appearance. The adult beetles are commonly found on flowers, where they feed on pollen and nectar. For this some of them have a special long, extensible filament on each maxilla. The flat, velvety-looking larvae live in the soil and are carnivorous, certain species being of value to man on this account. *Cantharis* and *Rhagonycha* are common European genera; *Chauliognathus* is common in North America. In the latter genus *C. pennsylvanicus,* about one-half inch in length and yellow and black in color, is often abundant on goldenrod flowers.

NET-WINGED BEETLES—Family Lycidae

These soft-bodied beetles have broad, flat, leathery-looking elytra that are often more or less covered with a raised network of fine lines. Some of the larger species are an inch or more long. Often the elytra are much wider at the tips than at the bases; and in general many of the species are even more unlike the typical compact beetle than their close relatives the soldier beetles and fireflies. Many are boldly colored, typically with broad bands of orange and black, or orange and blue, across the elytra. As a result they are very conspicuous, whether during their slow flight or when climbing on plants or visiting flowers.

Many of the species are highly protected by acrid, burning body juices that render them, to say the least, highly unpalatable. Their bold colors and patterns function as recognition marks whereby predators can easily learn that they are to be left strictly alone. Such warning, or aposematic, coloration occurs in a great many groups of insects where there is genuine protection of the individuals by bad taste, poison, stings etc. It is often very common to find that these protected insects are mimicked by others, which, themselves perfectly good food and unprotected by special devices, thereby gain a great advantage through being mistaken for the protected ones. Other outstanding examples of this kind of mimicry are found in the butterflies and moths (Chapter XI) and the bees and wasps (Chapter XIII).

The net-winged beetles serve as models for several groups of insects. Moths of various families, particularly the Syntomidae and Pyromorphidae, day fliers and flower-visitors like the beetles, thus have evolved some extraordinarily faithful mimicry of net-winged beetles that are common in regions where they fly. In North America the black-and-orange beetles are mimicked by a whole host of other insects, including moths, bugs and ichneumon wasps. In many instances these other insects are, however, more or less genuinely protected themselves, in which case the mimicry is the "Mullerian" type in which the warningly colored insects, both protected, reinforce each others' effects.

CHECKERED BEETLES—Family Cleridae

The checkered beetles are an extensive family of about three thousand species, mainly tropical but with numerous temperate zone members. The majority of the species are quite brightly colored, being spotted or checkered with various combinations of black, green, red, orange or yellow. The adults are elongate and often covered with very fine, short hairs. Some of the smaller species are quite antlike in appearance. They are most frequently found in flowers, to which they repair in search of the small insects on which they feed. Here their bright colors are frequently quite concealing.

The larvae are likewise predaceous, a good many being beneficial to man because they feed on wood- and bark-boring beetle larvae, some of them very serious forest pests. A few are found in carcasses and skins as scavengers and predators on maggots. Others are known to infest the nests of honeybees and of certain solitary European mason bees.

TUMBLING FLOWER BEETLES
—Family Mordellidae

The rather unusual and somewhat mystifying common name of this small family is due to the fact that the adults of a great many of the species are most commonly found in flowers, and that when disturbed they are extremely active, jumping and tumbling about in a most erratic fashion. The commonest species are small, being little more than an eighth of an inch long, with a wedge-shaped body that is stout and arched anteriorly but tapers posteriorly to a point. They are densely covered with fine, silky hairs and are most commonly black, although some are brightly spotted or banded with yellow or silver. The hind legs are strong and adapted for jumping. The larvae live in rotten wood or hollow, pithy stems, where they are predaceous on the larvae of small moths or other beetles.

BLISTER BEETLES and OIL BEETLES
—Family Meloidae

In this widely distributed family of about two thousand species occur some of the most peculiar and interesting of all beetles. The family is divided into two subfamilies, the Lyttinae, which have long elytra and usually have hind wings, and the Meloinae (Plate 40), which have very short elytra and no hind wings. It is the Lyttinae that were long known as Cantharids, a name now properly applied elsewhere. These beetles secrete a substance, known medically as cantharidin, that acts as an extremely powerful blistering agent, even a tiny drop being sufficient to produce large, watery blebs and an intense burning when applied to the skin or other soft parts of larger animals. The substance is found in greatest concentration in the elytra of the dried beetles. A well-known European species, *Lytta vesicatoria,* serves, under the name of Spanish Fly, as the chief source of medical cantharidin. The substance was very widely used during the last century, when blistering and bleeding were almost the standard remedies for every disease, being applied to the skin in a solution. Later this was displaced by the mustard plaster, and nowadays by the heating pad, lamp or deep-wave therapy. We do not, however, try to cure everything from appendicitis to cholera by such means. The burning effect of the Spanish Fly also led inevitably to its employment in love potions, a dangerous proceeding in view of its toxic nature when taken internally.

The majority of the Lyttinae are quite brightly colored, as befits insects so well and so genuinely protected. As we might expect, the beetles make little or no attempt to hide, but clamber over plants in plain sight. A great many may have metallic-looking blue or green elytra; others are predominantly banded or striped with black and yellow, or are jet-black, a conspicuous color among flowers and foliage. The beetles can be extremely bothersome, since even the touch of one to the sensitive human skin will produce a blister, and their habit of coming to lights at night often brings them into our houses in considerable numbers. We have highly unpleasant memories of many contacts with them since, as entomologists, we spend much time collecting insects at bright lights set out in favorable places. In such circumstances it is often impossible to avoid having blister beetles crawling about on one.

The oil beetles of the subfamily Meloinae are heavier-bodied and flightless, having the elytra much shorter than the abdomen and the hind wings missing. The males of many species have the antennae curiously modified to serve as forceps with which the females are held during mating. The oily secretion that oozes from various apertures when the beetles are disturbed does not have the blistering powers of the secretions of the Lyttinae, but does apparently make the beetles distasteful to predators and permits them to roam conspicuously over the flowers on which they feed. The adults of both subfamilies are sometimes injurious to crops by feeding on the foliage. Before the advent of the Colorado potato beetle made other potato beetles seem minor by comparison, some of the blister beetles were major potato pests, being called as a result "old-fashioned potato bugs." Others occasionally do damage to alfalfa, tomatoes, beans, corn etc. Before modern insect poisons were available it was customary to try, by beating on pans and thrashing the plants with leafy branches, to drive the beetles out of the fields into the hedgerows, which were then burned.

Some of the most interesting of the oil beetles are the members of the genus *Cysteodemus* that inhabit the deserts of the Southwest and Mexico. They are an inch to an inch and a half in length and are metallic blue-green, with extremely hard, impervious elytra and exoskeleton. The elytra are fused together and so expanded and curved as to make the abdomen almost perfectly hemispherical and to enclose a considerable air chamber. The

spherical shape offers a minimum of surface area for evaporation, and the air chamber serves for heat insulation. By these means the beetles are excellently adapted to withstand the hot, desiccating effect of their environment.

It is for the complexity of their life histories, however, that the blister beetles and oil beetles are best known. The larvae are parasites (or rather, parasite-like predators) on other insects, chiefly locusts and solitary bees. In the former instance it is the locusts' egg masses, deposited in the soil, that are attacked; in the latter it is the food supplies that the bees have laid up, as well as the bees' eggs. Their metamorphosis differs from that of conventional insects in that the Meloid larvae pass through a set of extremely distinctive larval stages; it is therefore called hypermetamorphosis, since it goes beyond the complexity of ordinary metamorphosis.

The eggs are laid in the soil or on the surface of the ground. It is then up to the larvae to find suitable hosts for themselves, a difficult task in which the great majority probably fail, and so perish. In compensation for this, very great numbers of eggs are produced, a single female depositing from two to ten thousand. This follows the customary pattern of many parasites, which make up for the hazards of their developmental periods and the consequent death of a large proportion of their offspring by having a bountiful egg production.

The newly hatched larvae are extremely active, minute, bristly creatures known as triungulins. They may spend the winter in this stage, but in due course scatter in search of hosts, those that will feed on locust eggs running actively over the ground, and those that will parasitize bees climbing up on flowers to await the passing of any hairy insect. They are of course very tiny in comparison with a bee, and many of them were, in fact, described as "bee lice" before the facts were known. They will seize upon any insect that comes within reach; those that happen to get a ride on flies, honeybees and other unsuitable hosts will never be able to complete their development and will die; but those that attach themselves to male bees of the right kind may be able to transfer to a female during the bees' courtship; and those fortunate enough to attach directly to a female of the host species of bee need do no further changing. They remain on the female while she is preparing her nest (page 254) and provisioning it with pollen and nectar, clinging tightly to her body hairs. Then, as she is laying an egg in the provisioned cell, one of the triungulins slips aboard the egg and clings to it. It is thus sealed inside the cell by the female bee. Its first act is to eat the egg, thus affording itself its first meal and removing a future competitor.

The species that feed on locust eggs lead much simpler lives in this early stage, since the triungulins merely cruise about until they find a pod of locust eggs in the soil. In either case, having had a small first meal, the triungulin then molts, changing to an entirely different-looking larval form that has short legs and limited powers of locomotion. So different are this and the leathery, active triungulin that one would never suspect them to be successive stages. Other molts are accompanied by still other radical changes, one form being even shorter-legged and having its abdomen curled under like that of a larva of one of the scarab beetles, and still another pupa-like and immobile. This last is the stage in which the winter is passed. After that, another, more active larval form appears; and finally the larva changes to a real pupa from which the adult emerges in due time. No more complex insect development is known, although comparable hyper-metamorphoses occur in other groups. The Meloidae remain the classic example of this, each succeeding form being exquisitely adapted for the part it plays in the life cycle.

Sitaris is a common European genus of blister beetles, the investigation of which by the great French naturalist Fabre produced one of the classics of his *Souvenirs Entomologiques.* Its larvae, like those of the European and American oil beetles of the genus *Meloë,* parasitize mason bees. The blister beetles of the many species of the North American genus *Epicauta,* as well as of its larger relatives of *Macrobasis,* attack locust egg pods.

POWDER-POST BEETLES and other borers
—Families Lyctidae, Anobiidae and Bostrichidae

Here are grouped together a number of beetles that range from minute to small in size, the majority of which are often extremely destructive during their larval stages as borers of wood. Quite a few other similar groups could also have been included. A number of the species attack other substances, some being quite well-known pests of dried food and stored substances.

The powder-post beetles of the family Lyctidae are so called because of the dry, powdery dust that is extruded from their burrows in wood at the time of the emergence of the adults. The burrows communicate with the exterior as small round holes, the "worm holes" that are so respected by certain collectors of antique furniture as signs of authenticity that they are often faked. The somewhat larger augur beetles of the family Bostrichidae live similarly. Many of the species work in naturally dead wood out of doors, and some even bore into the living terminal growth of trees. Millions of dollars' damage annually is done by species boring in practically anything man-made of wood. Houses themselves may be so weakened that they collapse, and even painted and varnished furniture may have larvae

busily working inside, the first evidence of which may be the telltale accumulation of powdery dust from the almost invisible exit holes. Stored lumber, boxes and crates, wine barrels and even the corks of wine bottles are frequently infested. In this work these beetles ecologically replace in the north temperate regions the termites of the tropics, few of which occur in significant numbers in the temperate zones. One Bostrichid in California has such unusual powers and habits that it regularly perforates the lead sheathing of electric cables, just as one of the termites also does, thereby earning for itself the name "lead cable borer" or "short-circuit beetle."

The death-watch beetles of the family Anobiidae are similar borers in wood, especially in old buildings and furniture. The best-known species, the death watch, *Xestobium rufovillosum,* often makes clicking sounds that are plainly audible to humans by striking the head or jaws sharply against the walls of its burrows. This has given rise to many superstitions, the chief one being that someone's days are numbered and the moments are being counted off by the ticks emanating from the wood.

Other Anobiids are pests in stored foods and products of all sorts. The cosmopolitan drugstore beetle, *Sitodrepa panicea,* not only infests a great many kinds of drugs and stored herbs and spices, but is a general pest in cereals. It has even been known to flourish on diets composed of opium and aconite. The cigarette beetle, *Lasioderma serricorne,* is another world-wide pest, living not only on tobacco but also on such condiments as ground pepper, mustard, chili pepper, cloves and other "hot" spices.

Closely related to the Anobiids and, in fact, combined with them by many entomologists, are the Ptinid beetles, another world-wide group of household and stored-product pests. Many of the species are quite globular in outline and wingless. A number of species of the spider beetles, such as the white-marked spider beetle, *Ptinus fur,* and the shiny American spider beetle, *Mezium americanum,* are often abundant household pests. Even a heavy infestation of these insects may be unsuspected until some of them fall into a slippery container, such as a bathtub or wash basin, from which they cannot climb.

LARDER BEETLES and CARPET BEETLES
—Family Dermestidae

As far as the average person is concerned, these might as well be called the "domestidae," since the best-known species are pests in nearly every household. The family as a whole evolved as rather specialized scavengers feeding on dried, mummified skins, fur, feathers and similar animal refuse; some species quite naturally evolved the habit of living

A **Click Beetle** (*Melanactes densus*), showing the hinged body by means of which it can snap up into the air to right itself.

in mammal nests where such residues would occur bountifully; and from this it was a short step to taking advantage of the abundant economy of man. The majority of species still live out of doors. The adults are small, oval and covered with minute scales that give them a velvety appearance. Many species are plain gray or brown and have indistinct markings, but others are quite brightly colored in red, black and white. The larvae are extremely different from those of any other beetles, being covered with a complex vestiture of hairs that form long pencil tufts in some species and can be raised and lowered. Pupation takes place in the last larval skin.

The adult larder beetles, *Dermestes lardarius*, are about a third of an inch long, oval, dark brown with a lighter yellowish cross band. The larvae, a very hairy brown, feed on dried meats, cheese and animal products of all kinds. As in all these species, the adults leave the house when they emerge from the pupa and remain outdoors for a time, there feeding on pollen. Their presence in a house is often first detected when specimens are found on the window sills where they are attempting to get out to the light.

Much more abundant and destructive are the various carpet beetles and buffalo bugs of the genera *Anthrenus* and *Attagenus*. The adult beetles are no more than an eighth of an inch long, oval and often checkered with brightly colored scales that rub off easily. The very hairy red-brown or golden-brown larvae, which do the damage, are seldom seen because of their light-avoiding habits. They feed on nearly any substance of an animal nature, being especially harmful to fabrics and furs, and will chew holes in even cotton or synthetic fibers if these have been rendered the least bit greasy by spilled foods. Upholstered furniture and carpets often swarm with them, burrowing away unseen until suddenly the householder discovers that irreparable damage has been done. In recent years these

beetles appear to have very largely replaced the clothes moths as household destroyers, especially in urban regions, although the sellers of household insecticides still advertise their products chiefly as moth-destroyers, apparently going on the principle that the public has heard of moths and is incapable of learning about beetles. The professional pest control operators of many of our large cities, in fact, regard clothes moths as now comparatively unimportant.

Perhaps the "most unkindest cut of all" (although there is an element of fundamental justice in it) is the fact that these beetles, especially *Anthrenus musaeorum*, are the worst pests in museums where collections of birds, mammals and insects (including themselves) are maintained. Every museum in the world is forced to spend a large part of its budget for pest-proof cabinets and cases, and for constant fumigation, in order to protect its collections of dried animal materials of every kind. Private collectors are even more handicapped, since the possibilities of infestation are much greater. A great many of the most valuable collections of the world have been irreparably damaged by these museum beetles. Some museums do a little to balance the account, however, by using the larvae to clean skeletons of the soft tissues adhering; but this is not considered good practice, since it greatly enhances the danger of infestation in the collections.

CLICK BEETLES—Family Elateridae

Because of their habit of coming in to light at night the elongated but quite flat beetles of this large and world-wide family (Plate 44) are familiar insects to nearly everyone but the most confirmed urbanite. When one falls or is placed on its back it struggles for a while, perhaps, to turn itself over, but to no avail since its short legs cannot reach the ground. Suddenly it stops trying, lies immobile for a second, and then arches its body strongly so that the central part is bent away from the ground. There is a loud click—and the whole beast shoots up into the air, perhaps for several inches. When it lands it may be right side up and scurry actively away; or it may land on its back again and have to make another try. Certainly it will succeed in righting itself in a short time. The many popular names, such as skipjack, snapjack and snapping beetle, attest to the wide interest that this unusual performance never fails to awaken.

Included in the family are some eight thousand species, ranging from less than a quarter of an inch to nearly four inches in length. The head is small and more or less hidden beneath the large prothorax. The latter is joined to the rest of the body by a very loose, crosswise joint, which gives the flexibility necessary for the arching. A sharp spine on the prothorax slides along a groove on the lower side of the mesothorax and, passing over a ridge, drops into a deep hollow, thus forming the snap mechanism that, suddenly released when the body is arched under strong muscle tension, throws the beetle up into the air.

Perhaps the majority of the species are rather plain, being unmarked or faintly mottled with brown or black. Some, however, are quite brightly variegated with red, yellow, black or white. Some of the tropical species are metallic, although in this respect they do not approach their near relatives, the metallic wood-boring beetles of the family Buprestidae. One of the most striking is the large, eyed elater, *Alaus oculatus,* of eastern North America, two and a half to three inches long, and black, white and gray. On the prothorax is a pair of large black-and-white eyespots that make this part of the body look like the head, and the whole beetle, at first glance, resemble the front part of a much larger animal. It is, of course, problematic whether this resemblance is of any practical value to the beetles in protecting them from the attacks of birds, lizards and similar predators, since such animals do not have the powers of recollection or mental imagination possessed by man. At any rate the eyed elater looks very unbeetle-like. It and the other large click beetles must benefit to some degree from the value of the click mechanism as a defense. When seized and squeezed, the beetles always click hard; and the force exerted by this effort, to say nothing of the surprise, is quite enough to make a bird or lizard relax its grip, allowing the beetle, with a few more clicks, to bounce into shelter.

Adult click beetles feed on leaves, chiefly at night. Their flight, like that of most beetles, may be described as adequate but far from skillful. They are often attracted to sweet liquids, a feature that is used in the control of some injurious species by

Eyed Elater (*Alaus oculatus*). A large Click Beetle with prominent, eyelike spots on its body.

putting out sweet baits in the early spring to attract the adults that have overwintered in the ground.

The elongate, brown, rather hard-shelled larvae are known in general as wireworms because of their slender, cylindrical shape. They are not only very difficult insects to control but are among the most destructive and widespread pests of nearly all of our cultivated crops, including corn, small grains, grasses, potatoes and other root crops, vegetables and flowers. In fact, some kind of wireworm damages practically every crop except those grown on trees. Wireworms attack seeds almost as soon as they have been planted, preventing many from germinating. Later they bore into the underground parts of the stems, causing the plants to wither and die; and still later they feed on the roots of what is left. The larvae are quite long-lived, various species spending from two to six years in the soil. Adults may live for ten to twelve months, a large part of which time is, in most species, likewise spent in the soil. Some species, like the big-eyed elaters, are general scavengers during larval life, living chiefly in rotting wood.

Among the most remarkable of the click beetles are the species of *Pyrophorus* of the New World tropics, which we mentioned when describing the fireflies. More than a hundred species are known, of which many are small and not brightly luminescent, but many others are famous for their brilliant luminosity and are described by every naturalist. The adults have a roundish yellow spot on each side of the prothorax (in the position of the eyespots of *Alaus*) that gives off a whitish to greenish light, and an area at the base of the abdomen that emits a warmer-toned glow that may be orange or even reddish. The colors of the lights vary with the species and also with the age of the specimens. Like most click beetles the adults spend the day in retirement but become active at night. *Pyrophorus noctiluca* has been described as floating out of the treetops in the dark of the forest at night like a golden ball or a flying saucer. Three or four of the insects give enough light to read by; and a dozen will serve to enable a nocturnal traveler to follow along a trail. The natives sometimes, in fact, tie them to their ankles when they have to travel at night. Perhaps the most unusual use of these insects occurred during the building of the Panama Canal, when a doctor performed an emergency operation by the light of a number of these beetles, all other sources of illumination having failed.

METALLIC WOOD-BORING BEETLES
—Family Buprestidae

The beetles of this large, world-wide and important family of fifteen thousand species are most closely related to the click beetles. Like them they are elongate; but they lack the click apparatus, are usually less flattened, taper more markedly to the rear and are consistently more hard-shelled. They well deserve their common name, for a large proportion of the species are more or less metallic (Plate 43). Some are as brilliantly so as anything imaginable, far exceeding any real metal surface in depth of color and iridescence. Only the most outstanding of the tropical birds, butterflies and moths can equal some of them. In many of the species the elytra are dull-colored and cryptically marked, the metallic colors being pronounced only on the lower and upper surfaces of the abdomen and therefore showing only in flight when the wings are spread. It is most disconcerting to a collector (probably also to a bird) to have a bright emerald green, flying insect suddenly disappear. Not knowing what to expect, who would think of looking twice at the flat lump on the tree trunk, colored and roughened just like the bark?

The larvae are just as distinctive as the adults, although in a strictly utilitarian way. The great majority are soft, white or yellowish, small-headed and legless grubs with the thorax flattened and greatly expanded sideways. Because of this wide anterior they are commonly known as "flat-headed borers," and have been likened in form to tadpoles. Most of them depend on wood for nutriment and make wide, flat galleries as they gnaw their way about. Their borings are thus easily recognized, being oval or almost ribbon-shaped in cross section, in contrast to the cylindrical tunnels of most other wood-boring insects. After tunneling for some months, sometimes for a year or more, the larva cleans out a chamber just beneath the bark and pupates there. As a result the adult, on emerging from the pupa, has but a thin wall to break through to reach the outer world.

Not all species are wood-borers. Quite a few tunnel in soft herbaceous stems; others, such as some of the species of *Agrilus*, cause the formation of stem or twig galls in which they live; and still others, such as species of *Brachys* (and needless to say, very small forms), mine in leaves, a habitat for which their flat shape fits them very well. Some species have the habit of tunneling just beneath the bark of twigs, which are thereby girdled and ultimately killed.

The flat-headed apple borer, *Chrysobothris femorata,* is one of the most injurious forms in North America, attacking more than thirty species of fruit and shade trees besides apple, although to its credit we must say that it generally selects trees that are already not in a healthy condition. The beetle is half an inch long, dark brown, banded and spotted with gray, with bronze reflections at certain angles and metallic greenish blue under the wings. The genus *Agrilus* contains more than seven hundred species, many of which are severe pests. The red-necked *Agrilus, A. ruficollis,* causes the raspberry gouty gall that seriously weakens or kills raspberry and blackberry canes. The worst is perhaps the bronze birch borer, *A. anxius,* the cause of enormous loss in the Canadian forests. Everywhere one sees thousands of birch trunks showing ghostly white, especially along hillsides where they are exposed by the death of the foliage of the trees below them.

The great genus *Stigmodera* has more than three hundred species in Australia alone, and includes some of the most resplendent of the family. *S. macularis,* for example, a species that is commonly found visiting the flowers of the tea tree, has a purplish head and pronotum and golden elytra pitted all over with shining black dots. Another species, *S. gratiosa,* has the elytra dark metallic green, pitted with spots of bright metallic emerald, the whole sparkling and reflecting light like a jewel; while *S. roei* is similar with the addition of three pairs of orange spots. These last two are frequently mounted in brooches. *S. suturalis* has the head, prothorax and edges of the elytra iridescent, metallic violet and the rest of the elytra golden. In South America the very large *Euchroma gigantea* is nearly three inches long and metallic green, crimson and coppery, the colors changing with the angle of the light. The tough elytra of this beetle were collected by the thousands and used by the ancient Incas in ceremonial regalia, being arranged in overlapping rows. They are still used similarly by some natives today.

LADYBIRD BEETLES—Family Coccinellidae

The names ladybird, ladybug and lady beetle have been applied to these little insects since the Middle Ages, when they were dedicated to the Virgin and called "beetles of Our Lady." The admonition of the well-known nursery rhyme to the ladybird to "fly away home, your house is on fire, your children alone" is said to refer to the European custom of burning the hop vines after the harvest. The vines were doubtless heavily populated with ladybird larvae feeding on the aphids that abound on the hop. The second stanza, "Except little Nan, who sits in a pan, weaving gold laces as fast as she can," refers to the brightly colored larva forming its yellow pupal case. The incantation of these lines whenever a ladybird alights on the hand or is seen on the window sill still serves to make us pause and check the impulse to kill every small, moving creature. And it is interesting that it is completely justified, for it enables us to send on her way the lady (or gentleman) to continue a life of extremely beneficial predation on countless numbers of aphids, greenflies and scale insects. For with only a few exceptions, the more than four thousand species of ladybirds are thus predaceous in both larval and adult stages, ranking among our most beneficial insects and fully deserving all the encouragement that we can give them.

The majority have a characteristic shape (Plate 42), very flat beneath, but with the body strongly arched, almost hemispherical in side view, and often almost circular when seen from above. Most of the species are brightly colored, pink, orange or red, with black dots. Some, however, are unmarked, and a few are black with red or orange dots. Only a few exceed a quarter of an inch in length. The bristly, active larvae are boldly colored and patterned, typically with black, orange, blue or red, and taper slightly to the posterior end. They and the adults are voracious predators on small Homoptera, chiefly the often destructive aphids, mealy bugs and scale insects, frequently joining forces with the larvae of the flower flies to destroy severe infestations of these insects. A single female may lay as many as a thousand eggs, although the average is considerably less; and the entire life cycle may require as little as four weeks, so that there may be several broods a year even in temperate regions. One individual was recorded eating ninety adult and three thousand larval scale insects during its own larval development, and doubtless a great number during its adult life as well.

It is no wonder, then, that many species of ladybirds have been enlisted by economic entomologists as an important means of biological control of such harmful insects. Nearly every country in the world now has species that have been imported and liberated to control aphids and scale insects; and in nearly every case these importations have proven of the greatest benefit. One of the outstanding examples is *Rhodolia cardinalis,* an Australian ladybird that was imported to California and South Africa, where it does excellent work in keeping under control the cottony cushion scale, *Icerya purchasi,* a very destructive pest of citrus trees.

Many species of ladybirds have a curious habit of gathering in very large numbers (Plate 41) to hibernate together in some dry, sheltered crevice. In nearly any part of the temperate zone considerable assemblages of this nature can be found in winter beneath loose stones or dead bark. In some parts of the world these groups number scores of thousands of individuals assembling, year after year, in the same place. In California certain hilltops are famous as winter quarters of ladybirds, which annually gather to the extent of a bushel or more from the surrounding territory. Such spots are highly valued by their owners, who collect the beetles and sell them to owners of citrus groves. When liberated in the spring they set to work on the scale insects; and the next autumn a new generation seeks refuge in the same winter quarters, to be collected and distributed in turn.

Sad to relate, one small group of the ladybirds, the subfamily Epilachninae, consists of plant-eating forms of which a few are sometimes quite destructive to plants valuable to man. In Europe, *Subcoccinella 24–punctata* is sometimes destructive to clover; and in North America the Mexican bean beetle, *Epilachna varivestis,* is frequently a serious pest on beans, especially in the southeastern states. The few harmful species, however, do little to detract from the deservedly fine reputation of most members of the family.

DARKLING BEETLES—*Family Tenebrionidae*

The common name of this family refers to the nocturnal habits of the species and not to their color, although it is true that a large proportion are dark. The family is one of the largest, containing upward of twelve thousand species, widely distributed in every continent but much commoner in the tropics and warm regions in general. A great many species inhabit deserts and arid areas, some of these being among the most distinctive members of the family. Practically all feed on plant material, chiefly as scavengers. Many are borers, usually in dead and decaying wood; many others are fungus-borers; a few live in ant nests; a few are scavengers on dead animal matter; and a few are predatory on other insect larvae. The larvae are typically long, slender and cylindrical, and are often quite heavily sclerotized. They often closely resemble wireworms but do not have the last segment of the abdomen so elaborately formed.

The adults (Plate 54) vary in size and form, ranging from species no more than an eighth of an inch long to others two inches in length. Many are extremely flat, others are cylindrical, and still others, especially in desert regions, are almost spherical. In many species the wings are absent and the elytra completely fused together down the back. This, combined with a very compact form and thick shell, characterizes many of the desert species, greatly reducing evaporation by minimizing the surface area of the beetle and sealing all unnecessary joints and pores.

Several species are widely distributed, sometimes serious pests in grain and stored food products. The best known of these is the mealworm, *Tenebrio molitor,* the larva of which when full grown is more than an inch and a quarter long, and the adult over a half an inch. Man makes considerable use of this beetle, since it is very easily reared in large numbers in captivity, all that is necessary being to start a number of beetles or larvae in dry bran or some such cereal, keep them dry and fairly warm, and wait for results. Since the life cycle requires a year, one's culture of mealworms should be started well ahead of the time when the beetles or larvae will be needed; but the very high reproductive rate pro-

The **Pinchbuck** (*Harpium sycophanta*), an unusual Longicorn Beetle of Europe.

duces a large number of individuals. Mealworms are a standard diet for soft-billed cage birds, enormous numbers being reared and sold at pet stores for this purpose, as well as for giving the fish in an aquarium an occasional taste of fresh food. They are also extensively used in biological research, and are perhaps one of the best-known animals because of the great amount of investigation that has been done on them. A number of smaller species such as the so-called confused flour beetle, *Tribolium confusum,* are also pests in dried foods.

Our favorites among the Tenebrionidae are the forked fungus beetles, *Boletotherus cornutus,* which may be found in the woody bracket fungi that grow from dead trees and logs. The larvae burrow in these fungi, and the adults may often be found in and about them. They are short, compact, cylindrical beetles about a quarter of an inch long, black and extremely rough-surfaced. On the pro-

thorax is a pair of long, rough, blunt horns that point forward and that are very much more prominent in the males. Perhaps the most unusual members of the family are the large black species of *Eleodes,* some an inch long, that often abound in the arid regions of North America. They are commonly known as pinacáte bugs (a Spanish word, so pronounce all four syllables). When disturbed they defend themselves by elevating the rear end of the body as high as possible, while the head nearly touches the ground, and discharging a very pungent defensive liquid. One of the beetles staggering across the desert with its body sticking almost straight up in the air is a most absurd sight.

LONG-HORNED BEETLES or LONGICORNS
—Family Cerambycidae

This is one of the very large, widely distributed and extremely important families. Although perhaps only sixth in rank in number of species, its ecologic significance is greater than this figure would seem to indicate, for it contains a disproportionate number of the major wood-boring beetles. It is well represented in the temperate zones but reaches its peak of abundance in the tropics.

The longicorns are great favorites with collectors, for not only are they exceedingly beautiful, with slender bodies and very long legs and antennae (sometimes several times the length of the body), but they offer an almost infinite variety of color and design. Many are strong fliers but often sit motionless, as though in a catatonic state. At such times they may be picked up easily with the fingers; but they can then retaliate by biting hard and can express dissatisfaction by squeaking loudly. Some species produce the sound by rubbing two parts of the body together, others by scraping the hind femora against the edges of the elytra. The Hawaiian *Plagithymsus* uses both methods.

The white or yellowish grubs have extremely powerful, hard jaws with which they can easily bore tunnels in the hardest heart woods as well as beneath bark. They are often somewhat enlarged just behind the head but are quite cylindrical, and are therefore called round-headed borers, in distinction from the flat-headed larvae of the Buprestidae. Many of the species live in their tunnels for two, three or even more years, destroying a great deal of wood in the process. When almost ready to transform to the pupal stage the larva prepares an exit tunnel that will permit it to get out of the tree when it has transformed to the adult beetle; for although the adult has strong jaws it is singularly incapable of gnawing its way through any but the feeblest bar·rier. The exit tunnel is then stopped up with loose, shredded wood fibers or chips. Some species secrete calcium carbonate (lime) with which they either make a neat cap over the exit tunnel or an eggshell lining for the pupation chamber.

A great many longicorns visit flowers as adults; in fact this is one of the chief places for collecting the adults of certain large groups. Among these the bodies are often very slender and the elytra narrow, cut away or strongly curved at the sides to facilitate slipping the hind wings out from beneath them. Many of these species are noted for their mimicry of wasps, having black, yellow, orange or red colors and patterns that are without doubt very efficacious in protecting them from predators. They are of considerable importance as pollinators. The European *Clytus arietes* not only looks like a Vespine wasp but behaves like one, hurrying about actively in plain sight and waving its antennae. Some of the tropical species of *Clytus* are incredibly close ant mimics. The North American *Cyllene robiniae* (Plate 51), a black-and-yellow-banded species an inch in length, is also a noted wasp mimic; furthermore its coloration is cryptic when it is feeding in the flowers of goldenrod, as it does in great abundance. Many other longicorns the world over are well-known mimics, not only of wasps and ants but of brightly colored, protected bugs. A few species have been recorded living with ants.

The longicorns show an enormous range of size, for while some of the smallest species are less than a quarter of an inch long, the giants may be fully six inches in length without counting the antennae. If we include the length of the antennae of the big species they will span some twelve inches, which is a figure that compares favorably with the giant walking sticks of the Orient. The largest belong to the Asiatic *Macrotoma,* which includes such species as *heros* and *luzonum,* and to the South American *Titanus,* species *giganteus* and *mundus.* These genera have antennae as long as the rest of the beetle, short jaws, and brown coloration. They are armed with a number of long, sharp spines along the sides of the thorax as well as on the head and legs, making it a hazardous operation to pick one up.

Even more remarkable, and perhaps somewhat larger in body size, are the New World tropical species of *Macrodontia,* such as *cervicornis* and *dejeani.* The antennae are relatively short by longicorn standards, that is to say a little shorter than the rest of the body; as though to make up for this, the jaws are extremely long, as in some of the stag beetles, and studded all along with many teeth, large and small. The thorax is brown and the elytra chestnut brown with elaborately scrolled and scrawled designs in black. This makes the beetles very difficult to see even when they are in plain sight, for the colors and design harmonize with the confused details of the bark, twigs and dead leaves among which they may be found. We would probably have passed by the first (and only) specimen of *M. cervicornis* that we ever encountered in life if it had not happened to move at just the wrong moment for its own safety.

Many of the other large longicorns are also noted for their cryptic appearance. The African *Pterognatha gigas* is so mottled and colored that when resting along a twig with its antennae extended it looks like a patch of withered moss or lichen with a couple of twisted strands projecting. Even more remarkable is the big *Acrocinus longimanus* of South America, with a body and elytra three inches long covered with a most intricate Paisley sort of design in gray, black and dull pink. Not only its antennae but its front legs as well are much longer than all the rest of the body, and are stretched out straight in front when it is resting along a branch.

None of the temperate zone longicorns even approximate the size of the many large tropical species, but some of the members of the same subfamily, the Prioninae, are nevertheless large beetles. *Prionus laticollis* of North America, more or less flattened, brown and leathery looking, is sometimes more than two inches long, excluding the antennae; so likewise are *P. imbricornis* and *Ergates spiculatus* of the Rocky Mountains and Pacific Northwest. The larvae of the Prionids live in the roots of various plants or in dead logs. Those of the large *Prionophus reticularis* of New Zealand are greatly relished as food by Maoris, whose name for them is "hu-hu."

The longicorns do not run to brilliant metallic, iridescent colors as much as certain other families of beetles, but some are as bright and attractive. Among the finest are some of the species of the South American genus *Pyrodes,* two inches long and emerald green with coppery shadings. Some of the other species of the same genus, however, are quite dull and cryptically colored.

Among the more important North American longicorns are the members of the genus *Monochammus,*

Broad-necked Prionus (*Prionus laticollis*). A large and powerful Longicorn Beetle, common in eastern North America.

variously known as sawyers. The larvae bore in the wood of many coniferous trees, making large cylindrical tunnels that ruin a great deal of wood and produce considerable quantities of sawdust. The large and powerful adults have exceptionally long antennae and are colored in dark grays, browns and black, matching the bark on which they rest.

The widespread Eurasian and North American genus *Saperda* contains many species that often do a great deal of damage by boring in various deciduous trees. One of the commonest and most destructive in North America is the round-headed apple tree borer, *S. candida,* a very attractive-looking beetle that is brightly striped with brown and white. The black-and-yellow *Cyllene robiniae* mentioned above is often very harmful to locust trees when it is in the larval stage. There is, in fact, no deciduous tree of any importance to which damage is not done by the larvae of one or more longicorns. Many of the beetles attack dead wood, and may thus do harm to trees that have been felled and are being seasoned in the log. Such species, together with the metallic wood-borers, are the chief reason why such cut timber can be stored safely only under water. Even cut and sawed lumber is sometimes not immune, so that the damage goes on until the wood has finally been fashioned into finished articles; and then the powder-post beetles take over and continue the job of destruction.

Not all of the longicorns are root-eaters or wood-borers, for many species invade the pithy stems of shrubs or even of annual plants. A large, stoutly built black species of *Moneilema* specializes in attacking the pulpy stems of the ferociously spined cholla cactus. A number, such as the extremely elongate species of the genus *Oberea,* are serious pests in the canes of blackberry and raspberry. The very interesting longicorns of the genus *Tetraopes* attack milkweed. Their generic name is based on the fact that each of the compound eyes is divided into two separate parts, making the beetle "four-eyed." They are brightly colored scarlet and black, and thus, like so many other insects that feed on the acrid juices and tissues of milkweed, warningly colored (Plate 53).

A longicorn that is representative of another way of living is the oak-pruner, *Hypermallus villosus.* The larvae live in oak twigs, which they eventually bore in such a manner that the twigs are severed and drop to the ground with the larvae inside. The larvae then remain in the twigs during the winter, and transform to the pupa and adult in the spring. The twig-girdler, *Oncideres cingulata,* does much the same kind of thing, but in this case it is the female who, at the time of laying an egg in the twig, cuts a groove around it so as to girdle and kill it and thus cause it to fall eventually. Needless to say, the drastic pruning that a heavy infestation of such beetles may give a tree is often very harmful.

LEAF BEETLES—Family Chrysomelidae

It has been estimated that there are more than twenty-five thousand species of these beetles (Plate 56) in the world, which makes this probably the second-largest family of the order. Like so many other large groups it reaches its maximum development in the tropics, but still contains thousands of temperate zone species. The majority of the species feed on leaves in both the adult and larval stages, the two often living and feeding side by side. They are usually diurnal and sun-loving, preferring to rest on exposed surfaces of the foliage. When disturbed, the beetles often fold up their legs and drop to the ground.

Many of the species are extremely attractive (Plates 54–57), often, especially in the tropical regions, being among the most brilliantly colored of all beetles. Few are large, a specimen an inch long being exceptional; but hundreds of species are living gems that more than make up by their beauty for what they lack in size. The majority are rather broad, oval or rounded, and quite stoutly formed. A few are flat. Quite a number, including one whole subfamily, have the hind legs adapted for jumping; many of these are appropriately known as flea beetles or, in Australia, kangaroo beetles.

The subfamily Donaciinae contains many species that strongly resemble longicorns (to which the leaf beetles are indeed very closely related), having the body more slender and the antennae more elongate than most leaf beetles. They are aquatic during the early stages, the larvae feeding on the leaves of such plants as water lilies. The adults, too, may be found around the water, often crawling beneath the surface to feed. They are covered with a short, silky pile that repels water and carries a film of air when the beetle goes under the surface.

The largest members of the family belong to the Sagrinae, most of which are tropical although a few occur in Europe and North America. The deep metallic blue *Sagria papuana* of North Queensland is called the kangaroo beetle because of its enlarged hind legs and jumping ability. Its larvae live in swellings in plant stems.

The subfamily Criocerinae is world-wide, containing many hundreds of species. The larvae of some disguise themselves by carrying about a load of their own excrement over their backs, a habit that is also characteristic of the tortoise beetles. Two extremely well-known pests that belong to this group are the old-fashioned potato beetle, *Lema trilineata,* and the asparagus beetle, *Crioceris asparagi.* The former, and the blister beetle that has the same common name (page 116), are black and yellow striped; both were the major pests on potatoes until the Colorado potato beetle came along and displaced them from this position of honor. The asparagus beetle, a native of Europe, was introduced into New York about 1862. Leaving behind the predators and parasites with which they have evolved a system of more or less mutual checks and balances, such introduced species often extend their ranges almost explosively and become excessively injurious in a very short time.

The Clythrinae, Chlamisinae and Cryptocephalinae include a large number of very small species. In some of the species the female lays the egg in a case made at the moment by coating it with her excrement. When the egg hatches, the larva adds to this its own excrement, making a neat, smooth, flask-shaped or gourd-shaped structure in which it lives and which it carries about. The larvae of the European *Clythra quadripunctata* and the North American *Coscinoptera dominicana* live in ant nests, presumably as scavengers. Many of the beetles of this group are very compact, rough-surfaced and hard-shelled. When disturbed they pull their appendages close to the body and fall; and their resemblance to the droppings of caterpillars is so marked that they must benefit from it.

The largest and most characteristic of the subfamilies is the Chrysomelinae. Typically almost hemispherical, and often brightly or brilliantly colored, the adults and larvae often live together on the same foliage. Many have boldly marked patterns of dark and light, and show great individual variation, a feature that makes them favorites with many collectors. The famous Colorado potato beetle, *Leptinotarsa decemlineata,* is a representative member of this group. It was first discovered in the upper Missouri River region about 1823 during Long's expedition to the Rocky Mountains. At that time it was merely an ordinary, far from abundant, and quite local species that fed on the buffalo bur *Solanum rostratum.* This plant is a member of the nightshade family, to which the potato and the tomato also belong. As the West became settled, potato culture was introduced into the region occupied by the beetle, which promptly took to the new food plant with great enthusiasm. Its spread eastward was at first gradual, but soon accelerated; and by 1874 it had become well established along the Atlantic coast. Since then it has become established wherever potatoes are grown, and has proven a major pest everywhere. It was responsible for severe damage to the all-important potato crop in many European countries during the nineteenth century, causing widespread famine and heavy emigration to America. As recently as World War II it was the subject of German propaganda, the United States Air Force being accused of deliberately liberating large numbers of live potato beetles over Germany, even though Germany itself had been having outbreaks of the species for over sixty years.

A close relative of the Colorado potato beetle is

Colorado Potato Beetle (*Leptinotarsa decemlineata*). An extremely injurious pest in Europe as well as in its native North America.

the orange-red and black *Labidomera clivicollis* (Plate 55) that feeds on milkweed nearly everywhere in temperate North America. Its coloration suggests the similar appearance of other milkweed feeders so strongly that it may be of the warning, or aposematic, type although this is not certain.

The subfamily Galerucinae contains many more serious pests. One of the worst is the imported European elm leaf beetle, *Galerucella xanthomelaena,* that often skeletonizes nearly every leaf of many elms. The small black-and-yellow adults often attain prominence by entering houses in the autumn in great numbers to spend the winter. A related species, *G. nymphaea,* feeds on the leaves of water lilies. Also members of this subfamily are the striped cucumber beetle, *Diabrotica vittata,* and the spotted cucumber beetle, *D. duodecimpunctata,* both native garden pests that attack a wide variety of plants.

The flea beetles, the subfamily Halticinae, are all small, few being longer than a quarter of an inch and the majority even smaller. The femora of the hind legs are greatly thickened, containing powerful muscles that are used in jumping. Many have metallic colors. There are hundreds of species, some of which are severe garden pests. In addition to the damage they do by eating leaves, some of the species are the carriers of serious plant diseases such as the early potato blight and the bacterial wilt of corn.

[125

The subfamily Eumolpinae contains many species. Some of the best known and most attractive are the brilliantly metallic members of the genus *Chrysochus* that feed on dogbane, *Apocynum*. *C. auratus* of eastern North America is bright green with a golden, coppery or sometimes even crimson metallic sheen. It is to be found, often in great abundance, on the leaves of the food plant. The Western *C. cobaltinus* is less brilliant and a dark cobalt blue.

The wedge-shaped leaf beetles, the subfamily Hispinae, are characterized by the peculiar shape of the body, which is narrow in front and broad behind. Many of them have the elytra and body roughened by either pits and ridges or by long, protruding spines. Some of the large tropical species, such as the Australian *Monochirus multispinosus*, are as prickly as any hedgehog or porcupine. Many of the species are leaf-miners in the larval stage, the North American *Chalepus dorsalis*, for instance, forming large, blotchy, whitish mines in the leaflets of locust. We have seen trees so heavily infested by these larvae that not more than 5 per cent of the leaf area was untouched.

Finally, the Cassidinae or tortoise beetles (Plate 50) contain some of the most interesting as well as beautiful members of the family. The beetles are typically quite flat-looking, due to the expansion forward and sideways of the margins of the body and elytra. Many of the tropical species are particularly large and brightly colored, often being strongly iridescent. Some of these, such as the little green South American *Desmonota variolosa*, have been used in jewelry. The roughness of the surface of this beetle only enhances the depth of its deep emerald iridescence. A related group, *Tauroma*, are unusual among tortoise beetles in having a long horn protruding laterally from each side of the thorax. The common North American gold bug, *Metriona bicolor*, is brilliantly metallic while alive. The appearance is due to such delicate structural adjustments of superimposed layers in the integument that the drying and shrinking of the specimen after death causes the total disappearance of the metallic appearance; and what was a living bit of burnished metal changes in a few hours to a rather dull, brownish beetle.

Quite a few of the tortoise beetles are destructive to garden plants. The larvae of many of the species have a long, flexible, forked structure at the posterior end, which can be held forward and above the back. On this is accumulated a mass of the larva's excrement which it holds above itself like a parasol, effectively shielding itself from view.

PEA and BEAN WEEVILS—Family Bruchidae

These beetles became known as weevils because as larvae they bore and feed within dried seeds, a way of life practiced by hundreds of species of true weevils of the family Curculionidae. This is all that the two groups have in common, the pea and bean weevils being, in fact, most closely related to the leaf beetles. There are over nine hundred species, nearly all of which live as larvae in various seeds. The best known are the worst pests, the pea weevil *Bruchus pisorum* and the bean weevil *Acanthoscelides obtectus*. Both, like so many other insects that live in man's foods, are practically worldwide. Small, round holes in dried beans and peas show that a larva has been living in the seed but has emerged. All of us have probably eaten many, thus getting an unsolicited bit of animal protein. As many as six generations a year may be produced, so that it does not take long for an infected batch of seeds to become thoroughly riddled. Other species attack many other seeds used by man as food, some living in coconuts and palms.

BARK BEETLES, WEEVILS and THEIR ALLIES
—Superfamily Rhynchophora

The families of this group have a number of characteristics in common that set them apart from all other beetles. Chief of these is the tendency for the mouthparts to become smaller and set out at the end of a beak projecting from the front of the head. In some of the families this is no more than a tendency, but in others, including the very large family of true weevils, the whole front of the head may be prolonged forward to form a slender proboscis longer than the rest of the insect. There is no question of this being a sucking proboscis such as we see in many other orders of insects; the jaws remain jaws, although they are out at the end of the beak. The beetles of this superfamily are never large, and the majority are very small. They are, however, of the utmost importance both in the ecology of any region in which they occur and in man's economy; for many of the most serious pests of our forest, agricultural and stored products belong to this group.

PRIMITIVE WEEVILS—Family Brenthidae

Although a world-wide family of nearly two thousand species, almost all of these beetles are tropical. They are long and slender, often excessively so, not only the body and the elytra but the head as well being drawn out into a projection straight forward that may be as long as the rest of the insect. The jaws and antennae are set in the front portion of this. In many species the sexes are quite different from each other in this respect, the male having a short beak with large mandibles but the female having a long one with small mandibles. With it the female bores deep holes in wood, in which she lays her eggs. Occasionally she gets her snout caught in the hole; and in such cases the male has been known to help her get loose, displaying considerable ability as an insect engineer in prying down on the end of her abdomen while she braces her front legs and pulls. There often is an extreme, yet apparently normal, variation in size, some individuals being no more than one-third the length of others.

The adults frequently are gregarious, more than a hundred having been found gathered beneath the bark of a fallen tree. The males are pugnacious and eager fighters, contending with each other for the females. The larvae bore in the woody tissues of trees, some in dead wood but others in living trunks. They have been known to do considerable damage in this way, even in solid oak.

Only one species, *Eupsalis minuta*, is widely distributed in North America. It is a deep red-brown with yellow markings, and ranges from one-quarter to nearly three-quarters of an inch long. A few other species occur in the extreme southern states. Perhaps the finest, and one of the most grotesque of all beetles, is the big New Zealand *Lasiorrhynchus barbicornis*, of which large specimens may be nearly four inches long. The small *Cordus hospes* of Australia lives in ant nests.

The family Belidae consists solely of the New York weevil, *Ithycerus noveboracensis*, a fairly large, stocky species about three-quarters of an inch long that is widely distributed in Canada and the United States. The larvae are somewhat destructive by boring in the twigs and branches of many trees, ranging from oak to apple.

Several other small families are known which do not, however, contain any members of other than technical interest. The following major groups contain the great majority of the Rhynchophora.

TRUE WEEVILS—*Family Curculionidae*

Known also as snout beetles, elephant beetles and billbugs, the weevils are the largest family, not only of the Coleoptera but also of the whole animal kingdom. About forty thousand species are now known; but considering the rate at which new ones turn up every year and the relatively small amount of study that has been done in enormous tropical areas, it is fairly conservative to estimate that probably double that number actually exist. Although the largest are as much as three inches long, the weevils as a group average less than one-quarter of an inch in length, and many are extremely minute. The proboscis is usually quite prominent, although it is very short in some. The antennae are almost always conspicuously bent or elbowed, and usually project from the side of the proboscis or may be folded in special grooves. The integument is extremely hard. Many of the species are wingless, but many others fly well. The majority of the species are plainly or quietly colored,

often cryptically, and frequently have very rough integuments. A few groups, however, are very bright. Some of the big Papuan species of *Eupholus*, an inch to an inch and a half long, are bright, sky blue. In both the Old and the New World tropics are found a number of weevils, up to an inch or more in length, that are known as diamond beetles because of the brilliant, almost flashing, reflections of the metallic scales on the elytra. *Chrysolophus spectabilis* is the best-known Australian diamond weevil, and *Cyphus* and *Entimus* the chief genera of the South American ones. A great many of the weevils are covered with tiny flat scales that are chiefly responsible for their color patterns. Sometimes the colors are due to a fine, powdery dusting that can be rubbed off by the weevil and then renewed.

The larvae are usually legless and often blind, curved and blunt-ended. Nearly all are burrowers or borers, most commonly in sound or rotting wood or in fruits and seeds. There is, however, no part of a plant from the roots to the topmost leaves that may not be provender for some weevil larvae. Those that mine leaves tend to be hairy and equipped with special swellings used for locomotion. The few that feed exposed in the open encase themselves in a sticky secretion that keeps them from falling. A few genera are aquatic as larvae; and in a few of these, such as *Bagous*, *Eubrychus* and *Litodactylus* of Europe, the adults are also aquatic. Some of the species that bore in stems or roots cause the formation of galls, inside which the larvae live. When about to pupate the larvae of some weevils make cocoons from a substance that is formed in the excretory organs, excreted from the anus and then worked up with the mouthparts. Some other larvae have spinnerets near the mouth with which the cocoons are made. The majority of species, however, simply pupate in a cavity in the substance in which they have been burrowing. Parthenogenesis, the development of unfertilized eggs, occurs regularly in some species.

Literally thousands of species of the weevils are injurious to man's interests, making it impossible for us to do more here than to mention a few representative ones; and even then we will have to omit some of the major insect pests of the world—so many of these are weevils.

The grain weevil, *Calendra granaria*, and its congener the rice weevil, *C. oryzae*, occur wherever man stores grains—wheat, corn, barley, rye, millet, rice, and even beans and peas. They are the traditional weevils (the word comes from the old Anglo-Saxon "wifel") that we read about in the tales of old days at sea. If you were very fussy you tapped the ship's biscuit hard to drive out the weevils before you ate it.

The famous cotton boll weevil, *Anthonomus grandis*, is perhaps the best-known member of the group in the United States, where it first appeared in 1892 in southernmost Texas, having come in from Mexico. It spread toward the north and east at an average rate of about sixty miles a year, and now occupies practically every important cotton-growing area in the country. The weevil winters chiefly in the adult stage, hiding in almost any sort of rubbish or protected place. It is a chunky, brownish insect about one-quarter of an inch long, with a prominent, stout, downcurved beak. The females attack the blossom buds, or squares, of cotton when these are about six days old. They eat cavities in them and lay a single egg therein, each female laying from one hundred to three hundred eggs. Later in the season eggs may be laid in the ripened fruits, the bolls. The infested squares usually fail to develop, and if they do are useless for producing any worthwhile cotton. The entire life cycle from one adult generation to the next takes an average of three weeks, so that there may be, depending on the location and season, from two to ten generations in a single year.

The larvae spend their entire developmental period inside the single square or boll where they began, boring about and destroying not only the seeds but the fibers of cotton that are packed around them, and pupating there also. They cannot, therefore, be reached with any insecticide. Some control is obtained by making as early a crop as is practicable, in order to get the cotton fruits past the vulnerable square stage before the full numbers of the weevils are around to lay eggs. Cleaning up all rubbish and burning it destroys many overwintering weevils. Finally, dusting the crop with poison that kills the adult weevils, best done from airplanes, gives excellent results if done thoroughly and at exactly the right time.

Despite all control methods the boll weevil continues to be one of the most expensive of all insects. It is estimated that it causes an annual loss of from three to five million bales of cotton a year, amounting to a monetary loss to the growers of one hundred to two hundred million dollars annually. It is safe to say that since the weevil first entered the United States it has caused a total loss of between four and five billion dollars. This does not include financial losses due to depreciated land values, the closing of cotton gins and oil mills, and all of the other economic dislocations that have occurred wherever a district has been hard hit by the weevil.

On the other hand, people who look beneath the surface feel that the cotton boll weevil has, perhaps, not been such a bad thing for the South in the long run. It has been realized for generations that Southern agriculture has been too intensively concentrated on the two cash crops, cotton and tobacco. As a result the economy has been too closely tied to the fluctuations in prices of these products, with practically no other major crops to cushion the shock

when prices went down. Moreover, both of these crops are extremely soil-exhausting, so that concentration on them has had the effect of wearing out the soil, removing from it at great speed the major elements necessary for plant growth. Much of the soil of the South is today thus badly depleted. For a long period the old, worn-out soils could be abandoned, since there was ever new land to the west. When this possibility ended, Southern agriculture faced a crisis; and the invasion of the boll weevil capped the climax. It caused, it is true, great loss and suffering, for in many regions it reduced the productivity of whole communities far below subsistence level. But it forced much of the South to stop concentrating on cotton, and cotton alone, and to diversify its agriculture. As a result the rural South is today in a far healthier condition, growing many other crops; perhaps not making so many dollars per acre as in the best of the old days, but living on a much broader and more secure basis. There is one famous statue to the boll weevil in a Southern city, erected by the citizens who realized that despite the initial shock, the weevil has supplied a stimulus for a better-balanced agricultural economy.

In the tropical regions of both hemispheres the big palm weevils of the genus *Rhynchophorus* bore in the tender, growing heads of palms and kill the new shoot on which depends all future growth of the tree. These are among the largest of the weevils, being brown or black, short-beaked beetles as much as two inches long. *Rhynchophorus ferrugineus* is a very serious pest in the coconut and wine palms of Pacific regions, sometimes threatening the economy of a complete island where the entire agriculture is concentrated on raising copra, the dried meat of the coconut. A similar species, *R. cruentatus,* occurs in the palmettos, or cabbage palms, of the southern United States and throughout tropical America. The eggs are laid in the delicate tissues at the base of the growing leaf sheath, and the larvae burrow about within. Curiously enough, while burrowing they make a rather loud noise that sounds like a clucking hen. The big, two-inch-long, mature larvae are much relished as food by many natives, being eaten either raw or fried crisp.

A great many weevils are borers in woody stems, some in mature wood and others in tender shoots. One of the most widely known is the white pine weevil, *Pissodes strobi,* of eastern North America, which quite regularly kills the terminal shoots of young white pines by riddling them with burrows. It is this central, terminal shoot that each spring sends its growth upward, and thus is responsible for the growth of the trunk of the tree, while the whorl of shoots around it grow out to the sides to form the branches. When the central shoot is killed the tree cannot grow upward until one of the side shoots bends around and takes on the task of continuing the linear growth of the trunk. This means that not only does the tree lose a year or two of upward growth but also that it will always have a kink in the trunk where this happened. As a result, when the tree has grown large enough to be cut, the log will not be straight but will have places where the grain is bent, wherever the weevil killed a central shoot.

The acorn and nut weevils of the genus *Curculio,* of which there are various species common to Eurasia and North America, are noted for the length and slenderness of their beaks, which in the females may be nearly twice as long as the body, with the jointed antennae arising prominently from their sides part way out. Those of the males, although much shorter, are still very prominent. As their common name implies, these weevils live as larvae inside acorns and various nuts. The species tend to specialize, *Curculio proboscideus,* the large chestnut weevil, and *C. auriger* being chestnut and chinquapin feeders; while *C. rectus* and *baculi* are acorn weevils, preferring the fruits of the black and red oaks. There are many others. The female bores a hole in the young nut or acorn with her beak and then turns around, backs up to the hole and lays an egg in it. Some species of acorn weevils make a number of branch tunnels inside the acorn radiating from the single entrance hole, the curve of the female's beak making this an easy matter, lay an egg in each and then seal the entrance hole with a pellet of fecal matter. The larvae feed in the nuts and acorns, fall to the ground with these in the autumn, and then cut their way out and spend the winter in the soil. In the following summer they pupate and emerge as adults in time to mate and infest more nuts and acorns.

A final species will serve to illustrate still another way of weevil life as well as another serious pest. The plum curculio, *Conotrachelus nenuphar,* is the best-known member of its large genus, which includes more than fifty American species. It is a stout-bodied weevil about one-fifth of an inch long, with a fairly long beak that is turned down beneath its body, a prominent hump on each elytron, and a cryptic brown, gray and black coloration. It looks, in fact, very much like a caterpillar dropping. The adult beetles hibernate among rubbish and debris and become active in the spring when the fruit trees are flowering. The females lay their eggs in the young fruits, attacking peach, cherry, apple, pear and others, as well as plum. The larvae complete their growth in the fruit in from three to five weeks, emerge and pupate in the ground. In about a month they emerge as adults, feed for a time from the fruits and then seek places in which to spend the winter. For some reason the female cuts a crescent-shaped gash partly around the hole where she lays the egg in the fruit; and this may enlarge and form a prominent scar on the fruit even though (as is com-

An **Acorn Weevil** (*Curculio*). The female uses the grotesquely elongated beak to bore holes in acorns in which to lay her eggs.

mon in apples) the egg fails to hatch. The feeding punctures of the adult weevils often make bad scars on the fruit also. Even more important is the fact that the weevil is a carrier of the serious infectious disease, brown rot. Other species have similar habits, attacking many fruits and nuts; *C. juglandis* is often a bad pest of walnuts, butternuts and hickory nuts, causing the nuts to fall when they are about half-green; and *C. crataegi,* the quince curculio, lives also in hawthorn fruits. One reason that many such weevils are so hard to control is the fact that they can feed on many of the common wild fruits or nuts in an area and thus maintain a sizable population that serves as a source of continual infestation for cultivated crops.

BARK, ENGRAVER and AMBROSIA BEETLES
—Family Scolytidae (*Ipidae*)

Only the giants of this group are more than one-quarter of an inch long, the majority being less than half that. Most of the species are compact, blunt-ended and very short-beaked, and are red-brown to black with no markings. Many bore tunnels in or under the bark of trees; a few bore in roots, twigs or solid wood; and a few tunnel in shrubs and herbaceous stems. Some live within seeds or fruits, such as those of the palms, and in fir cones; and some even bore in the wood of casks and barrels. The food of the wood-eaters is primarily the carbohydrates in the wood cells or, in some groups, the fungi that they cultivate in the galleries hewn out of wood. They are often sociable and gregarious; and some species are truly social, although in a primitive way. Among the sociable species there are all gradations from

[129

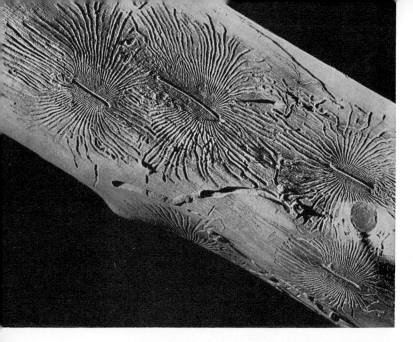

Tunnels of a **Bark Beetle** (*Scolytidae*) shown in the sap wood of a dead branch from which the bark has been stripped. No group of insects is more destructive in forests.

what has been termed a simple and unorganized but intensive polygamy to a specialized, organized polygamy and even a simple monogamy. The males of some species of *Xyleborus* have sixty or more females (!) while those of *Ips* will have no more than two, and those of *Scolytus* only one.

The true bark beetles tunnel either in the bark itself or between it and the sapwood. In this they are frequently destructive out of all proportion to their size, for this is a vital region in most trees. The layer known as the vascular cambium is a sheath no more than two cells thick, upon the existence of which is dependent the tree's ability to form new wood and other conductive cells. Just outside the cambium is the phloem, the thin layer of cells along which food materials are carried from the leaves to the roots. It is only necessary to make a cut through these thin layers completely around the trunk, thus girdling the tree, to cause its death. This frequently happens when the bark beetles are abundant in a tree, as they usually are, their burrows connecting up to extend around the trunk. A few tiny beetles only one-eighth of an inch long may thus cause the death of a tree two hundred feet high.

Many of the bark beetles are known as engraver beetles because of the intricate pattern of lines that their tunnels make in the inner surface of the bark and the outer surface of the wood. To some degree they are distinctive for different species. Each set of tunnels is the work of the progeny from a single batch of eggs. The beetles bore in through the bark, making a single gallery or chamber which, for the social species, serves as a nuptial chamber. The female of each species deposits her eggs in a distinctive way: sometimes at the ends of the cham-

ber, sometimes in a considerable number of niches all along both sides of the central gallery. When the eggs hatch each larva bores its own tunnel away from the original tunnel, which thus serves as the starting point for a whole series of more or less parallel or radiating, and enlarging, larval burrows. The whole often forms a pattern that looks like a gigantic twisted centipede. Each larva pupates at the far end of its tunnel, and then when it transforms to the adult bores out through the bark to the outer world. When the beetles are abundant, the bark is often peppered with emergence holes that look like the holes made by fine birdshot. *Scolytus rugulosus,* about two millimeters long, is, in fact, known as the shot-hole borer for this reason. It is a European species that was introduced into the United States and by 1878 had become a well-established pest on all cultivated fruit trees as well as wild plum and wild cherries.

Another well-traveled species is the smaller European bark beetle, *Scolytus multistriatus,* widely distributed in Europe, introduced into North America before 1909 and now occurring throughout the East and the Midwest. A serious pest by itself, it has teamed up with our native elm bark beetle, *Hylurgopinus rufipes,* in transmitting the spores of the fungus that causes the exceedingly serious Dutch elm disease. The eggs of the beetle are laid in recently cut, broken or dying elm branches, but the newly emerged adults feed on the bark of healthy twigs, a habit that accounts for the rapid dissemination of the disease to uninfected trees. The beetle may have as many as three generations a year, hibernating in the larval stage. Infected trees can be recognized by the wilting of the leaves, the curling of the ends of the twigs, the presence of many small sucker twigs shooting out from the larger limbs, and the brown color of the thin, soft layer beneath the bark. Where it is practicable, trees can be protected from infection by sprays that kill the beetles; a task, however, that requires expensive high-power apparatus and is quite beyond the financial means of most people. But the cost of spraying every elm in North America would be prohibitive, even if such a job could be done. The best hope is that resistant strains of the elms will be selected by the killing off of all nonresistant ones. We have already lost to a similar disease one of our most valuable native trees, the chestnut. It would be equally tragic if our elms were also to go.

Members of the large Eurasian and North American genus *Dendroctonus* are perhaps the worst of all pests in the coniferous forests of Canada and the United States. Some of the most destructive species are: *D. piceaperda,* which destroys large areas of the spruces in eastern North America; *D. monticolae,* the most destructive species of the Western white, lodgepole and yellow pines; and *D. ponderosa,* a bad pest on Engelmann spruce as well as on Western pines. An important part of forest management is to find all trees infested by the beetles and to cut and burn them when it is safe to do so. In many cases the beetles are attracted to fresh wounds in trees, as are other borers such as Buprestids and longicorns. It is therefore important to prevent unnecessary cuts in the bark, for even a small "blaze" made to mark a trail may thus bring about the death of the tree.

In contrast to the bark beetles, the timber or ambrosia beetles (often put in a separate family, the Ipidae) bore deep into the wood, thus riddling much valuable timber with their holes. Their tunnels can be distinguished by their uniform diameter throughout their entire length, their freedom from wood dust, and the fact that they are usually stained brown. The female first excavates a long main gallery in the solid wood and then makes short egg galleries all along this at right angles. In the main gallery the female prepares a bed or layer of chips and excreta on which she cultivates a fungus. Each species of beetle raises but a single species of fungus; and it is interesting to note that closely related species of beetles have closely related species of fungi. In some species the spores of the fungus are carried in the excreta of the beetle; in others they are stored in the female's crop and then regurgitated on the newly made fungus beds; in still others they adhere to brushes on the front of the female's head or to globules of fatty substance that forms in pores on her prothorax. This is reminiscent of the fungus-growing termites and the leaf-cutter ants, which also cultivate fungi but have large, highly organized societies. The ambrosia beetles are thus of special interest in showing us a primitive insect society in which the same thing is done. The young ambrosia beetles do not stay around and cooperate with the mother or with each other but scatter, each on its own, the young females bearing the spores of the distinctive fungus of their species.

Cases are known where the fungus has proved a veritable Frankenstein monster when, for some reason, the beetles were unable to keep it cut back enough to check its too exuberant growth. Spreading throughout the tunnels, it has been known to choke them, entrapping the occupants in a meshwork from which they could not escape.

The ambrosia beetles contain many species harmful to forest trees. In addition, one species is often destructive to wine and beer casks, and one is the carrier from tree to tree of pear blight.

LAMELLICORN BEETLES
—Superfamily Lamellicornia or Scarabaeoidea

The next four families belong to this major division, one of the most easily recognized groups of the

beetles and also one of the largest. The group name is descriptive of the antennae, each of which has at its tip a club composed of a number of flat plates. These are on separate antennal segments, and can be moved so as to be brought close together to form a tight club or spread apart more or less fanwise. This structure greatly increases the surface area on which are scent structures, so that these beetles have a very keen sense of smell. The group is primarily a burrowing one, this habit persisting in the majority of species.

The adults are mostly stout and compact in form, extremely powerful but seldom agile, walking in an ungainly manner and flying clumsily but strongly. Many are ornamented with most striking spines, horns and other protuberances on the head and thorax. In many members of the group the colors are unusually brilliant. The males and females often differ in a great many features, in some cases so extremely that they have been described as members of different genera. The larvae are equally distinctive, being pale-colored with long, heavy abdomens curled beneath them to the form of the letter "J." They feed, chiefly underground, on decaying plant matter, roots or dung. Since their lives are spent surrounded by the substance on which they feed, they lie on their backs or sides and use their short legs but little. The posterior segments of their abdomens are usually considerably swollen and darkened because of the fecal matter that accumulates there.

In this group are found perhaps the majority of the most beautiful or bizarre members of the order, as well as the largest. Some of the worst insect pests, as far as man is concerned, also belong here. In the general economy of nature these beetles are of primary importance, being excelled by no other group in the volume of dead plant matter that they return to circulation in the world of life. Much has been written about the importance of scavengers on animal matter, but it must be realized that there is actually a far greater volume of dead plant material that must be processed before it can be reused by life as a whole. In this plant-scavenging the beetles play a major role; and among them the lamellicorn scavengers are pre-eminent.

BESSY BUGS—*Family Passalidae*

There are several hundred species of this family in the tropics of both the Old and the New World, but none in Europe and only four in North America. One of these is common and widespread, whereas the others just barely get in from the south. They are rather large beetles, the common North American *Passalus cornutus* being nearly an inch and a half long, elongate and flat and rather square-ended; the prothorax is very large and square and set off from the rest of the body by a prominent, deep indentation. There is a small horn on the head; the elytra are shiny black and deeply grooved.

Both adults and larvae live together in family groups in rotting logs, showing a definite, though primitive, social organization, something that is very rare in beetles. The adults disintegrate the wood and prepare it for the consumption of the larvae by chewing it thoroughly and mixing it with digestive secretions. Both male and female seem to take part in this, a most unusual thing in social insects other than the termites. A noted feature of the colonial life that is quite obvious to anyone finding a colony is the ability of both the larvae and the adults to make sounds. In the larvae this is accomplished by means of the vestigial hind legs, which are reduced to short, toothed organs. These are rubbed against the basal joints of the middle legs. The sound of the adults is produced by rubbing the inner surface of the bases of the wings against rough places on the upper surface of the abdomen. In both cases the squeaking, grating noise is plainly audible to a human, often if he merely listens to the rotten log in which the colony lives.

Although they have powerful jaws the adult's bite is not at all to be feared, so that they can be handled with impunity. We do not know how the old country name of "bess" or "bessy bug" originated for these beetles, but it is obviously a folklore sort of term and greatly preferable to "horned passalus," a stilted translation of the scientific name. They are also known as "patent leather beetles," in reference to their shiny elytra. An old country superstition has it that a sure cure for earache can be obtained by chopping off the head of one of these beetles and allowing a drop of the exuding fluid to fall on the offending eardrum. Some of the tropical species are very large, reaching a length of three inches; these are often used as food by natives.

SKIN BEETLES—Family Trogidae

This is a small but widely distributed group that is often classified as a subfamily of the Scarabaeidae. Most of the species are less than one-quarter of an inch long, chunky, dirty gray or black and very rough-surfaced. The adults as well as the larvae are mostly found in old, dried animal carcasses, where they feed on all the residues but the bones. They are thus frequently in company and competition with Dermestid beetles, but unlike the latter have never become household pests. Some notably large species of the genus *Trox* occur in deserts, where their compact, tightly sealed, shell-like exoskeletons are important in preventing dessication.

STAG BEETLES—Family Lucanidae

The majority of the nine hundred members of this family have gone in for the development of mandibles in a big way. Even in the females these are large and powerful and capable of giving a hard bite that will draw blood. There is little doubt that the "pinch bug" that Tom Sawyer took to church was a stag beetle, very likely the common North American *Pseudolucanus capreolus,* which attains a length of as much as an inch and a third.

It is in the males that the mandibles show a grotesquely exaggerated development, being in many species fully as long as all the rest of the beetle and ornately branched and toothed. This is responsible for the name "stag beetle," since the mandibles can be compared to nothing else as well as to the antlers of a stag. In still others the mandibles are just as long in proportion but straight and plain, or perhaps sharply bent inward at the tips. The conventional idea is that the jaws serve the males as weapons in sexual life, chiefly in combat among themselves for the females. In some cases this is very possibly true, but in the species where the mandibles are exaggeratedly large and ornate they are so clumsy, and so incapable of giving a really hard bite because of the inefficient leverage of their muscles, that they are a severe handicap in fighting and everything else that the beetle does. If any sexual selection of the best fighting male is taking place it should favor the ones with the shorter, more efficient jaws; and this is directly opposed to the classical idea that the large jaws have evolved through a long period of selection, as successful mates, of the largest-jawed individuals. Very possibly the stag beetles have evolved successfully in spite of their large jaws and not because of them, the inheritance factors for the jaw development being somehow linked, in the hereditary pattern of these insects, with some other vital factor or factors. Perhaps we shall have the answer to this puzzle, one of the classics of biology, when someone investigates the genetics of the Lucanids.

The majority of the species do not have the exaggeratedly developed male mandibles, but many do. The common European stag beetle, *Lucanus cervus,* and *L. elaphas* of the southeastern United States, may reach a total length of two and one-quarter inches, of which the mandibles are more than one-third. The largest is the East Indian *Odontolabis alces,* with males more than four inches long. The giraffe stag beetle (what a hybrid creature one can visualize from such a name!) *Cladognathus giraffa* of India and Java, is nearly as long, the male's jaws being fully half the total length. Most of the species are rather plain brown or black in color; but the Chilean *Chaisognathus granti* is dark metallic green with red iridescence; and the Australian *Phalacrognathus muelleri* is burnished metallic carmine edged with green. The Chilean species mentioned and the European *L. cervus* are among the very few insects shown on postage stamps, the former on a Chilean airmail and the latter on a stamp of Hungary.

There is nothing else in the lives of stag beetles to set them apart from other lamellicorn scavengers. The adults are often attracted to lights at night but otherwise are found mostly in the woods where there is plenty of rotting wood. In this the larvae live in conventional lamellicorn fashion.

THE SCARABS and THEIR RELATIVES
—Family Scarabaeidae

The word "scarab" immediately calls to mind the sacred scarab, *Scarabaeus* (or *Ateuchus*) *sacer,* the beetle that was regarded as possessing divine attributes by the ancient Egyptians, who figured it on many monuments and bas-reliefs and made conventionalized images of it for use as seals and jewelry. This is only one member, although one of the most interesting, of an enormous family, completely worldwide and containing more than twenty thousand species. Various attempts have been made to split the group, the subfamilies that we list below, as well as a number of others, having been considered separate families by various authors.

The subfamily Coprinae (or Scarabaeinae) contains the sacred scarab and its other dung beetle relatives, pre-eminent as pill-makers and ball-rollers. There is no finer nor more interesting description of the habits of any animal than the chapters on the sacred scarab in Fabre's *Souvenirs Entomologiques.* Finding a pile of relatively fresh manure of a large grazing animal, the big black scarab tears off a mass of this and shapes it into a hard, compressed ball. The beetle itself is little more than an inch long, yet the ball may be as large as a small apple or a man's fist. This the beetle then rolls away, standing behind it, facing backward and down, and pushing with its long hind legs while its forelegs are braced against the ground. During the early part of the season the dung thus rolled away is used for food by the beetles. Often another individual, sometimes of the same sex, joins one that has already made and started to move its ball and helps to roll it along. Sometimes robbery is attempted successfully; mostly, however, the two beetles share the provender. Eventually when a suitable spot is reached the beetles bury themselves and the food in a chamber underground, and there dine with no danger of disturbance. They eat continually until the food is all gone, a scarab eating more than its own weight in twenty-four hours. The beetle or beetles then ascend to the surface of the ground and set out in search of more dung.

Later in the season the beetles, now grouped into mated pairs, are more selective, preferring fresh, rich sheep or goat manure. Again the ball is formed and rolled along to a spot suitable for burying it. In the underground chamber the female then shreds the material and molds it into a beautifully symmetrical pear. The main body of this is solid, but the narrow neck contains a small cavity in which is laid

A Stag Beetle (*Lucanus elaphus*). The enormously overdeveloped jaws of this male are not as efficient weapons as the much shorter ones of the female.

the egg; and this cavity communicates, by means of a loosely filled canal through which air can enter, with the outside at the point where the stem of the pear would be. The main body of the pear is hard-packed; and this, together with its spherical shape and its underground position, insures—as well as the work of a beetle can—that it will not dry up and become too hard for the larva. The scarabs now leave, filling in the tunnel as they go. In due time the egg hatches and the larva lives inside the pear, eating away everything but a thin rind. In this it then pupates and eventually, when the rains come, softening the ground and the shell of the pear, emerges as an adult. The new scarab digs its way up to the surface and, after a short period of drying out and warming up, sets about finding dung and making and rolling a food ball of its own.

The big beetle rolling its ball along fitted in with the ancient Egyptians' ideas of cosmogony. The ball, which they believed the beetles rolled from sunrise to sunset, represented the earth. At the front of the beetle's head are a number of sharp, radiating projections; these were supposed to symbolize the rays of the sun, and the beetle was the sun itself. (Actually the radiating projections are used as a dung rake and triturator.) The thirty segments of its six tarsi represented the days of the month. (There is a bit of a mix-up here, since the sacred scarab actually has no tarsi on its front legs, and so has a total of only twenty tarsal segments. Closely related beetles, however, have the full complement of thirty.) The beetles was supposed to bury the ball for twenty-nine days and then on the thirtieth to cast it into the Nile, whereupon a new beetle sprang from it fully formed.

As a result of the excellent provisions for their welfare, a very large proportion of the larvae succeed in growing up, as is evidenced by the fact that a female scarab will prepare only two to four pears during a season. Other species are not so successful, for we see them making a larger number of underground stores, in some species separately and in others in the same chamber. Nor do all make pear-shaped food masses for their larvae, some forming egg-shaped ones, others simple spheres and still others merely packing a more or less cylindrical mass into the underground chamber. Some Indian scarabs of the genera *Heliocopris* and *Catharsius* make very large balls for the eggs and larvae, which are covered with a coating of hard, compressed clay. These become firm when they dry out, so much so that some that were dug up from as much as eight feet underground were once believed to be ancient stone cannon balls.

The male and female of the European Spanish Copris, *C. hispanus,* work together to make a number of ovoids, each containing an egg. The male then waits above, but the female stays in the chamber with the ovoids and constantly crawls about and over them, removing any signs of incipient mold and repairing any cracks that may develop through drying. When the young larvae have completed their development and emerge as adults the mother accompanies them up to the world above. They then separate without any sign of family cohesion. Since many of these beetles are long-lived, perhaps surviving for three years, there is plenty of opportunity for contact between parent and children, the primary requisite of true insect societies. But in none of these beetles is there any evidence of even the most rudimentary type of social organization or of the contacts being anything but the most casual meetings.

Both the larvae and adults of many of the dung beetles and other Scarabaeids have sound-making structures very similar to those of the bessy bugs (*Passalus*).

Every continent has many dung beetles. The great majority of this family and of the next two subfamilies, the Aphodiinae and Geotrupinae, however, are not ball-rollers but simply excavate the underground chamber whether for feeding or rearing, close to or beneath a pile or mass of dung. But every continent has at least some ball-rollers, although these are proportionately more poorly represented in Australia (where there are very few large mammals to supply suitable dung) and South America than in Europe, Africa, Asia and North America. They are chiefly warm-climate and tropical beetles. One of the most extraordinary members of the subfamily is *Macrocopris symbioticus,* a small Australian species that lives in the anus of wallabies and feeds on the excreta, holding onto the host by means of extremely large, hooked claws.

The best-known American tumblebugs, as the ball-rollers are familiarly called, are members of the genus *Pinotus,* formerly called *Copris.* They are an inch or so long with stocky bodies. In the southern parts of the United States the common species is *P. carolinus* (Plate 46). Other prominent dung-feeders, which do not roll balls however, are such members of the genus *Canthon* as *C. laevis* and of *Phanaeus* as *P. vindex* (or *carnifex,* Plate 48). The last-named is a beautifully iridescent beetle, the head bronzed, the thorax coppery and the elytra green or blue-green. The male has a long, curved horn on the top of his head, which the female lacks. Many other species of *Phanaeus* occur throughout tropical America, some being brilliantly and iridescently colored with blues, greens, black, gold and bronze. They are favorites with beetle collectors.

The work done by the dung beetles is of great importance in the general ecology of a region, as well as in sanitation. Enormous quantities of manure are buried promptly, in many instances without being eaten by the beetles. Underground it is promptly acted upon by various cycles of bacteria, and soon transformed into substances that can be absorbed and utilized by plants; aboveground it might dry and be useless for months. Fabre recorded a dozen *Geotrupes,* a beetle less than an inch long, as burying sixty cubic inches of manure *apiece* in a single night! Each beetle measures less than one-quarter of a cubic inch itself. The next night, and the next, and as long as Fabre's supply of manure held out, the beetles repeated their startling performance. This is indeed work of importance to all of the plants and other animals of the environment. Moreover, in view of what we know about the transmission of many diseases by fecal matter and by the feces-visiting flies, the work of these beetles is seen to be also of prime sanitary importance. Human excreta, especially in the tropical regions, may contain not only such bacteria as that of Asiatic cholera but the eggs of many parasitic worms and the cysts of the *Endamoeba* that causes amoebic dysentery. When it is promptly buried the danger of transmission is minimized, the pollution of water supplies is lessened, and the pathogenic organisms themselves may die much sooner. The small *Geotrupes* and *Aphodius* and their relatives are the chief agents in this; small but mighty, they occur in countless numbers everywhere.

The subfamily Melolonthinae contains many of the most abundant and familiar of the Scarabaeids. The heavy-bodied cockchafers of the Old World and the June bugs and May beetles of North America are the large brown beetles that come to lights so abundantly, banging and buzzing against window screens or entering and circling clumsily about the room. During early summer they sometimes swarm in great numbers; and although the adult beetles do no harm, they are an indication that somewhere in the neighborhood their larvae are living in the soil and eating the roots of plants in large quantities. The larvae are the curled, flat, white grubs, an inch or so long, that are most frequently turned up in shallow digging. They take as long as three seasons to mature in the ground, although the adults live for only part of a year. They are most often seriously destructive to crops when land that has been under grass for some time is plowed and planted to something else. Their one virtue is that they make good fish bait; in fact we have known bass to take them eagerly when they were refusing the conventional worm.

Smaller editions of the June beetles, about one-quarter of an inch long, are the various species of *Serica*, chunky beetles that also often come to lights. In the eastern United States the Asiatic beetle, *Anomala orientalis,* and the Asiatic garden beetle, *Autoserica castanea,* often appear at night in immense swarms, the latter being a particular nuisance. Both of these are recently introduced pests that are spreading out from the New Jersey–Connecticut area and promising to become of greater importance. The larvae in the soil, ordinary-looking, curved, white grubs one-quarter to one-half inch long, are very destructive to the roots of many garden plants; and those of the Asiatic beetle are particularly injurious to lawns where they add their efforts to those of the Japanese beetle.

The June beetles are also harmful in an unexpected way, since they are intermediate hosts of a giant thorn-headed worm, *Macroacanthorhynchus hirudinaceus,* that lives in the intestines of hogs. The hogs become infected with the worms by eating the beetles or their grubs, the grubs having picked up the infection by eating infected hog manure.

The leaf chafers, *Macrodactylus,* are also members of this subfamily. The best known is the rose chafer, *M. subspinosus.* The adults are more slender than the June beetles, about half an inch long, gray, and long-legged, and are frequently abundant, doing serious damage feeding on the flowers of roses. They are much more harmful, however, on grape and many other garden plants. It is the adults of this species that do the chief damage, although the subterranean larvae may be abundant enough to damage the root systems of many plants. Like the June beetles, rose chafers are sometimes harmful in an unexpected way, since young poultry are liable to be poisoned by eating them.

The big June beetles of the genus *Polyphylla* (Plate 49) have the elytra prominently striped with dark and light colors. They are especially noted for the length and flexibility of the plates that form the very prominent antennal club and for their ability to squeak noticeably when picked up and held. In the dry and arid parts of North America they are sometimes abundant and harmful. Like many of their relatives they often come abundantly to lights at night.

Most of the Melolonthinae are rather plain, brown being the commonest color. Some of the species of *Serica* and *Autoserica* have a slight iridescence that can be seen best when the beetles are held between one's eyes and the source of light. Although by no means pronounced, it is interesting to the student of color because it is a physical color, not a pigment, and is of a type very rare in insects. It is produced by structures in the integument which consist of very fine parallel ridges and grooves—what the physicist calls a "diffraction grating." A great many insects have structural colors, the great majority of blues, greens and all iridescent and metallic effects being of this general nature; but diffraction gratings are rare.

The subfamily Euchirinae contains only a few species, occurring in the Old World tropics. The most famous is the big *Euchirus longimanus* of Indonesia, as much as two and one-half inches long. The females have all the legs normal, but the males have greatly lengthened front legs that are nearly four inches long and curved and knobbed fantastically. Very likely these unusual structures serve some use in mating. The beetles are quite sluggish and pull themselves along clumsily with the long legs. They are especially fond of the fermenting palm sap from which the natives make wine.

The subfamily Rutelinae contains a great many species known in general as shining leaf chafers, since they run to metallic and iridescent colors that are largely lacking in the Melolonthinae. These effects are produced by structures in the integument, although they may be combined with pigments; they are of the conventional type found in the majority of structurally colored insects, being caused by very thin, slightly separate layers, one beneath another, that break up or refract the light to give the appearance of color and iridescence. Many of the most beautiful of all beetles are members of this group. So also are some of the most destructive pests. The great majority of the species are tropical or subtropical.

Not all of the species are metallic, although they may have bright colors derived from pigmentation. The common vine Pelidnota, *Pelidnota punctata,* that occurs over much of North America, is a bright orange-brown with black spots. It is quite destructive at times, the larvae being root-feeders and the adults eating the leaves of grape. Another related species, the goldsmith beetle, *Cotalpa lanigera,* about an inch long and shaped like a June beetle, is greenish yellow and yellowish, with the thorax quite metallic.

The most brilliant North American species of this group belong to the genus *Plusiotis*. Our favorite is *P. gloriosus,* the size and shape of a June beetle but longitudinally striped with brilliant green and incredibly metallic silver. Our first acquaintance with this beetle came more than twenty years ago, when very few specimens were known, while we were collecting insects in the Huachuca Mountains of Arizona, a high, isolated mountain range in which are found many Mexican plants and animals. A gasoline pressure lantern suspended in front of a vertically stretched sheet was bringing in thousands of insects, far more than we could handle, so that we were forced to hastily pick and choose. We could not believe our eyes when suddenly the first *Plusiotis* crawled up on the sheet; but it was soon followed by others, and we reaped a rich harvest. Now it is known that this and other species are relatively common in certain spots in Mexico and the Southwest, and that considerable numbers can be collected at light—but at that time our series created a minor sensation.

The Japanese beetle, *Popillia japonica* (Plate 52), is beautiful too, in a more sober way, dark bronzy green and chestnut. But its looks fail to appeal when we think of its despoliation of our fruit trees, ornamental shrubs, gardens, lawns and (crowning insult) our golf courses. It was a sad day in 1917 when the first specimens in North America were discovered at a nursery near Philadelphia, where they had been accidentally imported in the earth with a shipment of Japanese iris roots. It is sad, too, that both the requisite knowledge and authority with which it might have been then and there extirpated were lacking. By the next year it had extended its range to less than three square miles; the next year it occupied seven square miles; but by the end of the third year it was found in an area of more than forty-eight square miles and was then too widespread to be brought under control. Now it is getting well down below the Mason and Dixon line and up into northern New England, and has hurdled the unenforceable quarantine barriers and invaded the Midwest. It has good years when it swarms in such numbers that a mass can be seen across the Hudson River taking off for a fresh invasion of New York; in its bad years it is merely a very serious pest but even then occurring in such numbers that 278 beetles have been counted on a single apple. A swarm has been known to defoliate completely a bearing peach tree in fifteen minutes, leaving nothing but the bare twigs and the peach stones stripped of their pulp. In lawns one may suddenly see that the grass is all dead; and, picking it up, one finds that the roots and turf have been eaten away.

People often ask, quite justifiably, why all of our modern scientific knowledge and resources have apparently been unable to cope with this and other similar imported insect pests. The answer is a complex one, involving many factors, from politics to just plain bad luck. Lack of ability is not a part of it, for some of the finest entomologists in the world are the men in the United States Department of Agriculture and the various state entomological agencies. A good part lies in the fact that necessary funds and authorizations for control, quarantine and study were not forthcoming until the beetle had become so firmly established that nothing short of the eradication of all insects and most other animal life in the Philadelphia–New York area could have accomplished anything. The politicians who control appropriations are often a most timorous crew, who will take necessary drastic action (that might offend a constituent) only when it has been long apparent to everyone else that something must be done.

The use of poisonous insecticides on such a large scale is, of course, impossible. The underground larvae of the beetle are, moreover, especially difficult to control by such means. The trapping of the adults is only a local palliative. Poisonous sprays for the adults do some good, but their use is necessarily limited and hazardous in one of the rich fruit- and vegetable-growing sections of the country. It was early recognized that some form of biological control was about the only promising possibility. This meant making exhaustive and detailed studies of all natural enemies of the beetle, both existing and potential, both predators and parasites, in the hope that one or more could be found that would control it. This was done as fast as funds were forthcoming, in a thorough series of projects that involved sending skilled American entomologists to China and Japan, where the beetle is native. Scores of thousands of beetles were collected alive and bred in laboratories; and all enemies were likewise bred and then tested on populations of the beetles to ascertain their worth. Every detail of the lives of all stages of the beetle in every possible environment was also studied, in the hope that some ecologic means might be found whereby control could be obtained. Such work takes time; and meanwhile the beetle was spreading. Short of practically paralyzing all traffic on some of the busiest railroads

Hercules Beetle (*Dynastes hercules*). Awesome-looking horns on the male's head and thorax are used only in combat at mating time.

and highways in the country, local quarantine could not be made more than a slight delaying action.

A vast number of parasites and predators have been found and tested, first in the laboratory and then, reared in sufficient numbers, in the field. Ichneumonid, Braconid and Chalcid wasps, Tachinid flies and nematode worms have all proved somewhat helpful, but by no means sufficient. This has been largely a matter of accidental bad luck, for there are such parasites in the home region of the beetle that keep its numbers strictly under control there. It is, in fact, merely another rather scarce and attractive beetle in the Orient. But unfortunately the beetle has been able to thrive in the somewhat different conditions in North America, whereas the natural parasites have not. Nothing can be done about this except to keep trying, in the hope that either some of the known parasites will undergo mutations and evolve a new, more efficient strain; or that some other natural control will turn up. For a while it was thought that infectious disease to which the beetles were susceptible might be the answer; but this has not yet worked out well be-

cause of the difficulty of getting such diseases established and distributed. Everything that the brain of man can devise has been or is being tried. And still the beetle keeps spreading.

The story has a moral—one that should be evident by now. If only adequate quarantine and inspection had been possible in 1916, the whole dilemma could have been prevented at very small cost. We must strengthen such measures, in spite of the anguished howls of the tourist who resents not being able to bring home the tulip bulbs given her by that nice lady in Holland, or the political pressure of the foreign government that wants its fruits admitted to this country, even though its orchards are swarming with a dangerous fruit fly. And we must see to it that the skilled entomologists who guard our country against hundreds of pests every year—pests that, but for their constant vigilance, might prove far worse than the Japanese beetle— are not hamstrung by lack of funds. Instead, they must be allowed to prepare properly in advance to mobilize their forces against the inevitable species that occasionally slips through.

The subfamily Dynastinae (Plate 48) contains the giants of the beetles (although the Goliath beetle, a Cetoniine, has the largest body) as well as a great many smaller species. More remarkable even than the size of some of these beetles is the excessive ornamentation of the males, consisting of one or more horns on the thorax and one or more on the head. The horns are almost always lacking in the females, and not all species have them in the males. There may also be considerable individual variation within a species, some males being very short-horned. The ornaments occur in various combinations of number, size and degree of complexity.

In the giants of the New World tropical genus *Dynastes,* such as *hercules* and *neptunus,* the central thoracic horn is enormous, curving forward and down and sometimes meeting or even crossing the very long, upward curving head horn. The two horns thus form what looks like an enormous pair of pincers, one above the other. In some of the species the horns are almost as long as the rest of the beetle; a big male *neptunus,* for example, may be six inches long over all, of which the horns make up two and one-quarter inches. In this species and in the equally large and heavier-bodied *hercules* the horns are lined near their tips with a short pile of bright orange hair.

The horns of these *Dynastes* are quite smooth and simple; but in the equally bulky *Megasoma elephas* the one arising from the head is forked at the tip and has a basal prong, and on the thorax there are two long, lateral horns but only a short central one. In the genus *Golofa* the somewhat smaller species *pizarro* has the central thoracic horn abruptly thickened and curved forward near the tip, and forked. In *Allomyrma* both the head and the central thoracic horns are widened toward the ends and forked. Still other genera and species show other complexities.

Many of the medium-sized and smaller species of the subfamily occur in the North Temperate Zone, but none of the really large ones do. *Dynastes tityus* is sometimes quite common in the southern United States, with a related form in the Southwest. Large males are about two and one-half inches long, with a long head horn and a long thoracic one, and are olive-gray with black spots and markings. Smaller species such as the dark brown, short-horned ox beetle, *Strategus antaeus,* and the small rhinoceros beetle, *Xyloryctes jamaicensis,* both occur widely. The small (about half an inch) carrot beetle, *Ligyris gibbosus,* is something of a pest on garden plants, the larvae being root-feeders; and the small sugar cane beetle, *Eutheola rugiceps,* is a pest on the full-grown cane. The small *Oryctes nasicornis* is found in Europe in the decomposing bark refuse of tanneries.

The larvae of most of the rhinoceros beetles, especially the larger ones, are dwellers in rotting wood and rich leaf mold. Many of the smaller species eat roots while burrowing about in rich soil, and some have been found living in the stems of palms. The large *Oryctes rhinoceros* is sometimes a serious pest in Oriental coconut groves, the larvae destroying the leaf bases and opening the way for decay.

The chief interest in these beetles attaches, of course, to the extraordinary development of the horns of the males, a feature paralleled by the similarly exaggerated jaws of many of the stag beetles. There can be no doubt in the mind of anyone who has ever watched one of the beetles cumbrously making its way about that, despite its great strength, it is definitely handicapped by the awkward structures. As weapons against an attacker the horns are quite useless, for all their impressiveness; for the only way in which they can be brought together is for the beetle to raise its head, thus lifting the lower horn toward the upper one. At most, a hard pinch or squeeze can be given. Nor are the beetles lithe enough for the horns to be used as a stag uses its antlers.

It is known that in at least some of the species the horns are used by the males at mating time in combats with other males. After a good deal of clumsy pushing and prying, one male will manage to get the other gripped between the horns and will then either slam him down on the ground or will first carry him off and then slam him down or perhaps simply drop him. The loser in the tussle, being thoroughly armored, just draws his appendages in close and seems to suffer little or not at all from the treatment. Sometimes a female is thus picked up and carried about, and she too is perhaps flung down—observation of which has given rise to the idea that the males use the horns to carry the females away to a more suitable place for mating. However logical this may seem to the human mind, it is quite un-insect-like, and it is definitely not as an obligatory part of a courtship ritual that the males thus treat the fair ones.

Conventionally, such structures as these horns, like the jaws of male stag beetles, are regarded as having arisen through a process of sexual selection. According to this theory the males that have the largest horns, because of varying inheritance factors, will more often secure mates and thus will more frequently be successful in passing on their large horns to offspring. In actuality, this does not seem to be always true, since males with smaller horns are often just as successful in mating. Perhaps the inheritance factors for large horns are linked with other less obvious characteristics that may be of very practical service to the beetles. If this is so, it is the other characteristics that are subject to the laws of natural selection since they have survival value, and the cumbersome horns are merely fortuitous survivals. However, the horns must not become so large as to constitute a handicap great enough to offset the benefits derived from the other characteristics, for in that case the balance would be tipped in favor of males with smaller horns. Doubtless this is the case in some, at least, of the beetles that have the horns small or only moderately large.

The Cetoniinae (Plate 47), often called flower chafers, are a great world-wide group containing many species famous for their brilliant, often metallic and iridescent colors. They are compact, but rather flatter than most other Scarabaeids. Many species are less than one-half inch long and only a few are very large. The adults of many species fly quite freely, some being among the most consistent and skillful fliers of the beetles, and often visit flowers actively. A great many of them are also fond of fruit and at times may be serious pests.

Among the commonest of European chafers, *Cetonia aurata* and *metallica,* although small, are brilliantly metallic green and gold, colors repeated by many hundreds of species in various combinations the world over. The great majority of the brilliantly colored species are tropical. The abundant North American green June beetle, *Cotinus nitida,* is nearly an inch long and dull, velvety green, with its elytra widely margined with yellowish brown. The adults often do considerable damage by feeding on ripe grapes, figs and other fruits. The soil-inhabiting larvae sometimes damage grasses; they are conventional-looking white grubs of the usual scarabaeid type, and like other Cetoniine larvae travel on their backs by means of special muscular pads, not using their legs for locomotion at all. The large brown to black species of *Osmoderma* are known as odor-of-leather beetles because of their characteristic scent. Their larvae live in rotting wood. The large genus *Cremastocheilus* consists of blackish species one-quarter to one-third of an inch long that live in ant nests.

It is especially in spring and early summer that many of the flower beetles are most active in flying from blossom to blossom. Later in the season many turn their attention to fruits. The most consistent flower visitors are often extremely hairy and have the side edges of the elytra cut away or curved to allow the hind wings to slip out from beneath them in flight. The five-eighths-of-an-inch-long, hairy, yellow *Euphoria inda* and its relatives have a very strong resemblance to the bumblebees that are busy at the flowers at the same time. They even buzz loudly when flying. They and the smaller species, such as those of *Trichiotinus,* undoubtedly are important agents in cross-pollinating the flowers they visit, their hairiness being a decided asset in this. The most famous member of the subfamily is the African Goliath beetle, *Goliathus giganteus,* whose larvae live in rotten logs. A large specimen may be more than four inches long and have an even greater mass than the biggest of the rhinoceros beetles, although the impressive horns of the latter make them seem bigger. It is a brightly colored species, but with no iridescence, covered with a short, velvety-looking pile that rubs off. The thorax has a bold design of curved black lines on a white ground, and the elytra are chestnut brown. A number of related species are smaller but similarly marked. Native children sometimes catch the big beetles and make them fly around on the end of a string. Their great black leathery wings are much larger than those of many sparrows.

The Goliath beetles, like many other Cetoniines, have a short, rounded, forked process at the front of the head, but relatively few have really prominent horns like those of so many of the Dynastiines. The Bornean *Theodosia,* however, has long horns on both head and prothorax like a rhinoceros beetle. The two-and-one-half-inch *Chelorrhina* of the Congo, spotted with black and orange or silvery white and green, has a long, Y-shaped horn on the head; and so do the species of *Eudicella* from the Congo, some of which are striped lengthwise with green and orange while others are silver and black and still others have rows of orange polka dots on the green elytra.

There is no end to the combinations of color, iridescence and pattern found in the tropical Cetoniinae. Many are brown or black, with cryptic patterns of dots and scrawls that certainly serve to disguise them most efficiently. Others, apparently just as successful, or at least as common, are not merely brightly colored but show a depth of iridescence and a play of changing colors that is almost unparalleled. The bright emerald green *Ischiopsopha lucivorax* is such a species, glowing with a luster that seems to come from deep beneath the surface. This beetle, which is about an inch and a quarter long, is used ornamentally by the natives of the Waugi Valley in the highlands of the interior of New Guinea. Specimens are strung side by side between two strands of plant fibers, like the rungs of a ladder, to make headbands that are often worn with wonderful headdresses of bird-of-paradise plumes. Even more incredible, and to our minds one of the most beautiful of all living things, is the Sumatran *Hetorrhina dohrni,* which combines black with broad areas of green-gold that glow like a burning ember with deep orange-red, a living color that changes with every tiny shift of the light or the angle of view. Such color effects are literally three-dimensional, and can be truly appreciated only on the insects themselves.

[139

CHAPTER XI

Moths and Butterflies

(*Order Lepidoptera*)

A SWALLOWTAIL CATERPILLAR

THE moths and butterflies make up the second-largest order of insects, with perhaps a hundred thousand species. Some representatives of the order live in every part of the world where insects exist except in Antarctica. The order includes a great many of our most beautiful and familiar insects. Although they may be extremely destructive in the larval stage, they are not only completely harmless but often beneficial and desirable as adults. A great many gardeners, in fact, feel that their flower beds could not be complete without butterflies visiting them, and make special efforts to attract them. No less a person than Sir Winston Churchill once obtained from a dealer in butterflies a large number of living specimens, which were released in time to ornament a garden party. Far more people are interested in moths and butterflies than in any other group of insects, often making the collection and study of them their chief avocation. The international Lepidopterists' Society is the most thriving of any of the organizations devoted to a single group of insects, with hundreds of members all over the world.

In comparison with other insects, the moths and butterflies show a curious mixture of the primitive and the advanced, of great conservatism and extreme progressiveness. In their complete metamorphosis and in the extremely specialized characteristics of the adult they are highly advanced insects. Yet their larvae, commonly called caterpillars, are in many ways very primitive. In their food habits almost all members of the order have been very conservative and with almost complete unanimity have remained simple feeders on plants. In comparison with other great orders in which successive families may be terrestrial or aquatic, or may be plant-eaters, scavengers, parasites or predators, the Lepidoptera are almost uniform. This is not to say that some groups have not in the past experimented with different ways of life; for they have, and have left descendents that lead unusual lives. These, however, are but a small proportion of the whole; and the great majority of moths and butterflies munch away at leaves when they are young, and when they are grown up, sip a bit of nectar from flowers or else do not feed at all.

Practically all moths and butterflies have the wings completely covered with tiny scales that overlap like shingles on a roof. The body, too, is covered with similar scales, or with longer hairlike scales, or with hairs. Many other groups of insects have scales also, notably the weevils and the mosquitoes. The caddisflies often have wings thickly covered with short hairs, and a few have simple, primitive scales which make some of them very mothlike, especially since they may also have brightly colored wings. But in these and the other insects with colored wings, the colors are in the actual membrane of the wings, while in the moths and butterflies the membrane is almost invariably uncolored and the color patterns are due to colors in the scales. Each wing is a mosaic of tiny units. Considering the small size and the great number of these that are needed to cover a wing, the intricacy of the patterns and the uniformity with which they occur in each species of moth and butterfly is all the more remarkable. In a few groups the wings are nearly devoid of scales, and in a few others they have bare transparent areas; but these are the exceptions. It is interesting to note that in at least some of the groups where the wings appear to be transparent, the scales completely cover the wings during the pupal stage but are shed after the transformation to the adult.

The mouthparts of the adults are also very characteristic, the chief structure being a tubular proboscis, often called the tongue, through which liquids can be sucked up into the mouth. This is usually carried coiled spirally like a watchspring beneath the head; when feeding it can be straightened out quickly and thrust deep into a flower or other source of liquid food. In some of the moths it is as long as, or even longer than, the rest of the insect. On the other hand, in quite a few families of moths it is vestigial and cannot be used. These moths do not feed at all as adults, but exist on the basis of the food that they ate and stored in their fatty tissues when they were larvae.

The tongue is double in origin, being composed of two half-tubes, each a greatly lengthened part (the galea) of one of the first maxillae. These develop separately from each other and are still separate when the adult emerges from the pupal shell. After spreading and hardening its wings the butterfly or moth must fit together the two structures so that they form a long tube. Sometimes this takes several minutes, the two parts twisting and writhing about until finally they interlock properly and form the tongue, which is then coiled beneath the face. In addition to the tongue there are two pairs of jointed palpi, sensory mouthparts that serve chiefly for taste. In many of the higher groups of moths, and in all of the butterflies, one pair of these is either very minute or lost altogether.

Curiously enough, the chief sense of taste that causes the uncoiling of the tongue prior to feeding is not located on the head at all, but on the soles of the feet. Extremely sensitive taste organs located there react to the sweet secretions that cover parts of flowers and touch off an automatic reflex mechanism that uncoils the tongue; so that when a moth or butterfly lands on a flower, attracted to it by sight or scent or both, it is immediately stimulated through its feet to straighten out the tongue and thrust it down into the nectary. Monarch butterflies have been shown experimentally to be able to react thus to solutions of sugar containing no more than 1/120,400 part of sugar per 1000 parts of water, a sensitivity of taste 2408 times as great as that of the human tongue!

Although such sucking mouthparts characterize the moths and butterflies as a group, there are some very primitive little moths that still have the simple biting mouthparts, with functional jaws, that were possessed by the ancestor of all the Lepidoptera. Even if we did not know about these moths, the family Micropterygidae, we would infer that the ancestors of the order must have had separate, paired jaws and other mouthparts; but these jawed moths are living testimony to this, being perfectly unmistakable moths in all ways. The caddisflies show many characteristics of structure in common with the primitive moths, and must be regarded as a group of distant cousins whose ancestors took up life in fresh water during the larval period.

The antennae are the chief organs of smell from a distance, being used by a great many moths, for instance, as the chief means of finding the females in darkness. Most moths have simple, tapering, hairlike antennae; a few have antennae that end in a swelling or club, like those of the butterflies, and in these the seat of the smell organs is in the club; but some male moths have extraordinarily elaborate antennae, with many branches that form great feathery, plumy structures. Since these have an enormous total surface area closely set with small sense organs, these moths are extremely sensitive to the odors of the female, which they can locate from as much as several miles away. Females use their antennae chiefly to identify suitable kinds of plants on which to lay their eggs; where the antennae of the males are very elaborate, those of the female are much smaller.

In contrast to the adults, the larval moths and butterflies are quite simple, primitive insects. They are practical, humdrum, hard-working individuals who concentrate on just one thing—eating, digesting and storing as much food as possible. This they do with great efficiency. In their simple lives delicate sensory organs, long legs or spreading wings would be not only superfluous but a handicap. So they have none of them.

Instead of the great compound eyes of the adult, the caterpillar has on each side of its head a curved line of tiny simple eyes, or stemmata, usually six in number. With these it can do little more than distinguish light from darkness and form extremely crude images. Some caterpillars, for instance, can distinguish between a dark, vertical bar such as a tree trunk, and a horizontal one; but that is about all. Color perception, if present at all, is of the simplest sort. The jaws are large and well developed but quite short; excellent tools for grinding plant tissues, but useless as weapons. The other mouthparts and the antennae are extremely short, being useful for little more than simple touch perception. We know that the sense of taste is fairly well developed, since most caterpillars will eat only certain foods, firmly refusing all others to the point of starvation.

On the center of the lower lip, or labium, is the spinneret, a small structure at the opening from the silk glands. The glands may be extremely large, extending back almost to the rear of the abdomen in some caterpillars, and amounting to more than

25 per cent of the body weight in a mature silkworm. The silk is formed as two different liquids that harden as they are extruded from the spinneret and strike the air, and are so manipulated that one forms a sheath around a core of the other. The silk is then a compound thread in which there may be coloring matter derived from pigments in the caterpillar's food. Some strains of the silkworm produce yellow silk; others form a silk that is fluorescent; and a great many regularly form brown silk, some of the Asiatic species whose silk is used commercially and known as tussah being examples of this.

The lives of most caterpillars, at least when they are small, are concentrated along the thread of silk that is continually formed with every movement. Always as the caterpillar moves along, its spinneret extrudes the thread, which fastens to the surface on which it is crawling. To this its feet cling, so that it is able to hold fast and move along on anything, no matter how slippery. If it falls or drops, the spinneret continues to pay out the silken thread, from which the caterpillar may swing in midair. This is often a very useful means of escaping attack, especially from predaceous insects, although even birds often seem to lose sight of the caterpillar when it is dangling from the thread. After the danger has passed the caterpillar climbs back up the thread, thriftily eating it as it goes. The silk also serves as a guide, especially valuable to caterpillars that form nests to which they retire at night or during bad weather, and to the communal species. Often the burrows of boring or tunneling caterpillars are completely lined with silk; and of course a great many species use large quantities in forming the cocoons in which they·transform to the pupa.

The three pairs of true legs on the thoracic segments of a caterpillar are short, each ending in a one-jointed tarsus that bears only a single claw. On the abdomen is a series of paired fleshy legs called prolegs, each of which has at its tip a group of small hooklets. Typically the caterpillars of Lepidoptera have five pairs of these prolegs, one pair each on the third, fourth, fifth, sixth and last segments of the abdomen. Part of these are reduced or missing in some families, e.g. in the measuring worm caterpillars of the Geometridae and the larvae of the prominent moths. The larvae of many sawflies look and act very much like caterpillars, also having fleshy prolegs, but the sawfly larvae never have the hooklets at the ends of the prolegs and never have five pairs arranged as noted above, having either more or fewer. They also have but a single simple eye on each side of the head.

A great many caterpillars are elaborately colored and patterned, and many have the body grotesquely shaped or ornamented with warts, spines, tubercles and projections of many shapes, or covered with hairs. These are usually protective, tending to mislead or misdirect predatory enemies. Some also have special organs that can be protruded when the caterpillar is attacked or annoyed, and diffuse strong, repellent scents and tastes. In fact the caterpillars show us better than any other insects a great variety of passive defensive specializations of color, shape and habit. This is quite to be expected in so large and successful a group of harmless plant-eaters, most of which have practically no means of fleeing from their enemies or fighting back. Without such highly elaborated means of defense most caterpillars would have slight chance of survival in a world full of predators hungry for insect food. We shall take up some outstanding defensive adaptations as we consider the families that illustrate them best, and do the same with the protective colors and patterns of adult moths and butterflies.

Within the Lepidoptera we see an enormous range of size, perhaps greater comparatively than in any other order. The smallest moths are members of the family Nepticulidae, tiny insects with a wingspread of no more than one-eighth of an inch, that live as larvae in leaf or bark mines. At the other end of the scale are such species as the great owlet moth of South America, *Thysania zenobia,* with an expanse of some eleven to twelve inches, and the hercules moth, *Coscinoscera hercules* of Australia, with a wingspread nearly as great and a wing area of almost a hundred square inches.

One of the first questions asked by nearly everybody is how to tell moths from butterflies. This is not easily answered, for the differences do not depend on any one single factor. The majority of moths fly at dusk or during the day, while almost all butterflies are diurnal and many fly only when the sun is shining. There are, however, many families of moths that are consistent daytime fliers, being most commonly seen visiting flowers along with the butterflies. Many of these day-flying moths are just as brilliantly colored as any butterfly. Perhaps the most striking member of the order, in fact, is the day-flying Uraniid moth *Chrysiridia madagascarensis,* sometimes called the most magnificent living creature. Many butterflies, on the other hand, are extremely plain and dull-colored.

Again, it is sometimes said that the caterpillars of moths spin silken cocoons in which to pupate, while those of the butterflies form their pupae (chrysalids) naked. This is only partially true, for many thousands of species of moths have no cocoon, the caterpillars simply pupating naked in the soil; while in many skippers and some butterflies a crude cocoon-like network of silk is formed.

One also hears that the antennae of butterflies end in a club while those of moths do not. This is another half-truth, for there are moths with just as strongly clubbed antennae as any butterfly, many of which are large, brilliantly colored day fliers; and the clubs of some butterfly antennae are so slender that they are far from obvious. It is true, however, that most moths do have antennae that either are hairlike and taper to a very fine point or are feathery. Again, we may hear that moths always rest with the wings flat over the back while butterflies when at rest hold the wings vertical with the upper sides together over the back. This is not always true, for some butterflies rest with the wings flat out to the sides, and so do many moths; and some moths rest with their wings vertical over the back like most butterflies.

The majority of moths have a wing-coupling apparatus that consists of either a lobe on the front wing (the jugum) that slips over the edge of the hind wing, or (most of the species) a strong bristle or bundle of bristles on the front base of the hind wing (the frenulum) that catches in a special mass of scales and hairs or a hook on the corresponding front wing. None of the butterflies (except a single Australian skipper) has such a structure for coordinating the wings, this being done by their broad overlapping at the bases. But there are many moths that have neither jugum nor frenulum.

The order is divided into a number of superfamilies of which the true butterflies are one, the Papilionoidea; the skippers, usually considered to be butterflies, are another, the Hesperioidea; while the others are moths. The superfamilies are classified on the basis of combinations of a great many characteristics of the early stages as well as of the adults. Most people are not interested in such technicalities, and so will simply learn the various families of the butterflies and skippers, of which there are some sixteen, and realize that everything else lepidopterous is a moth. Since there are from eighty to a hundred or more families of moths, depending upon the opinions of various authors, the classification can get very complicated and technical.

It is inevitable that many members of a group so large and so devoted to plant foods should be harmful to man's interests. A few of these are scavengers that invade the home and that feed upon our woolens, furs and foods. The majority, however, are of agricultural importance, attacking crops; and among these are many of the worst of all insect pests. Considering the potentialities of the strong-jawed larvae, it is surprising that relatively few Lepidoptera are wood-borers; but a few are, and some of these do considerable damage to trees and woody plants. By far the greatest harm to trees, as to crops, is done by leaf-eating larvae, some of which are veritable scourges of the forest. Finally, a few caterpillars are equipped with spines and poison-secreting glands, because of which they cause severe rashes if brought into contact with the human skin. Fortunately none of these is regularly abundant enough to be a serious problem.

On the other side of the picture, the adults of a great many moths and butterflies, being consistent flower visitors, are responsible for the cross-pollination of many flowering plants, and are thus more or less essential for the formation of many of the seeds and fruits upon which man feeds. Although they are secondary to bees in this, they are nevertheless of major importance. It is also to certain moths that we owe silk, still a major article of commerce despite its partial displacement by synthetic fibers. The chief source is the silkworm moth, *Bombyx mori,* the only insect we can call truly domesticated to such an extent that it cannot any longer maintain itself in a state of nature. Other large moths are also used in Asia as the source of special silks, such as tussah.

One of the most valuable insects in the world, as any Australian will agree, is a small moth that is native to South America, the cactus moth *Cactoblastis cactorum.* During the last century the introduced, flat-stemmed prickly pear cacti took over more than sixty million acres of the best Australian grazing and wheat lands, driving out the grasses and covering the areas with an almost impenetrable thorny growth. Every possible means of controlling the plant was tried without avail, including the introduction of more than 150 different cactus-feeding insects. Nothing worked until in 1925 this moth was introduced from Argentina. It proved to be what was needed, since its larvae tunnel in the pulpy stems, opening up the way to disease organisms that complete the ruin of the cactus. Many millions of acres that were abandoned are now reclaimed and are producing crops and sheep. One enthusiast has even suggested that the cactus moth should be given a place on Australia's coat of arms!

It is interesting to note here how circumstances alter cases. During the last two centuries the red dye cochineal was of major commercial importance, although nowadays, because of the manufacture of synthetic dyes, it is of little more than historical interest. Since it was derived from scale insects that lived on the cactus, great acreages were devoted to raising cacti and the scale insects on them. At that time any insect that attacked cactus was considered a serious pest—but now one of them is the benefactor of a great island continent.

THE PRIMITIVE MOTHS
—*Suborder Homoneura*

In these moths the front and hind wings are much like each other, with similar numbers and arrangement of veins. This is in accordance with the condition found in more primitive insects and in sharp contrast with that of all the rest of the moths and butterflies, in which the hind wings have become much smaller than the front ones and have lost a

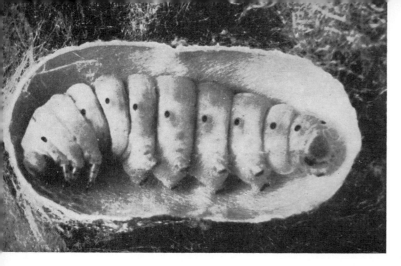

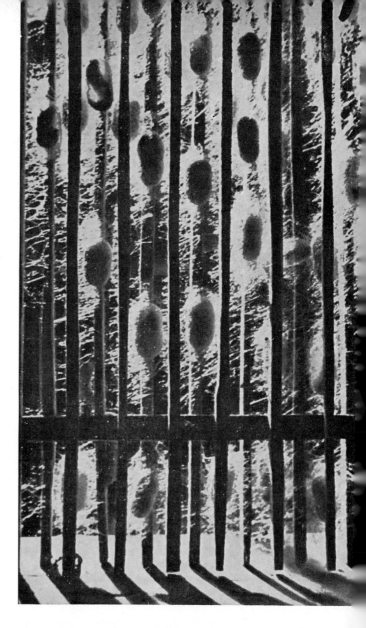

(At right) Frame on which **Silkworms** (*Bombyx mori*) spin their cocoons. This species, the true silkworm, is the chief representative of the family Bombycidae. It is entirely domesticated and feeds only on Mulberry leaves. (Above) **Silkworm** cocoon opened to show the caterpillar before pupation, and (below) an intact cocoon from which the female moth has just emerged.

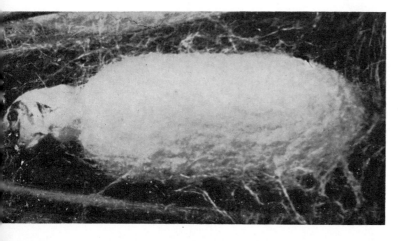

number of the veins. The members of this group are primitive in other ways as well, some of them exceedingly so, although the various families differ from each other in details. In one family, as we have seen, there are functional mandibles in the adults; in another there are functional mandibles in the pupae but not in the adults; and in others the mouthparts are so reduced that the adults do not feed. The wings are thickly covered with microscopic bristles (aculeae) under the covering of scales, another character found in more primitive insects.

The Homoneura are, in fact, a hodgepodge of primitive survivals, remnants of formerly widespread and prosperous groups of moths that have managed to survive the competition of more advanced insects only in odd, widely separated corners of the globe. This is exactly the kind of distribution that we almost invariably find in similarly primitive animals and plants of any group. Australia and New Zea-

land are especially rich in these primitive moths, as they also are in the primitive egg-laying and marsupial mammals. We know that Australia and New Zealand were long ago separated from the continent of Asia by the subsidence of the lands that formerly connected them. When this happened the existing primitive animals and plants were able to survive there in considerable numbers, since the more advanced forms, which evolved later on the main continental land masses, could not get to Australia, now an isolated island. In this connection the primitive moths, of which there are more families and many more species in Australia and New Zealand than anywhere else, have been much studied.

MANDIBULATE MOTHS
—Family Micropterygidae

These are the moths that are equipped with jaws, with which they chew solid food. They chiefly eat pollen and the spores of primitive plants, the other mouthparts as well as the mandibles being specially adapted for grinding such tiny units. The larvae live in damp places and, as far as is known, feed on mosses and liverworts. They have definite, although small, compound eyes, unlike other caterpillars; and have a number of abdominal appendages, a very primitive characteristic that they lose during growth. The moths are all small, none having more than one-quarter of an inch wingspread. Many are obscurely colored, but many others are iridescent blue, purple or greenish, sometimes with yellow or orange marks. They are widely distributed, some occurring in every continent, but in a patchy and unpredictable fashion, as befits archaic survivals.

SWIFTS and GHOST MOTHS
—Family Hepialidae

In sharp contrast to the other primitive moths, the members of this family are large, some having a wingspread of nine or ten inches or more, thus ranking among the largest of the moths. Those of Eurasia and North America are mostly rather plain brown and gray; but in Australia, New Zealand and Africa many are extremely handsome, with wings boldly patterned with brown, pink, red, blue, green and silver in various combinations. These moths have swift but sometimes erratic flights and are usually abroad in the dusk. Some are daytime fliers.

The larvae are either borers in wood or woody stems or roots, or else live in turf. Some of both types are injurious, especially in Australia and New Zealand, where there are many species. The enormous larvae (up to six inches long) of the Australian bent-wing moth, *Leto staceyi,* often do serious damage by tunneling in eucalyptus wood. The adult of this moth, which has a seven-inch wingspread, has a very large, prominent eyespot on each front wing. As a result, when the wings are folded back the moth does indeed bear a strong resemblance to the head of a much larger animal; and it is perfectly possible that this is occasionally a source of some protection. In New Zealand the larvae of the various species of *Porina* are known as grass grubs because of their destructive habit of tunneling in turf and eating the grass roots.

Several other families of primitive moths are known, consisting of only a few species, but all of these are small moths. Most of them are confined to Australia, New Zealand and South Africa, but one, the Eriocraniidae, has representatives in Eurasia and North America. Aside from the interest resulting from their primitiveness, these moths are noted for their peculiar pupae, which are formed in the soil. These are equipped with enormous crossed mandibles, which are used in cutting the way up to the surface of the ground, after which the adult emerges, spreads its wings and flies away.

THE MORE ADVANCED MOTHS and THE BUTTERFLIES
—Suborder Heteroneura

This suborder contains the vast majority of the moths and all of the butterflies. In all of them the hind wings show a considerable reduction compared with the front wings, and in some they are reduced almost to the point of uselessness. In many of the best and fastest fliers, such as the hawk moths, the hind wings are extremely small. It is interesting that this same tendency rose independently in the ancestry of the flies, also skilled aerialists; but the flies have completely lost the hind wings as wings, transforming what is left of them into organs of equilibration. There is no sign of this in moths and butterflies.

Beyond this it is almost impossible to characterize the suborder, so greatly do many of its members differ from one another. It is divided into some fifteen superfamilies and up to a hundred or more families. Many of these are small and of limited distribution, or are composed of small and ordinary moths that are of interest only to the specialist. We will omit these or touch upon them lightly.

THE SMALLEST MOTHS
—Family Nepticulidae

The smallest of all moths are members of this family, some having a wingspread of no more than three millimeters and the largest little more than twice that. They are very attractive mites, flying fast (although not far) and running actively. Many have bands or other markings of bright metallic silvery scales. Most of the species mine as larvae in leaves or under thin bark or epidermis, chiefly of deciduous trees and shrubs; but a few are known to cause the formation of galls on twigs or leaf petioles, in which the larvae live. Typical mines are long, very narrow pathways that wind and twist about a great deal, gradually increasing as the larva grows larger, or suddenly enlarging into a blotch. The family is world-wide and contains some three hundred or more species.

YUCCA MOTHS and OTHERS
—Families Prodoxidae, Adelidae etc.

Here belong a number of small but widely distributed families of small, rather primitive moths. Most of them are leaf-miners, leaf-eaters or scavengers when they are larvae, sometimes living in flat cases. The Adelids are noted chiefly for the great length of the antennae of the males in some species, these being four or more times as long as the head and body, very thin and hairlike. Many of the species are brilliantly colored, having metallic and iridescent shades of gold, green, purple etc. Quite a few fly in the daytime, even in bright, hot sun.

The yucca moths, a small, entirely American family, are small and white, sometimes with slight dark markings. They are famous for the closeness of their mutually dependent relationships with various species of yuccas. In the best-known species, *Tegeticula yuccasella,* the female has on each first maxilla a special long tentacle with which she collects from the anthers of the yucca flowers a ball of pollen that is sometimes larger than her head. This she carries to another flower and pushes down on the end of the stigma, thus effectively cross-pollinating the flower, since each of the pollen grains can send a pollen tube down into the ovary. We can only call this act of the moth's a "deliberate" one, with the reservation that by this we must not in any way imply that she is conscious of what she is doing as the term would imply if applied to a human. What we mean is that it is not merely a by-product of other activities of hers, like the pollination that results from the food-gathering activities of bees and other insect flower visitors.

Having done this, the moth lays one or two eggs in the ovary of the flower. When the ovary develops into a fruit with many flat seeds inside, which it could not have done without the moth's activity, the eggs hatch and the larva or larvae eat part of the seeds. Since there are only one or two larvae, there remain plenty of uneaten seeds to start new yucca plants. The plant benefits from the moth's actions, and the moth benefits from the food and shelter provided by the yucca. No better example is known of the mutual dependence of an insect and a plant.

SCAVENGER and CLOTHES MOTHS
—Family Tineidae and others

A good many moths in quite a few families are essentially scavengers, the majority feeding on miscellaneous plant and animal debris, often when it is being disintegrated by bacteria and fungi. Despite the competition of many other groups of insects, there is so much food of this sort available that it was inevitable that some moths would evolve the ability to take advantage of it. The two outstanding groups of these scavengers are members of the large, quite primitive, world-wide family Tineidae, and a large group of species of the enormous, also world-wide but quite advanced family Pyralididae. All of these are "microlepidoptera." The Tineids are small, seldom being more than one-half inch in wing expanse, while none of the scavenging Pyralids expands more than an inch. Included in both groups are several species that at times are destructive household and industrial pests.

Several of the Tineids are known as clothes moths

because of their larval habit of eating fabric of animal origin such as wool, mohair, cashmere, fur felts etc., as well as fur. Clean fabrics made from plant fibers and the various synthetics are usually immune, but may be eaten if soiled with grease, sweat or other animal substances. The larvae of the common clothes moth, *Tineola bisselliella,* make more or less continuous silken webs along the galleries that they excavate in fabrics; those of the carpet moth, *Trichophaga tapetzella,* also spin some silk; but those of the case-bearing clothes moth, *Tinea pellionella,* make small, oval, flattish cases in which they live and which they carry about with them. The same case-making habit is also characteristic of a great many other Tineid larvae, such as some of the genus *Monopis* that occasionally enter houses and scavenge about. The clothes moths listed are, however, the only serious household pests of the group; and for some reason, perhaps because of the much greater incidence of dry cleaning, they are becoming much less of a problem than they were formerly. If people would only realize that the adult clothes moths are actually very small, with narrow wings that scarcely expand half an inch, they would save themselves a great deal of worry and, often, expense. There are literally hundreds of species of moths that fly into houses, attracted to lights (which the adult clothes moths are not), or living as relatively harmless scavengers on debris. The sight of these is often enough to raise the cry, "There's a clothes moth—kill it," and perhaps to cause a quite unnecessary treatment by an exterminator. The larger the moth the more dangerous it seems. The adults of the common clothes moth and the case-bearing clothes moth are pale straw yellow to gray and almost unmarked; those of the carpet moth are blackish with the outer half of each wing white. The last species has been found breeding in bat refuse, owl pellets and similar trash of animal origin.

One Asiatic member of the genus *Monopis* is extremely interesting as being one of the very few Lepidoptera in which the larvae are born alive. Females have been found with as many as a dozen larvae in a specially enlarged duct in the abdomen. Some groups of insects such as aphids and flesh flies are quite regularly ovoviviparous, but aside from these small moths there are only one or two other instances of this in the Lepidoptera.

The family Pyralididae contains two main groups of scavengers, belonging to the two subfamilies Pyralidinae and Phycitinae. In the former, the grain-snout moth *Pyralis farinalis* is a rather brightly colored, reddish and olivaceous species that may expand nearly an inch. As its name implies it is often a pest in stored grains and cereals. Several other species of the genera *Pyralis, Aglossa* and *Herculia,* some of which are known in general as grease moths, often scavenge in houses. The clover hay worm, *Hypsopygia costalis,* a dull rose and yellow moth, is sometimes injurious in stored hay.

The Phycitinae contains a number of destructive and widely distributed invaders of our houses, warehouses and food depots. Some are of European origin, others American; but all have followed man about the world and now are practically cosmopolitan. The Indian meal moth, *Plodia interpunctella,* has about a half-inch wingspread, with the bases of the wings clay color and the outer parts brownish red with leaden metallic bands. It is one of the moths most frequently mistaken for the clothes moth. The other harmful pests are the Mediterranean flour moth, *Ephestia kuhniella,* the tobacco moth, *E. elutella,* and the almond moth, *E. cautella.* All three of these are gray and comparatively unmarked, and are very injurious in warehouses and factories. The last is particularly addicted to dried fruits.

There are many other scavenging moths in various families. The Pyralids also include the world-wide bee or wax moth, *Galleria mellonella,* and the lesser bee moth, *Achroia grisella,* both of which invades beehives to lay their eggs. The larvae burrow about in the hive, fundamentally scavenging, but also eating young bees and in general webbing up the hive with silk tunnels. Related species of the genus *Aphomia* live in wild bee nests. The family Blastobasidae also contains many scavengers, one of which is the acorn moth, *Valentinia glandulella,* whose larvae burrow in acorns, sometimes perhaps as the primary invader but often at least as a scavenger after the acorn weevils.

BAGWORMS and OTHER CASE-BEARERS
—Family Psychidae and Others

A considerable number of larvae of several families have evolved the habit of constructing portable cases in which they live, and which they carry about wherever they go. For unprotected caterpillars this is a very useful habit, since the case serves not only for protection against the elements but also as a means of escaping the attentions of predators. In many instances the cases are elaborately constructed and covered with bits of twigs and leaves, often in an erratic pattern that gives excellent camouflage. They seem, however, to be of little or no use as a protection against parasitic wasps and flies.

The case-bearers of the family Coleophoridae are a widely distributed group of small, very narrow-winged moths. Like those of a great many of the small "microlepidoptera," the wings have very long fringes of hairs that are often wider than the wing membrane itself. Few have a wing expanse of more than one-half an inch. Most of the moths are light-colored, from white to pale brown, but some

Yucca Moths (*Tegeticula alba*), female, in a Yucca flower. The plant is entirely dependent on these moths for cross-pollination.

are dark and brightly metallic. The larval cases are quite varied in form, ranging from plain oval sacs to elaborate structures that look like an old-fashioned horse pistol in miniature, with a thick barrel and a butt that curves down and back toward the muzzle end. Some of these species are, in fact, known as pistol case-bearer moths.

The bagworms, the family Psychidae, are the best known of the case-bearers the world over. Even before it eats, a larva just hatched from the egg scrapes together fibers and fastens them with silk to make a case. Thenceforth it will probably never leave the case until it transforms into an adult moth, for as it grows it simply adds more materials in a larger size at the front end. The rear end tapers back to the oldest part of the case and is left open for excretion. At the front the head and thorax protrude when the caterpillar is eating or moving about; but when it is resting, molting or transforming to the pupa it fastens the case to a solid object with silk. A strong silken attachment is spun before pupation or before the winter. Cases are extremely durable and may often be seen hanging in numbers from the bare winter twigs. They are frequently mistaken by beginning naturalists for the cocoons of larger moths. Some of the species are very small, the cases being not more than one-quarter of an inch

[147

long; but others, especially in the tropics, have cases that are as much as six inches long. Bits of leaves and twigs are cemented to the outside, often so thickly that the case looks like an irregular bundle of debris. Although there is quite a bit of variation, the caterpillars of each species generally make distinctive cases; sometimes, in fact, the cases are of more value in the identification of the species than are the adult moths themselves. One species may attach flat bits of leaf or small whole leaves; another uses pine needles fastened at the front end and trailing back; another does the same sort of thing with twiglets; and another may use short pieces of twig fastened crosswise and built up atop each other in log-cabin style.

Aside from their cases the bagworms are noted for the degeneration of the females. This is very unequal in different species, the females of the more primitive groups being as well developed as the males. In all of the advanced groups, however, the females have lost the wings, and in many species have lost the legs as well. When they emerge from the pupal stage, which was formed in the case, they may do no more than crawl out of the case and rest upon it waiting for the male to come along. If one comes, the female, after mating, crawls back into the case, lays her eggs in it and then dies, thus leaving her dead body, the egg mass, her pupal shell and her last larval skin in the case. Such females are often covered with a thick layer of fluffy hairlike scales that surround the eggs and insulate and protect them. In still other species, however, of which the common bagworm, *Thyridopteryx ephemeraeformis,* of eastern North America is one, the female not only never leaves the case but actually does not emerge from the pupal shell. When she has transformed to the adult stage she apparently gives off a characteristic scent, for the males fly to the cases at this time and mate with the females through the open end. The eggs are fertilized without leaving the mother's body, and since she is little more than an egg bag, she simply dies within the pupal shell. Eventually the eggs hatch and the caterpillars emerge from the body of the mother, from the pupal shell and from the case, and immediately set about making cases of their own.

There has long been considerable speculation as to how a species with such almost completely degenerated females ever gets dispersed from one locality, or even from one tree, to another; for the larvae may never crawl more than a few dozen feet during their lifetime, especially if they get their start on a suitable tree. The males are often fast but not strong fliers, but of course can do nothing about dispersing the eggs or larvae. Yet such bagworms are widely distributed despite the lack of any obvious mechanism for it. It has been shown recently that in an African species the eggs are extremely hard-shelled and impervious; and that when a bird eats the contents of an egg-filled case, as must often happen, the eggs are unaffected by its digestive processes and are returned to the outer world, perhaps many miles from where they were eaten. When in due time they hatch the species has been effectively dispersed by the agency of the bird. It is possible that this distribution mechanism works for many other moths and other insects that have wingless females.

SLUG CATERPILLAR MOTHS
—Family Eucleidae

This family of about five hundred species is widely distributed, although the majority of its members are tropical. It is best known for the very peculiar caterpillars, which have lost the abdominal prolegs and have the true legs somewhat reduced. The head is strongly bent down beneath the thorax, which is expanded above and around it, concealing and enclosing it except for a slit through which the caterpillar does all of its feeding and spinning. Replacing the prolegs, the under surface of the body bears a number of pairs of muscular suction pads, with which the caterpillars crawl. Many of them are smooth-skinned and look very sluglike, gliding along without the apparent use of any legs. Many others, however, are spiny or hairy, and are sometimes very brightly colored.

In quite a few genera the caterpillar bears barbed, stinging hairs that produce a burning rash if they come in contact with the human skin. One of the most unusual of these is the caterpillar of the hag moth, *Phobetron pithecium,* of eastern North America, which is nearly an inch long when full grown. It is flat and has several irregularly curled, pointed, paired processes covered with brown stinging hairs. It is perhaps the most uncaterpillar-like caterpillar in the world, resembling a very tattered bit of dead leaf. With its slow, gliding motion and the protection of its stinging hairs, it would seem to be as perfectly protected from its enemies as a caterpillar could be, and so it probably is, at least from predators; yet the moths are far from abundant. When the caterpillar spins its cocoon it somehow manages to transfer the curled processes to the outside of the cocoon, which is then effectively camouflaged and protected. The cocoons of all of the slug moths are oval, sometimes almost spherical, and equipped with a hinged lid that the moth pushes open when it emerges.

The moths of the slug caterpillars are mostly small, but some of the larger species expand an inch or more. They are stoutly built and densely hairy, with broad, thickly scaled wings. A great many have extremely attractive color patterns, often of green or silvery markings or broad bands combined with orange brown. They are great favorites with collectors, especially since they are attracted to lights in numbers and thus easily obtained. The closely related flannel moths of the family Megalopygidae average a bit larger, are even more densely hairy, and run to light pastel shades of cream and tan. The very hairy flannel moth caterpillars have the usual prolegs and, in fact, two extra pairs that lack hooklets. They are well equipped with stinging spines, some of the tropical species being so virulent that contact with one of them can practically disable a human for a while.

Also closely related to these moths are the small, almost wholly American family Pyromorphidae and the largely Old World family Zygaenidae which consists of the small day-flying moths with narrow, often brightly colored wings. The adults are often seen visiting flowers. Many are smoky brown or black, sometimes with metallic iridescence and an orange collar. Others have the wings boldly marked with yellow, orange or scarlet. There is little doubt that mimicry is involved, some of the species being very wasplike and others strongly resembling the protected, warningly colored moths of the almost wholly unrelated family Syntomidae that also visit flowers in the daytime.

MICRO MOTHS of MANY FAMILIES
—Miners, Leaf-tyers and Borers

There are probably over twenty-five thousand different "microlepidoptera" in the world that as larvae feed on leaves in various ways. Many are miners, while others roll the edges of the leaves into tubes in which they live, make tiny cases or tie one or more leaves together into minature nests or tents. The foliage of the world undergoes an enormous total attack from these moths, although in individual size they are small, seldom having a wing expanse of more than one-quarter to three-eighths of an inch. A great many of them have extremely narrow wings with long hair fringes. These are the so-called "tineoid" micro moths, members of many different families. Many species have attractive, complex patterns in a great variety of color combinations. Some have an extremely beautiful, shining metallic or deep velvety iridescence in gold, silver or blue, purple and green. If it were not for their small size many of these tiny moths would be as well known and as eagerly sought by collectors as any of the big tropical butterflies.

The leaf-mining larvae of many of the micro moths, especially of many of the world-wide Gracilariidae, a family of over a thousand species, are highly modified for their peculiarly restricted lives, having the whole head and body flattened, the eyes greatly reduced and the legs often mere vestiges or missing altogether. The jaws are short and protrude horizontally in front of the head, where they serve as shears with which the soft internal tissues of the leaf are sliced away. When they are full grown some of the caterpillars leave the mine and spin a cocoon elsewhere; but others spin and pupate inside the mine. We often can trace the progress of the caterpillar within the mine from the time when it hatched from the egg, through its molts as evidenced by the shed skins and head capsules, to pupation and emergence of the adult.

The mines themselves are often extremely distinctive in shape and extent. It is not infrequently more practical to identify the species of moth responsible for a mine by the appearance of the mine and the species of plant than by having specimens of the moth itself, since many of the moths have few distinctive characteristics. Some mines are simple and linear, winding about in characteristically tortuous ways. Others are trumpet-shaped, starting small and widening abruptly. Still others may have a number of finger-like branches radiating from a central blotch. Some are made only close beneath the upper surface of the leaf; others close above the lower. Each species is restricted to a single species of plant or to plants of a certain group such as oaks, or the closely related willows and poplars.

Far more species are leaf-rollers or -tyers, especially during later adult life, since quite a few caterpillars mine in a leaf when they are small and then come out of the mine as they grow older. The very large, almost universally distributed families, Pyralidiidae, Tortricidae, Olethreutidae, Gelechiidae and Oecophoridae, which together contain upward of twenty thousand species, include a great many leaf-rollers and -tyers, some of which are at times pests on plants valuable to man. Many of the caterpillars are not powerful enough, especially when young, to eat leaves entire, and so merely feed on the soft tissues between the network of veins, thus skeletonizing the leaf. Many species of various Tortricid genera such as *Archips* and *Cacoecia* are often thus destructive to ornamental shrubs and fruit trees; especially harmful are the species that live a more or less colonial existence as caterpillars, spinning big, untidy nests with the silk of which is incorporated much debris of dead leaves, cast skins and droppings. The cherry tree ugly nest caterpillar of North America, *Archips cerasivorana,* and the apple tree species, *A. argyrospila,* are examples of this. In Europe the bright green *Tortrix viridana* sometimes abounds so as to strip the oaks of their leaves in large areas, swarms of millions of the adult moths rising like clouds.

The worst pest of this type, however, is the spruce budworm of North America, *Harmologa fumiferana,* a dingy, sooty, gray-brown moth from one-half inch to three-quarters of an inch in wing expanse. It has more than once been voted one of the three most destructive North American insects. The larvae completely defoliate spruce and related trees over areas of hundreds of thousands of acres in all of the northern forests, particularly in Canada. Incalculable loss is thus caused to the lumber and pulpwood industries. It was estimated that more than two hundred million cords of spruce and fir were destroyed in the United States and Canada in one fifteen-year period. Control is, of course, exceedingly difficult since there are so few roads in the northern forests, and ordinary spraying with insecticides from the ground is prohibitively costly in any event. Spraying or dusting from airplanes, especially using some of the synthetic insecticides such as DDT, has been effective; but this, too, is costly and not entirely satisfactory, since concentrations of spray heavy enough to do a clean job are destructive to all of the other animal life of the forest. The use of parasites, such as certain of the parasitic wasps and flies, is more promising although slower.

By no means all of these small moths are leaf-eaters, a great many species boring in seeds, fruits, twigs and cones. The most widely known is the codling moth, *Laspeyresia pomonella,* originally a native of Europe, that has spread everywhere in the world where apples are grown. The moths have about one-half inch of wingspread and are brown with very pretty coppery reflections or a bronze iridescence. In the spring they lay their eggs in the flowers of the apple, so that the larvae are already in the fruit when it begins to develop. Apples thus infected show no entrance holes. Later in the season the eggs are laid on the developing fruit, and the larvae that hatch from these bore into the apples and tunnel about. When fully grown they emerge and pupate in a shallow cocoon under debris or loose bark. All too often, however, the fruit is first picked and bitten into. Many millions of dollars of fruit are destroyed annually by this moth in every country where apples are grown. This, however, is far from the only loss due to its activities, since often as many as eight sprays a year must be applied in order to protect the fruit—a very expensive business indeed. Large and valuable orchards in Oregon and Washington, in fact, have been abandoned because the infestation of the codling moth was so heavy that the cost of control was prohibitive. The cost does not stop with the spraying, either, since many states and countries have stringent laws regarding the amount of insecticides that can be allowed to remain on the fruit; therefore fruit that has been sprayed must be washed before it can be marketed; and the cost of this plus the cost of the fruit damaged in the cleaning process is another heavy charge against the codling moth. There are various other fruit "worms" that infest apples. Of these the lesser codling moth, *L. prunivora,* a closely related species, is some-times quite serious. The Oriental fruit moth, *L. molesta,* is another member of the same genus that attacks stone fruits, especially peaches, boring in the growing twigs as well as in the fruit.

Another member of the same family (Tortricidae) is the European pine shoot moth, *Evetria buoliana,* now widely introduced in the rest of the world. The rather pretty red-orange moths lay their eggs in the terminal buds of "hard" pines, including such valuable forest and ornamental species as the red, Scotch, Austrian and mugho pines. The caterpillar bores in the developing shoot when growth starts in the spring, effectively hollowing it out and preventing any growth that season from that shoot. In heavy infestations the brown, dead shoot may show on nearly every twig of the tree, the equivalent of a complete pruning of all new growth; and such an infestation two or three years running may kill the tree. A number of other related species similarly infest other pines.

WASP MOTHS—*Family Aegeriidae* (*Sesiidae*)

A very distinctive family of seven hundred or so species, the wasp moths (Plate 65) are world-wide. As the name implies, they are wasplike in appearance. The majority have the wings more or less devoid of scales but the borders colored. Many have the body brightly banded with black and yellow, orange or scarlet. The front and hind wings are locked together by a series of short curved spines. Of course it is pure coincidence, but this coordinating mechanism, so different from that of the other moths, is very similar to that of the bees and wasps that the moths mimic. Nobody has yet suggested that this, too, is involved in the mimicry. The hind legs frequently bear prominent masses of yellow or orange hairs and scales that resemble the balls of pollen carried by the bees; and some of the species have a long orange or yellow process streaming out behind from the end of the abdomen that strongly resembles the ovipositor of many of the parasitic wasps. Some of the moths are almost perfect mimics of specific wasps that fly in the same regions, although many others are merely general mimics. The big hornet clearwing, *Sesia apiformis,* of Europe and eastern North America, is a most convincing yellow-and-black hornet. The North American peach-borer, *Conopia exitiosa,* is an excellent mimic of some of the steely blue and orange pepsid wasps. The adult moths have quick flights and are seldom seen in numbers, even though we may know that by the criterion of larval abundance they are common in the area. They are mostly day fliers, frequently visiting flowers.

The caterpillars are borers in trunks, stems roots and rootstocks of many plants, chiefly woody perennials. Some live in galls of their own making, others in galls formed through the agency of gall wasps. A number are injurious to plants useful to man and are quite difficult to control. They attack such plant tissues as squash and pumpkin stems, blackberry and raspberry canes and roots, grape roots, clematis rootstocks, oak trunks and that beneath the bark at the base of the trunk of peach, plum and apricot. The larvae of most of the species pupate in the burrow. The pupa has a number of backward-directing spines on the abdomen, which drive it forward when it wiggles; this it does when the adult is fully formed and ready to emerge, traveling along the burrow to an exit hole prepared in advance and protruding part way out to permit the emergence of the adult.

WOOD-BORERS—Family Cossidae

This rather small but world-wide family consists of medium-sized to very large, heavy-bodied moths that as larvae are borers in wood or pithy stems. The moths are most commonly drab gray or brown with many small, inconspicuous marks. The enormous *Xyleutes boisduvali* of Australia is certainly one of the largest and perhaps the most massive of all moths, having a wing expanse up to ten inches and an abdomen as large as a small banana. Most of the species are much smaller, the Temperate Zone ones seldom exceeding four inches in expanse and often being little more than an inch.

The pale, fleshy larvae often do considerable damage by boring in the trunks and branches of valuable trees. Some of the smaller species bore in perennial herb stems. They spend at least a year, and in some species three or more years, in the larval stage. The adults, and particularly the females, are heavy-bodied and not strong fliers. Their mouthparts are so reduced that they cannot feed. The leopard moth, *Zeuzera pyrina,* of Europe and (introduced) eastern North America, is quite woolly and white and has regular, small, steely blue dots. It is a considerable pest in trees in city parks. The large goat moth, *Cossus cossus,* of Europe, is a pale brownish gray, irregularly marked moth that may expand four inches. The caterpillars, which bore in tree trunks, are noted for their strong goatlike odor.

BUTTERFLY MOTHS—Family Castniidae

Fairly closely related to the Cossids, which are generally regarded as a rather primitive family, the Castniids are confined to the tropics of the Old and New Worlds. We have taken the liberty of calling them butterfly moths in the absence of a more appropriate common name, since their chief interest to us arises from the many ways in which they resemble butterflies. They are considered to be very closely related to the ancestral stem of at least the skippers, and possibly more remotely to that of the true butterflies. They must be regarded as moths because of their larval and pupal characteristics and their possession of a frenulum for coupling the wings. But they are very broad-winged, fast-flying, daytime flower visitors, and have strongly clubbed antennae and often very bright colors. The adults are frequently extremely difficult to catch, not only because of their fast, erratic flight and expert dodging ability, but because they may visit only the flowers of tall trees of the tropical forests and scarcely ever come near the ground. The males are often bold, active and quarrelsome, darting out from a favorite perch to drive other males away; in South America we have caught specimens by tolling them within reach with a cardboard lure painted to resemble the pattern of the species. Some of the larger species, which may expand three or more inches, are very attractively colored and patterned in yellow, black, white, and iridescent blue. Others are noted for their close mimicry of the highly protected Heliconiid and Ithomiid butterflies that abound in tropical America and are mimicked by moths and other butterflies in many groups. Even the wing shape of the Castniids that mimic these has been modified, being much longer and narrower and blunter than that of the nonmimetic ones. The Castniids are a favorite group with collectors, some of the rare species being sold by dealers at quite high prices.

PYRALID MOTHS—Family Pyralididae

The name of this family comes from the Greek word for fire, and touches on an ancient legend about the moths not only flying into fire but perhaps being born of it. The fertile imagination of the ancient Greek would not have been satisfied with our prosaic modern knowledge that the moths are simply attracted to light. The family is enormous and world-wide, containing upward of twenty thousand species and being the third largest in the Lepidoptera. Technically the Pyralids are microlepidoptera, belonging on the primitive side of the order; and while a few are medium-sized, with wing expanses of as much as three inches, the majority average decidedly less. Some specialists split the family into a number of small ones.

As we might expect, a great variety of habits and habitats are found within the limits of this large group. We shall touch on only a few of these here, the others having already been mentioned along with moths of other families as scavengers, leafrollers and -tyers, etc. The majority of the members of the family are really quite ordinary moths with little that is distinctive about them to interest anyone but a specialist in their classification.

The grass moths and sod webworms of the subfamily Crambinae are found in every continent, to a total number of several hundred species. Some reach the Arctic, others live in Tierra del Fuego.

A **Pyralid Moth** (*Galasa rubidana*) in its characteristic resting position. The tiny front legs are folded against the body.

The caterpillars of the majority live in silken tunnels in turf and among grass roots, where they often do considerable damage. Some attack corn, cutting the seedling plants. Members of the genus *Chilo* are serious rice pests in tropical countries, and *Diatraea saccharalis* is exceedingly injurious to sugar cane. The adults are narrow-winged moths that characteristically roll the wings back around the abdomen, giving them a slender appearance. Their palpi are quite long, sometimes three times the length of the head, and protrude straight out in front, making them very obvious "snout moths" and still further enhancing the slenderness of their bodies. They usually rest along a grass blade or other thin leaf and are not easily detected.

One of the most infamous members of the subfamily Pyraustinae is the European corn-borer, *Pyrausta nubilalis*. In its native home in southern and central Europe it is of relatively little consequence; but transported to the United States in 1908 or 1909, certainly at least twice, it immediately became an exceedingly injurious pest in corn. Despite attempts to limit its spread by stringent quarantine (many of us can remember being stopped along a road and asked if we had any corn or living plants of various kinds) it spread into the great corn-growing regions of the Midwest. It is now definitely corn enemy number one. The larvae bore in the stalks, after an early period of external feeding, and seriously weaken or kill the plants. In one genetic strain there is one generation a year, in another two. The winter is passed in the pupal stage in the hollow corn stubble, so that one of the most important control measures is to destroy or plow this under deeply in the autumn. Con-

trol is made difficult by the ability of the species to live in a great many other plants, some of them common weeds found everywhere, such as burdock.

The most biologically distinct group of Pyralids is composed of the small moths of the subfamily Nymphulinae, whose caterpillars are aquatic. Although there are no more than a few hundred species at most, some occur nearly everywhere that there is fresh water. One group occurs chiefly in lakes, ponds and quiet waters. Caterpillars of *Nymphula* and the European *Cataclysta* make flat cases of pieces of plant fastened together with silk, in which they live while crawling about among the plants and feeding. Some of those of *Elophila* and other genera, however, spin silk webs, under which they live on the surfaces of rocks; and some of these are found in extremely swift water, where they feed on the diatoms and other small aquatic plants that are caught in the web. While young, the caterpillars respire directly through the body wall or get oxygen from the tissues of the aquatic plants. They have slender tracheal gills, however, which are chiefly used when they are living in the cases. The webs of some of the stream-living species are so constructed that they catch and hold air bubbles in the water. The moths, though small, are attractively marked with bold patterns, and often have a row of metallic eyespots on the hind wing.

PLUME MOTHS and FEATHER-WINGED MOTHS—Families *Pterophoridae* and *Orneodidae*

In the majority of members of these two curious families the wings are deeply cleft lengthwise. In the plume moths (Pterophoridae) the front wings thus usually form two plumes and the hind wings three, while in most of the feather-winged moths each wing is cleft so that it forms six plumes. The two groups are not at all closely related to each other, and so have evidently developed the splitting of the wings independently. In some of the plume moths, e.g. the European *Agdistis,* the wings are not cleft. We can assign no reason for the strange condition on the basis of worth or usefulness to the moths, since they are in general very weak fliers. The plume moths in particular have very long, extremely fragile legs, and impress one as most delicate and inefficient insects. Yet there are some six hundred species of them, they appear in nearly all parts of the world, and many of them are extremely common. They have been noted for their occurrence in bleak alpine environments such as at 15,200 feet in the Andes. Some are quite small, expanding little more than one-quarter of an inch; the giants may expand two inches. The feather-winged moths consist of less than a hundred species, chiefly Asiatic. The larvae of both families are relatively ordinary leaf- and flower-eaters.

URANIID MOTHS—Family Uraniidae

The Uraniids (Plate 64) are a relatively small family almost limited to the tropical regions of the Old and New Worlds. The majority are small to medium-sized and quite ordinary-looking moths. A few genera, however, are large day fliers of the utmost brilliance of coloring and form, rivaling almost any of the butterflies. It is often difficult for people who do not know them to realize that they are indeed moths and not swallowtail butterflies of unusual beauty. The hind wings bear tails, sometimes a single one half as long as the wing, sometimes as many as three shorter ones. The species of *Alcides* and *Nyctalemon* of the Indo-Australian region have the wings crossed by broad bands of a pale satiny blue that changes to pale green or yellow with shifting light. The *Urania* species of the New World have somewhat more slender wings, with long tails on the hind ones. Their iridescent colors are more intense, shifting from green shot with gold to sapphire blue, sometimes set off by broad white fringes. The famous *Chrysiridia madagascarensis* of Madagascar is the largest and most brilliant member of the family. In addition to the gold-to-green-to-blue bands of both wings it has the hind wings deeply scalloped and long-tailed, with broad white fringes, and glowing with great patches of an almost three-dimensional iridescence that shifts from gold to copper to purple. No painting or reproduction can give more than a fractional impression of the play of its colors, for they shift, blend and then change again with every minute variation of the angle of light falling upon them.

Such colors, which occur in many insects but in few with a brilliance that matches that of these moths and some of the butterflies, are due to structures and not to pigments. Pigment colors are present, but they are usually negligible. It is the structural colors that show the iridescent changing of apparent hue. Blues, greens and all the metallic effects are almost invariably caused by structures, the blue pigments being almost completely absent, and greens limited to caterpillars and a relatively few, inconspicuous moths. Pigment colors usually fade, and can be washed out with solvents. Structural colors on the other hand change greatly or disappear when the surfaces are wetted but reappear, with no change, on drying out.

The structural colors of insects as well as of most birds and other animals are the result of four main types of structures. One consists of very small particles dispersed in a different medium; this is the "Tyndall blue" of the physicist and explains the phenomenon of the blue of the sky; it is also responsible for the white of snow and of milk, and for the bluish tinge of dilute milk. A second type consists of very fine lines or ridges, closely parallel to each other. This is the "diffraction grating" of the physicist. It is never brilliantly iridescent, but may show a play of quiet colors. Some of the scarabaeid beetles, genus *Serica,* show it plainly.

The other two types, which are really variants of a single kind of structure, produce most of the brilliant insect color effects. They are caused by the presence of two or more very thin layers or films, slightly separated from each other by a medium of a different refractive index. We have all seen such thin film color effects, the commonest being caused by a film of oil on water. In moths and butterflies and some weevils the films are in the scales, in other insects in the wing membrane or integument. The *Urania* type has the thin films located in the actual body of each scale itself, and all parallel to the surface of the scale. The other type, named for the *Morpho* butterflies, which display it most prominently, has the films located in the fine ridges that rise from the body of the scale and set at an angle to the surface. In many forms this produces a more glittering effect; but it is impossible to say which type is more beautiful.

EMPERORS and GIANT SILKWORM MOTHS—Family Saturniidae

These are the giants of the order, nearly all of the species being large, while some exceed any other moths or butterflies in wing area if not in actual wing expanse. A few are relatively small, with an expanse of as little as an inch and a quarter; but even this is far above the average of Lepidoptera. The wings are usually quite thickly scaled, the bodies hairy or woolly, and the antennae of the males broadly plumy, those of the females being much narrower. In the majority of the species there is a prominent crescent-shaped, round or oval mark in the central region of each wing; and in many this is devoid of scales and is transparent, sometimes forming a large, conspicuous window. In quite a few groups the hind wing bears a prominent tail, sometimes extremely long. In others the hind wing has a large, often brightly colored eyespot. The males are usually strong, powerful fliers, but the heavier females are relatively sedentary.

The caterpillars, as one would expect, are large and prominent. They differ considerably from group to group, some being almost naked and unornamented, others bearing prominent tubercles that may be scarlet, blue or yellow, and still others being more or less thickly covered with spines or hairs. One group bears powerfully stinging spines. Some have extremely brilliant color patterns. Most of the group spin large silken cocoons that may be very tough and enduring or may be thin and flimsy; others spin none at all but enter the ground to pupate. In general there is but a single generation a year, as befits large, slow-growing insects. (See Plates 62 and 63.)

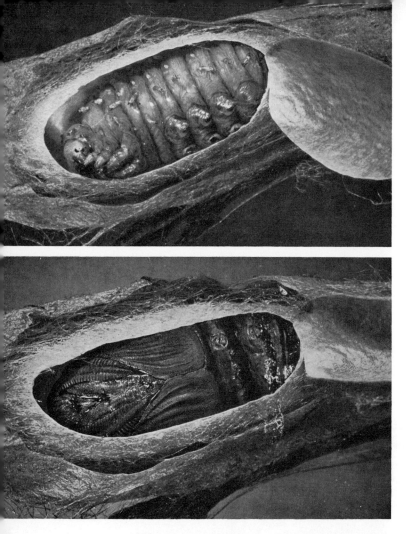

(Above) an opened cocoon of the **Cecropia Moth,** showing the caterpillar before its transformation to a pupa, and (below) the same cocoon showing the pupa to which the caterpillar has just transformed.

Europe has relatively few Saturniids, the best known being the emperor moth, *Saturnia pavonia,* a rather small but very beautifully patterned species, and the great peacock, *S. pyri.* It was with the latter that Fabre made his classical experiments, showing that the males were attracted in great numbers by the distinctive scent of the female. Instances have been recorded of these moths locating a female from as much as five miles away. Cages and other objects with which the female has been in close contact retain their attractiveness to males for some time, in some instances for several months or a year.

North America is the home of more than sixty species, a considerable number of which are tropical in origin and occur only in the extreme southern parts. The luna moth, *Actias luna* (Plates 70, 75, 77), is a lovely pale green with a maroon edge on the front of each fore wing and a long, gracefully curved tail on each hind wing. The largest species are the strikingly marked cecropia moth, *Hyalo-*

phora cecropia (Plates 68, 69), which has a bold pattern of black, white and red on its broad wings, and the tan polyphemus moth, *Antheraea polyphemus* (Plates 71, 74), with a transparent blue eyespot on each hind wing. Even more prominent are the enormous eyespots on the bright yellow hind wings of the io moth, *Automeris io* (Plate 72); the males of this species have bright yellow front wings, while those of the females are brown and more cryptic. The caterpillar of the io moth (Plate 73) is bright green with a prominent red and white stripe on each side, and bears numerous bunches of stinging spines that cause an intense burning pain and an annoying rash on the human skin. It is a member of a tropical group containing more than a hundred species in Central and South America. An introduced Chinese species, *Samia walkeri,* the ailanthus silk moth, was brought to North America along with its food plant, the Chinese ailanthus tree, a tree that has proven extremely hardy in the New York City region, where it is the characteristic tree of back yards, vacant lots and waste places. The moth seems to be able to flourish in the city, presumably because of the slightly higher temperatures there, but has extended its range very little elsewhere. It is large, expanding up to five inches, with an olive-green color and a bold pattern that includes prominent crescents on the wings. The cocoons of the ailanthus moth and the native promethea moth are suspended from twigs, often inside a rolled leaf; those of the cecropia are securely fastened along a twig or in a fork; but those of the polyphemus and luna, although spun with one or more leaves wrapped around them, are not otherwise fastened, and fall to the ground in the autumn.

The New World emperor moths (Plate 76) are a distinctive group that is sometimes classified as a separate family, the Citheroniidae. The moths have more slender, pointed wings than most other Saturniids, with less development of the eyespots or crescents. The caterpillars have longer, more slender horns, and enter the ground to pupate without spinning a cocoon. The royal walnut moth, *Citheronia regalis,* is a large species with the wings an indescribable orange-red-brown with yellow spots. Its caterpillar, known as the hickory-horned devil, is a thick-bodied, most awesome creature as much as five inches long, with several pairs of long spines on the head and thorax, and a bold pattern of white or yellow rectangles on a green body set off by bright blue or scarlet patches. It is completely harmless, despite its striking appearance. A similar, slightly smaller species is the imperial moth, *Eacles imperialis,* largely bright yellow. The much smaller members of the genus *Anisota* include the common and very beautiful rosy maple moth, *Anisota rubicunda,* which is yellow with a broad pink band across each wing. Its caterpillars are sometimes minor pests on maple.

The New World tropical species are numerous. The moths of the genus *Rothschildia* are especially noted for the enormous size of the crescent-shaped, transparent windows in their wings, combined in many with bold patterns and bright reddish or orange-brown colors. *R. splendida, zacateca* and *aurota* are perhaps the most impressive. A few species enter the very southern United States, but the real home of the group is in Central and South America. The sizable genus *Rhescyntis* (*Arsenura*) contains some very large species, with as much as nine or ten inches of wing expanse and with hooked front wings; while *Copiopteryx semiramis* is noted for the extremely long, graceful tail on each hind wing.

Africa has many Saturniids, the majority of which, as elsewhere, have little but their size to recommend them. The large genus *Nudaurelia*, for example, contains many rather plain brown species. The extremely impressive *Argema mittrei* from Madagascar, however, is one of the world's most striking moths. It is large (up to six and a half inches expanse) and bright yellow with dark markings, and has extremely long, graceful tails, more or less twisted and enlarged at their tips, on the hind wings. Its lacework cocoon is an extraordinary thing, since the silk has a strongly silvery, metallic luster. Despite its small size the little *Eudaemonia argiphontes* is even more curious, for a specimen with a wing expanse of two and a quarter inches will have a tail four and a half inches long, with an enlargement at the tip, on each hind wing; and the tail is so slender that one wonders how it can possibly survive a moment's flight. The extremely small species of *Ludia* and *Holocera* expand no more than an inch and a half, yet are very attractive moths with strongly hooked fore wings and sober colors.

The Indo-Australian region is the home of many more impressive Saturniids. The large green or yellow-green *Actias,* such as *A. maenas,* have long, curved tails, like the smaller North American *A. luna.* Some have an expanse of seven inches; and in some there is a strong sexual dimorphism, the males being bright brown while the females are green. The genus *Antheraea* contains some very large species, such as *A. paphia,* that are reared commercially in India as the source of tussah or tussore silk. The most famous, however, are the enormous, boldly patterned hercules moth, *Coscinoscera hercules,* and the atlas moth, *Attacus atlas.* The latter has strongly hooked front wings and the larger wingspread, ten inches or more; but the former has tails on the hind wings, much longer in the males than in the females, and very broad wings, so that it unquestionably has the largest wing

A **Cecropia Moth** (*Hyalophora cecropia*) cementing her eggs to a twig as she lays them.

area of any insect. One in flight looks quite as large as a pigeon. Only the giant owlet moth of South America, *Thysania agrippina,* and the females of some of the *Troïdes* swallowtail butterflies exceed these moths in wing expanse.

The Saturniids have long been favorites among naturalists and moth-collectors, one reason being the hardiness of the pupae in the strong cocoons. These are often sold by dealers in all parts of the world, so that the collector can have the double pleasure of seeing the moths emerge and of having absolutely perfect specimens.

COMMUNAL NEST DWELLERS
—Families Liparidae Lasiocampidae etc. (in part)

None of the moths or butterflies exhibits, at most, more than the barest rudiments of social behavior, the caterpillars of some species living together and sometimes sharing communal webs or nests. These gatherings are, however, quite impermanent, since the caterpillars never do more than pupate together in the nest, and when transformed into adults scatter and act wholly as individuals. In many instances they separate before pupation, or even when only partly grown caterpillars. In no instance is there

Large caterpillar of **Regal Emperor** or **Royal Walnut Moth** (*Citheronia regalis*) of eastern North America. Aptly known as the **Hickory Horned Devil.**

anything of the association of parent and offspring that marks the foundation of the highly evolved insect societies. Nor is there any evidence of any specialization of individuals in division of labor, since each caterpillar does what every other one does. No particular family is especially distinguished for such communal life.

In the microlepidoptera some species of *Yponomeuta* (Yponomeutidae) and a number of Tortricids thus live in webs. Sometimes, as in the genus *Archips* of the Tortricidae, these may become rather large and firmly bound together, each caterpillar continually spinning a thread of silk as it moves about; but there is no planning or design, the nests and webs merely marking the nightly return of the caterpillars from their feeding grounds. The same is true of the North American tent caterpillar *Malacosoma americana* (Plate 90), whose white webs often form conspicuous objects in the trees that are frequently defoliated by a resident colony. However, the European species of the same genus, *M. neustria* and *castrense,* and the North American *M. disstria,* form only temporary aggregations and relatively little if any, communal web, so that we can see that the habit is not very deeply ingrained in the group.

Most famous of the communal caterpillars are those of the European processionaries, *Thaumetopoea.* Here the caterpillars not only live in a communal web in which they spend the winter, but also march in more or less consistent formations when leaving the nest to feed. The processionary of the pine, *T. pityocampa,* marches in long, single files, each caterpillar following the one in front closely and blindly. To a great degree the trail of silk, laid down as a thread by the first caterpillar of the procession and added to by each succeeding one, is the guide; but recent work has shown that great importance is also attached to the physical presence of one caterpillar immediately ahead of another. In a classical experiment Fabre led a procession onto the rim of a large pot and then destroyed the trace left by their arrival. For eight days the pro-

White-marked Tussock Moth (*Notolophus leucostigma.*) A winged male and wingless female are shown resting on the cocoon of the female.

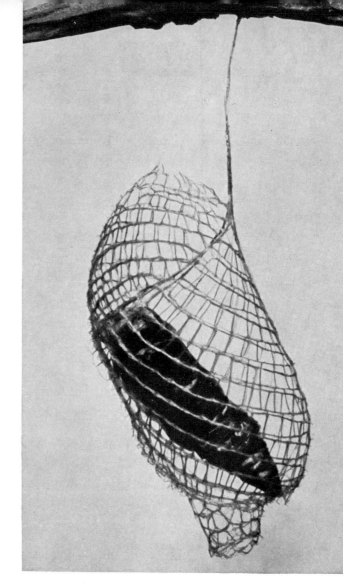

The lacelike cocoon of an **Yponomeutid Moth** (*Urodus parvula*) is unusual in that it is suspended by a long, hairlike stalk.

cession, forming a closed circle, proceeded around and around the rim, moving at a rate of some seventeen feet per hour, and stopping only during darkness or very cold weather. Finally, starved and worn out, it broke up when some individuals laid a new trail down the outside of the pot. The files may consist of several hundred individuals. No particular caterpillar acts as leader, chance dictating which is first; and each one, when placed first in the line, acts just like each other.

Communal nests are also formed by various members of Liparidae (Plates 88, 89), such as the browntail and goldtail moths of Europe, *Euproctis phaeorrhoea* and *Porthesia chrysorrhoea,* the former of which has become established in the eastern United States, where it is something of a pest. The fall webworm, *Hyphantria cunea* of the family Arctiidae, often forms immense, untidy sheets of silk that drape entire small trees. And the caterpillars of quite a number of butterflies, such as the

North American Baltimore, *Euphydryas phaeton,* the European peacock, *Nymphalis io,* the small tortoiseshell, *Vanessa urticae,* and the tropical Morphoes, live in similar communal webs or nests. Sometimes pupation takes place in the nest; sometimes the caterpillars scatter and pupate individually. The most strongly constructed nests are the flask-shaped ones made by the caterpillars of the Mexican Pierid butterfly, *Eucheira socialis,* which are used by the natives as purses or even containers for liquids.

MEASURING WORMS and INCH WORMS
—Family Geometridae

The scientific name of this family, which means "earth measurers," is very appropriate. The caterpillars progress with a looping gait, extending the front end forward, taking hold with the legs, and then bringing the rear end forward with a sharp vertical loop of the body. Various little superstitions have grown up around this curious habit; one being that an inch worm, allowed to crawl over you unmolested, is measuring you for a new suit of clothes that will soon be forthcoming.

The Geometrids (Plate 67) are the second larg-

American Tent Caterpillar (*Malacosoma americana*). Gregarious and sometimes destructive pest of trees in eastern North America.

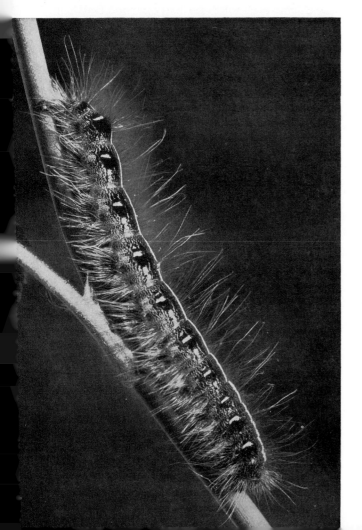

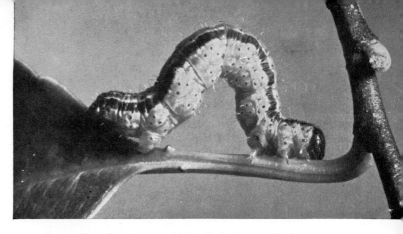

Caterpillar of a **Geometrid Moth** (*Geometridae*). Lacking prolegs in the middle of the body it progresses with a looping gait that has given it the names Inch-worm and Measuring-worm.

est family of the Lepidoptera, containing thousands of species on every continent. Some specialists split them into a number of families. Their chief characteristic is the loss of at least many or most of the larval prolegs that normally occur on the third to the sixth segments of the abdomen. In most groups the front two pairs are missing, and some lack the third pair as well and have the fourth pair set far back toward the rear end. It is this lack of most of the central legs that causes the looping gait.

The moths themselves are usually broad-winged and of medium size, e.g. from three-quarters of an inch to an inch and a half in expanse; but there are many small species that expand no more than three-eighths of an inch. The largest are seldom more than two inches across. Their flights, while often fairly fast and erratic, lack the power and speed of those of many of the other macro-moths. The antennae of the males are usually narrowly plumed, but may, like those of most of the females, be almost hairlike. All have a pair of tympanic hearing organs located on the base of the abdomen facing forward, a characteristic that separates them from most similar moths of other families. The majority are colored in rather sober shades of browns and grays with finely and closely detailed patterns, although there are some strikingly colored species, particularly in the tropics. The adults of two small subfamilies are mostly pale green, being colored, incidentally, with green pigments—a rare thing in adult Lepidoptera, although there are many that have structural green colors. The pigments of these green Geometrids fade very quickly. A great many species have their wing margins irregularly notched or scalloped, giving them quite broken outlines that enhance their resemblance to dead leaves and bits of bark.

The moths of the majority of species rest with the wings out flat at the sides, the fore wings partly covering the hind wings; or they hold the fore wings back flat, covering the hind wings and abdomen. Since the patterns of most of these species are highly cryptic, the moths blend excellently with the

A **Geometrid** caterpillar (*Geometridae*), showing the twiglike form and resting position characteristic of many members of the family.

notably the peppered moth, *Biston betularia,* are furnishing exceedingly valuable information about what Professor E. B. Ford of Oxford calls the "most striking example of evolution which has ever actually been witnessed in any living organism, plant or animal." The normal variety of this moth is white, peppered and scrawled with dark marks in a cryptic pattern. There is, in addition, a black, or melanic, variety, *carbonaria;* and the appearance of these varieties is a matter of inheritance. Until about a hundred years ago the normal, i.e. the characteristic, variety was the pale one, the melanic being exceedingly rare. With the growth of great industrial centers, yearly pouring forth thousands of tons of sooty residues that deposit on all surfaces for many miles around, the tree trunks and other surfaces on which the moths rest during the daytime have become steadily darker. Coincidentally with this the melanic variety has increased greatly in proportionate numbers in these areas, until in some of the worst-polluted regions it has almost entirely replaced the pale variety. The latter is now the rare one. Exceedingly thorough studies demonstrate conclusively that it is the darkening of the environment that is responsible for this, by exerting a selective pressure on the moths through the agency of the birds that prey upon them during the daytime. In the darkened, polluted areas the birds capture far fewer of the black variety and far more of the light one, since the latter cannot find light, matching backgrounds on which to rest. With such a steady drain on their numbers, fewer and fewer of the light-colored moths survive to reproduce, the opposite being true of the black ones. We are thus able to witness, study and measure the change of a very light-colored species into an almost wholly black one in the polluted areas, while in unpolluted or lightly polluted regions the species remains unchanged. Most of the significant studies have been made in England and Germany. It is hoped that similar work can be instituted in North America around some of the great and heavily polluted industrial areas, where very likely the same sort of change is taking place.

The long, slender looper caterpillars are often noted for their protective resemblance to twigs and leaf stems. In many instances the similarity, which has a good start because of the inherent slimness of the caterpillars, is greatly increased by peculiarities of coloring and irregularities of shape. A great many loopers consistently hold on with only the single pair of prolegs at the very rear end while resting, the thin body protruding stiffly from the surface and looking like a short, stiff twig. In many instances the caterpillar spins a few strands of silk that support its head and body in the rigid position, in which it can then remain for hours without strain. Brown caterpillars thus usually rest on brown

backgrounds on which they rest. In those that partially cover the hind wings with the fore wings, the lines and other pattern elements of the fore wings run uninterruptedly onto the hind wings when the wings are in the normal resting positions, although there may seem to be no relation between the two when the wings are unnaturally extended in the conventional position for spreading specimens in a collection. The moths very definitely exercise some kind of choice as to the general tone of the surfaces on which they rest during the daytime, most frequently settling finally on a surface that matches them in tonal value. This is accomplished by an automatic reflex mechanism that does not, of course, involve anything similar to consciousness or the exercise of a deliberate choice that characterizes human mental processes. The deciding factor seems to be the tone of either a fringe of hairs and scales surrounding the eyes, or of scales at the base of the front wing. The moth will seldom come to rest on a surface that differs strongly from these, being uneasy on a surface that causes two different regions of the eye to be differentially stimulated.

A considerable number of European Geometrids,

twigs, green ones on green twigs or among leaves. A number of species that feed on pine have green and whitish lengthwise stripes and are thus practically undetectable when lying in a bundle of pine needles. Still others, particularly the caterpillars of the green Geometrids, are brown, with irregular pointed and twisted projections along the sides of the body; and these look almost exactly like crumpled bits of dead leaves, especially since they usually hold themselves in very contorted positions.

A number of Geometrids are serious pests, although as a whole the family is not nearly as injurious to man as many smaller groups. Here belong some destructive enemies of forest and shade trees such as the spring and fall canker worms, *Palaeacrita vernata* and *Alsophila pometaria;* the snow-white linden moth, *Ennomos subsignarius;* and the lime tree looper, *Erannis tiliaria,* in North America: and the winter moth, *Operophtera brumata;* the mottled umber, *Erannis defoliaria;* and the currant moth, *Abraxas grossulariata,* in Europe.

Death's-head Sphinx Moth (*Acherontia atropos*), a mating pair. The prominent skull-like design on the thorax has given rise to many superstitions.

A **Sphinx Moth** (*Phlegethontius carolina*), showing the extremely long, coiled tongue through which it sucks nectar from flowers.

The last mentioned is a boldly marked black and white moth, and is equally conspicuously colored and patterned in both the larval and pupal stages. There is no doubt that it is distasteful to birds, and that the coloration serves as a warning of this.

A number of Geometrids have wingless or nearly wingless females, the North American canker worms and the European winter moth mentioned above being the best-known examples. These species pupate in the ground. When the females emerge they climb up tree trunks. Here the winged males find them, the matings take place, and the eggs are laid in masses. An outstanding problem, which we have discussed at some length in connection with the bagworms, has been how such species ever get distributed when the females are incapable of travel for any effective distance.

SPHINX or HAWK MOTHS
—Family Sphingidae

The members of this cosmopolitan family (Plates 80, 81) are among the best known of the moths to naturalists and entomologists, since both the larvae and the adults are large, extremely distinctive and unusual. The smallest species have a wing expanse of about two inches, but these are exceptions, since most members of the family average from three to four inches, and some of the largest expand as much as eight. The front wings are very long, narrow and usually pointed, but the hind wings are very small. The bodies are large and packed with powerful wing muscles and are often beautifully streamlined. The moths have a very rapid and strong flight in which the wings beat so fast they seem a mere blur. Some of the day-flying species resemble hummingbirds when flying, the similarity being greatly enhanced by their consistent habit of hovering in front of flowers while feeding from them. They can do this because the tongue is very long and strong and can be uncoiled and thrust deep into a flower to the nectary while the moth is

[159

Caterpillar of **Death's-head Sphinx** in characteristic "sphinxlike" position.

still on the wing. Although many of the species are day fliers, the majority do not awake and begin to fly until dusk.

The sphinx moths are of major importance in the pollination of many flowering plants. It is not unusual to find the special adhesive pollen masses of such plants as orchids and milkweeds fastened to their tongues, evidence that they have been visiting these flowers. Some plants, in fact, have evolved such closely integrated, mutually beneficial relationships with certain of these moths that they ac-

A **Bumblebee Hawk Moth** (*Hemaris fuciformis*), so called because of its resemblance to a large bee.

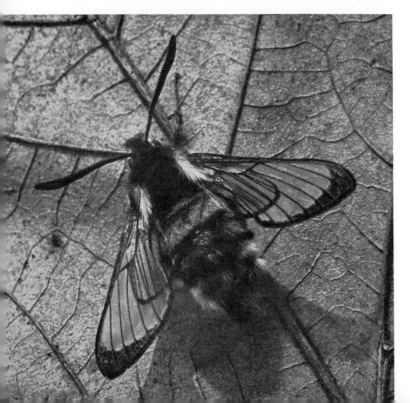

tually bar other insects from gaining access to their flowers. Often this is accomplished by having the nectaries located at the bottom of tubes so deep that only a long-tongued hawk moth can reach into them. In 1891 Alfred Russel Wallace noted that in Madagascar there was an *Angraecum* orchid with the nectaries at a depth of from ten to thirteen inches, but that no hawk moth was known from the island with a tongue long enough to reach that far. He therefore predicted that such a moth must exist, since the plant was certainly being cross-pollinated by something and only a hawk moth could have so long a tongue. In 1903 the moth was discovered and found to have, as Wallace had predicted, a tongue long enough to reach the nectaries. It was appropriately named *Macrosilia morgani predicta*.

At least one of the sphinx moths has departed from the flower-visiting habits of the family. The famous death's-head sphinx of Africa and Europe, *Acherontia atropos,* has the tongue very short, strong and pointed. With it the moth pierces the honeycomb of beehives and sucks the honey. This moth has on the thorax an excellent facsmile of a human skull; and since it is a large and common species, this has given rise to all kinds of superstitions, its presence being believed to presage death. It is also peculiar in being able to make a quite loud squeaking sound when disturbed, forcibly expelling air though the tongue.

A number of sphinx moths have the wings more or less lacking in scales and thus transparent, usually only the outer border being scaled. In at least some of these, the day-flying North American species of *Hemaris,* the wings are formed in the pupa with a full covering of scales, but these are shed very soon after the moth's emergence. Some of the smaller species of this group and of others in all continents are called hummingbird hawk moths, as is the small *Macroglossa stellatarum* of Europe.

Many of the sphinx moths are very beautifully colored and patterned, and are eagerly sought by collectors. Among the tropical species green or green-and-yellow wings and bodies are not uncommon, having a decided cryptic value in concealing the moths while they are resting among foliage during the daytime. This they usually do with the front wings hanging back, more or less covering the hind wings and body. In a number of species, such as the North American *Smerinthus* (Plate 80) and *Paonias* and the New World *Pholus,* the hind wings may be very brightly colored while the fore wings are cryptic. In such cases the hind wings, which are hidden while the moth is resting, are suddenly exposed when it is disturbed, giving something of a surprise to the disturber and perhaps enabling the moth to escape. Such "flash coloration," which by its sudden appearance may confuse a predator, is common in many groups of

[continued on page 177]

62 and 63. Two caterpillars of South American **Emperor Moths** (*Automeris*) closely related to the North American Io Moth. The spines are barbed and poisonous, and produce a burning rash on contact with human skin.

64. Urania Moth (Family Uraniidae). A day-flying moth of the New World Tropics that flies faster and is more brilliantly colored than most butterflies. (About natural size.)

65. Hornet Clear Wing Moth (*Sesia apiformis*). A strikingly effective mimic of the large yellow and black Hornet. (Magnified several times.)

66. **Ilia Underwing** (*Catocala ilia*). When the moth is at rest during the day the brilliantly colored hind wings are normally concealed by the bark-like front wings.

67. **A Geometrid Moth** (*Lytrosia unitaria*). The cryptically colored and patterned wings make this moth difficult to see.

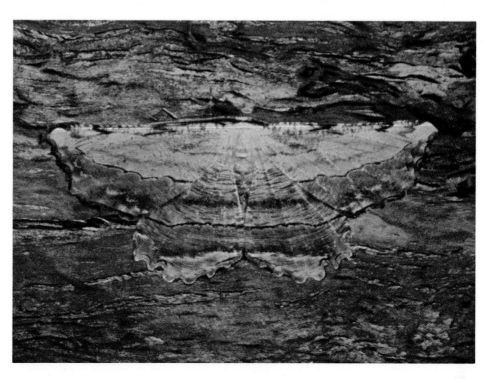

68. **Cecropia Moth** (*Hyalophora cecropia*). This big Cecropia and its relatives are common in nearly all parts of the United States. Fastened to a twig, its cocoon, shown at the right, becomes conspicuous during the winter.

69. A brightly colored **Cecropia** caterpillar covered with impressive tubercles and spines.

70. **Luna Moth** (*Actias luna*). The wide-spreading plumes of the male's antennae enable him to scent the female miles away.

71. **Polyphemus Moth** (*Antheraea polyphemus*). The eyelike spots on the hind wings of this moth and of the Io Moth, below, may sometimes confuse their enemies.

72. **Io Moth** (*Automeris io*). Its thin cocoon is usually found on the ground amidst leaves.

73. Caterpillars of the **Io Moth** eating their own eggshells.

74. Caterpillar of the **Polyphemus Moth** which, despite its size, is difficult to see among foliage.

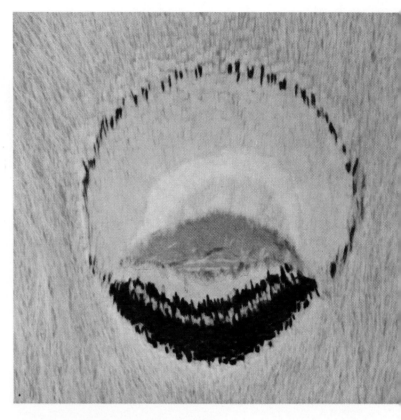

75. Eyespot on the hind wing of a **Luna Moth.**
(Greatly magnified.)

76. **California Silk Moth** (*Calosaturnia mendo-cino*) laying eggs on its food plant, manzanita.

77. The long-tailed **Lu**
(*Actias luna*), one
the most beautiful
North America's E
peror Moths. Its o
cocoon is thin a
parchment-like.

78. Caterpillar of the **Striped Morning Sphinx** (*Deilephila lineata*). When full grown it is about three inches long.

79. **A Sphinx Moth** caterpillar. Many in this family have this hornlike process at the rear of the body. The eyelike slit is really a breathing aperture or spiracle, one of the last abdominal pair.

80. **A Hawk Moth** (*Smerinthus geminatus*),
a common large North American species.

81. **Eyed Hawk Moth** (*Smerinthus ocella-tus*). A mating pair from Europe.

82. Caterpillar of a **Prominent Moth** (*Symmerista canicosta*). Its brilliant colors signal its inedibility.

83. Caterpillar of a **Prominent Moth** (*Notodonta stragula*) bearing a striking resemblance to a dead leaf.

84. A **Puss Moth** (*Cerura scitiscripta multiscripta*) caterpillar whose pattern is an excellent example of disruptive coloration. The lashlike filaments at the rear of the body are greatly modified hind legs.

85. Adult **Puss Moth** showing its bold black-and-white pattern.

86. **Garden Tiger Moth** (*Arctia caia*). This big European moth is highly distasteful to birds. Recently it has been found to have poison glands and spines on the hind legs that produce sharp pain in some humans.

87. **American Tiger Moth** (*Isia isabella*). Its caterpillar is the familiar black and brown "woolly bear" often seen scurrying across the road in the autumn.

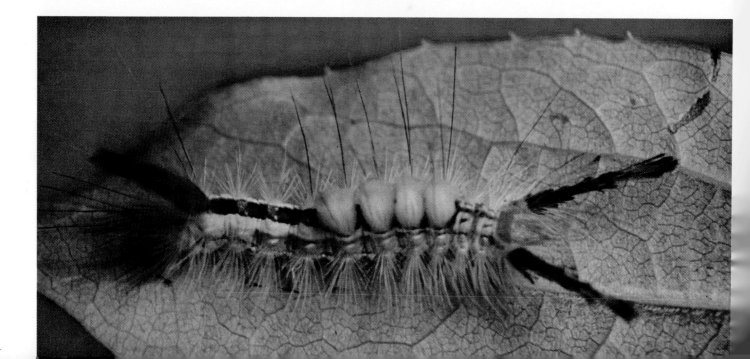

88 and 89. (Left) A **Tussock Moth** (*Hemerocampa leucostigma*) caterpillar. (Above) A head-on view. This caterpillar ranks among the worst pests of city shade trees.

[continued from page 160]

animals. The prominent eyespots on the hind wings of such sphinx moths as the species of *Paonias* are a good example, as are the eyespots on the hind wings of io moths and their relatives, caligo butterflies, and the brilliant colors of the hind wings of most underwing moths.

Few of the sphinx moths seem to migrate or make long-distance flights, which is surprising in view of their potential ability to do so. A few, however, are well-known migrants. The death's-head sphinx regularly migrates far northward into Europe from Africa; and a New World tropical sphinx with gray front wings and brick-red hind wings, *Erynnyis ello,* quite frequently flies as far northward as Canada.

The caterpillars of the sphinx moths are most unusual creatures, which characteristically rest with the whole fore part of the body and the head reared up in front. It was a fancied similarity of this position to the Egyptian sphinx that gave the name to the group. The relatively small head is curved down below the large thorax when the caterpillar is in this position; the thorax then looks like a very large head, and the whole caterpillar like the front part of a much larger animal. In some species markings on the thorax look like eyes. On the rear end of the abdomen many sphinx moth larvae have a rather prominent backward-pointing horn (Plate 79), which is not, however, of any use as a weapon but is simply an ornament. In many other species the horn is lacking and is replaced by a rounded tubercle. Many sphinx caterpillars have a series of parallel oblique lines on the body that are definitely cryptic, helping the larva resemble a brown or green leaf with parallel veins. It is surprising how hard it is to detect a big sphinx caterpillar three or four inches long even when it is in plain sight, so perfectly do its colors blend with those of the plants on which it is feeding.

A few of the sphinx caterpillars are pests. The most injurious are the big green caterpillars of the tobacco and tomato sphinxes, *Phlegethontius sextus* and *quinquemaculatus* of North America. Both species will eat the leaves of tomato and potato; and both are a familiar and unwelcome sight in many gardens. On the other hand some, such as the very common and beautiful lined morning sphinx, *Deilephila lineata* of North America, feed on such weeds as purslane, and are thus mildly beneficial (Plate 78).

PROMINENTS—Family Notodontidae

The prominents (Plate 85) are a small but widely distributed family of medium-sized moths that are quite closely related to the owlet moths (Noctuidae). The adult moths are in general relatively undistinguished, although they exhibit a wide range of colors and patterns, from white through

Caterpillar of **Tomato Hornworm** (*Phlegethontius quinquemaculatus*), often destructive to tobacco and tomato plants.

practically every combination of the pigmental colors. Many are extremely hairy, and many are cryptically colored in grays and browns that make them very inconspicuous when they are resting flat on bark. The North American species of *Datana* and *Melalopha,* and the European buff tip, *Phalera bucephala,* have the head and thorax differently colored from the rest of the body; this gives the moth, which rests with the wings more or less rolled about the body, a striking resemblance to a short twig with a broken end. In the buff tip the head and thorax are a light, buffy brown, the color of freshly broken wood; in the North American genera they are very dark and look like the shadow under a sharp end. Some of the species of *Schizura* have a most unusual resting position, rolling the wings around the body and projecting the whole at a sharp angle, the head almost touching the branch. In this position the moth is an almost perfect facsimile of a short, blunt, projecting twig, for its colors are a judicious blend of grays, browns and greens that enhance the resemblance.

It is in the larval stage, however, that the prominents are most unusual, because of the great multiplicity of protective devices that they have. The

A Prominent Moth (*Nadata gibbosa*). The tufted thorax and brown wings serve to disguise it.

). **American Tent Caterpillars** (*Malacosoma americana*). A sociable species often highly destructive to Wild Cherry trees in the Spring.

The bright, black and yellow caterpillars of the **Yellow-necked Apple Worm** (*Datana ministra*) adopt a characteristic group, warning position.

larvae of many prominents have the last pair of prolegs greatly reduced in size and useless as legs. They therefore constantly hold the rear of the body up in the air, thus achieving a most unusual posture. In some genera, such as *Schizura* and *Cerura,* some of the larvae secrete powerful acids from a gland that opens on the lower surface of the prothorax, and can squirt droplets of this some inches when disturbed. Others lack the ability to squirt the acid but are obviously highly distasteful to birds and are seldom eaten by them. Such larvae are often very boldly and warningly colored, like that of the red-humped apple worm, *Schizura concinna,* which has a bright red head and patch on the body that cannot fail to catch the eye. They emphasize the effect of the bright colors by throwing both front and rear ends up in the air when disturbed, holding on by only the middle prolegs. The droplets of acid

Caterpillar of a **Prominent Moth** (*Schizura unicornis*) almost buried in the cocoons of parasitic wasp larvae that have emerged from it.

are extremely painful if they get in the eye of a human, and presumably the same holds true for birds, lizards and other caterpillar-eaters.

The larvae of the puss moths of the North American *Cerura* (Plate 84) and the European *Dicranura* are even more unusual. They are boldly marked, being colored light greenish or yellow with a dark diamond-shaped saddle on the back. When disturbed they throw both ends up and wave them about, like other prominents; but they also retract the head under the thorax, which swells greatly and bears two prominent eyelike humps. The last pair of prolegs has been greatly modified by transformation into two very long, slender whiplashes; and these are extended to double their normal length and whipped about in the air over the caterpillar. The boldly striped black-and-yellow larvae of *Datana* adopt the curled-up defense position at the slightest annoyance; and since they are gregarious, living and feeding in large groups, the effect of the whole group displaying their bright colors and violent, double-ended twitching is a very noticeable and effective warning. Such defense mechanisms are certainly effective against predators and even have some value against parasitic wasps and flies that are seeking to lay their eggs on or in the caterpillars. In the latter case, however, the value is only partial, apparently, since many of these caterpillars are parasitized by ichneumon wasps and tachinid flies. We once watched a wasp lay her eggs in every one of a batch of red-humped apple worm caterpillars, despite being obviously bothered by their secretions. She was very methodical and took some hours to complete the job. She also paid no attention to us, allowing us to photograph her repeatedly while she was laying her eggs in the larvae.

Many other prominent caterpillars, in fact the great majority, seem to have no such acid spray defense, but have evolved cryptic colors and forms that disguise them. Some of the species of *Schizura* (Plate 82) are brown, and have one or more large green patches and one or more large, pointed humps on the back. The combination most effectively breaks up the outline of the caterpillar, making it look like a twisted piece of partly dead, partly green leaf. This effect is increased by the caterpillar's habit of eating out a part of a leaf on one side of the midrib and resting in the eaten-out space. The caterpillars of the genus *Notodonta* of both Europe and North America (Plate 83) have still more contorted body forms, colored in several shades of brown. Even when feeding in plain sight they so resemble a twisted bit of dead leaf that we, even when looking for them and knowing that they were there, have gazed all around one for several moments before realizing what we were seeing.

The mirror-back caterpillars of the genus *Pheosia* are most unusual in being quite brightly shiny. The

The **Beautiful Wood Nymph** (*Eudryas grata*), an Owlet Moth, has iridescent scale tufts on the body and enormous, hairy "mittens" on its front legs.

North American *P. rimosa* has a long horn on the rear of the abdomen and thus looks like a small sphinx moth caterpillar; but the European species lack this.

OWLET MOTHS—*Family Noctuidae*

This enormous group of over twenty thousand species is by far the largest family in the order. Many workers have broken it up into a number of families, but others have promptly reassembled these in various ways. As we might expect in such a large group, there are immense differences between many of the species. Some of the smallest have no more than one-third of an inch of wing expanse, while at the other end of the scale there is a species of the New World tropical genus *Thysania* that expands a foot. The great majority of owlet moths are relatively soberly colored; but there are many brilliantly and iridescently colored species, especially in the tropics, that vie in sheer gaudiness with any other members of the order. The vast majority are nocturnal, although some groups are confirmed day fliers. One of the outstanding characteristics, which, however, is shared with several closely related families, is the possession of a pair of hearing organs located on either side of the posterior part of the thorax. These consist fundamentally of a tightly stretched membrane, or tympanum, connected internally with sensory organs, that lies in a cavity more or less covered or protected by an expanded hood. Most of the adults have the tongue well developed and feed from flowers, fruit, sap or other available sweet liquids. The majority are quite strong and fast fliers, some species making long migratory flights.

The caterpillars are as varied as the adults. Many are almost completely naked except for minute bristles, while others are clothed in dense coverings of very long hairs, sometimes with long pencils of hair several times the length of the rest of the vestiture. Some are very brightly colored, while those that feed at night, burrow in the soil or trash, or bore in plant stem tissues, are very plain. The majority are simple leaf-eaters, but many feed on all other kinds of plant material, living or dead; and a few, such as the European *Cosmia trapezina*, are consistent predators on other caterpillars. A few are aquatic. Perhaps the majority enter the ground to pupate, and do this in a simple cell with little or no cocoon; but others form very strong cocoons in which are incorporated not only much silk but the larval hairs, wood chips and other substances. In such an enormous group we can touch upon only a few high-lights.

Certainly the best known and most favored by collectors are the striking underwing moths of the great genus *Catocala* (Plate 66) of the northern hemisphere. The species range in size from little more than an inch and a half to over three inches in wing expanse. The front wings are highly cryptic in color and pattern, so that when the moth rests on bark with these wings laid back flat, covering the hind wings and the abdomen, it is often extremely difficult to perceive. The hind wings, on the other hand, are usually brilliantly colored with bold black bands and spots on a yellow, orange, scarlet or red background. When these wings are exposed the moths are as conspicious as they are inconspicuous when only the front wings are visible. Such "flash coloration," as it is called, is of great value in confusing attackers. When the moth is resting it is largely by chance that a bird, for example, may disturb it. As this happens the dull creature, indistinguishable from its background, is suddenly transformed into a brilliant flash of color. Perhaps the surprise is momentary, but only a split moment is needed for

[179

The **Green Marvel** (*Agriopodes fallax*). A nearly perfect match in both pattern and color for the pale green lichens on which it rests.

the fast-flying moth to make good its escape or at least to gain a good start. Flash coloration also works equally well in reverse; for a pursuer's attention is fixed on the most prominent feature of the moth, the bright hind wings. When, therefore, the moth dodges around a tree trunk and plasters itself flat against the bark, hiding the bright colors and showing only the cryptic ones, the confusion of the predator is very likely to make it dash past still looking for the bright colors. The essential feature is the sudden transition from a bright object, on which the attention is concentrated, to an inconspicuous one, or vice versa. This is, of course, the fundamental technique of the "magician" or prestidigitator who keeps our attention focused on a bright handkerchief or spangle-clad assistant while the trick is performed inconspicuously. The various species of *Catocala* and their relatives differ greatly in the tones and colors of their front wings, some being almost white and resting on white-barked birches; others being various shades of brown or gray, often with darker or lighter patches that simulate such objects as lichens; and still others being very dark. All species tend to come to rest on more or less matching backgrounds, a reflex mechanism something like that described for the European peppered moth probably being responsible. Some species have the hind wings black, or black and white, and a few have them pale blue. The very large tropical genera *Ophideres* of the New World and *Phyllodes* of the Old World

have the same type of brilliantly colored hind wings combined with cryptic front ones; but in their cases the front wings are much more pointed and leaflike. Some of the *Ophideres* have been recorded as doing damage to bananas and citrus fruits by puncturing them and sucking the juices, since almost alone of the Lepidoptera they have tongues that are hard and sharp enough to be used for piercing.

The genera *Thysania* and *Erebus* of the New World tropics contain some very large species, the South American owlet moth *Thysania agrippina* having been recorded as having a wing expanse of a foot, making it the greatest known in the order. It is a very pale whitish moth with many dark reticulations and with relatively narrow wings. The big, black-brown *Erebus odorata*, known as the black witch, not uncommonly flies far northward in the autumn from its tropical home, sometimes even reaching Canada.

It is especially among the tropical owlet moths that we find many species with extremely bright colors and bold patterns. The African peach moth, *Egybolis vaillantina*, for example, has the fore wings iridescent gray-green and the hind wings bluer; the base of each fore wing has a large bright orange patch, and across the middle is a band composed of dark lines and orange spots. It is probably the most beautiful of all pest insects. In the New World tropics *Noropsis hieroglyphica* has fore wings that shade from orange to cream, bearing a bold geometric design in black and metallic blue with rows of polka dots on the outer half. Such patterns may in actuality be not nearly as revealing as would seem at first glance. The North American green marvel, *Agriopodes fallax*, has pale green wings bearing a sharp design of irregular black lines and scrawls. Seen by itself, a specimen is most conspicuous. However, when one is seen resting against a background of lichens on a tree trunk, it is immediately obvious that the markings almost duplicate the shadow pattern of the crenulated edges of the lichens. Since the colors also match, the moth is actually a marvel of concealing coloration.

A large group, the subfamily Plusiinae, contains many day-flying species that may often be seen visiting flowers in company with bees and butterflies. The genus *Plusia* includes many members with bold patterns, sometimes streaked with silver and burnished with greenish or golden metallic lusters. Other groups fly during the daytime at high altitudes on mountains and in the Arctic, and some of these have brightly colored wings. The genus *Anarta*, in fact, contains some species that occur in the extreme Arctic regions where there is no night during the brief warm season.

The majority of owlet moths are, however, small to medium-sized and relatively soberly colored, typically with cryptic patterns that match them to natural backgrounds of bark, wood and dead vegetation. Many are extremely flat as adults and worm their way into very thin cracks beneath bark, where they lie concealed during the daytime or, if they hibernate as adults, during the winter. These moths are the "millers" or "dusty millers" that abound everywhere, their name originating in the abundant dust of scales that is shed from the wings when one of the moths is seized. The caterpillars of many species are destructive "cutworms" living among trash or loose soil on the surface of the ground and feeding on young sprouting plants. To the gardener they are among the most pestiferous of insects, perhaps killing an entire crop that has just begun to grow. Others, such as the New World *Leucania unipuncta* and related species on other continents, may live as cutworms when they occur in relatively small concentrations, but at times build up their numbers to form great migratory hordes of caterpillars known as "army worms," which march across country laying waste the vegetation.

The cutworms are only one harmful group, for there are many owlet caterpillars that attack other parts of plants. Many, like the cabbage looper, *Plusia ni* and its subspecies *brassicae*, are leaf-eaters. Others are fruit-borers, such as *Heliothis obsoleta*, whose caterpillar is variously known as the cotton boll worm, corn worm and tomato fruit worm, depending on what plant it is attacking. Still others are stem-borers, such as the European potato stem-borer, *Hydroecia immanis*, the columbine-borer, *Papaipema leucostigma* and the widely injurious stalk-borer, *Papaipema nebris*. Although few of the

An **Owlet Moth** (*Acronycta longa*) almost perfectly camouflaged.

owlet moth caterpillars stage such mass attacks as earn a bad name for the army worm and for many pests of other families, the group contains hundreds of species that are a steady drain on many of man's valuable plants.

Some owlet moths are well-known mass migrants, occasionally moving across large areas in great swarms. In the Old World the abundant day-flying *Plusia gamma* regularly starts northward from Africa, crosses the Mediterranean Sea and reaches Europe about the end of May. The dark sword grass, *Agrotis ypsilon*, whose larva is the destructive greasy, or black, cutworm, a cosmopolitan moth, makes great migratory flights from India northward into the cooler foothills of the Himalayas. In the New World the cotton moth, *Alabama argillacea*, a serious pest on cotton, is a very active migrant in the tropics, and in North America stages mass migrations of millions of individuals northward in October. The migrant moths fly a thousand miles beyond where any cotton can grow, and therefore can leave no progeny; but year after year the flights continue. We have seen dozens of the moths flying in the cars of New York City subway trains during a heavy migration.

Closely related to the owlet moths is the small family of the foresters, the Agaristidae. Relatively few species occur in the North Temperate Zone, the best known in North America being the small black moths with white spots of the genus *Alypia*. In Africa and the Indo-Australian regions, however, are numerous species, many of which are day fliers, that have a most imposing array of bright colors and patterns. One of these, *Agarista agricola* of India, is a striking-looking moth with a two-inch wing expanse. The wings are jet-black with narrow bands of pale green and greenish blue, and have white tips or edges. On the front wings are brilliant orange patches and rows of spots, and on each hind wing is a bar of bright scarlet. The abdomen is black and has an orange tip. Although this sounds garish, the colors actually harmonize to produce a very attractive moth.

TIGER MOTHS—*Family Arctiidae*

The tiger moths (Plates 86, 87, 99) are a large family with common representatives nearly everywhere; but like so many other similar groups they are especially abundantly represented in the tropical regions. The name comes from the appearance of a considerable number of species in the temperate zones that are colored very brightly with black and yellow or black and orange bands, spots or patches. The members of the family run strongly to such colors, although some are soberly or dully clad in browns and grays. One group is made up of species that are pure white, sometimes relieved by black and orange bands on the body, or sometimes by orange legs. An enormous variety of very brightly colored and patterned species is found in the tropics, particularly of the New World. The body and legs of many of the species are thickly garbed in dense hairs. Characteristically the front wings are rather narrow and pointed.

The caterpillars, like the adults, run strongly to hairiness; some, known as "woolly bears," are very thickly clothed with dense, bristly spines or long hairs. The best known of these are the caterpillars of the widely distributed tiger moth *Arctia caia,* of Europe and northern North America, and of the common North American *Isia isabella.* The latter, typically rich chestnut brown with jet-black ends, is frequently seen scurrying along in the autumn, seeking a suitable place in which to hibernate. A widespread superstition holds that the length of the black ends is indicative of the coming winter, short ends meaning a short, mild winter. The idea has been tested, in a humorous way, by making annual counts of considerable numbers of the caterpillars; but unfortunately for the reputation of the woolly bears as weather prophets, the records show that they are more often wrong than right, with considerable disagreement between those of neighboring localities. Tiger moth caterpillars tend to be rather less particular about their diets than those of most groups, many species feeding on a large variety of herbaceous plants. Fewer eat the leaves of trees and woody shrubs. The long hairs are usually employed in making the cocoons, being bound together by relatively small amounts of silk, to which excretory secretions are sometimes added, to make quite loose cocoons.

The most attractive group of the northern tiger moths, members of the genus *Apantesis* and related groups, have the veins of the black front wings white, creamy or yellow, and often have pink, scarlet or orange hind wings with prominent black borders and spots. When the wings are spread they are very conspicuous; but when the front wings are laid back over the hind wings they present a very fine imitation of a shadow pattern among grass blades, and quite effectively conceal the moths. The species of the genus *Utetheisa,* sometimes called calico moths, some of which abound nearly everywhere from the middle temperate regions to the equator, are delicately but very brightly colored, with orange and white front wings that bear lines of tiny dots, and white to orange or bright pink hind wings. One species, *U. pulchella* of Africa and Europe, is a well-known migrant, regularly flying northward in great numbers. Large swarms have been observed from ships; one was seen 960 miles southwest of the Cape Verde Islands.

Relatively few species are serious pests, although a great many do a bit of damage in the vegetable garden. The North American fall webworms of the genus *Hyphantria* occasionally do considerable local damage to trees, the caterpillars sometimes being abundant enough to cover the trees and shrubs over a considerable area with sheets of filmy silk webs. Some of the tiger moths of the genus *Halysidota* also may cause local damage to trees.

Very closely related to the tiger moths, and in fact often classified with them in the Arctiidae, are the lichen moths of the family Lithosiidae. They constitute a widespread group that is particularly rich in species in the Indo-Australian region. Like the tiger moths they run to bright colors and patterns, characteristically in pastel shades. The caterpillars are almost exclusively feeders on lichens.

DAY-FLYING MOTHS
—Families Syntomidae, Pericopidae etc.

There are a good many families of moths that consistently fly by day and have bright colors that rival those of the butterflies. In general they form two major groups, one rather primitive and the other quite highly specialized. The former, the Pyromorphidae and the Zygaenidae, have already been touched upon in this chapter. The latter consists of a number of families related to the owlet moths, some of which are cosmopolitan, others essentially of the New World tropics, and still others limited to the Old World. The classification has been variously split and reassembled. The large family Syntomidae and the smaller family Pericopidae are largely New World tropical, the Nyctemeridae, Callidulidae and others Old World tropical.

The Syntomids (Plates 94, 96, 100) are a group of medium-sized, narrow-winged moths, usually with small hind wings, that commonly have bright colors and bold patterns. Many are exceedingly wasplike; and those that have more or less transparent wings frequently have bright patches of color on the body. Probably the vast majority, if not all, of the species are genuinely protected against predators by bad-tasting body fluids. Their bright colors therefore are warnings. In a great many cases their colors also represent mimicry of other similarly protected insects. This type of mimicry is called "Müllerian," after the distinguished German naturalist Fritz Müller, who first formulated his ideas about it during many years of field and laboratory studies in South America. It supplements but is quite different from the more obvious Batesian mimicry, named for Englishman Henry Bates, in which an edible, unprotected species or group gains a certain immunity from attacks of predators by mimicking the appearance of a species that is genuinely protected by poisonous or bad-tasting secretions, stings or other real weapons. In Müllerian mimicry the resemblance is between two or more species or groups that are genuinely protected. By looking alike, instead of each having its own distinctive appearance, they simplify the process of learning by the local predators that they should be left strictly alone. Birds, lizards and monkeys have been shown by many experiments to have the mental capacities to learn that insects with certain appearances are inedible. But their learning ability is relatively limited, so that anything that cuts down the volume of memory work will aid the protected species. (Of course, nothing like the conscious memory of the human mind is involved here.) When, therefore, instead of having a large number of different, distinctive warning appearances, the protected species of a locality concentrate on a small number, not only do the predators learn more surely, but fewer of the protected species are killed during the educational process. This is one of the primary principles of modern advertising: to concentrate on one or a relatively few distinctive trade-marks or brand names, which are brought to the attention of the customer as often as possible. Müllerian mimicry is this in reverse, conditioning the customer *not* to sample the product!

Many of the Syntomids are brilliantly colored, with distinctive patterns that make them very conspicuous. There are many iridescent blues and greens variously combined with black, white, orange and scarlet. The same is true of the Pericopids and other families. For example a widespread Pericopid of the New World tropics that is not uncommon in southern Florida, *Composia fidelissima,* has the wings black with a deep sapphire iridescence that is quite strong on the hind wings. On both pairs of wings are borders of large white spots, and on the front of each fore wing are large scarlet patches. It is an extremely conspicuous object, whether flying or resting, effectively advertising its inedibility. Such patterns are of the warning, or aposematic, type.

The Syntomids in particular also contain a great many Müllerian mimetic groups. The majority of these Syntomids imitate wasps, having clear wings with perhaps only narrow dark borders, and spots or patches of brilliant colors on the bodies and legs, just as do many of the wasps that fly in the same regions. Sometimes the resemblance is an almost exact one to a particular species of wasp; in other cases the mimicry is merely of a general wasplike appearance. In some species the mimicry goes far beyond mere form and color, for the moths imitate the actions of the wasp, even pretending to sting by bending the abdomen around and jabbing it against an attacker although there is really no weapon there at all. The narrow-waisted appearance of the wasps is sometimes simulated by a patch of light color on either side of the base of the abdomen, making the broad-waisted moth look wasp-waisted. Some species even have a long, slender process extending out behind from the rear of the abdomen that simu-

Silver-spotted Skipper (*Epargyreus clarus*). Its robust head and body, pointed wings and hooked antennae are characteristic.

lates the long ovipositor of the Ichneumon wasps. Others have evolved an almost perfect mimicry of the distinctive appearance of the strongly protected Lycid beetles, having the wings orange with dark or blue crossbars. And quite a few of the Pericopids, as well as some Castniids, Geometrids and Dioptids, have evolved largely transparent wings, with dark, sometimes iridescent, borders and veins, that represent mimicry of or with the abundant Ithomiid butterflies that are one of the most characteristic protected groups of the New World tropics. Altogether there is a bewildering mélange of protected groups, mimicking each other and being mimicked by unprotected ones, that is sufficient to confuse utterly most students of insects. It is small wonder that the predatory birds, lizards and monkeys learn very quickly, after a small number of literally bitter experiences, to avoid practically every brightly colored insect.

SKIPPERS—Families Hesperiidae and Megathymidae

There is always a slight question whether the skippers (Plate 98) should be regarded as butterflies or not. The matter is really of little more than academic interest since, although they are unquestionably a group distinct from the true butterflies, they are nevertheless more closely related to them than to any other members of the order, fly with them, behave like them and are collected and studied with them by most naturalists. The skippers are primitive in many ways, especially in their early stages and in their wing venation. The caterpillars typically live primitively in individual silken nests or tubes, and pupate in a slight approximation of a cocoon in which the pupa is suspended by silk strands. The adults are large-headed and stout-bodied, with powerful wing muscles and relatively small, often pointed, wings. Their flight is invariably very fast and darting, whence the common name. Nearly all are active flower visitors. Their antennae

A Japanese **Skipper** (*Parnara guttata*) extends its long tongue to feed from a flower.

are clubbed like those of the true butterflies, but are almost always hooked at the tip and usually have a slender portion beyond the club. Most skippers are fairly small as butterflies go; the smallest may expand little more than one-quarter to three-eighths of an inch, while the largest, with the exception of the giant skippers (Megathymidae) seldom exceed two inches in wing expanse. The majority are rather plainly colored with browns and dull yellows; but especially in the New World tropics, the great center where more species occur than anywhere else, there are numbers of bright, sometimes iridescently, colored forms. A few are very strikingly metallic.

The true skippers are divided into a number of subfamilies, of which some are small and similar enough to others to be of interest only to specialists. A single species, *Euschemon rafflesiae*, found only in Australia, makes up the Euschemoninae. It is of great interest because, although it is undoubtedly a skipper, the males have a frenulum, the wing-coupling structure characteristic of most moths but not otherwise found in any skipper or butterfly. In this respect, therefore, it adds another to the list of curiously archaic survivals found in Australia.

The small subfamily Pyrrhopyginae of the New World tropics contains the largest and most powerful of the skippers. A large female of such a species as *Pyrrhopyge spatiosa* may have a wing expanse of nearly three inches. This does not seem large compared with the eleven- or twelve-inch expanse of one of the big owlet moths; but when we realize that the skipper has just as much wing muscle, that

is to say as much flying power, as the big moth, but only a tenth or so of the wing area, we can see that the skipper is like a terrifically powered, supersonic fighter plane with its wings cut down to a minimum, while the moth is by comparison merely an underpowered, broad-winged glider. The bodies of the skippers are usually beautifully streamlined for the speeds at which they operate, being blunt in front and tapering to a sharp, often rigid point in the rear. Their flight is extremely fast yet wonderfully controlled, as anyone can testify who has attempted to net them on the wing, for they can dodge and be out of sight before the collector has had time to realize that he has scored a miss.

Skipper caterpillars tend to be quite plain, although there are some exceptions. They often have distinctive patterns on the head (Plate 97), sometimes with a pair of large spots that look like big eyes. A prominent characteristic is the conspicuously narrow neck, making the head seem well set off from the body instead of being broadly joined to it, or even partly sunken in it, as in most other caterpillars.

The subfamily Pyrginae is rather large, containing more than six hundred species in the New World alone but less than half that many in the Old World. The species of the temperate regions tend to be plain in appearance, running to browns and checkered grays. The dusky wings, *Erynnis,* are a familiar group in North America but have far fewer species in Europe. The checkered skippers, *Pyrgus,* on the other hand, are the dominant group of the subfamily in Eurasia, but have relatively few species in North America. One circumpolar species, *Pyrgus centaureae,* occurs widely in the subarctic and southward in alpine zones on mountain tops to New Mexico. It is in the New World tropics, however, that the majority of the species are found; and here are many large, powerful, exceedingly handsome forms. In the genera *Elbella, Jemadia* and *Phocides* are numerous species, some as large as two and a half inches in expanse, with the wings crossed by white, black and iridescent blue stripes; some of the *Phocides* add orange stripes, and others are all dark with shining blue on the hind wings. Numerous species of *Astraptes* have black wings with brilliant blue basal areas; and the smaller species of *Quadrus, Pythonides, Sostra,* etc. have the hind wings iridescent blue crossed by bold black bands.

Such widespread genera as *Urbanus* and *Chioides* have the wings brown to black with light spots and often dull green or blue iridescence, and very long, gracefully curved tails on the hind wings. The peculiar South American *Phareas celeste,* on the other hand, has the wings very broad and rounded and a pattern of small white spots on the dark fore wings that makes it resemble very strikingly some of the satyrs. It is a most un-skipper-like skipper.

Eutheus and *Cabirus* have the black wings crossed with orange patches, making them resemble the common day-flying Dioptid moths that are involved in so many mimicry groups in the New World tropics. It is hard to believe that mimicry is not involved in the appearance of these skippers, even though the group in general is almost unique in taking no part in mimetic relationships. In contrast to all others, *Haemactis* has very angulate black wings with broad pinkish red borders cut by black veins. Having no part in this riot of color, the species of *Heliopetes* are silky white with black borders and those of *Aethilla* are plain jet-black with sharp white edges. With their sharp fore wings and streamlined figures, the last are fully as distinguished as the bright colored groups.

It is both difficult and unsafe to generalize about such a large group, especially when so many of the life histories are totally unknown. Nevertheless the Pyrginae, in general, feed on a great variety of broad-leaved plants but favor the legumes (Fabaceae), at least in the temperate zones. The caterpillars often prepare nests, when they are young cutting loose a piece of a leaf to form a flap which they fold over, and when they are older rolling up a whole leaf or tying several together. In contrast, again at least in the temperate regions, the caterpillars of the next subfamily, the Hesperiinae, are largely grass-feeders, and often dispense with definite nests though they may web some grass together.

The Hesperiinae are the largest group, containing over a thousand species in the New World, but fewer than half of that in the Old World. They tend on the average to be much smaller in size than the Pyrginae and, especially in the temperate regions but also considerably in the tropics, to be brown, orange-brown or yellow. The males of many of the genera have a very characteristic line of special scales, called the brand or stigma, running diagonally on the front wings. This presumably acts as either a recognition mark or an attraction to the females during courtship. It is often a very prominent object. Many of the species have exceedingly rapid, darting

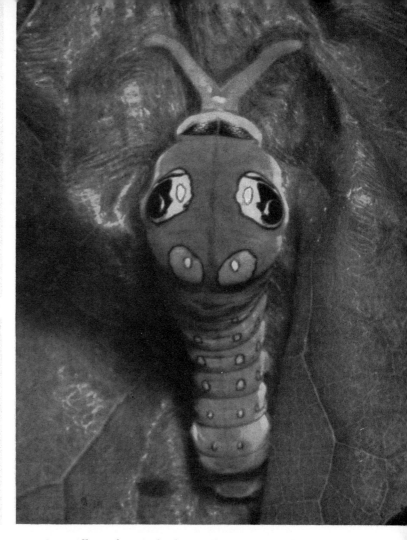

Caterpillar of **Spicebush Swallowtail** (*Papilio troilus*) extending its orange scent organs as a defensive reaction. (See also color plate 91.)

flights that seem much faster than they really are because of the small size of the skippers and the erratic course followed. We know of no exact measurements of rate, but it is doubtful if any exceed thirty miles an hour at any time, even in short bursts; and the average of even the fast species is probably less than twenty miles an hour.

Two genera of the New World tropical Hesperiinae stand out from all the others because of extraordinary colorings that would be unusual in any group. The species of *Argopteron,* whose wings are dark brown on the upper surface with a few orange spots, are solid, metallic golden underneath. And *Dalla semiargentea* has the fore wings solid brown, but the hind wings iridescent silvery to pearly white.

The giant skippers (Megathymidae) are a small family limited to the northern tropics of the New World, a few species occurring in the southern and Great Plains regions of the United States and others in Mexico. They are very large, some families having a wingspread of as much as three inches, and are extremely heavy-bodied. Their colors typically consist of large yellow or whitish spots or patches on a brown background. The caterpillars are all borers

Caterpillar of **Evemon Swallowtail** (*Graphium evemon*) has small but realistic eyespots on the body.

(Left) Caterpillar of **European Swallowtail** (*Papilio machaon*), preparing to change to the chrysalis, has spun a silk girdle and pad that will hold it in place; (second from left) it sheds its skin, exposing front end of chrysalis; (second from right) completely exposed chrysalis; and (right) adult emerging from chrysalis and spreading its wings. The trans-

in the stems or fleshy leaf bases of yuccas (Spanish bayonets) and agaves, characteristic plants of the arid regions. They may make a silk-lined tube running off to some distance to one side of the plant, from which they dispose of their excreta. They pupate in this or in the tunnel, the adult emerging through the already prepared exit hole. The pupae have considerable power of motion along the tube. The adults are extremely fast-flying and difficult to net, but the larvae and pupae can be found at the bases of the spiky leaves of the yuccas.

SWALLOWTAILS and THEIR RELATIVES
—Family Papilionidae

Although a relatively small family of butterflies, the swallowtails (Plates 92, 93) are widely known, at least some of the species being prominent in nearly every part of the world. Only in the Arctic regions are none found. The great majority have usually been placed in the genus *Papilio*, but in recent years this has been split into a number of genera. The species differ enormously in size, some being among the largest of butterflies while others expand

no more than two inches. Despite the common name of the family and the fact that we think of these butterflies as having tails on the hind wings, there are many tailless species of *Papilio*, and some entire genera lack tails. In fact, in *Papilio memmon* of Asia and *P. dardanus* of Africa, some females are tailed and others tailless.

Swallowtail caterpillars (Plate 91) show a wide variety of colors and patterns, but all agree in having, in the groove between the head and the thorax, a protrusible, usually yellow or orange, Y-shaped organ, the osmeterium. This connects with glands in the thorax in such a way that when the caterpillar protrudes it, as it does when disturbed, a powerful scent is disseminated. In many cases this is extremely pungent and repulsive to humans, but in others it emits a rather pleasant aromatic odor. It definitely functions as a defense weapon, repelling such enemies as birds.

A number of swallowtail caterpillars have a characteristic pattern consisting of a pair of eyelike black and yellow spots on the thorax that are sometimes incredibly like real eyes. Since this part of the body

formation to the chrysalis takes ten to fifteen minutes; the transformation to the adult butterfly within the chrysalis requires from ten days to seven months depending upon the season. The emergence of the adult and the expansion of its wings may take place in fifteen minutes to a half-hour.

is quite swollen and the true head is small and more or less tucked down below it, such a caterpillar does look, to a human at least, like the front end of a snake with big eyes. Of course, a bird suddenly confronted with such an apparition is likely to start back or at least to fail to eat the caterpillar, or to delay long enough for the scent mechanism of the osmeterium to come into play. It is doubtful if any birds, lizards or similar predators think that the caterpillar is a snake, or, for that matter, think at all. The eyespots are found in caterpillars of many species of both Asia and the New World, being, perhaps, most realistic in the common spicebush swallowtail, *P. troilus,* of eastern North America.

The pupae or chrysalids of the swallowtails are often angulate objects that resemble green leaves or irregular bits of twig or bark. They are suspended by the rear end of the abdomen, where a structure called the cremaster is engaged in a firmly attached button of silk, and also by a silk girdle that passes around the thorax. Like the great majority of butterfly pupae, they are otherwise unattached and not covered by a cocoon.

The kite swallowtails, most of which are placed in the genus *Graphium,* are mostly light-colored, ranging from white and pale yellow to light greenish, with extremely long, slender, pointed tails. The wings are typically crossed by a number of thin, dark bands. The pale yellow *G. podalirius* ranges from central Europe through central Asia and China, and the pale green *G. ajax* ranges over much of central and southern North America. There are, however, tailless and darker-colored species such as the common *G. sarpedon* of Asia, which is black with a band of large green spots crossing the wings. In the tropics there are many of the kites, at least one or two being common in nearly every region in both the Old and New Worlds.

The Aristolochia swallowtails, many of which belong to the genus *Battus,* are another world-wide group, although there are many more in the New World tropics than elsewhere. Along the inner margin of the hind wings of the males is a large fold, inside which are thick, felted masses of scent hairs and scales. The caterpillars feed on plants of the world-wide family Aristolochiaceae, as a result of which they acquire highly distasteful and poisonous qualities that last through to the adult. They are therefore well protected from predators and are much mimicked by other swallowtails and butterflies of many groups. None occurs in Europe, and only one consistently lives in North America, the black-and-blue Dutchman's-pipe swallowtail, *Battus philenor*. Asia has a number of species and the New World tropics a great many. Some of these are tailed; many are tailless. In general they are black and have brilliantly colored patches, bands or rows of spots of iridescent blue, green and red. A characteristic South American group, containing such species as the widespread *B. erlaces, aeneas* and *childrenae*, has a bright green patch on the front wing and a bright red patch on the hind wing. The latter is structurally colored in some of the species, for when one looks at it at a very acute angle the red changes abruptly to a brilliant iridescent blue.

Very closely related to the Aristolochia swallowtails, and feeding on the same plants as larvae, are the magnificent bird-winged butterflies of the genus *Troïdes* (*Ornithoptera* in many books) of the Indo-Australian region. The wings of the males of most of the species are velvety black, with bands, rows of spots or large areas of intensely colored iridescent blue, green or gold, sometimes with a patch of crimson on the head and body or with the whole abdomen golden. The front wings are very long and graceful and the hind wings small. Most of the species have the hind wings tailless, but in *T. paradisea* there is a very thin, peculiarly bent tail. The males of some of the species expand as much as seven inches. The females are considerably larger, some expanding ten inches or more, and usually lack the bright iridescent colors of the males, having the wings crossed with rows of white spots. Ever since people began collecting butterflies, the *Troïdes* have been among the most desirable of all prizes, sums amounting to several hundred dollars having been paid for single specimens. We now know that few, if any, of the species are really rare in their proper habitats, but since some live in extremely inaccessible regions in interior New Guinea and other Australasian islands, and are difficult to catch because of their habit of flying at great heights in the forest canopy, several species are still, when in perfect condition, exceedingly choice collectors' items.

One of our favorite descriptions, and one that gives better than any other a feeling for the dramatic beauty of these butterflies, was written by the great Alfred Russel Wallace about his collecting in the Aru Islands: "The next day . . . I had the good fortune to capture one of the most magnificent insects the world contains, the great bird-winged butterfly, Ornithoptera poseidon. I trembled with excitement as I saw it coming majestically toward me, and could hardly believe that I had really succeeded

Spicebush Swallowtail (*Papilio troilus*), adult.

in my stroke until I had taken it out of the net and was gazing, lost in admiration, at the velvety black and brilliant green of its wings, seven inches across, its golden body and crimson breast. It is true I had seen similar insects at home, but it is quite another thing to capture such oneself—to feel it struggling between one's fingers, and to gaze upon its fresh and living beauty, a bright gem shining out amid the silent gloom of a dark and tangled forest. The village of Dobbo held that evening at least one contented man."

The final group, the genus *Papilio,* contains many more species than any of the others. They are known as the fluted swallowtails because of the curved, fluted inner margins of the hind wings, which, however, lack scent scales such as occur in the Aristolochia-feeding group. Here belong the most familiar species of the north temperate regions. The only widely spread European swallowtail is *P. machaon,* whose caterpillar, banded with pale green and black, feeds on parsley, fennel, carrot and similar umbelliferous plants. It has several close relatives in North America, the most widespread being the common black swallowtail, *P. polyxenes asterius* of the East, and *P. zelicaon* and others of the West. More widespread in North America are the tiger swallowtails, the Eastern *P. glaucus* and the Western *rutilus* and others, big yellow species with narrow black bands across the wings, which occur almost everywhere and are familiar sights visiting flowers or sailing overhead. In the tropics of all countries there are dozens of common and familiar species and quite a few rare ones as well; and so varied is the group that it would be futile to try to describe even the chief types of patterns and colors.

Many swallowtails are mimics of protected butterflies. The most famous of these is *P. dardanus* of Africa, normally a tailed species with broad areas of white on dark wings. In some regions both males and females conform to the normal appearance; but in others the females have lost the tails and developed totally different patterns, mimicking the highly protected, bright orange-brown, black and white Danaids. Another widespread species, the common *P. clytia* of Asia, likewise mimics protected Danaids, but in this case simulates a group that has the veins dark and the areas between them whitish, greenish or yellowish broken by cross lines. Until he comes to know them well a collector can never be sure whether he is seeing mimic or model until he catches it. Even more surprising a mimic is the South American *P. zagreus,* which has evolved a bright orange-brown and black pattern unlike any other swallowtails but closely mimetic of the Heliconiids and Ithomiids, the dominant protected butterflies of the region.

One of the swallowtails most desired by collectors is the big *P. homerus* of Jamaica (nearly a six-inch wingspread and very broad wings). Its black wings are crossed by broad yellow bands and have a row of iridescent blue spots on the hind ones. It flies only in certain restricted regions of the one island, has only one generation a year and is quite difficult to collect except when the males alight in wet dirt (a common swallowtail habit) to suck the moisture.

The widespread genus *Parnassius* contains a considerable number of tailless species found in the alpine regions from Europe across Asia to New Mexico. White and thinly scaled, the butterflies have fine black-and-gray markings and black-and-red eyespots pupiled with white on the hind wings. *P. apollo* is the best-known European species, *P. smintheus* the most familiar in North America. A few are yellow, a few others add blue eyespots as well. They are great favorites of collectors, partly because of their restricted high mountain habitats, partly because of their real beauty and partly because they offer interesting studies in variation. A few species are extremely rare, being known only from a handful of specimens from the wild and inaccessible mountain ranges of central Asia.

Other genera show still greater divergences of color, pattern and shape. The very plain, dull yellowish brown *Baronia brevicornis,* a relict of some ancient glacial age, is found only on a few mountains in the Mexican highlands. The Asian *Armandia* has three tails on each hind wing. The Indian *Teinopalpus imperialis* is iridescent green with sharply pointed fore wings and bright orange marks and tail tips on the hind wings. On the other hand, the little *Leptocircus* of the Indo-Australian region expand as little as one and one-eighths inches and have considerable transparent area on the black wings and disporportionately large, pointed tails;

while the enormous *Drurya antimachus* of Africa has long, slender fore wings that expand eight inches and is tailless and orange-brown with black borders and rounded spots and bars. In truth, within this single family there is so much variety that one never wearies of studying swallowtails.

SULPHURS, ORANGES and WHITES
—Family Pieridae

This large, world-wide family of more than a thousand members contains many of the most familiar butterflies everywhere. The very name "butterfly" is based on one of the common European sulphurs, very likely the species known as the brimstone, *Gonepteryx rhamni.* These butterflies have, in general, fairly strong, often vigorous flights and are mostly common flower visitors; they are therefore likely to be prominent. The caterpillars of perhaps the majority are cylindrical, green, and covered with a short pile or down; but those of some groups bear numbers of short, spiny tubercles, although none is as spiny or hairy as many other butterfly larvae. Most of the pupae, which are suspended by a silk girdle around the body as well as by attachment of the rear end of the abdomen to a silk button, have a projecting horn on the center of the head that often makes them resemble sharp twigs or spines.

The colors of this family are unusual in being pigments derived from the uric acid excretory products. We have no clue as to why this one cosmopolitan group should have evolved these chemically distinctive pigments, but the fact remains that it is perfectly feasible to identify a butterfly as a member of this family by chemical analysis of the scales without ever having seen the specimen. A few members have structural colors that produce a satiny or silvery effect, particularly on patches of male sex scales, and a few others have some iridescent blue or pur-

Veined White (*Aporia crataegi*). A familiar European Butterfly.

ple, sometimes strikingly combined with underlying orange or red pigments; but the majority have only pigment colors that alone are enough to make them extremely attractive. Sexual dimorphism is quite marked in a number of groups, the males and females differing, sometimes very greatly, in pattern and even color. In many such instances the differences are not great enough to be of any protective significance, but in others the females are protectively colored while the males are showy and prominent. In some instances the females mimic distasteful, protected butterflies of other families, and in others they are concealingly colored. Even when they most resemble other butterflies their pigments are still of the uric acid type.

The whites of the subfamily Pierinae contain many species, some common nearly everywhere. In the North Temperate Zone the small white, *Pieris rapae,* known in North America (where it was introduced) as the European cabbage butterfly, and the large white *P. brassicae,* fortunately still limited to Europe and Asia, are serious pests on all cultivated plants of the cabbage-mustard family (Cruciferae). They are the most destructive members of the family; but another that sometimes does considerable damage is the pine white, *Neophasia menapia,* of western North America, a member of a small group that has adopted the habit, unusual for a Pierid, of feeding on coniferous trees. Some of the most interesting of the whites are the small, drab species of *Phulia* and *Piercolias* of the Andes and *Baltia* of Central Asia that live only at very high altitudes up to eighteen thousand feet or more, where scarcely any other butterflies or moths exist.

Most familiar of the sulphurs are the members of

Chrysalids of **Falcate Orange Tip** (*Anthocaris midea*) are slender, sharp and mottled brown. They strikingly resemble thorns or short twigs.

Chrysalis of **Orange Barred Sulphur** (*Phoebis philea*) is pale green with greatly expanded, leaf-like wing cases.

the widespread genus *Colias,* yellow or orange with black borders. Most common in Europe are *C. hyale* (yellow) and *C. edusa* and *myrmidone* (orange); and in North America *C. philodice* (yellow) and *C. eurytheme* (orange). The former of these North American species is the often abundant "mud puddle" butterfly, so called because the young males rest in large numbers around puddles and on damp earth, sucking the moisture. The latter is the alfalfa butterfly (Plate 95), sometimes a serious pest. A related species in South America is likewise an occasional pest on alfalfa and clover. In central Asia occur the most magnificent species, highly desired by collectors, such as the flame-orange *C. romanovi* and the unusual blue *C. sagartia.* An orange species, *C. hecla,* is one of the most northern of all insects, occurring from arctic Scandinavia to Ellesmere Island and Greenland.

In the tropics of both the Old and New Worlds members of *Catopsilia* and *Phoebis* are both abundant and extremely prominent. They are relatively large, some expanding three inches. Some species are solid yellow, some white with yellow borders, and others orange. The magnificent *P. avellanada* of Cuba is intense orange, boldly marked with crimson. Some of these butterflies are among the most noted of all migrants, swarms of many millions often being seen steadily making their way in one direction. In some notable instances the migrations appear to be, in effect, mass suicides; for the swarms head out into the ocean, which they can never cross and from which they never return. Charles Darwin recorded such a migration of these butterflies when his ship, the *Beagle,* was off the eastern coast of South America. A much smaller species, no more than an inch and a half in expanse, is the least sulphur, *Eurema lisa,* which is common over most of the eastern United States and ranges southward in the tropics. It has been observed in great flocks over the Atlantic, at least some of which have successfully made the trip of about six hundred miles to Bermuda.

One of the smallest of the sulphurs is the dainty sulphur, *Nathalis iole,* of North America, which expands as little as three-quarters of an inch. Still smaller are the tiny whites of the tropics of the genus *Leucidia,* less than one-half inch. The angled sulphurs of the New World tropical genus *Anteos,* on the other hand, have a wingspread of three and a half inches; and *Hebomoia glaucippe* of the Indo-Australian region, which is white with broad, orange tips on the front wings, may surpass four inches.

The large genus *Delias* of the Indo-Australian region is one of the most interesting groups of the family. A few of the species are brightly colored above, but the majority are rather plain white with dark borders. Quite unlike most other butterflies and moths, however, they have an extraordinary assortment of colors and patterns on the undersides of the wings; and there is little consistency in this among various species, so that one simply cannot tell from looking at the upper surface what to expect on the lower. One will be orange with black borders; another black with orange and scarlet edges. Although some *Delias* are common in India, Australia and other well-known lands, many species occur in the mountainous and as yet more or less unexplored interior of New Guinea, along with the marvelous birds of paradise and bower birds. Many of them are still, therefore, exceedingly rare in collections and are much sought after; and there are doubtless many species as yet undiscovered.

The subfamily Dismorphiinae is almost wholly limited to the American tropics, the plain white European genus *Leptidea* being the only others known. The males are noted for their extremely unusual colors, patterns and wing shapes, quite unlike any others of the family. Some have the wings largely dark brown, with perhaps the tips of the front wings sharply pointed or strongly hooked. On the hind wings are enormous patches of sex scales

that may have a pearly or almost metallic luster. The females, on the other hand, are either relatively normal-looking Pierids, white, yellow or orange, or else they mimic orange and black Heliconiid and Ithomiid butterflies that fly in the same regions. Others mimic transparent-winged Ithomiids. It is very possible that the Dismorphias are themselves distasteful to birds, but this is by no means certain, so that we cannot say whether they are examples of Batesian or Müllerian mimicry.

BLUES, COPPERS and HAIRSTREAKS
—Family Lycaenidae

Many of our familiar butterflies belong to this world-wide family, most members of which are, for butterflies, small to minute. In every part of the world it is hard to be out of doors during the warm seasons without seeing some species of blue or copper. The blues and hairstreaks, although well represented in the boreal and temperate regions, are most abundant in the tropics; the coppers, however, are scarce or absent in the tropics, a very few in Africa and New Zealand being nearly the only ones outside of the north temperate regions.

The caterpillars are quite distinctive, being typically short, stout and sluglike, or shaped like the common sowbugs or woodlice. The legs are short and inconspicuous, and the head is bent down beneath the thorax, into which in many species it is retracted. A great many of the species show a strong development of honeydew glands, the sweet secretion of which is greatly relished by ants. These insects commonly attend the caterpillars on the food plant and often defend them against enemies. In quite a number of species the caterpillars are taken into ant nests and live there as welcome guests. Some others, however, invade ant nests and prey on the ant larvae. A small group in southern Asia has

Common Blue (*Polyommatus icarus*). Widespread and familiar European butterfly.

caterpillars that regularly feed on aphids, and one North American species does the same. Many other Lycaenid caterpillars, although not regularly carnivorous, are noted for their occasional cannibalism. This family, in fact, shows a more interesting variety of larval habits than any other in the order.

The blues (Plebeiinae) are the largest of the groups, containing several hundred species in all. In general they are small, fragile butterflies. Not all are blue, for many of the species are whitish or brown, and in a great many the females tend to be almost wholly brown. The undersides of the wings are commonly marked with one or two rows of fine, dark spots; and there is often a marginal row of orange and scintillant blue spots that may also occur on the upper side. Some groups have tails on the hind wings, and more strongly resemble hairstreaks. They are especially numerous in the Indo-Australian regions, such genera as *Lampides* being particularly prominent. The smallest of butterflies is the tiny pigmy blue, *Brephidium exilis,* of southern North America, which may have a wing expanse of less than half an inch. The larvae of many blues have a honey gland that opens on the back behind the seventh segment and secretes the ant-attracting honeydew. The European *Maculinea arion* is a good example of a species closely associated with ants. The eggs are laid on thyme, on which the larvae feed for some time until partly grown. The honey gland does not become functional until the second instar, but thereafter ants, such as the common wood ant, *Formica rufa,* visit the larva, caressing it with their long legs and antennae and thus stimulating it to produce a drop of honeydew. This continues for some time until the caterpillar ends its fourth instar, when it leaves the plant and wanders about. When it encounters an ant it is picked up and carried fo the ant nest. Here it feeds for a time on the ant brood, meanwhile giving drops of honeydew to its host ants; and in this stage it passes the winter. In the spring it transforms to a pupa and shortly to an adult butterfly, and then leaves the ant nest and sets about finding a mate and plants of thyme on which to lay eggs.

In the case of this blue, as well as of others in various continents, the relationship with the ants appears to have progressed to the point where the caterpillar is dependent on the ant. In some species the ant actually carries the caterpillar to fresh food plants. In the majority of the species there is no such dependence, although the caterpillars doubtless gain varying amounts of protection from the ants that attend them on the food plants. Some blue caterpillars lack the specialized honey gland. The largest number of species intimate with ants are known from South Africa, but many undoubtedly occur elsewhere. There is some evidence that even in the case of a species that is merely attended upon its food plant by the ants, it is more or less necessary for the proper growth of the caterpillar that it be stimulated to secrete honeydew.

The coppers (Lycaeninae) are small butterflies (Plate 114) that are usually more or less coppery and iridescent. They fly considerably faster than most of the blues, having proportionately larger bodies and more powerful wing muscles. The caterpillars do not have a single large honey gland like that of so many of the blues, but instead secrete honeydew from small, scattered glands. The most widespread and common species of both Europe and the northeastern United States, where it may be a very early introduction, is the small or American copper, *Lycaena phlaeas.* Many subspecies of this butterfly are known, ranging widely into Africa and across central and northern Asia; one of these, the subspecies *feildeni,* is known from nearly as far north as any butterfly, having been described from Ellesmere Island, and is one of the five species of butterflies known to occur in Greenland. New Zealand has three species that show a definite relationship to the North Temperate Zone species, although there are no "connecting links" in between; their ancestors must have gotten there at some remote time in the past when there was a land connection with Asia.

The hairstreaks (Theclinae, Plates 118, 119) are so called because of the presence in most of the familiar species of fine, hairlike tails on the hind wings, and of small, streaky marks on the undersides of the wings. They number many species in all continents, but are especially abundant in the New World tropics, where some of the largest and finest are found. Their flight is fast and erratic, often scarcely to be followed with the eye. Their caterpillars feed fairly consistently on the leaves or flowers of woody shrubs and trees, although some eat herbs; and the adults are much given to abruptly pitching down and resting on the leaves of such plants. They show very strongly a curious habit that is more or less characteristic of most Lycaenids, resting with the front wings held tight together up over the back but the hind wings spread slightly apart and moved forward and backward alternately with each other.

Many of the hairstreaks lack tails, having the rear margins of the hind wings merely rounded or scalloped. Quite a number of species are bright green beneath, this color being highly concealing when the butterflies are resting among foliage with the wings over the back. The European and North American species of *Callophrys* and most of the North American *Mitoura* are thus strongly green. Especially in the Indo-Australian and New World tropics are many species with intense blue iridescence on the upper side of the wings, few of the Temperate Zone species being other than plain brown with perhaps some orange. But the tropical hairstreaks contain many species that rival even the brightest of the big Morphoes in brilliance, and would certainly be as famous and sought after by collectors if they were larger. We, ourselves, prefer hairstreaks. In the Indo-Australian region such large genera as *Amblypodia*, *Rapala* and *Pontia* contain many beautiful species; and the same is true of the *Thecla* of the New World tropics. Some of them, such as the large *Thecla coronata*, which expands more than an inch and three-quarters and is a giant among hairstreaks, not only have the wings iridescent blue above, but underneath are iridescent blue or green, set off boldly with black and white lines and crimson and orange spots on the hind wings. This sounds too gaudy to be beautiful; and so it probably would be were it not for the fact that somehow the colors and patterns are exquisitely blended and proportioned. The hairstreaks, too, are a never ending source of surprise, for they seem to follow no rules as to pattern of the undersides. We can line up five specimens of different species with the upper side of the wings ranging from white through pure blue to a deep iridescent cobalt. On the underside one will have the wings deep, velvety brown-black; another will be black with broad metallic green-gold and blue bars curving across the wings; another will be white with a bold zebra pattern of black; another will be iridescent velvety green and blue, dusted with black scales, with a great scarlet patch on each hind wing; and another will be pale, pearly gray with rows of black dots across the wings.

The small subfamily Gerydinae of southern Asia, and the single species, the harvester, *Feniseca tarquinius*, of eastern North America, have carried the somewhat carnivorous habits of so many of the Lycaenids to its logical conclusion and have become entirely predatory. The caterpillars of both groups feed on the small, teeming and defenseless aphids or plant lice that abound everywhere. The caterpillars are squat, hairy creatures that often become thoroughly covered with the fragments and secretions of their prey. The chrysalis of the harvester is a surprisingly faithful miniature replica of a monkey's head. It is a pity that it is only about one-eighth of an inch long, for otherwise it would be a wonderful subject for speculation by some of our overenthusiastic naturalists, who are always seeing fanciful resemblances to crocodiles, snakes and owls in various insects, and then stating that these were developed for the purpose of frightening away birds and monkeys.

One extraordinary Australian Lycaenid, *Liphyra brassolis,* expands as much as three inches, nearly twice as much as any other member of the family. Its orange-and-black pattern, too, is unlike the others. Its caterpillar is an exceedingly thickly armored creature that lives in the nests of the viciously stinging tree ants (*Oecophylla*) and preys on the ant brood. The pupa, which is formed in the ant nest, is also armored. The soft, fragile adult butterfly, however, has no such protection; and as it emerges from the pupa the ants rush at it. But it has a covering of thick loose scales on the wings, and these clog the jaws of the ants as the butterfly heads for the exterior at a fast run. By the time it gets outside it is usually quite thoroughly stripped of the special scales (although occasional specimens show them in numbers) and down to the layer of normal wing scales beneath them. It runs away some distance,

(Left) Chrysalis of the **Harvester Butterfly** (*Feniseca tarquinius*) bears a striking resemblance to a tiny monkey's head. (Right) **Harvester Butterfly,** adult, after emerging from the chrysalis and expanding its wings. Its caterpillar is carnivorous.

spreads its wings and flies. It then mates and, if a female, lays its eggs near other ant nests. If ever an animal lived a life of continual danger, with no right to have survived, this is it.

METALMARKS—Family Riodinidae
(Erycinidae)

This cosmopolitan family of small butterflies (Plate 115) is in some ways intermediate between the Lycaenids and the great mass of brush-footed butterflies and their kin. But its real relationship is with the Lycaenids; perhaps they should together form a single family. It has some members in every continent, but is poorly represented in the Old World, the great majority of species being South American. North America has more than Europe, since a number of tropical groups have outlying members there. The common name arises from the presence on the wings of many species of small, metallic-looking flecks. The butterflies have fairly active flights and a habit of alighting on the underside of leaves upside down, and with the wings spread out flat.

The sole commonly and widely distributed European species is the Duke of Burgundy fritillary, *Nemeobius* (*Hamearis*) *lucina,* a small brown-checkered species. In the entire Indo-Australian region no more than sixty species are known, most of which are similarly small and dull-colored. We have some very attractive ones from New Guinea belonging to the genera *Laxita* and *Sospita* that have bright pink and red washes on the outer parts of the wings. The majority of the fifteen or so North American species are rather undistinguished.

In the New World tropics, however, the group simply runs riot, hundreds of species forming a completely bewildering mélange of pigmental and structural colors, patterns and wing shapes that defies any generalizations save that anything is possible. In most groups one gets accustomed to a certain family resemblance and can usually say with some certainty, "That looks like a satyr" or "That should be a nymphalid." Not so with the metalmarks—the most one can say is, "That is probably nothing else, so it must be a metalmark." A good part of the complication arises from the fact that a number of the groups have become mimics of the major protected groups of butterflies and moths. But aside from this, the various genera have evolved almost every possible combination of colors and wing shapes. A curious fact is that, although there are so many species, one seldom catches any one in numbers. In a single day's collecting in Brazil we have taken representatives of twenty-eight species (close to double the number found in all of North America) but no more than a half-dozen specimens of any one, and only a single specimen each of the majority.

The genus *Stalachtis* contains species rather large for metalmarks, with a wing expanse up to two and a quarter inches, that are very good mimics of some of the abundant, protected Heliconiid and Ithomiid butterflies. Thus *S. calliope* and *magdalena* mimic brilliant orange-brown and black striped models. On the other hand *S. lineata, phaedusa* and *zephyrites* mimic other species that have the wings largely transparent with black veins and marks, and a mere patch of orange-brown on the fore wing, *zephyrites* in particular being an excellent mimic of certain Ithomiids. Similarly good Ithomiid mimics occur in the genus *Ithomiola,* quite unrelated to *Stalachtis.*

The members of the genera *Rhetus* and *Chorinea,* some of which range northward in Mexico, are unusual even in this family for their very pointed, triangular fore wings and long-tailed hind wings. Some have a band of scarlet crossing each wing, others have the crossbands whitish, and in still others, such as *C. arsius* and *dysonii,* the crossbands are transparent. Then in *C. faunus* the transparent bands are so wide as to occupy most of the wing, leaving only a narrow black margin. The long tails are frequently brilliantly iridescent blue, set off by a scarlet patch at the base of each. These butterflies resemble strongly the little Indo-Australian swallow-tails of the genus *Leptocircus.* If the two groups only occurred in the same region we would undoubtedly lay the resemblance to mimicry of some sort; but since several thousand miles separate them the similarity is only a chance one. The species of *Ancyluris* have similar, though shorter, tails; and on the underside the wings have an intense, almost glittering, blue iridescence that is unsurpassed in brilliance by any other animals.

Many other genera have iridescent colors, some of the species of *Theope* in particular strongly resembling some of the blue hairstreaks in wing shape and other features as well. The small species of *Caria* are dusted with iridescent green and gold scales that give an unusually pleasing effect. In contrast the tiny species of *Mesene,* some with a wing expanse of less than three-quarters of an inch, are solid bright scarlet with narrow dark margins; and *Hyphilaria parthenis* is broadly zebra-striped with black, in the males on an orange ground, in the females on white. And as unusual as any are the species of *Helicopis,* with creamy to light orange ground color, dark borders, and several long tails on each hind wing, the longest tipped with white. We had to catch several dozen specimens of these in Brazil in order to get one that did not have some of the tails broken.

Related to the metalmarks are the members of the small family Libytheidae, known as "snout butterflies" because of the extraordinary length of the palpi, which project in front like a long, straight beak. The wings are angulate and patterned with darker and lighter shades of browns. One or two species occur in each of the major faunal regions of the world, ours in North America being *Libytheana bachmanii*. There are a few records of migrations of this butterfly in Texas.

MORPHOES—*Family Morphoidae*

Although a small family of less than fifty species that is confined to the New World tropics, the Morphoes (Plate 112) are one of the best-known and most famous of all the groups of butterflies. They and the owl butterflies are closely related to the Nymphalids. No other insects possess such great areas of astoundingly iridescent blue as solidly covers the wings of the males of some of the species. The first sight of even a dead specimen of such species as *Morpho rhetenor, cypris* or *sulkowskii* is breathtaking because of their combination of size and brilliance. We shall never forget our first sight of *rhetenor* flying swiftly toward us along a partly shaded forest trail in Brazil; each time the butterfly passed through a shaft of sunlight the flash of blue from the wings was like an unbelievably brilliant spark. We had barely presence of mind to swing the net and miss it by three feet as it shot past; and the fact that as it passed overhead we could suddenly see nothing but its dark, cryptically colored underside doubtless had something to do with our poor aim. Again, we have seen Morphoes from a low-flying airplane, soaring like jewels over the top of the forest canopy, the flashing blue of their wings plainly visible from several hundred feet above.

Morpho rhetenor is a solid, deep, unmarked blue above, while *cypris* has the wings crossed by a pattern of yellow or whitish patches that are, nevertheless, just as blue and iridescent. Both have slender, tapering and curving front wings, and expanses up to five and a half inches. The pearl morpho, *M. sulkowskii,* is much paler and translucent, with the pattern of the underside showing through above, and has an even more glittering iridescence that changes color like mother-of-pearl with every shift of the light or every changing angle. These three are the most famous for the extent and depth of their iridescence, which is strongly three-dimensional. Many others have broader black wings with a wide crossband of a duller yet still strongly iridescent blue. The largest of all, *M. hecuba,* with a wing expanse as great as seven inches, entirely lacks the hard glitter of the others but is an exceedingly beautiful butterfly in its own way, having its almost black wings crossed by a broad band that shades from an intense orange-brown to a lighter yellow. In all of these it is the males that are brightest; the females, the biologically less expendable producers and custodians of the eggs, are relatively plainly and cryptically colored, although many have considerable blue iridescence, and have broader, less graceful wings.

As was described under the Uraniid moths, the iridescent colors are due to microscopic structures in the scales which break up the light into different wave lengths by purely physical means. These are thin parallel layers in the fine raised ridges that lie along each of the scales; and in the Morphoes the layers are set at an acute angle to the plane of the flat scale, a feature that is responsible for the changeability and almost mirror-like reflecting quality of the iridescence.

The caterpillars of the Morphoes are hairy creatures that live and pupate communally in a jointly spun web. They bear poisonous hairs which, although not as toxic as those of some of the moths, are still able to produce a very irritating rash on the human skin. Despite this, large numbers of the showier species are bred and reared commercially in Brazil, since the wings are used in making jewelry, lampshades, pictures and the like. In fact tens of thousands of people have seen the brilliant blue glitter of pieces of the wings in such objects for every one who has seen the natural beauty of the entire butterfly. Some of the species are essentially inhabitants of the high canopy of the tropical forest and approach the ground so seldom that such breeding is the only practicable way to secure large numbers of perfect specimens. Individuals can sometimes be lured within net range by using a painted cardboard model or a dead specimen as a decoy, but the method is never reliable.

The big, broad-winged members of the Asiatic genus *Stichophthalma* are often classified with the Morphoes but are equally often regarded as Nymphalids. They have lovely but quiet colors, some being dull orange, while others are violet-tinted whitish above, with a row of eyespots like those of the Morphoes on the hind wings beneath. Although possessing none of the brilliance and showiness of the Morphoes, they are most attractive in their way.

OWL BUTTERFLIES—*Family Brassolidae*

The real owl butterflies of this family are members of the genus *Caligo*, the others being without the prominent "owl-like" feature. This is a pair of very large eyelike spots, one on the underside of each hind wing, that do indeed look strikingly like enormous eyes with yellow irises and big black centers. The rest of the underside of both pairs of wings is a cryptic scrawl of yellow, orange-brown and black lines and broad yellow bands. The upper side is completely different, that of *Caligo beltrao,* for example, being deep, solid brown with a fugitive blue iridescence on the fore wings and a light band that deepens and widens to a dull orange on the hind wings. The butterflies are all the more impressive because of the great breadth and area of the wings, the hind wings actually being larger than the

The caterpillar of the **Mourning Cloak** (*Nymphalis antiopa*) is spiny and black with bright red spots along the back.

front ones, so that the expanse of five and a half inches of *beltrao* tells only part of the story.

There is no doubt that, when the butterfly is turned upside down and rear end forward, the underside of a large *Caligo* does remind one strongly of an owl. This has led to fanciful statements that birds and other predators, seeing one of the butterflies unfold its wings when disturbed, think it is an owl and flee in terror. Photographs, undoubtedly faked, have been published purporting to show this. Such statements are at best rank anthropomorphism, attributing to birds that have probably never seen an owl the conscious recognition of an enemy and the capacity for imagination and fear. Most animals automatically follow a definite routine pattern in life; and sudden disruption of this invariably checks abruptly the trend of their behavior and in many instances, especially if they themselves are hunted at times, causes them to flee. It is the abrupt change, the sudden surprise, not the formation of any specific "mental picture" (of which most animals are incapable) that breaks up the little behavior pattern in which the bird is involved, or interrupts what it is doing. In this lies at least much of the benefit of the surprise mechanism of so many animals, from the sudden unveiling of the brilliant patches of color or eyespots on the hind wings of moths and butterflies to the erection of the great spreading jabot of the frilled lizard of Australia and the instantaneous appearance of the white rump patch of the flicker. The effect need not last for more than a split second to allow the displayer to get a head start on the delayed attacker and make good its escape; and if only one or two individuals out of a hundred are thus benefited, the characteristic will be sufficiently worth while to the species to be preserved and intensified as evolutionary change goes on.

Several genera of Old World tropical butterflies are sometimes included in the same family as the New World *Caligo* and their relatives, the family then being known as the Amathusiidae. The Old World forms include the Indo-Australian genus *Taenaris*, medium-sized to large butterflies with rather plain, sober colors of browns and light grays

196]

and one or two very striking eyespots on the upper and undersides of the hind wings.

BRUSH-FOOTED BUTTERFLIES
—Family Nymphalidae

This is by far the largest family of butterflies (Plates 113, 116, 117), containing several thousand members, of which some occur wherever any butterfly or moth can survive. In the past the satyrs, Heliconiids, Ithomiids and Danaids were regarded as members of this family; but even with them removed the brush-footed butterflies outnumber any others. The common name arises from the fact that in the adults the front legs are hairy and brushlike, greatly reduced in size and useless as legs, although they are sometimes used in the cleaning of the antennae. When resting or walking, therefore, the butterflies are functionally four-legged. The caterpillars are usually quite spiny, often with branching spines arising from prominent tubercles, and are sometimes ornately horned on the head. The chrysalids, too, are often irregularly shaped and studded with spines and tubercles. They frequently are very brightly colored, sometimes with brilliant metallic spots or tubercles; and from this fact came the

Mourning Cloak, adult, just after emerging from its chrysalis and spreading its wings. In England it is known as the **Camberwell Beauty.**

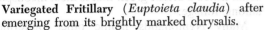

Variegated Fritillary (*Euptoieta claudia*) after emerging from its brightly marked chrysalis.

name "chrysalis" (*chrysos* being the Greek word for "golden") that is often used for butterfly pupae.

In Nymphalids of the North Temperate Zone one gets a strong impression of the dominance of orange-brown and black in more or less checkered patterns, due to the abundance of numerous species of the silverspots, fritillaries and checkerspots (*Speyeria, Boloria, Euphydryas* and *Melitaea*) and crescents (*Phyciodes*). The anglewings (*Polygonia*) and the tortoiseshells (*Nymphalis*) also have this general appearance, which has perhaps arisen more or less because of its value for concealment among brightly lit, brown, dead forest leaves. Some of the Temperate Zone Nymphalids, however, such as the unequaled peacock (*Nymphalis io*) of Europe and the admirals and emperors (*Limenitis*) of both the Old and New Worlds, have bold or brilliant, often iridescent, patterns and colors. But in all of the tropical regions, although there are many soberly colored species, the members of this family burst out in a riot of colors, both pigmental and structural, that quite rivals the accomplishments of any other group.

One of the most famous and certainly the best known of all butterflies is the painted lady (Plate 111) or thistle butterfly, *Vanessa cardui*. It is the most migratory of all insects, great swarms of travelers having been recorded in all parts of the world. Large numbers regularly cross the Mediterranean from Africa to Europe each spring; and sizable flocks have many times been seen hundreds of miles out at sea. In general it has no regular seasonal pattern in its migrations, which often seem to arise as the result of a surplus population building up in a limited area. But it is, as a result, the most cosmopolitan of all butterflies, having spread by its own efforts and without the intervention of man. Curi-

ously enough some of its closest relatives, such as the American painted lady of North America, *V. virginiensis,* show little or no trace of the migratory habit.

The anglewings and the tortoiseshells have the edges of the wings extremely irregular and jagged, with many short tails and crenulations. On the upper side their wings are bright orange-brown and black, but beneath they are mottled and scrawled with grays and browns. Therefore when they rest with their wings held tight together over the back they are excellent facsimiles of dead, crumpled leaves or pieces of rough bark. When alarmed in flight they often pitch down suddenly into this position. They spend the winter as adults, creeping into hollow trees, crevices or dark sheds or barns, or hanging up in a tree among dead leaves. Their cryptically colored and shaped wings are of special benefit to them during this period. Among tropical groups the New World butterflies of the genus *Anaea* and the Indo-Australian *Kallima* are famous as dead-leaf imitators. The front wings are sharply pointed, and the hind wings bear slender tails. The upper sides are brightly colored, often bright orange and iridescent blue, so that they are very conspicuous in flight. The butterfly alights along a stem or twig, clapping its wings together over its back and resting so that the tails of the hind wing just touch the stem while the tips of the front wing project out-

Small Tortoiseshell Butterfly (*Vanessa urticae*) just awakened from its winter's sleep and sunning itself.

An **American Painted Lady** (*Vanessa virginiensis*) struggling out of chrysalis shell.

Caterpillars of **American Painted Lady** (*Vanessa virginiensis*). They normally live in solitary nests made by webbing leaves together.

ward. Not only do its shape and position then exactly imitate a leaf, but the undersides of the wings are patterned with a dark line along the middle with other lines branching out from it, thus simulating the midrib and veins of a leaf; and in many species irregular spots imitate damaged areas such as are found on most leaves. The sudden transition from the brilliant, active butterfly to the immobile leaf is enough to confuse almost any pursuer, including even butterfly collectors. A great many other tropical groups are similarly brightly colored above and dull beneath, but none can quite match this leaf resemblance. One very striking group, the South American genus *Nessaea,* has the wings black above, crossed by a broad turquoise-blue band, and sometimes also an orange one, but underneath tinted a bright green that is most inconspicuous among foliage.

Many Nymphalids mimic other butterflies of protected, warningly colored groups. The North American viceroy, *Limenitis archippus* (Plate 105), has departed from the black, white-banded and iridescent blue colors of its relatives to become orange-brown with black borders, closely mimicking the very conspicuous monarch (Plate 106). Carefully controlled research (done with jays, which will eat almost anything) has shown that after one or two trials the birds learn to shun the monarch, and that the viceroy then enjoys an equal immunity. In the tropics many members of the genus *Phyciodes* and of the related *Chlosyne* and *Eresia* show similarly striking mimicries of protected forms. This seems peculiar to us in north temperate regions, where the dominant *Phyciodes* are our familiar little crescents with checkered brown and black patterns. In the tropics, however, some have become black

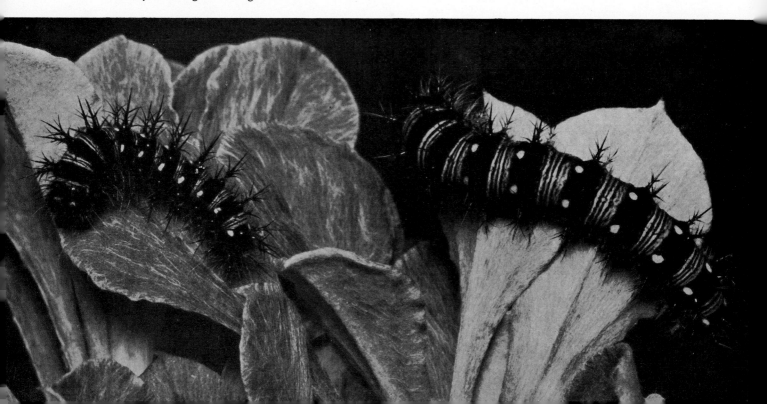

with red bands and others bright orange with black streaks, mimicking the protected *Actinote* and *Eueides* species. It is hard to believe that such exotic-looking butterflies are close relatives of our plain little crescents. In Africa the most famous mimetic Nymphalid is *Hypolimnas misippus*. The males are black with an enormous blue-tinted white spot in each wing; but the females have become orange-brown with a black border and a large white spot on each fore wing, very closely resembling the abundant, protected *Danaus chrysippus*, a relative of the North American monarch. This *Danaus* is the model also mimicked by the females of the African swallowtail *Papilio dardanus*.

Perhaps the most glamorous group of the Nymphalids are the genera *Prepona* and *Agrias* of South America, large, powerful butterflies having sometimes a wing expanse of four or more inches and occurring mostly in the densely shaded rain forests. Typically the *Preponas* are black above, with the wings crossed by a brilliant, iridescent blue band; but in *P. praeneste* the wings are flushed with a fugitive blue iridescence and bear large red markings. The *Agrias* often have brilliant blue iridescence and large scarlet patches or bands, while some add touches of bright orange. Beneath, the wings have a concentric pattern of dark and light stripes with a row of blue-pupiled eyespots near the margin. Their large size and striking color combinations alone would make these butterflies eagerly sought; but some of the species are exceedingly difficult to capture, flying consistently high above ground among the foliage of the tall forest trees. It was many years, during which the rarer species commanded very large prices, before it was found that even the rare ones could be baited with various mixtures of decaying and fermenting substances, and would then come down within net reach. Some of the forms are still, however, very rare in collections.

The clicking butterflies, or calicoes, of the tropical American genus *Ageronia* have been famous ever since Charles Darwin in the *Voyage of the Beagle* described their peculiar ways. They habitually rest on tree trunks with their wings out flat at the sides, but suddenly take flight, making a loud rattling noise as they do so. This appears to be made by means of curious organs on the wing veins that rasp together when the front and hind wings of each side are rubbed on each other in flight.

For the rest, there are so many striking combinations of color and pattern among the tropical Nymphalids that it would take a book to catalog them. Many are of the utmost brilliance; others have curiously shaped wings with hooked tips and long, slender tails; and still others are somberly and cryptically colored. In every part of the world the family is well represented, one of the lesser fritillaries, *Boloria chariclea,* occurring at the northernmost

Highly sculptured eggs of the **Emperor** (*Apatura ilia*), a widespread Old World Nymphalid butterfly.

limit of land on Ellesmere Island, fronting the Polar Sea, and thus sharing with a very few other insects the distinction of living at the farthest north possible for any land life. Other members of this same genus occur on high alpine summits far south of the Arctic.

WOOD NYMPHS and SATYRS
—Family Satyridae

This large, cosmopolitan family, very closely related to the Nymphalids, contains many familiar butterflies everywhere. The species are seldom prominent, however, since they are usually of medium size and dull-colored, generally fly low and near shelter, and therefore do not catch the eye of casual observers as do the sulphurs, nymphalids and swallowtails. Their flights are seldom rapid, but they are expert at dodging into cover and hiding when alarmed. Most of the species are some shade of brown, almost invariably with a number of round, ringed eyespots on the wings. The bases of the main veins of the wings are considerably swollen and hollow. There is some ground for belief that these

An **Arctic Bog Fritillary** (*Boloria eunomia*) laying her eggs.

Egg of an **Arctic Satyrid** (*Oeneis polixenes*) cemented to a blade of grass.

may act as resonating chambers in a sound perception apparatus. The club of the antenna is very gradually and sometimes but slightly enlarged, and so is often quite inconspicuous. The caterpillars of the Temperate Zone species are almost entirely grass-feeders. They are practically hairless, inconspicuously colored with browns or greens and frequently striped lengthwise. The last segment of the abdomen is more or less forked and tapers strongly to a pair of sharp points. In some groups the caterpillar more or less enters the ground to pupate, excavating a shallow cell among rubbish and using enough silk in this to almost warrant calling it a cocoon. The development of a great many of the species is very slow, some spending more than a year, spread out over parts of two seasons, in the larval stage.

Many of the genera of the Northern Hemisphere occur in both Eurasia and North America, and some species are common to both. Europe is quite rich in species, the grayling, *Eumenis semele,* the hedge brown, *Maniola tithonus,* the meadow brown, *Maniola jurtina,* and the wall butterfly, *Pararge aegeria,* being widespread and very common. In North America some species of the wood nymphs of the genus *Cercyonis* are almost ubiquitous, as are various members of *Euptychia,* which are known as wood satyrs. The latter is an enormous genus in the New World tropics. Both Europe and North America

A Wood Nymph (*Cercyonis pegala alope*), familiar Satyrid butterfly of eastern North America.

have a number of species of ringlets of the genus *Coenonympha,* small, ochreous butterflies often abundant in open meadows; *C. tullia* occurs widely across Europe, Asia and North America eastward to Quebec. In both Old and New Worlds are various of the alpines of the genus *Erebia,* chiefly dark brown butterflies with deep red patches or spots. Europe is particularly rich in these, and two of its species, *E. theano* and *E. callias,* extend into western North America, southward in the Rocky Mountains to Colorado. The alpines are primarily butterflies of cold mountainous, subalpine or alpine regions; but *E. rossi* occurs far northward in the Canadian Arctic. The true arctics of the genus *Oeneis,* however, live in even more rigorous environments, several species occurring around the Arctic regions from Scandinavia across Asia and North America to Labrador and Baffin Island. Of these, *O. melissa* has a famous isolated subspecies, *semidea,* that occurs only above timber line on the summits of the Presidential Range of New Hampshire; and *O. polixenes* has a similar subspecies, *katahdini,* in the alpine zone of Mount Katahdin, Maine. These Satyrid butterflies give us an enormous amount of information about geographic distribution since the last glacial cycle, because many of them were trapped, so to speak, on high mountains when the continental glaciers receded northward. Populations therefore still exist on high, southward alpine peaks, where they have been isolated for several thousands of years from their cousin populations in the Arctic; and the linking up of all the related populations, and comparison of them with one another, is one of the most interesting phases of butterfly study. Our knowledge of the alpine butterflies of the Rocky Mountains is still very incomplete, so that they offer a fertile field for study by collectors who also like to climb mountains.

In the tropics the Satyrids, like the other large families, are so numerous and varied as to defy any short description. Some of the most interesting are the large *Taygete* of South America, dark-colored butterflies with purple or bluish spots on the wings, that fly only in the dense shade of the forests, keeping so close to the ground and dodging so expertly that they are most difficult to catch. Also flying in the same dense shade are found the very beautiful species of *Callitaera* and *Haetera,* whose broad wings are almost completely transparent, but flushed outwardly with lovely rose or bluish tints. They are extraordinarily difficult to see as they float over the forest floor in the gloom beneath the dense canopy of treetops. The silvery satyr, *Argyrophora argenteus,* which flies in open environments in Chile at altitudes of three to seven thousand feet, is one of the most unusual of the group, being solid, glossy, silvery white with no markings above. And in the high alpine regions of the Andean *altiplano* fly the species of *Pedialiodes,* living in the same environment and behaving the same as the alpines and arctics of the northern hemisphere. When pursued they drop sharply to the ground and hide in the grass, a habit that is characteristic of some of the *Oeneis.*

MILKWEED BUTTERFLIES and MONARCHS
—Family Danaidae

The milkweed butterflies are relatively few in number but of great interest, and some are among the best known of all butterflies. All are relatively large, from two and a half to four inches in wing expanse. The great majority are tropical in both Old and New Worlds, but some, notably the North American monarch, occur in temperate regions. The larvae (Plate 101) feed chiefly on various plants of the milkweed family (Asclepiadaceae) and to a lesser degree on others, most of which have milky, more or less poisonous juices. The insects are distasteful, and perhaps even poisonous, in all stages; as a result they are seldom attacked by predators. The caterpillars tend to have bold warning or "advertising" patterns of transverse stripes or rows of spots, and typically bear two pairs of long, fleshy filaments which they lash about in the air when they are disturbed. The chrysalids (Plates 102–104) are broad, blunt and rounded, hang only by the cremaster at the end of the abdomen, and are often brightly colored and ornamented with metallic gold markings.

The butterflies show a wealth of color and variety of patterns, nearly all of which are definite warnings of their inedibility. Their actions, too, do the same, for they fly slowly (but powerfully) with much soaring, out in the open far from any shelter. If they were endowed with human mental attributes we would say that they "flaunt" their distastefulness and "dare" predators to attack them, secure in the "knowledge" of their protection. Like most such genuinely protected butterflies, they are exceedingly tough and rubbery, so that even a very hard pinch of the body, that would kill an ordinary butterfly, merely stuns them temporarily.

Because of their large size and powerful flight with no attempt at concealment, the North American monarch, *Danaus plexippus* (Plate 106), and its tropical relative, *D. plexippus megalippe,* are familiar butterflies wherever they occur. The monarch is probably the most famous of migratory butterflies, and is the only one that has a regular seasonal migration with a subsequent return flight. In the autumn the butterflies may be seen almost everywhere, working their way southward in great numbers, often concentrating along the seacoasts but flying through even the largest cities. We have watched a large flight passing over the heart of New York City. At night swarms of the migrants numbering many thousands may roost together, some-

Monarch Butterflies (*Danaus plexippus*) at a resting place where large numbers gather to sleep during migration.

A **Monarch** expanding its wings after emerging from the chrysalis. At right is another chrysalis.

times occupying the same locations that other swarms have in many past years. The butterflies go far southward to subtropical or tropical regions, where they spend the winter, often in an only partially active state. In the spring they begin drifting northward again, although this is by no means as compact and uniform or extensive a mass movement as that of the autumn. The females lay eggs on milkweed plants as they go, and their progeny, after reaching the adult stage, continue the northward flight, even far into Canada. We are still ignorant of most of the details of the monarch's migrations. It is hoped that various cooperative projects now under way, involving the capture, marking and release of specimens and their subsequent recapture elsewhere, will teach us a great deal.

It is uncertain how much of the monarch's spread about the world has been by its own unaided efforts and how much help it has received by being transported by man. It has spread across the Pacific to Australia and beyond, and turns up occasionally in Africa and Europe. Enough specimens have been seen flying along far out at sea to warrant the belief that occasionally, at least, it crosses the oceans under its own power.

In Africa and the Orient are closely related species, golden brown like the monarch, without its numerous white spots in the black borders but often with a large white patch on each fore wing. The most widespread is the golden Danaid, *D. chrysippus,* extending from Africa to Australia. It is mimicked by edible, unprotected butterflies of other families such as the females of *Papilio dardanus* and *Hypolimnas misippus.* Other Danaid genera in the Orient have other distinctive patterns, some like *Euploea* being black or very dark brown with white markings, while others like *Danaïda* are pale blue or bluish green with black veins and cross marks. These, too, are much mimicked by various edible butterflies, some of the swallowtails (*Papilio*) being especially striking mimics.

In the New World tropics are a few genera, such as *Lycorea* and *Ituna,* that are exceedingly different in color and pattern from the other members of the family. This has come about through their taking part in a complex Müllerian mimicry with a great many species of the protected Heliconiidae and Ithomiidae.

MIMICS and MODELS—Families Heliconiidae and Ithomiidae, etc.

Limited to the tropical regions of the New World, except for a few species that stray into temperate regions, these two families are famous as the centers of the most bewildering complex of mimics and models. They are highly protected, having odors and body juices distasteful, if not actually poisonous, to predators. They also are very rubbery, able to stand abuse that would kill most butterflies. In many parts of the tropics they are among the most conspicuous, if not the most abundant, of the butterflies, so that they almost always form a large part of collections.

Along with their distastefulness these butterflies have evolved characteristic, distinctive, bright colors and bold patterns that make them easily and instantaneously recognizable to predators such as lizards, birds and monkeys. They thus are excellent examples of warning, or aposematic, coloration. Involved in mimicry with them are many other, likewise warningly colored, groups of insects that are also protected by various means, notably bees and wasps, Lycid beetles, stink bugs and various dayflying moths such as the Zygaenids and Syntomids. As is usually the case, the Heliconiids and Ithomiids actually seem to make a point of displaying themselves, flying slowly, gliding a great deal out in the open, and passing from flower to flower, with no attempt to keep under cover or even to remain near shelter. They are usually extremely bold, too, and

Caterpillar of the Japanese national butterfly (*Sasakia charonda*), one of the Emperors.

are thus easily caught. They remind us of the almost fearless actions of the skunk, another warningly colored and extremely well-protected animal.

As we have already seen, such large, protected groups are usually mimicked by various unprotected species, which thereby gain a certain immunity from predators that cannot distinguish them from the genuinely protected models. This is Batesian mimicry (Plates 105, 106). In addition to this, the protected species tend to mimic each other and thus not only to reduce the number of distinctive appearances that a predator must learn, but also to share the cost of training predators to leave them alone. This, the mutual mimicry of genuinely protected, warningly colored species, is Müllerian mimicry (Plates 107–110).

The commonest pattern among the Heliconiids and Ithomiids is one of black stripes and edges on a bright orange-brown ground color. Sometimes yellow or white spots or patches are added to this basic pattern, which is subject to considerable variation. Dozens of species of nearly every genus of the two families, as well as some of the likewise protected Danaids, have this general appearance. On the wing they are very difficult to tell apart. Another common type of Ithomiid and Danaid has transparent wings with black markings and borders, sometimes with a bar of yellow or white across the apex of the front wing. This type of pattern is not a truly warning one, perhaps, since its possessors often are butterflies of the deeply shaded forests where they are extremely difficult to see or keep in sight. They are, however, mimicked by a considerable number of moths and of butterflies of other families, including a swallowtail, a number of Dismorphiine sulphurs, and quite a number of metalmarks and moths of the families Castniidae, Pericopidae, Dioptidae, Geometridae and probably a few others. The difficulty is to know whether the mimicry is Batesian or Müllerian. Probably most of those mentioned are themselves distasteful, so that they and the Ithomiids and Danaids reinforce each others' effects; but the metalmarks and Geometrids are almost certainly edible, so that their mimicry is in all likelihood Batesian.

It is in their Müllerian mimicry of each other, however, that the Heliconiids and Ithomiids, and a few Danaids, are really outstanding (Plates 109, 110). They tend very strongly to have developed local patterns, on each of which the members of several species in a region have converged so that they resemble each other strongly. This acts as cooperative training for the predators of that region. Then in another locality, where the same species occur, some or all of them will be found to have converged on a totally different pattern; and perhaps others will be over in a still different mimicry group. This has proven to be quite baffling to lepidopterists whose aim is to classify all of the members of a species together. It was not until it was realized that, quite contrary to the usual rules, colors and patterns may mean very little, and that the only way to determine which butterfly is really which is to examine its fundamental structures, that the classification of these mimetic groups began to be straightened out. When this was done it was found, for example, that a number of butterflies that all looked alike might really belong in several different genera, or even in different families; and that their closest relatives might look very different. The understanding of Müllerian mimicry was the key to the understanding of their classification.

One of the most striking mimicry groups has black wings, with a wide orange-brown band with some black spots across it on the fore wings, and a small orange-brown patch at the tip of each hind wing. This is shown by *Heliconius aristiona* (Heliconiidae) and *Melinaea mothone, Mechanitis deceptus* (well named), *Ceratinia bicolora, C. semifulva,* and *Hyposcada fallax* (all Ithomiidae). In some instances one is forced to examine minor details of wing venation to identify specimens of this mimetic group; so that it is hardly to be wondered at if a mere bird cannot distinguish one flying butterfly from another. Yet all of these belong to genera in which each has close relatives that are members of other totally different-looking mimicry groups.

The large genus *Heliconius* contains many of the most beautiful of these butterflies, as well as many of the most puzzling mimics. Some of the species show iridescent blues or greens, but a great many are black with simple but bold patterns of bright red, yellow or white. Let us see how two of the widespread species, *H. melpomene* and *H. erato,* pair off with each other in mimicry. The typical *melpomene* and *erato* form *hydara* are both black, with a single large scarlet patch on the fore wing. (In this, incidentally, they are mimicked by a swallowtail, *Papilio euterpinus,* the females of a white, *Pereute charops,* and a nymphalid, *Eresia castilla.*) Then, elsewhere, *H. melpomene amaryllis* and *H. erato demophoön* add to this a bright yellow stripe on the hind wing. In *H. melpomene cybele* and *H. erato cybellina* the patch of the fore wing is bright yellow and broken into a number of spots, and the base of the wing is red. And, finally, *H.*

melpomene form *aglaope* and *H. erato demeter* have a single small patch of yellow on the fore wing with the base of this wing red, and on the hind wing have a bold set of radiating red bands. Looking at such a set of eight specimens, one would say that four totally different butterflies were represented by two specimens of each; in actuality there are only two different species, each occurring in each of the four different guises. *Melpomene* also has some two dozen other appearances, *erato* somewhat fewer.

Finally, to show what another very attractive *Heliconius* can do in the way of local mimetic variability, let us look at the widespread *H. cydno* that ranges from Honduras to Peru. Its different forms are by no means all geographic subspecies, some being variations that may occur in the same locality as others; but all are duplicated in mimicry by other species. *Galanthus* has the wings steely blue-black, crossed by a very wide band of pure white. To this *chioneus* adds a broad white border on the hind wings. In typical *cydno* the band of the front wings is bright yellow, the border of the hind wings white. In *hermogenes* the band of the front wing is broken into a dozen small white spots and the hind wing border is yellow. And in a variety of *hermogenes* the front-wing spots are yellow.

The Heliconiids are particularly noted for their acrid odor, noticeable to some humans as far as ten yards away. It is not certain, of course, that it is the odor that repels birds, monkeys etc., although it is likely that it is. It is certainly some repellent quality that makes it possible for *Heliconius* to sleep together in groups in a favored tree or shrub, returning night after night to the same spot. One individual, recognizable by a distinctively damaged wing, was recorded coming back nightly to the same dormitory for over a month, at the end of which period it was obviously greatly weakened and dying of old age. Only butterflies that are genuinely and efficiently protected could thus gather in a way that would otherwise make them an easy target for any predator. Probably the accumulation of the odor multiplies its effectiveness. For technical anatomical reasons these highly protected groups are considered to be among the highest, if not the very highest, of all butterflies; and in their marvelous success and freedom from predatory enemies they are likewise perhaps the most advanced members of their order.

CHAPTER XII

Flies and Mosquitoes

(*Order Diptera*)

A GALL MIDGE

THIS is the fourth-largest order of insects, containing upward of sixty thousand species. It is as nearly cosmopolitan as any group of insects can be, occurring in every part of every continent; and it contains many of the most abundant and familiar species, including a large proportion of the insect parasites of man and the carriers of some of the most dangerous human diseases. The adults are easy to recognize as members of the order since they have a single pair of wings only; but the larvae of various families differ so greatly from each other in appearance that it is impossible to characterize them in general terms. Both larvae and adults show a great range of differences in food habits and environments.

Many groups are aquatic as larvae, although the majority are terrestrial. Some larvae are scavengers, perhaps living in the foulest ordure; many feed in living plants, boring in stems, mining in leaves or living in galls; others are predators on insects and other small animals; and still others live, parasite-like, in the bodies of other insects. The adults of many groups are blood-sucking parasites of vertebrates, some visiting their hosts only occasionally while others live permanently upon them. In fact, the chief direct importance of the order to man comes from the transmission of diseases of both man and domestic animals by such parasites, to say nothing of the irritation caused by their bites. A great many species are destructive agricultural pests. On the credit side of the ledger, however, a great many of the parasitic flies are of incalculable value because of their destruction of harmful insects; and members of many large families are very important as pollinators of flowers.

The outstanding characteristic of the order, which gives it its scientific name, is the possession by the adults of only a single pair of functional wings. These are the front ones, the hind pair having been transformed into two short, knobbed structures known as halteres, which serve as organs of equilibrium, especially in flight. Despite this functional loss, many flies are perhaps the fastest of all insects in the air and show exceptional skill and control in flight. All of the usual mouthparts are present in adults, but modified so as to serve as sucking, piercing or lapping structures through which only liquid foods can be taken. In a number of the families they form a long, slender, tubular proboscis; in others this is short; and in still others it is so reduced as to be nonfunctional, such adults never feeding but subsisting on what they ate as larvae.

The larvae of all are greatly reduced, the majority to the point where they have lost many of the fundamental characteristics of insects. None possesses legs. In only a few families do they have a recognizable, well-developed head, and in the majority the eyes are lacking. As we progress up the list of families, starting with the most primitive and working toward the most advanced, we see the head and mouthparts becoming more and more reduced until in the highest groups the head is nothing more than a tiny, pointed structure around the mouth, and the jaws have been replaced by a pair of hard, sharp hooks. With these, solid foods can be loosened and shredded, facilitating the digestive action of salivary fluids that are poured out of the mouth. The liquefied food is then sucked in, so that we see the maggot first shredding its food out ahead of it and then digesting it and, last of all, ingesting it. In such larvae all that remain of the numerous paired spiracles are a single pair at the front end and a single pair at the rear; and in some even the front pair is missing. Headless, jawless, eyeless and legless, and covered with only a soft, wet skin, the larvae of the higher Diptera seem at first glance to have sacrificed most of the evolutionary gains of hundreds of millions of years—yet with their specialized, external digestive techniques and secretive habits they are mighty transformers of plant and animal substance into fly protoplasm.

The pupae are extremely simple, even in the least-reduced primitive groups. In the advanced groups pupation takes place within the last larval integument, forming an oval barrel-shaped "puparium" with few visible structures. The adults of the higher families emerge from this by means of a most unusual apparatus. While the fly is still inside the puparium it everts from the front of its head a large, liquid-filled bladder, which cracks and pushes off the front end of the puparium. Through this opening the fly crawls out; the bladder is deflated and withdrawn into the head; and only a closed suture of the face marks the site of the hydraulic apparatus.

The order is divided into more than a hundred families, a great many of which are of interest only to the specialist. As in the other orders, we shall omit reference to the majority of such families and concentrate on those that are of most general interest because of abundance, medical or economic importance or the possession of unusual structures or habits.

CRANEFLIES—Family Tipulidae

This large, world-wide family contains thousands of species, ranging in size from some no larger than a good-sized mosquito to others with a wingspread of more than three inches. All have extremely narrow wings and long, thin bodies and legs, giving rise to the common name "daddy long legs" (a name that is more often used for the still more long-legged spider relatives, the harvestmen or Phalangida). Even the layman who knows nothing about insects can hardly help wondering, as he looks at a cranefly, how it manages to get along without breaking off its legs. The same thought is in the mind of the entomologist, since even the largest species are notoriously fragile and difficult to collect intact. Some of the larger craneflies often stray, quite unintentionally and harmlessly, into houses, where they may worry people who mistake them for giant mosquitoes.

The larvae are characterized by radiating fleshy processes surrounding the blunt anal end. The majority live in wet or damp environments, which range from the mud and sand of marshes and shores to the humus of woodlands and the soil of meadows and pastures. Those of some of the larger species, such as of the genus *Tipula,* are known as "leather jackets" and are hated by the farmer for the damage that they do in grasslands or grainfields by destroying roots and turf. The larvae of some aquatic genera have protrusible gills and fringes of hairs on the anal segment. Among these are *Dicranota,* which live in streams and ponds, preying on the little *Tubifex* worms; and *Antocha,* which live in swift streams in silken cases attached to rocks.

A number of smaller families are more or less closely related to the true craneflies. One of these is the Liriopeidae (Ptychopteridae), or phantom craneflies, of which the unusual North American *Bittacomorpha clavipes* is the best-known species. The extremely slender legs of this insect spread more than an inch, and are black with white bands. The tarsi are flattened and hollowed beneath; and when the legs are spread like the spokes of a wheel they catch the rising air currents to aid the small, inconspicuous wings in a slow rising and falling flight. In shady woods one can often see only the black-and-white tarsi, which look like disembodied circles of dots drifting about in the air. In the family Anisopidae, or false craneflies, the adults of *Anisopus* often feed on rotting fruit, while the larvae revel in manure and sewage. Swarms of *Trichocera* adults may often be seen in spring or autumn forming dense, drifting clouds; the larvae of this genus sometimes do damage to roots and tubers, especially potatoes, stored in cellars.

A **Cranefly** (*Tipulidae*). Noted for its incredibly long, fragile legs.

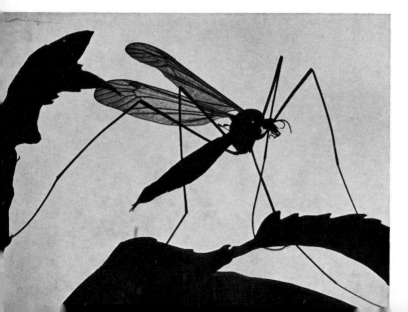

MOTH FLIES—Family Psychodidae

Nearly all of the members of this widely distributed family are small to minute flies with the wings so densely covered with short hairs that they appear opaque and make the flies look like tiny moths. A few species have very beautiful iridescent colors. The larvae and many of the adults feed in decaying liquid or semiliquid organic matter. Many species are very abundant around sewage plants; and some of these (e.g. of the genus *Psychoda*) are not infrequently found in bathrooms and kitchens, and around septic tanks and outhouses, from which they may emerge in swarms. The larvae of some species live in fermenting sap flowing from wounded trees.

One large group, chiefly tropical, is represented by the blood-sucking adults of the genus *Phlebotomus*. These are the sand flies that in some regions are among the worst pests of the tropics. In addition to the almost intolerable nuisance of their biting, to which some people are particularly sensitive, a few of the species are carriers of dangerous diseases of man. In the Mediterranean and southern and western Asiatic regions *Phlebotomus papatasii* thus transmits three-day or pappataci fever; the same and other species transmit Kala-azar and oriental sore in Asia; and other species in the New World are the carriers of Carrion's disease in the high Andes and espundia from Mexico through much of South America. The flies are quite difficult to control, since as adults their small size allows them to penetrate ordinary screening, and as larvae they breed in large numbers in even small bits of decaying vegetation.

NET-WINGED MIDGES
—Family Blepharoceridae

The small adults are distinguished by the many creases that cover the wings with a faint network. The very flat larvae are unusually well adapted for their life in swift mountain streams by the possession of six ventral suction discs. By means of these they hold themselves fast to stones in even the swiftest currents, where they feed on the film of algae and other minute plants. The pupae are also held fast to the stones by similar discs. The wings of the adult develop fully before it emerges from the pupa, so that it rises to the surface of the stream and takes flight instantaneously as it reaches the air. The adults of some species are bloodsuckers (not of man); of others, predatory on small flies.

MIDGES—Family Chironomidae
(Tendipedidae)

The name "midge" is applied loosely to a number of groups of small flies but is most commonly used for the members of this large, abundant and very widely distributed family of about two thousand species. The adults are slender, fragile insects that look much like mosquitoes; but they are almost always much paler-colored, do not have the wings fringed with flat scales and never suck blood since they lack the elongate piercing beak. They often form tremendous courting and mating swarms consisting of incalculable millions of individuals, visible from afar as dancing clouds and producing a humming that can be heard hundreds of yards away. Great numbers often come in to lights at night, worrying people who do not realize that they are completely innocuous.

The larvae live, often in enormous numbers, in nearly all fresh waters from swift streams to deep lakes. A few, such as the little *Eretmoptera browni* of the Pacific coast, the adults of which have reduced, straplike wings, live in tide pools; and some have been found living in the sea at depths as great as twenty fathoms. Many live in gelatinous tubes or in silk or sand cases; they burrow in the mud or swim about freely, feeding on algae and other microscopic plant life. The larvae of *Symbiocladius* are found only under the wing pads of the mayfly *Rithrogena;* those of *Xenochironomus* live as inquilines in sponges. Larvae of some species of *Chironomus* are bright red because of the presence in the blood of hemoglobin, almost unknown in other insects; others are yellow or even black. Most of the larvae have retractable tubular blood gills at the end of the abdomen, another unusual feature since the tracheal gill is the characteristic respiratory organ of aquatic insect larvae. Many species can exist in highly polluted waters where other insects cannot live. The larvae as a whole are of tremendous importance in the economy of nature in the fresh waters, transforming enormous quantities of plant matter into animal matter. They certainly constitute the main food of the young of many of our most valued fresh-water fishes, and are also eaten in great quantities by larger predatory aquatic insects, which themselves are a major part of the food of larger fishes. The whole animal life of the fresh waters, in fact, is very largely supported upon a foundation of these midges and the mayflies.

BITING MIDGES or PUNKIES
—Family Ceratopogonidae (Heleidae)

These minute, pestiferous flies, which all too often abound in many regions, are sometimes classified as a subfamily of the true midges. Unlike the midges, however, they have absolutely nothing to recommend them to man, for they are vicious bloodsuckers. Although so small that it can barely be seen with the naked eye, a punkie may leave an intensely itching welt larger than that produced by the bite of a mosquito or deer fly a hundred times its size. Their vernacular names in the north woods of America, "no-see-ums" and "red-pepper gnats," testify to their powers of making people miserable. They fly, not only all night long, but also at dawn and dusk and during the day in shaded woods; and can penetrate any screening coarser than cheesecloth. The one good feature is that they stop flying when the wind blows. As larvae they live at the seashore in the intertidal zone, in water holes in trees, in mud, wet sand or damp leafmold, or in shallow, quiet water. The majority of the best-known species belong to the genus *Culicoides*. Only a few species transmit diseases of man and domestic animals, but some are known to carry filarial worms that infect man. The adults of some species suck the blood of caterpillars and other insects. In the Orient there is a species that sucks from mosquitoes the blood the mosquito has just sucked from a vertebrate.

MOSQUITOES—*Family Culicidae*

These insects are undoubtedly the best-known blood-sucking fly pests of man the world around, swarming even in the Arctic in numbers that rival the populations of Temperate Zone and tropical salt marshes and swamps. They are also as a group the most harmful to man because of their transmission of serious diseases, of which yellow fever and malaria are the worst. Especially since the Second World War, when mosquito control became a vital military necessity in many unexpected areas, they have been studied more intensively than, perhaps, any other group of insects. Despite this, new species are still being discovered; and a vast amount of information about life histories, distributions and disease transmission remains to be found out.

Of the more than two thousand world species all but fifty or so belong to the subfamily Culicinae, the true mosquitoes. These have long, tubular proboscises, adapted for piercing and blood-sucking. As in most of the other externally parasitic Diptera it is only the females that suck blood, but in some of the mosquitoes not even the females do this. The two chief groups are the tribes Culicini and Anophelini, the distinction of which is essential for any understanding of the parts that the mosquitoes play as disease carriers. The ordinary, often abundant pest mosquitoes are Culicines, chiefly of the genera *Culex* and *Aedes* (Plate 135); certain species of these, as well as some other, genera are disease-carriers. The Anophelines are famous as carriers of various malarias, but actually only a few species are of importance in this respect. The larvae of Culicines usually hang head downward from the surface film of the water, while those of Anophelines lie more or less parallel to and just below the surface; all of them respire by sucking air at the posterior end, the Culicines through a siphon-like tube. In both groups the males have prominent feathery antennae, while those of the females are threadlike and short-haired. Culicine females have very short palpi, hardly visible without magnification, lying alongside the base of the proboscis. Anopheline females, however, have prominent palpi as long as the proboscis. The resting or feeding Culicine female stands with her body more or less parallel to the surface, her beak projecting downward from below her head; while the Anopheline female tends to point her head and proboscis in a straight line toward the surface on which she is resting, her abdomen pointing out away from it. Culicines tend to have transparent or simply tinted wings; Anophelines tend toward wings pictured with dark or light spots caused by differently colored flat scales. In all of these characteristics there are some exceptions and many degrees of intergradation.

The eggs are typically laid on the surface of the water, although many species deposit them in places where there will be water in the future when the wet season comes. Each species, except for a few generalized ones, tends to be extremely limited in its habitat. Some are restricted to salt and brackish marshes, but the majority live in fresh water. Some specialize in highly polluted waters where there is much organic decay; others in the highly acid water in rot holes in tree trunks; others in water in the natural reservoirs of tropical air plants growing far above the ground on trees, or of pitcher plants in northern bogs. Some prefer the margins of lakes or ponds, perhaps only where there is shade; others prefer brightly illuminated water; still others prefer temporary seepages, perhaps from a dam or irrigation ditch; and still others lay their eggs in wheel ruts or the water-filled hoofprints of cattle. Some actually prefer man-made containers and, like *Stegomyia fasciata,* the classical carrier of the dreaded yellow fever, will enter houses and lay their eggs in the water of flower vases, perhaps in the sickroom of a yellow fever patient. During the great yellow fever clean-up of New Orleans it was found that one of the most productive breeding grounds of this mosquito was in the funeral urns that marked the graves of so many previous victims of the mosquito and the virus.

The great majority of mosquito larvae live as general scavengers, sweeping into the mouth the tiny particles of organic matter found in the water. However, some have been shown to be able to exist on dissolved organic substance. The larvae of some groups, such as the giant *Megarhinus* that live in tree holes, are predators on other small aquatic insects, often on other mosquito larvae. Some develop extremely slowly, so that there is but a single generation annually; but others require only a week to complete larval growth, the whole life cycle taking as little as ten days.

[continued on page 225]

91. Caterpillar of the **Spicebush Swallowtail** (*Papilio troilus*). The huge "eyes" shown here are merely patches of color; the true eyes are very small and hidden beneath the head.

92. **Black Swallowtail** (*Papilio po-lyxenes asterius*) is common in North America. As a caterpillar it feeds on carrot and parsley.

93. **Common Swallowtail** (*Papilio machaon*). The only Swallowtail found commonly in Europe and the only one found in England.

94. Virginian Ctenucha (*Ctenucha virginica*). A day-flying, flower-visiting moth widespread in eastern North America.

95. Alfalfa Butterfly (*Colias eurytheme*), female, albino. Normal females are orange.

96. A Syntomid Moth (*Corematura chrysogastra*) which, like many of its relatives, is an excellent wasp mimic.

97. Caterpillar of the **Silver Spotted Skipper** (*Epargyreus clarus*). The eyelike spots on the head are merely patches of color.

98. **Leonardus Skipper** (*Hesperia leonardus*). A common autumn species of eastern North America.

99. **Cinnabar Moth** (*Hypocrita jacobaeae*). Like its caterpillar, it is brightly and warningly colored and highly distasteful to birds.

100. **Polka Dot Moth** (*Syntomeida epilais*). As a caterpillar it feeds on oleander, a shrub poisonous to most animals.

101–104. (Left) Caterpillar of **Monarch Butterfly** (*Danaus plexippus*) hanging head down, just before molting and transforming into a chrysalis; (bottom left) week-old chrysalis showing the butterfly wings forming within the shell; (center) fully-formed adult breaking out, and (right) beginning to spread its wings.

105 and 106. **Viceroy** (*Limenitis ar-chippus*). Resembling the **Monarch** (below), which is distasteful to birds, it shares the latter's immunity from birds.

107 and 108. (Above) A tropical **Danaid**(*Lycorella cleobaea*), highly distasteful to birds. Its warning colors are mimicked (below) by a **Nymphalid** (*Eresia eunice*), an edible species, which may thus escape certain predators.

109 and 110. An **Ithomiid** (*Mechanitis*), a close relative of the Monarch and also distasteful to birds. (Below) A **Heliconiid** (*Heliconius novatus* f. *aristiona*), itself distasteful, mimics the **Ithomiid** above. Such mimicry of each other by species that are both distasteful is very common in the New World tropics.

111. Virginia Painted Lady
(*Vanessa virginiensis*).
A close relative of the
cosmopolitan **Thistle
Butterfly** (*Vanessa car-
dui*).

112. A Morpho (*Morpho*). Its
brilliant iridescent wings are
often used in jewelry.

113. Weidermeyer's White Admiral
(*Limenitis weidermeyeri*), a
close relative of the Viceroy, is
common in western North
America.

114. **Large Copper** (*Lycaena dispar*), female. This species is widespread in Europe and was common in England until exterminated over 100 years ago by too avid collecting.

115. **A Metal Mark Butterfly** (of the *Eurybia nicaea* complex), greatly magnified. There are more of this family in South America than in all the rest of the world together.

116. A **Peacock Butterfly** (*Anartia amathea*) that is widespread throughout the New World tropics.

117. A **Dagger Wing Butterfly** (*Marpesia coresia*) sucking moisture from the mud. It, too, is confined to the New World tropics.

118. A **Hairstreak** (*Theritas tuneta*), greatly enlarged. The dainty form and exquisite coloring of many Hairstreaks make them popular with collectors.

119. **Gray Hairstreak** (*Strymon melinus*). Found throughout temperate North America, it is one of the few harmful butterflies, its caterpillars destroying beans and hops.

120. A **Horsefly** (*Tabanus*), female, with eye color patterns characteristic of the species. These colors disappear soon after death for they are caused by structures, not pigments, and thus vanish when the eyes dry and shrink.

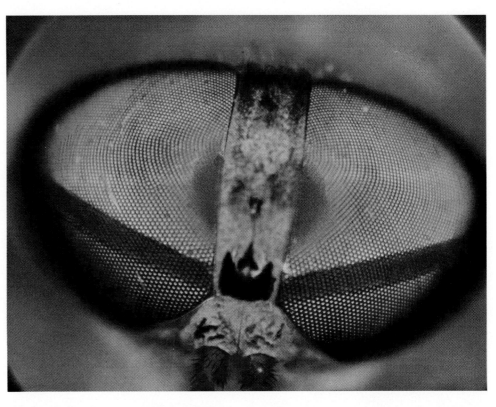

121. A **Horsefly** (*Tabanus*). The female is a blood-sucking pest of man and other warm-blooded animals but the male is content with honeydew and plant juices.

122. A **Horsefly** (*Tabanus*). Another species with characteristic eye colors. Each of the notably distinct facets is the lens of a separate unit.

[continued from page 208]

The pupae of mosquitoes, unlike those of nearly all other insects, are quite active, swimming fast and erratically when disturbed. Like the larvae they respire by means of air sucked down at the surface film. Most mosquitoes spend but a few days in this vulnerable nonfeeding stage, no matter how long the entire life cycle may be.

The adults usually mate soon after emerging from the pupal stage, after which the males die. The females seek a blood meal, without which they may be unable to mature their eggs, although in some species this can be done on the nourishment taken in as larvae, and in others from nectar or plant juices. Many species are just as narrowly specialized in this as in other ways, perhaps being restricted to amphibian or bird blood, or showing strong preferences for certain species of mammals. After a time the eggs are laid and perhaps other blood meals taken. Each species has its own pattern of activity, perhaps differing in populations of the species in different latitudes or regions. In the Temperate Zones the females may seek sheltered places in which to spend the winter, emerging from hibernation and laying eggs in the spring. Or the eggs may be laid during the autumn in places that are then entirely dry but will be flooded in the spring. In many such instances the eggs can withstand not merely the cold of the winter, but even months of drying. Sometimes, in fact, the eggs will not hatch until they have been subjected to a certain minimal amount of cold or dryness.

We have given the above details, only a small fraction of the multiplicity of factors in the lives of mosquitoes, to illustrate a few of the things that must be learned by the medical entomologist. Often such variable factors must be extensively studied during an attempt to control a serious outbreak or epidemic of an insect-borne disease, as happened in the 1930's when an African mosquito, *Anopheles gambiae,* was somehow introduced into northeastern Brazil. In the new environment it proved an even more dangerous carrier of malaria than in Africa (where it was bad enough) and caused the death of more than sixty thousand people before it was brought under control and finally exterminated with the aid of the Rockefeller Foundation. Needless to say extraordinary precautions were taken during the Second World War, when military aircraft were shuttling back and forth between Brazil and Africa in large numbers, to prevent a repetition of the calamity.

Another example of the same sort of thing, which occurred in Colombia during the Second World War, illustrates the unexpectedness that must always be expected when we are dealing with insect-borne diseases. Yellow fever suddenly appeared in villages where yellow fever had no right to exist, since no cases had been recorded that could pos-

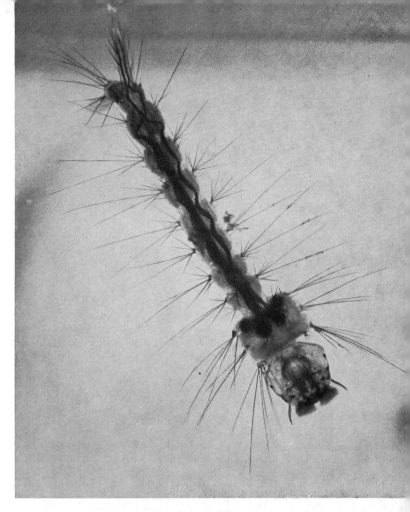

Larva of the **Pitcher Plant Mosquito** (*Wyeomyia smithii*) hanging by its breathing siphon from the surface film. This mosquito breeds only in the hollow water-filled leaves of the pitcher plant.

sibly have gotten the infections started. No "reservoir" of the disease was known, from which the yellow fever mosquito could have picked up infections to transmit to other humans. After much intricate research it was found that monkeys living high in the forest canopy had been carrying an infection, perhaps for millennia, and therefore constituted a reservoir. The disease was transmitted from monkey to monkey by *Haemagogus* mosquitoes which also lived in the forest canopy, breeding in water caught at the leaf bases of epiphytic plants. The infection had been brought down to ground level by woodsmen felling the great trees and being bitten by the mosquitoes that were thus carried down. Even with this knowledge, it was far from easy to control the epidemics and to prevent their spread into large areas where a potential ground-level carrier, *Stegomyia fasciata,* existed abundantly but the infection did not. The hazard is still present, without doubt, in many parts of tropical forests; and the problem still exists of how to utilize the great and valuable trees without starting new epidemics of yellow fever. It is now known that the same problem with jungle fever occurs in Africa.

A great many other diseases are known to be

transmitted by mosquitoes. These include filariasis (such as the infection by the roundworm parasite that causes the dreaded elephantiasis), dengue fever, human and equine encephalitis and the often fatal dog heartworm. In all, control is almost entirely aimed at the insect carrier, both by attempting to exterminate it and by rigidly isolating all infected individuals to prevent their infection of other carriers. Sometimes the isolation alone will suffice, as is the case of yellow fever in the United States, where the yellow fever mosquito occurs commonly in the South but is merely a minor pest as long as it cannot become infected by biting infected humans.

Considerable control of mosquitoes, whether pests or disease-carriers, can be obtained by means of chemical sprays. It is realized by experienced entomologists, however, that this is only to be done during emergencies, since widespread spraying not only is merely temporary but also does great harm to beneficial insects and other animals. The best and most lasting control is obtained by modifying the environment in which the mosquitoes breed and live, by such means as ditching, draining, raising or fluctuating the water level, clearing shaded areas etc. Larva-eating fish are often introduced into an area with very helpful results. There is no more complex subject than the control of such disease-carrying insects nor any better example of the difficulty of man's struggle to control his environment.

BLACK FLIES and BUFFALO GNATS
—Family Simuliidae

These are stout-bodied, humpbacked flies, about one-eighth of an inch long and usually blackish in color. They occur in countless millions, from the tropics to the far Arctic Circle, wherever there is suitable running water in which they can live as larvae. They are so persistent in their search for blood that they will crawl up trousers legs and shirt sleeves and burrow through any possible opening in clothing, so that the only way to defeat them is to tie the clothes tight around the neck, ankles and wrists and use zippers for fastenings. Although people vary considerably in their susceptibility, each bite is likely to produce a bloody red spot that will itch for days. Some of the modern chemical insect repellents usually keep them from serious biting, but these cannot be put on the eyelids, lips or other delicate areas, where the flies then bite with concentrated enthusiasm.

The eggs are laid near or in running water, sometimes in such abundance as to form a mosslike covering. The female of *Simulium maculatum* has been seen to go a foot beneath the surface of the water in laying the eggs. The larvae attach themselves so firmly by means of holdfast hairs, suction discs or silken cords that they can live even in the fastest-flowing water on the lip of a waterfall, straining out particles of organic matter from the water by means of a pair of large fanlike structures on the head. The elongate pupa lives in the same type of place. As the adult fly develops within the pupa a bubble of air is accumulated; the adult, after its emergence from the pupa, rises to the surface in this bubble and bursts up through the surface film with its aid. It then sets out in search of a mate and, if it is a female, of a blood meal, possibly traveling several miles for this purpose.

None of the North American species is known to carry disease, but several species of tropical America and Africa are the vectors of very troublesome roundworms that cause festering swellings of the skin and eyes. Many of the non-disease-carriers are, however, serious enough in their own right. *Simulium columbaczense* of Central Europe sucks the blood of man and domestic animals, penetrating every orifice of the body and sometimes causing death. *S. indicum*, the "potu" fly of the Himalayan region, is nearly as bad. *S. pecuarum*, the buffalo gnat of the Mississippi Valley, sometimes attacks mules and other domestic animals heavily enough to cause their death, and even sucks blood from other insects. And the black flies of the Canadian zone forests are proverbial deterrents to settlement in many regions, or to activities in the "bush" during their season. One of the most appropriately named insects is the African species that was christened *Simulium damnosum*.

FUNGUS GNATS—Family Mycetophilidae

More than two thousand species of these small flies are known. Occurring in nearly all parts of the world, they feed as larvae chiefly on molds and fungi as well as on decaying plant matter. As might be expected, some species are serious pests in mushroom cellars. The adults have exceedingly long coxae, threadlike antennae and hind legs adapted for jumping; when disturbed they often put on a very effective death-feigning act. The larvae of some species are famous for their gregarious habits; large assemblages sometimes are seen traveling over the surface of the ground in such compact files that the group resembles a single large worm or snake many feet long. The individuals in the moving group are often piled several deep on top of each other; those on the bottom layers go more slowly and then, when they reach the rear, climb up onto the top layer and go faster until they reach the front, when they again go down to the bottom. Such formations are known in Europe as "army worms," in America as "snake worms." A number of species are recorded as damaging stored grains, potatoes etc. In a few species the larvae are luminescent, one reputedly being so bright that when put in a cage the light streamed out through the openings a distance of several feet.

GALL FLIES and GALL GNATS
—Family Cecidomyiidae (Itonididae)

This is a large family of very small flies, world-wide in distribution and sometimes, despite their small size, of major economic importance. Several thousand species are known. The vast majority of the species cause the formation by plants of abnormal growths called galls in which the larva lives; but quite a few live on or within various plants without causing galls, others are general scavengers on decaying plant matter or animal excrement, and a few are predatory or parasitic on small insects.

The fragile adults have whorls of hairs around the antennae, and wings with very few veins. The gall-making habit is quite specialized, each species of fly confining its activity to one or a few related species of plants. Under the stimulus created by the insect the plant grows abnormally to form a gall, which is usually a compact, prominent structure of consistent size and shape. Inside this the larva lives, often eroding away the plant tissues with a special hard structure on the lower side of the body and feeding on the plant tissues and juices. A few of the gall gnat larvae live in galls originally formed as the result of the activities of other insects, but the majority are the primary gall-causers themselves. The galls are often invaded by insects of other groups, which are therefore called "inquilines"; sometimes these compete with or even kill the gall gnat larvae, sometimes both live in harmony or without actual contact.

Of the species that attack living plants but do not form galls, perhaps the best known is the infamous Hessian fly, *Mayetiola destructor,* so called in the United States because it is believed to have been imported from Europe in straw used for horse fodder by the Hessian soldiers brought over at the time of the Revolution. Its larvae bore in stems of growing wheat, weakening them so that they break as the head of grain becomes heavy. It causes losses of many millions of dollars annually and is extremely difficult to control. Like other introduced pests it is far more serious in its new home than in the land of its origin. The European pear midge, *Contarina pirivora,* and the clover leaf and clover seed midges, *Dasyneura trifolia* and *D. leguminicola,* are other destructive members of the family.

HORSE FLIES and GAD FLIES
—Family Tabanidae

This is another group that is noted for the blood-sucking habits of the females. Perhaps twenty-five hundred species are known, some occurring in nearly all parts of the world. None is very small, few being smaller than the common house fly, and some are very large and robust, being more than an inch long. The mouthparts form a short, powerful, piercing apparatus capable of penetrating tough skins and making a wound from which blood flows and is lapped up. The bites of many of the species are sharply painful and may drive humans and large game and domestic animals away from the areas where the flies abound. The species of *Tabanus* are chiefly large, brownish or blackish, with clear or smoky wings. Those of *Chrysops,* the "deer flies" and "moose flies," typically have dark bars or blotches on the wings; they are smaller but make up in numbers and persistence of attack for their size. The medium-sized species of *Haemotopota,* known as "clegs," are equally serious pests in many areas of northern Europe. In some parts of Russia they are so abundant that agricultural workers can carry on only at night during fly season.

The larvae hatch from large masses of eggs laid on the leaves or stems of plants in marshy or damp places, drop to the ground and burrow into the mud or soft soil. There they are carnivorous, devouring small earthworms, other insect larvae etc. The pupae are markedly elongate and cylindrical.

The compound eyes of Tabanids (Plates 120–122) are extremely prominent, those of the males in particular occupying most of the surface of the head. Those of a great many species, especially of *Chrysops,* are extremely beautiful, being colored with bands, patches and spots of brilliant iridescent hues that run the entire gamut of the spectrum. The colors are caused by microscopic structures in the integument that break up the rays of light into some of the component wave lengths, thus giving the impression of color even though no pigments at all are present. When a Tabanid dies and the integu-

A **Pantophthalmid** (*Pantophthalmus*), one of the largest flies. Although the members of this small tropical family are related to the Horse Flies they do not bite.

ment of the eye dries and shrinks, these structures are changed, and as a result the brilliant colors and patterns disappear. No satisfactory technique has been developed for preserving them, which is a pity both because of their beauty and because they are of some value in the classification of the different species.

Few Tabanids are carriers of human disease, but some species transmit rabbit fever (tularemia) in the western United States; and a West African species is a vector of the filarial worm that causes the painful Calabar swellings. This African species may bite, get a drop of blood, infect with the parasite and depart in only a fraction of a second, in contrast to some other species that, if undisturbed, will remain sucking blood on the host for as long as half an hour.

SOLDIER FLIES—Family Stratiomyiidae

The majority of the thousand or so species of this widely distributed group are brightly colored flies with white, yellow or light green stripings on the abdomen. The abdomens are rather flat and often covered by the wings, which are laid back flat over them. The adults are consistent flower visitors, especially favoring the flat flower clusters of umbelliferous plants (parsnip family). The larvae of the various species show a large variety of habits and habitats. Some are aquatic, scavenging or feeding on small animals. Many of these can live in extremely foul water such as that in privies, septic tanks and grease traps. They have a pair of spiracles at the attenuate posterior end, surrounded by a brush of radiating hairs that suspend the larva from the surface film and then, when it descends, carry along a bubble of air to be used beneath the water. Other larvae are terrestrial, many living as scavengers in the nests of bees or rodents, and many living as predators.

BEE FLIES—Family Bombyliidae

The name of the family originated in the resemblance of many of the species to hairy bees, the bodies of the flies being covered with dense coats of hairs or scales. Most of the species are quite robust, but some are rather long and slender. Many, especially of the sparsely haired species, have the wings beautifully pictured with bold patterns of black. Some of the species have metallic colorations of considerable brilliance. The adults commonly visit flowers to obtain nectar, perhaps sucking it through the extremely long proboscis while hovering in front of the flower instead of alighting on it. Many species are commonly seen hovering a few inches above roads or patches of bare dirt, the hotter the better, to vanish instantaneously, so fast and well controlled is the flight.

All of the known larvae of the two thousand or more species are parasitic on other insects, attack-

ing bees, wasps, locusts, and moth and beetle larvae. They show a distinct hypermetamorphosis, since the first stage is extremely different from the later ones. This is strongly marked in the species that parasitize solitary bees and wasps, for the female merely lays the eggs near the nest of one of these insects and the larva must find its way into the nest by itself. It is a tiny creature and an active one, and can penetrate the smallest crevices. Once inside, it molts and transforms into a heavier-bodied form that eats the bee's or wasp's eggs and the provisions stored in the nest. The bee fly puparium is armed with heavy spines, which serve the adult fly in breaking out of the nest.

MYDAS FLIES—Family Mydaeidae

Most of the species of this rather small family are large flies, some being an inch and a half long with a wing spread of nearly three inches. The adults are predaceous, but the larvae live on decaying wood. Some of the adults are boldly colored with steely blue and orange, quite definitely mimicking the large tarantula-hawk wasps of the family Pepsidae. Others superficially resemble large predatory robber flies (Asilidae). The adults of the neotropical family Pantophthalmidae are even larger, some, with a body length of nearly three inches, being the largest members of the order.

SNIPE FLIES—Family Leptidae
(Rhagionidae)

This is a widely distributed family of small to medium-sized flies. In the majority of species the larvae are general feeders and predators in leaf mold and soil, and the adults are predatory on other insects. In western North America the adults of *Symphoromyia* suck human and other large animals' blood; they are hairy, light gray and about the size of the common house fly. In both Europe and North America occurs the genus *Atherix,* the

A **Robber Fly** (*Proctacanthus philadelphicus*). A powerful predator that catches other insects in its bristly legs and punctures them with its short, strong beak.

members of which are aquatic as larvae. The females gather in large clusters on vegetation overhanging the water; there they lay their eggs and die. The mass of eggs, larvae and dead females may be very large. The larvae feed upon the remnants of the females, then drop into the water and continue life there. The Indians of Oregon were formerly able to collect as much as a hundred bushels of these masses in a day, and used them as food.

ROBBER FLIES—Family Asilidae

This is a large, world-wide family of predatory flies (Plate 129) that contains over four thousand species. The majority are medium-sized to large, although some are small and slender. The rather small head is dished out between the prominent eyes; the legs are long, strong and bristly, being used to hold the prey. The mouthparts form a short, stout, pointed beak with which even hard insect integument can be pierced. The flies seem astonishingly clumsy, occasionally catching their prey on the wing but more often dropping onto it from the air. They are able to master insects much larger and stronger than themselves, so that it is believed that they may inject a toxic substance into their victims with the beak.

Although the majority of species are relatively slender and not noticeably hairy, those of one group of genera (e.g. *Bombomima*) are very stout-bodied and thickly covered with short hairs. Most of these are colored yellow and black and are so patterned that they are almost perfect mimics of bumblebees. Experienced entomologists recognize them more easily by their behavior than by their appearance. There can be little doubt that this strong resemblance to bumblebees is of benefit to the flies, both in protecting them from predators that have learned to leave bumblebees alone and also in facilitating their approach to other insects that have nothing to fear from bumblebees. The bee mimics, and some of the other species as well, often buzz loudly while flying. Some of the large species prey upon bumblebees and honeybees quite regularly, and some even manage to catch dragonflies. They themselves, however, may fall victims to other smaller but better equipped predators. We have collected a number of specimens of the large bee mimics from the webs of spiders far smaller than they.

LONG-LEGGED FLIES—Family Dolichopodidae

The majority of the fifteen hundred or more species of this family are small but often brightly metallic blue, green or coppery. They are to be seen commonly on vegetation, especially in damp places and near water. Some of the adults feed from flowers, but the majority are predaceous upon other small flies. Most of the larvae live in the ground in rotten wood or humus, although a few are aquatic.

Those of the genus *Aphrosylus* live in the wash along the seashore. The majority are predaceous.

In many of the groups the males have special structures or ornamentation that the females lack. Some have especially bright or metallic hairs on the antennae or at the tip of the abdomen. Many have large flat expansions of the front or middle tarsi. These ornaments undoubtedly are used in courtship; and in at least one species the cup-shaped discs on the tarsi are clapped down over the eyes of the female during mating, thus blinding her.

DANCE FLIES—Family Empididae

This is a widely distributed family of over two thousand species of small to minute flies that are predatory both as larvae and adults. The flies may be found commonly over water and in shaded woodland, where in small swarms they perform the rising and falling courtship dances for which they are well known. The fundamental activity of the courtship is the presentation by the male to the female of a small fly that he has caught and killed. Acceptance of this by the female, who sucks its juices, is a necessary preliminary to the mating. A number of species, however, have developed interesting variations of this behavior that show a progressive evolution toward what subjective humans may stigmatize as very unfair practices. Primitive species, as mentioned above, give the female a choice bit of food, killed but otherwise just as it was when caught. In some species, however, the male wraps the prey in a slight web formed by secretions from his front tarsi. Still other males make quite a substantial web, the penetrating of which occupies more of the female's attention. So far there seems to be nothing more than an interesting analogy to human "gift wrapping." But the male of another group of species, which can only be termed degenerate, passes the female a dummy package consisting of only the wrapping, and mates with her while she is examining this.

HUMPBACKED FLIES—Family Phoridae

As their common name implies, these small flies have a curiously humped thorax. The adults are often quite active, running quickly about on vegetation (or windows) and occasionally forming dancing swarms. The family includes groups with a considerable variety of larval habits. Some species live in decaying vegetation, insects, snails etc. Still others live in fungi, and some of these may be pests in mushroom cellars. A good many others are parasites within the bodies of various insects, the hosts of the known species being chiefly bees, wasps, ants and sawflies. Still others live as guests or invaders in the nests of termites or ants, sometimes as parasites, sometimes as scavengers. In the genus *Termitoxenia*, which lives in termite nests, the wings are reduced to minute vestiges; and in *Ecitomyia*, which lives in the nestless, migratory colonies of army ants, the wings are narrow, useless, strap-shaped structures. The larva of *Metopina*, which lives as an ant guest, curls around the neck of an ant larva and obtains some of the food that is fed to its host by the worker ants. On the other hand, the larva of *Apocephalus* lives within the head of an ant, eating until the host's head finally falls off.

FLOWER FLIES and HOVER FLIES
—Family Syrphidae

This is one of the largest families of the flies (Plates 123–127), a cosmopolitan group that contains many abundant, beautiful and beneficial species, and only a few harmful ones. The adults of many of the species are quite small, but those of many others attain a length of three-quarters of an inch or more. The majority are brightly colored, some having steely or iridescent blue or green tints but others being variously spotted or banded with black and yellow or orange. The most distinctive characteristic of the adults is the presence of an extra vein, the so-called "spurious vein," through the central part of the wing.

The adults of most of the species are confirmed flower visitors. They may often be seen hovering apparently motionless in the air, perhaps above a blossom, their wings vibrating so fast that the eye cannot detect them. Suddenly the fly will vanish, perhaps to reappear a moment later as though materializing out of nothing. Because of this habitual flower-visiting the flies are of great importance in cross-pollination, some species being better suited to this than others because of their hairiness.

A great many of the species are best known for their mimicry of various wasps and bees. In the majority of these the mimicry is of a general type, consisting of the possession of a black-and-yellow or black-and-orange pattern that looks very wasplike without resembling any particular model. A goodly number, however, have evolved colors and patterns, and even body forms and behaviors, that make them so similar to specific wasps or bees that it is sometimes difficult for even an experienced entomologist, with all his powers of reasoning and recollection, to be sure whether he is seeing a fly or a wasp. In one region there may thus be one flower fly that mimics the large black-and-yellow hornets and another that mimics the smaller ones; another that mimics the black-and-white hornets; and still others mimicking one or more species of bumblebees. In regions where some of the bumblebees have red fur on the abdomens we may expect to find a flower fly similarly colored. A number of genera of the flies have gone in the opposite direction from their stout-bodied, hairy, bee-mimicking cousins and have evolved very long, slender bodies and clublike abdomens that almost perfectly simulate the "wasp-waisted" shapes of many hunting wasps. The smaller

solitary wasps and bees are also mimicked. In all of these cases the mimics doubtless benefit to a certain extent from being mistaken for their genuinely protected, stinging models by various predatory enemies. Some of the best mimics are also the loudest buzzers when caught, an additional feature that enhances their protective resemblance.

The larvae of the flower flies are as varied in appearance as the adults, and are even more so in habits. Perhaps the majority live in the more or less conventional fashion of larval flies, burrowing around in soft humus or decaying plant material. Such larvae live as general scavengers, as do also those that live in liquid or semiliquid environments. The larvae of the abundant and widely distributed drone fly, *Eristalis tenax,* and its relatives are interestingly adapted for life in highly polluted water. The posterior end of the body is greatly elongated to form a long, slender tube, at the tip of which is the last pair of spiracles. This apparatus, which is, in truth, an insect forerunner of the snorkel air tube of divers and submarines, can be kept at the surface of a mass of liquid sewage or putrescence while the larva is feeding down below. Because of it the larvae are often called "rat-tailed" maggots.

The drone fly (Plate 125), which in the adult stage resembles the honeybee quite closely, is responsible for the famous myth of the "bugula" that, first mentioned by Ovid, attained serious and wide credence for hundreds of years. This gave a simple formula for creating a swarm of bees: one merely killed an ox and left the carcass alone for some time. Upon returning, one would find bees swarming about it, supposedly generated in the carrion. Of course what actually happens in such a situation is that the drone flies lay eggs in very large numbers in the semiliquid putrescence and that a large number of adult drone flies develops from these. It was considered intellectual heresy to question the bugula during the uncritical Middle Ages, when practically anything with the sanctity of ancient authority was believed unquestioningly. The idea that flies or bees could generate spontaneously from nothing more than carrion seems naïve to us today, yet it was not until such greatly daring thinkers of the intellectual Renaissance as Redi and Spallanzani began questioning such dogmas and putting them to experimental test that the foundations of modern empirical knowledge were laid. And the ghost of the bugula persisted until practically our own times, being finally given the *coup de grace* by Louis Pasteur.

The larvae of a very large number of other Syrphids are predators. Despite their jawless, legless and eyeless condition, they wander about on plants and feed upon such small, soft-bodied and defenseless insects as aphids, piercing them with their mouth hooks and sucking the juices. Whereas the larvae that live in seclusion are pale and uncolored, many of these aphid-hunters are very brightly tinted, often with browns and greens that match them to their environment and help them to avoid the attentions of other predators. The aphids, because of their powers of multiplication, often become very serious pests on many plants; but the Syrphids, due to their own reproductive powers and voracious appetites, may almost completely exterminate an infestation of countless millions of aphids. A classic example of this occurred when aphids that were threatening the Long Island potato crop were brought under control largely by Syrphids. At the time many people complained of the inordinate number of "wasps" that filled the region, not knowing that these were really the adults of the flies that were saving the potato crop.

The larvae of a relatively small proportion of the flower flies live in or on plants, sometimes doing considerable damage. Examples of these are the narcissus and other bulb flies of the genus *Merodon,* the larvae of which often destroy bulbs and rootstocks of narcissus, hyacinth, iris etc.

Among the scavenging species, the larvae of some are particularly interesting because of their habits of living in the nests of social bees, wasps or ants. The various species of the genus *Volucella* thus feed upon diseased larvae and pupae in the nests of bumblebees or hornets. The adults are very stout-bodied, often metallic blue flies. The curious larvae of the genus *Microdon,* which live in ant nests, are so unlike conventional insect larvae in appearance that they have been described as slugs.

The large number of well-marked species and the attractive appearance of these flies makes them favorites with collectors. We have seen some extremely interesting collections of them that showed the chief mimetic species paired off with their bee and wasp models.

THICK-HEADED FLIES—Family Conopidae

The common name of this family is not a reflection on the mental ability of the flies (they have none) but is objectively descriptive, since the head is often broader than the thorax. The larvae live inside the bodies of other insects, chiefly attacking wasps and bumblebees but, in some species, locusts. There they feed on the host's blood, weakening it until it dies. They are thus really predators, but because of their relatively gentle internal method of attack are more commonly called parasites. The correct term is actually "parasitoid."

The adults (Plate 131) are not uncommonly seen visiting flowers. In some of the genera such as *Conops* and *Physocephala* they are quite long and slender and have petiolate, wasp-waisted abdomens that make them exceedingly good mimics of various small wasps that are usually common on the same flowers. Their actions on flowers are also extremely

wasplike, for they hold the abdomen up prominently in the air and often twitch it in a way that calls attention to their distinctive shape. The females of some species pursue the bees and wasps that will serve as hosts for their larvae and deposit eggs on them while in flight.

FRUIT FLIES—Family Trypetidae
(*Trypaneidae, Tephritidae*)

The twelve hundred members of this very widespread family are quite small flies that often are black or steely blue or green, with the wings pictured with black or brown mottlings or patches. The eggs are laid in clusters in plant tissues in cavities hollowed out by the sometimes very long ovipositor of the female. The larvae then burrow about in the living plant tissues.

The family is chiefly noted for the damage, sometimes serious, that is done by a considerable number of species that infest plants valuable to man. The majority, however, live in plants of no economic importance; and some, which attack weed plants, are of some benefit. Nearly all parts of the plants are infested by some species, some mining in leaves, others living in stems, flower heads, buds or fruits, and still others living in galls formed by the plant. Among economically important species are: the celery leaf miner, *Acidia heraclei;* the apple maggot, *Rhagoletis pomonella;* the cherry maggot, *R. cingulata;* the currant maggot, *Epochra canadensis;* and the Mediterranean fruit fly, *Ceratitis capitata.* The last is an especially destructive species, the larva of which attacks almost all succulent fruits. Its introduction into Florida created a very serious menace that was ended only at great expense and after drastic control and quarantine measures. At a total cost of hundreds of millions of dollars (including the value of the fruit lost and orchards destroyed) it was finally eradicated. Infestation by the Queensland fruit fly, *Chaetodacus tryoni,* has forced the abandonment of valuable stone-fruit orchards in Australia.

A common gall-making species is the round goldenrod gall fly, *Eurosta solidaginis.* The species causes the formation by the goldenrod plant of a ball-shaped gall nearly an inch in diameter in the stem. Inside this the larva lives, grows and pupates, emerging in May after spending the winter in the gall.

The picture-winged and peacock flies of the family Otitidae (Ortalididae) are a small but widely distributed family closely related to the fruit flies. Many of the species have boldly patterned wings, and some have brightly colored metallic bodies. Some have the head so produced out to the sides that the eyes are situated at the ends of short stalks. The larvae live in decaying vegetation, under bark or in excrement, except for a few species that infest growing plants.

The family Ephydridae contains a number of small to minute flies that live about wet places or in fresh water. Some of these are known as "brine flies," since the larvae live in salty or alkaline waters of such high concentrations that it is hardly conceivable that anything could survive in them. They are often abundant in pools about salt mines and salt works. In the Far West and in Mexico they develop in alkaline lakes in such numbers that the Indians collect them by the bushel, dry them and use them for food. Even more extraordinary is the petroleum fly, *Helaeomyia petrolei,* which lives in pools of crude petroleum in California and Cuba, swimming about and feeding on organic particles.

POMACE FLIES—Family Drosophilidae

The larvae of these small to very small flies live in decaying fruit or fungi or in fermenting sap or fruits. Some of them are abundant in houses and about wineries and cider mills, the adults being strongly attracted to the odors of fermentation. One of the species, *Drosophila melanogaster,* in particular, and a number of its relatives to a lesser degree, are of the utmost importance and value in scientific research, perhaps more so than any other animals. It is with these flies that a great many of the most fundamental studies of heredity have been made. Countless millions of them are reared in laboratories, where their small size, hardiness and great powers of multiplication make them almost ideal for genetic work. Fed on fermenting banana or similar foods, several hundred can be reared in a half-pint jar, the entire life cycle from generation to generation taking but two weeks. The adult flies are easily controlled since their strong attraction to light (positive phototropism) causes them to rush to the better-lighted end of a jar, where they can be led into another container without loss. They show a great many inheritable variations, several hundred major examples of which have been recorded and studied by experimental breeding. In this way the details of the relationships of genes, the units of inheritance carried by the sex cells, can be worked out on a trustworthy experimental basis. Since the hereditary mechanism is essentially the same in all plants and animals, the information obtained through studying *Drosophila* is applicable in corn, wheat or man himself. It has justifiably been said that *Drosophila* is to the science of heredity what the hydrogen atom is to nuclear physics.

LEAF- and STEM-MINING FLIES
—Family Agromyzidae

In the great majority of species of this widespread family of small to minute flies the larvae mine in plant tissues, most commonly in leaves but in many cases in stems. It will be readily appreciated that only a tiny insect can pass its entire larval life in a flat tunnel within the confines of a single leaf. The mines are often quite distinctive in shape and extent, some species being more readily identified by this than by the appearance of the insect itself. Heavy infestations may build up, since some species multiply rapidly, having several generations a year. The ugly whitish blotches spoil the appearance of the leaves of ornamental plants. In some of the stem-mining species the larva may mine completely around the outer layers of the stem, girdling it and weakening or killing the plant. On the other hand, such species as those of the genus *Leucopis* are predaceous on aphids and scale insects, and therefore in many instances beneficial to man. Two species of the genus *Cryptochaetum* were, in fact, introduced into California from Australia because of their value in controlling the cottony cushion scale, a serious citrus pest.

DUNG FLIES—Family Cordyluridae
(*Scatophagidae*)

Some of the long-legged, hairy, yellow members of this family are common in meadows and damp places, the genus *Scatophaga* being particularly widespread. They are about the size of house flies, but some members of the family are considerably larger. As the vernacular name of the family implies, many of the species are common about dung and manure, where they live and feed as larvae, perhaps also as adults. Some species are predaceous as adults, catching insects even as large as honeybees. A few are known to be parasitic in other insects during the larval development.

STALK-EYED FLIES—Family Diopsidae

Although this is a relatively small family of chiefly tropical flies, no account of the order would be complete without mention of it. The eyes are set on the ends of stalks that protrude sideways from the head, sometimes to an extent several times the width of the head. No possible reason of practicality or value to the fly can be assigned to this; in fact, the cumbersome extensions definitely handicap the flies in moving about. The stalks are not freely movable like those on which the eyes of crabs and other Crustacea are placed, and are many times longer than necessary to allow the fly to see to the rear. There is hardly a better example of the weakness of the view of evolution formerly held that all features of plants and animals must be beneficially adaptive, making them more fit for survival.

Only one stalk-eyed fly is known to occur in the United States, a species with quite short stalks. The majority of the known species occur in the Pacific-Asiatic or African regions, where the adults may be moderately common about the margins of ponds and streams, resting on stones or vegetation. The larvae feed on decaying plant and animal material.

BOT and WARBLE FLIES—Families Gastero-philidae, Oestridae etc.

The flies here included are variously classified in from one to four families, largely depending upon the opinion of the individual classifying them. They form a well-integrated group of medium- to large-sized, heavy-bodied flies that are in one way or another parasitic in mammals. Most of them are of Old World origin, but a number have been introduced into North America. Since quite a few of them attack domestic animals and man, sometimes with serious results, they are of veterinary and medical importance.

The true horse bot flies of the family Gasterophili-dae are robust, hairy flies somewhat larger than the common house fly. The proboscis is vestigial, so that the adults never feed. The females lay their eggs on the heads or bodies of horses, different species favoring specific locations about the mouth or on the forelegs. The eggs are fastened to hairs or skin with a cement that also acts as an irritant. The horse then rubs the place with its nose or licks it, and this causes hatching of the eggs. The larvae thus gain entrance to the horse's mouth, and pass down its digestive tract. Some remain in the pharynx, others in the stomach or various regions of the intestine, each species again favoring certain places. The larvae affix themselves to the wall by means of their mouth hooks, feed on blood and grow until mature. They then loosen their hold, pass out the anus with the feces, pupate in the soil and transform to adult flies. The presence of perhaps thousands of the larvae sometimes weakens a horse sufficiently to cause its death; and the nervousness caused by the presence of the adult flies (of which horses are very fearful), and by the irritation caused by the eggs, may also do considerable harm. It is possible to control the flies by thorough control of the horse manure and of the soil on which it falls, thus preventing pupation of the larvae, and also by consistent currying and brushing to remove the eggs from the skin.

The family Oestridae is best known for the sheep bot or sheep nostril fly, *Oestrus ovis,* widely distributed in both Old and New Worlds. Living larvae are laid in the nostrils of the sheep by the female without alighting. They migrate to the frontal sinuses and live there, causing nasal discharges, obstruction of breathing and serious fits of vertigo known as the "blind staggers." There are records of Oestrid infections in the Old World in camels, mules, donkeys and (rarely) man; and larvae have even been found living between the toes of elephants. Both these and the warble flies arouse the animals on which the female is diving to bursts of frantic running that may do great harm. Extravagant estimates of the flying speed of these insects have received much publicity. Estimates as high as eight hundred miles per hour have thus been made, which in actuality are probably ten to twenty times too high.

The warble flies of the genus *Hypoderma* were introduced into North America from Europe, the most serious being those known as ox warbles. From the eggs, which are laid on the skin, the larvae bore through the skin and enter the body. Here they migrate about for some time, spend a period in the esophagus and eventually come to rest just under the skin of the back, where they cause characteristic bumps or "warbles." When fully grown they may be two inches or more long. The terror that one of of the flies causes in cattle is evidenced by the name "bomb fly" that is sometimes applied to them, for a herd of placid cows will suddenly explode and dash frantically in all directions attempting to escape the tormentor, not only running chances of seriously injuring themselves but appreciably lowering the milk production. The physiological damage to the cattle is, of course, great; and the holes in the skin made by the emerging larvae seriously affect the value of the hide.

The warble and robust bot flies sometimes placed in the family Cuterebridae include the human warble fly, *Dermatobia hominis,* and a number of species of the genus *Cuterebra* that attack various mammals ranging from rabbits and hares to deer and caribou. All have essentially the same type of development as the ox warble fly described above, the larvae living under or near the skin of the host and causing serious swellings in which much pus accumulates. Rupture of one of these or of the larva may cause serious infections. The human warble fly infests cattle, dogs and cats as well as humans.

The method by which the human warble fly infects its hosts is most interesting. The female fly seizes mosquitoes, e.g. of the abundant and viciously biting genus *Psorophora,* and holds them unharmed while she cements a number of her eggs to their lower surfaces; she then releases them. The fly eggs do not hatch until the mosquito alights on a warm-blooded animal; but then the larva bursts out of the eggshell and fastens to the skin of the new host, later boring in. The mosquito is merely made the passive transportation agent for the eggs. Certain biting flies, ticks and even dung flies are also used; and there are records of flies laying their eggs on leaves against which a suitable mammalian host may brush in passing, enabling the waiting larva to catch onto it.

TACHINA FLIES—Family Tachinidae

It is something of a relief to turn for a moment from the unpleasant bot and warble flies to a group that bestows as great benefits upon man as any other family of animals, being one of his mainstays in controlling the numbers of many insects injurious to agriculture. As larvae these flies live within the bodies of other insects, feeding on their tissues and eventually causing their death; and among their victims are a great many of the species that are most harmful to man's economy. Since they are a very large and widespread family, occurring nearly everywhere that other insects live, these flies are of primary importance in the world of the insects as a whole, acting as one of the chief checks on the great reproductive powers of the plant-eating groups.

Some of the flies themselves are rather small, less than one-twentieth of an inch long, but the majority are about the size of a house fly, and some are several times as large. Characteristically they are very bristly, sometimes excessively so. The commonest color is gray, but many are black, yellow or orange, and some are most beautifully iridescent with blue-greens and purples that match the colors of any other living things. Many of them are common flower visitors, and thus to their other important activities add the cross-pollination of many plants.

Typically the eggs are laid directly on the host insect, most commonly being fastened to its skin. In many common species such an egg is a flat, white oval that can be seen plainly with the naked eye. Other species insert eggs (or living larvae) in the body of the host. Still others merely lay the eggs in the environment frequented by the host, and still others deposit the eggs seemingly more or less at random. In the last cases the larvae must find and penetrate the hosts for themselves, unless they belong to a species that depends upon the egg being eaten along with the leaf on which it is laid and hatching in the host's digestive tract. There is great differentiation of the various species as to the details of the larval life inside the host, especially as to its ways of respiration and feeding. In some types only a single Tachinid larva will develop inside each host; but in others a considerable number may live and develop to maturity. Sometimes, too, the Tachinid larva itself falls victim to other parasites, such as certain Chalcid wasps that can develop only in a host caterpillar in which they encounter a Tachinid larva that they can eat. It occasionally happens also that Ichneumon wasp larvae gain entrance to a caterpillar also parasitized by a Tachinid larva; in a number of such instances in our own experience the wasps were always successful, and nothing more was seen of the Tachinid.

The tachina flies have been very widely used by economic entomologists as a means of controlling noxious insects. Once it is established in a region where some pest is breaking out, the tachina fly or parasitic wasp may attain such abundance as to practically exterminate the pest. Thereafter it remains in the area, in reduced numbers to be sure, costing nothing but ever ready to cope with any future infestations. Many species have been im-

ported from the home regions of imported pests and, after a period of laboratory multiplication, turned loose at strategic places. It sometimes happens that, because of some feature in the environment that could not have been anticipated, the parasite is unable to adapt itself to the new region as well as the pest that it is expected to control. In such a case the entomologist keeps on trying with other parasites until he either exhausts the supply of possibilities, runs out of funds or finds one that will do the job. The great powers of multiplication of the flies (a single female may lay five hundred or more eggs or living larvae) make them well suited to cope with outbreaks of pests. Such biological control is enormously preferable to the wholesale use of poisonous insecticides. These should be used only on a small scale or to cope with genuine emergencies that demand drastic treatment, since they are extremely expensive, both initially and in the long run. Insecticides also have no lasting effect, and often do far more harm than good by killing off the beneficial insects of the area treated, to say nothing of their harmful effect on other forms of wildlife such as birds and fish.

Compsilura concinnata and *Sturmia scutellata* are two representative tachina flies that were imported from Europe to control the gypsy and browntail moths, serious imported forest pests. Control of the browntail has been most successful. Some species, such as the very common *Winthemia quadripustulata* of eastern North America, parasitize many species of hosts; others are more specialized, confining their attentions to those of a single small group. The principal hosts are the caterpillars of butterflies and moths, the adults and larvae of beetles and the larvae of sawflies; but some species attack Orthoptera, Hemiptera or even other Diptera. Their classification is a task for skilled specialists only.

FLESH FLIES, BLOW FLIES and MUSCID FLIES—Families Muscidae, Sarcophagidae and Calliphoridae

It would not be profitable to consider these families separately, since they all share the same variety of habits and are none too distinct from each other. They are from time to time combined in various ways by entomologists. Their classification is based on structures that are not always clear-cut and in many of the groups are difficult to see and use. We shall therefore consider them in one sequence, inasmuch as we are primarily concerned with the things that they do and with how these affect man and other animals.

The adult flies are relatively stout-bodied and bristly, averaging about the size of the common house fly although some are much smaller and many are considerably larger. They are most commonly gray or brown, often spotted or marbled with various darker shades; but, especially in the Calliphoridae (Plate 128), many species have bright metallic colors that are evidenced by such common names as "bluebottle" and "greenbottle." They are not nearly such consistent flower visitors as the closely related tachina flies (which many of them strongly resemble) but instead tend more to business in the environments where they feed as larvae and in turn will lay their eggs. It is in their life histories that we see the greatest variety.

Undoubtedly the best-known, most widely distributed and most infamous species is the house fly, *Musca domestica* (Plate 130), the most consistently dangerous animal the world over as far as man is concerned. The larvae of this fly are exceedingly general scavengers, being able to grow successfully and quickly in practically any damp, decaying organic matter from carrion and garbage to manure and even wet newspapers. This wide larval dietary has played an important part in allowing the house fly to accompany man everywhere in the world and to flourish in even our supposedly most sanitary communities. The tastes of the adult are similarly broad, being equally satisfied in the sugar bowl, the sickroom or the privy. The mouthparts of the adult form a short proboscis with a fleshy pair of expandable lobes at the tip. When it feeds, a drop of liquid, the "vomit drop," is first regurgitated on the food as the lobes gently rasp the surface; and then most of this drop is sucked back again. A residue remains, however, which probably contains bacteria from the previous foods; and these may range from excrement to infected sputum and the exudate from ulcers. Individual flies have been found to harbor as many as 33,000,000 organisms in the intestinal tract and 500,000,000 on the surface of the body and legs at one time; and their habits practically insure that these will be disease-causing if there are any such about the neighborhood. When we add to this a reproduction rate of a generation a month in warm weather, and the ability of each female to lay 120 to 160 eggs at a time, it is no wonder that this insect is the known carrier of nearly forty serious diseases (typhoid, tuberculosis and both bacillary and amoebic dysentery are the worst) as well as of intestinal worms. Despite this, we still tolerate flies in even our supposedly most sanitary homes, rather than hurt someone's feelings by forcing him to clean up his premises or control his dog.

A considerable group of the muscid flies have sharp, piercing mouthparts with which they penetrate skin and suck blood. The most widespread is the biting stable fly, *Stomoxys calcitrans,* similar enough in appearance to the house fly for the latter to be unjustly blamed for biting. It carries several diseases of man and domestic animals, in addition to being a severe pest of cattle and horses. The most serious of the blood-sucking muscids, however, are the tsetse flies of the genus *Glossina,* restricted to Africa, which act as carriers of human sleeping sickness and of n'gana, an important disease of cattle.

The majority of the other muscids and of the flesh flies and blow flies may be divided into two main groups: those that live as larvae in decaying, dead matter, and those that live in living animal tissues. The distinction between these habits, however, is not always at all clear; for many of the species that usually live as scavengers will also at times invade living bodies. In general the bluebottle flies, *Calliphora,* and most of the greenbottle flies, *Lucilia,* develop in decaying plant and animal material only, while the black blow fly, *Phormia regina;* the screw-worm fly, *Callitroga americana;* the greenbottle *Lucilia sericata* and many others will invade living tissues where they are invited by open wounds etc., and will often attack healthy areas. Some of the species of these, especially of *Lucilia,* have been considerably used in surgery to clean up infected wounds because of their preference for necrotic and decaying tissues. In recent years their use has been superseded by modern drug therapy.

A considerable number of these flies are able to develop in the human intestine when eggs or larvae are swallowed or otherwise gain entrance. Such cases of "myiasis" may be quite severe, but do not occur often enough to show that this is a normal way of life for the flies.

Within the Sarcophagidae is found an equally wide range of habits. In this family the majority of females deposit living larvae instead of laying eggs. In some of the flesh flies (*Sarcophaga*) these are deposited on meat by being dropped while the female flies past; and when the female is denied direct access to meat she may drop the larvae from as much as two feet above it, their minute size permitting them to penetrate screening.

A large number of the Sarcophagids and also many of the Calliphorids are internal parasites in insects or other invertebrate animals. The larvae of the Calliphorid cluster fly, *Pollenia rudis,* for example, live in earthworms. This fly often receives much attention in the autumn, since the adults enter houses in large numbers to spend the winter and sometimes form great clusters in attics and dark closets, to the horror of the housewife. Many of the species of *Sarcophaga* are internal parasites in a wide variety of insects.

The large larvae of *Sarcophaga fletcheri* and probably of related species are commonly found in the hollow, water-filled leaves of pitcher plants. These leaves serve the plants as traps for insects, which may often be found in them in very large numbers, drowned, disintegrating and being digested. The fly larvae, able to resist digestion just as their relatives are in animal intestines, feed on the trapped insects and thus parasitize the plant's hunting apparatus.

ANTHOMYID FLIES—Family Anthomyiidae

In this large, cosmopolitan family we find the same mixture of larval food habits that characterizes so many other groups of flies. The adults are chiefly small, brown or gray and very ordinary looking. Their classification is in quite a state of flux, as is usual in this section of the flies, many genera being much like muscid flies.

A great many of the species are plant-eaters, mining in leaves or boring in stems, roots and bulbs; and among these are some very serious agricultural pests such as the wheat, seed corn, cabbage and onion maggots of the genus *Hylemyia*. The majority of species, however, live as general scavengers in decaying plant matter. The lesser house fly, *Fannia canicularis,* which often invades our houses, is one of these. The adults, which look like miniature house flies, are often spoken of as "baby house flies" by people who do not realize that insects do not grow in size when once they have attained maturity and developed wings. A very interesting group of the plant scavengers is the genus *Fucellia*, the kelp flies, that breed in mats of the kelp seaweeds drifted up on beaches.

A number of these flies are predatory in either the larval or adult stages or both. An interesting group of Australian genera lives about running streams, where the adults catch mayflies in the air and suck their blood. Still others are parasitic on larger animals, the larvae of *Passeromyia* living in bird nests and sucking blood from the nestlings, while those of *Mydea* bore into birds' bodies and live beneath the skin like the larvae of warble flies.

THE DEGENERATE PARASITIC FLIES
—Section Pupipara

Four exceedingly interesting families of flies form this section, generally regarded as the most advanced of all the flies. All live parasitically as adults on the bodies of other animals, and as an adaptation for this kind of existence they have undergone considerable, sometimes total, degeneration of the wings. They show us, in fact, an almost exact parallel to the evolution of the biting and sucking lice in a very different group of insects; but some of these flies have not evolved as far as others, and so illustrate various stages in the development of parasitism. In the majority of species in the group, the larvae are retained within the body of the mother until they are practically full grown, being nourished meanwhile by the products of special glands. Here we see another parallelism, the evolution of the ability to bear the young alive having arisen independently in many groups of animals, of which we and our relatives the other mammals are merely one example.

The adult louse flies of the family Hippoboscidae live on various birds and mammals. They are typically flat-bodied, with strong, bristly legs that can grasp firmly the fur or feathers of their hosts. Some are completely wingless; others have wings but use them little and shed them when they have found a host; and others have and retain well-developed wings. All, however, depend for dispersal chiefly or entirely upon contact between individuals of their host species. Different genera and species tend to specialize on certain species or groups of hosts. Thus the species of *Olfersia* are found on such game birds as grouse and also on the hawks and owls that feed upon these. Many a hunter carrying the day's bag of ruffed grouse has been bothered by the large, flat flies running up through the short hairs on his neck, almost impossible to catch or pick off, and has wondered what they were. *Pseudolynchia brunnea* is found on the nighthawks and whippoorwills of the New World. The European *Ornithomyia* are found on many wild birds. The species of *Hippobosca* are found on mammals, the New Forest fly *Hippobosca equina* being a well-known pest on horses. Females of *Hippobosca camelina,* often abundant on camels, are said to lay pupae ready formed, each enclosed in an oval white case. The flies of this species are often a great nuisance to people riding camels. The best-known species is the sheep "tick" or "ked," *Melophagus ovinus,* a completely wingless insect that for long was regarded as a tick. It often causes serious skin irritations that result in greatly lowered wool production and value.

The bat ticks and bat lice of the families Nycteribidae and Streblidae live, as their names imply, on bats. On reaching a suitable bat host the winged female of the Streblid *Ascodipteron* penetrates beneath the skin and casts off both her wings and her legs. She then changes into a simple sac with the anal end communicating with the hole through which she entered; and from this the larvae to which she gives birth are projected. Many other Streblids are wingless, as are also the many species of the Nycteribids.

For centuries the family Braulidae was thought to consist of but the single species, *Braula caeca,* the well-known bee louse of the Old World; but recently another species was found in the Belgian Congo. The tiny, wingless flies cling to the bodies of honeybees, sometimes being found in great numbers. They apparently get their food directly from the mouths of the bees. The eggs are laid in the hives, where the larvae tunnel about and scavenge. In this as well as in other respects the bee lice are different from the bird and mammal parasites described above; and it is believed that they may really have evolved quite separately from an unrelated group of flies. Certainly they are one of the most striking manifestations of the infinite variety of insect life.

CHAPTER XIII

Wasps, Ants, Bees and Others

Order Hymenoptera

A CHALCID WASP

THIS, the third-largest of the orders, is perhaps the most widespread and pervasive, and certainly the most diversified. Its members are to be found everywhere on land. Arctic bumblebees live in the northernmost edges of Greenland and Ellesmere Island, while ants swarm in the hot, arid deserts (and nearly everywhere else) and wasps and stingless bees teem in the tropical rain forests. Parasitic wasps abound everywhere, some even penetrating the fresh waters, where they have followed their hosts beneath the surface.

Some groups are primitive plant-eaters, boring in stems or feeding on foliage, while others bore in seeds and still others are gall-makers on special plants. A great multitude are parasites that destroy vast numbers of other insects. Many are predators, catching other insects as food for their larvae and for themselves. Many of the ants are scavengers, living on unconsidered trifles of plant and animal debris, while others live on the sweet honeydew secretions of other insects. And many, especially the bees, are consistent flower visitors, subsisting solely on nectar and pollen.

No other order of insects has such a profound effect on all other forms of land life. The ceaseless subterranean activity of the ants has a far greater effect in loosening, mixing and aerating soil than that of the much publicized earthworms. The bees make possible the production of seeds by great numbers of plants, including many of the greatest value to man. And the parasitic wasps are perhaps the greatest natural check on the teeming hordes of plant-eating insects, as well as counterchecks on predators and other parasites.

In the complexity of their societies the Hymenoptera excel all other insects. At least three great groups of them have independently evolved high degrees of social organization. Some, in fact, have gone far beyond the bounds of ordinary socialization and have evolved intricate types of social parasitism and degeneration that almost strain our credulity and are unique in the world of life.

Estimates of the number of species of Hymenoptera run around one hundred thousand, but there is no doubt that when, if ever, all of the species are known, this figure will be enormously increased. At present only a very small part of the parasitic forms of the tropics are known, so that these alone will add many thousands of species.

The chief groups are the sawflies, parasitic wasps, ants, solitary wasps, social wasps and bees. Despite the great diversity that is found among them, all have many important characteristics in common, so that most of them appear obviously related, even to the non-entomologist. Typically there are two pairs of wings, of which the hind pair is considerably the

Horntail Sawfly (*Tremex*), showing the drill used by the female to bore holes in wood in which to lay her eggs.

smaller and is fastened to the rear edge of the front pair by rows of minute hooks. There is a relatively small number, often greatly reduced, of rather tortuous wing veins. The mouthparts are of the biting type, and in the more primitive groups are, like those of the Orthoptera, quite primitive. The jaws (mandibles) are usually strong and used for chewing food, at least in the larval stage. In the adults of many groups they are somewhat reduced and functionless. In the higher wasps and bees they are used chiefly as tools. In the bees, which are highly specialized for flower-visiting, the rear lip (labium) is more or less elongated, forming a sucking tube. These insects thus have both chewing and sucking mouthparts, a feature that permits great diversification of their habits.

The first segment of the abdomen is strongly joined to the thorax, appearing to be a part of that region. In the majority of groups the succeeding segments, or segment, of the abdomen are extremely slender, after which the abdomen broadens again. The appropriately termed "wasp-waisted" appearance of these insects is characteristic. The females of the majority have a tubular ovipositor, sometimes much longer than all the rest of the insect. In the higher groups this is modified as a sting. The metamorphosis is complete. The larva is generally a

rather simple, soft-bodied, legless grub with a well-developed head. When readying for pupation it usually prepares a cocoon of silk, parchment or both. The pupa has its appendages free (exarate), not tightly bound to the body as in the Lepidoptera.

General Classification

The suborder Clistogastra or Symphyta consists of those Hymenoptera that have the abdomen broadly joined to the thorax. It includes the sawflies, all of which we classify as the superfamily Tenthredinoidea (although some authors make further subdivisions) and a very small group of parasitic wasps, the superfamily Oryssoidea.

The other suborder, the Chalastogastra or Apocrita, contains all the rest (the great majority) of the order, in which the abdomen appears to be joined to the thorax by a slender stalk or petiole. The classification of the Chalastogastra is extremely complex, since it includes a number of important superfamilies, containing many families, which are distinguished by highly technical characteristics of body structure and wing venation. It is necessary for our purpose only to recognize the chief subfamilies and families, in order to appreciate the interest and significance of their exceedingly varied habits.

The three superfamilies Ichneumonoidea, Chalcidoidea and Proctotrypoidea together contain more than half of the known species of the order. Almost all are parasitic on spiders and other insects; but a few groups attack plants (chiefly boring in stems and seeds) and some live as invaders (inquilines) in the galls or nests of other insects.

The superfamily Cynipoidea contains some twelve hundred species of very small wasps, the majority of which live in plant galls. Some, however, are parasites.

The superfamily Formicoidea consists of the wholly social ants. Only one family is recognized (so compact a group do the ants form) but a number of important subfamilies differ greatly from one another in habits and structures.

The superfamilies Vespoidea and Sphecoidea contain the "true" wasps. The great majority are solitary in habit, each female provisioning her own nest or otherwise attending to the future welfare of her offspring. It is only in one relatively small group of the Vespid wasps that we find a social life, which is not nearly as highly developed as that of the ants and bees.

The superfamily Apoidea consists of the bees. Here, as in the wasps, the great majority of the species are solitary, each female preparing her own nest and provisioning it with nectar and pollen. Only in two families are there truly social bees: in the Apidae, the honeybee and its few relatives and the small stingless bees of the tropics; and in the Bombidae, the bumblebees.

Wasp "Parasitism"

Before going further it is well to note again, as was done in discussing the so-called "parasitic flies," that these insects are not, in the strict sense, true parasites. They almost invariably cause the death of their hosts, which is something that a typical parasite does not do. Their method of attacking the host, however, is the relatively gentle one, sucking from without or boring within, of the parasite. Strictly they are predators, which is an important matter, since it is by killing their hosts that they exert an enormous influence in the world of insects and are of great importance to man. But even among entomologists they are almost invariably termed "parasites," although sometimes the term "parasitoids" is used.

THE SAWFLIES
—Superfamily Tenthredinoidea

These are the essentially plant-eating, primitive members of the order, easily recognized by the broad joining of the abdomen and thorax. The ovipositor of the female is often very prominent, looking like a sting although it is not. It consists of a pair of slender appendages that function as a tube through which the eggs are laid, and another pair that act as a sheath. It is frequently armed with rows of teeth (whence the name "sawfly") and thus may form a powerful boring or drilling tool with which deep holes may be made, even in solid wood, for the reception of the eggs. The adults range in size from small forms less than a quarter of an inch long to large species that may attain a length of two inches.

The larvae are often greatly like the caterpillars of moths in form and coloration. They are, in fact, sometimes collected and reared by inexperienced amateurs of the Lepidoptera, who are greatly surprised and disappointed when the results turn out to be sawflies instead of moths or butterflies. Sawfly larvae have only a single tiny eye on each side of the head instead of the group of four to six on each side possessed by Lepidopterous larvae. They also never have the same pattern of abdominal prolegs as caterpillars, most of them having from six to ten pairs or lacking them altogether. Most caterpillars have a group of four pairs on abdominal segments 3 to 6 and a pair on segment 10; or else (as in the "loopers" and "measuring worms") a pair each on segments 5, 6 and 10, or 6 and 10. There are a few rare exceptions in each group, chiefly borers and leaf-miners.

Many sawfly larvae that feed out in the open are brightly colored with greens, yellow and blacks, their coloration being effectively concealing in numerous cases. Many others are covered with cottony, mealy or slimy secretions, which probably have a protective value. Some are able to squirt out a defensive liquid through variously located openings. A few

species live sociably in silken webs, thus still further enhancing their similarity to moth caterpillars that do the same.

The larvae of some species live as leaf-miners, and are correspondingly flattened and more or less legless. Those of others live in plant galls. These are particularly interesting since there is good evidence that the plant forms the gall in response to a substance injected by the female sawfly at the time she lays her eggs and not to a stimulus caused by the egg or the larva itself. We shall discuss plant galls at some length under the gall wasps (Cynipidae) because of the very special interest attached to the study of these abnormal, almost tumor-like growths.

Sawfly larvae almost all pupate inside a cocoon, which is characteristically formed of a parchment-like substance and is a rather blunt oval in outline. It may be attached to a plant or made in the soil, in rotting wood, or in the tunnel in the case of boring forms. The larva typically emerges by breaking loose a cap at one end.

The larvae of the small family Cephidae are borers in shoots and stems of various plants. Those of the wheat-stem borer, *Cephus pygmaeus,* a European species introduced into North America, are often exceedingly injurious, weakening the stem below the head of grain so that it breaks.

The adults of the horn tails (Siricidae) may be

A female of the very large **Ichneumon Wasp** (*Megarhyssa lunator*) laying her eggs. She may drill as much as three inches into solid wood with her long ovipositor.

An **Ichneumon Wasp** (*Heteropelma flavicorne*) parasitizing the young caterpillars of a **Prominent Moth** (*Schizura*).

more than an inch and a half long and brightly colored. The females use their powerful ovipositors to lay their eggs deep in solid wood, where the larvae tunnel for perhaps two years, greatly damaging the wood. The pigeon tremex, *Tremex columba* (Plate 139), is a common American species. It is often parasitized by the large, striking-looking ichneumon wasps of the genus *Megarhyssa*.

Also very large are the sawflies of the family Cimbicidae, some being heavy-bodied insects with stout, clubbed antennae and bright black-and-yellow or metallic colors, an inch and a half long. Their conspicuous larvae, which can shoot out a jet of protective spray, are often seen coiled more or less spirally on various plants on which they feed.

The great majority of the sawflies belong to the large family Tenthredinidae and are much smaller insects, the adults seldom exceeding one-half inch

Larva of a **Pine Sawfly** (*Diprion*) in its characteristic warning position.

in length. Many are brightly colored with black and red, green or yellow. The larvae of the majority are leaf-eaters on a wide variety of plants, chiefly trees and shrubs. Some are exceedingly injurious to plants valuable to man. The currant sawfly or imported currant worm, *Pteronidea ribesii,* is a very abundant pest, originally introduced from Europe, on currant and gooseberry. The slimy larva of the "pear slug," *Calirhoa cerasi,* which looks much more like a true slug than an insect, is also a European introduction. So is the pine sawfly, *Diprion simile,* which, with some close American relatives, frequently damages pines seriously. The birch-leaf miner, *Fenusa pumila,* often ruins the appearance of nearly every gray birch in the eastern United States by browning the leaves in June. The often abundant "rose slugs" are really the larvae of sawflies, *Cladius isomerus* and *Endelomyia aethiops.* And the infamous larch sawfly, *Nematus erichsonii,* is one of the most serious pests of boreal forests, regularly defoliating the larches over wide areas. There are dozens more similar pests in North America, feeding on plants from plum and cherry to pansies and ferns. One species, however, is not wholly bad from the viewpoint of many hay-fever sufferers: the raspberry sawfly, *Monophadnoides rubi,* sometimes feeds on ragweed!

THE PARASITIC WASPS

As we noted above these wasps are contained in four superfamilies, the Ichneumonoidea (Plate 9), Chalcidoidea, Proctotrupoidea and Cynipoidea, with some thirty or more families in all. They form a bewildering mélange that shows nearly every imaginable type of activity. The great majority engage in some type of parasitism, or rather of parasite-like predation; but in some of the families many, in some cases the majority, are plant-eaters, while other obviously closely related groups live as parasites or inquilines.

The most common and relatively most simple type of parasitism is, with minor variations, characteristic of many thousands of species. The female wasp, tirelessly searching in the specific environment to which her instincts lead her, finds an individual of the particular species or group of insects or spiders that are the normal hosts of her species. She pierces it with her ovipositor and lays an egg within it. In due time her larva hatches and sets about feeding within the host. It first attacks such nonvital parts as the blood and fatty tissues, so that the host continues its activities in seemingly normal fashion. Often the host is able to grow to full size and, if it is a larva, even to pupate. Inside it, however, the parasite also grows, and toward the end of its development attacks the vital organs. Eventually it emerges from what is left of the host, which by now probably consists of little more than the skin and hard exoskeleton. It spins a cocoon within which it

An **Ichneumon Wasp** (*Ophion macrurum*), an important parasite of large moths and butterflies.

pupates, and in due time emerges as an adult wasp.

Whereas perhaps the majority of parasitic wasps live thus, as single, simple larvae within a host, many thousands of species have evolved special departures from this basic pattern. One of the commonest of these lies in the presence within the host of more than one parasite larva—sometimes of a large number. Most commonly each of these arises from a separate egg, in which case all of the eggs may have been laid by a single mother, or, less commonly, by more than one mother. The latter situation is often avoided by the ability of the egg-laying females to sense the fact that a host has already been parasitized, and as a result to pass it by. This, of course, prevents wasteful competition between larvae of the same species. In many other cases, however, successful multiple parasitism does take place and may, in fact, be the rule; but this is usually only when the host is large and the individual parasite small, so that there is plenty of food

for a large family. One of the most valuable to man of all of the parasitic wasps, the little Braconid, *Apanteles glomeratus,* consistently develops in large numbers (up to 150) in relatively large host larvae such as those of the cabbage butterflies. Its larvae spin a mass of fluffy silken cocoons when they emerge from the remnants of the host, which are often very prominent.

A most interesting specialization, which in fact insures the production of a great many parasites from a single host, is the ability of a single wasp egg to develop into a great many separate individuals. This is accomplished by the fragmentation during early growth of the original embryonic mass to form a number of separate cells or cell masses, each of which then develops into a separate larva. The individuals that are thus formed from a single egg are, of course, all of the same sex, since they all have an identical inheritance. This phenomenon of "polyembryony" occurs in most or all groups of animals

[241

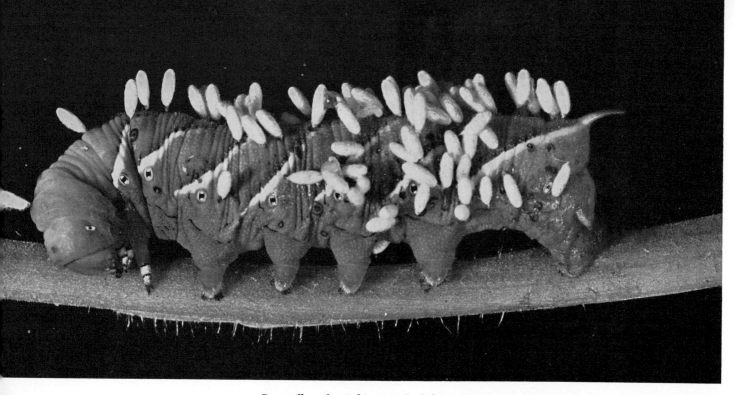

Caterpillar of a **Sphinx Moth** (*Phlegethontius*) bearing cocoons of the many **Braconid Wasp** larvae (*Apanteles*) that developed inside the caterpillar.

only as a rare accident. The so-called "identical twins" or "identical triplets" in human families are of this nature. Curiously enough, the armadillos are a group of mammals that regularly and normally reproduce polyembryonically. In parasitic wasps, where the task of finding more than one host larva may be beyond the abilities of the mother, it has an obvious special advantage. It also enables very small wasps to utilize relatively very large hosts with maximum efficiency. It is particularly prevalent in some of the Chalcid family.

Many of the parasitic wasps are extremely small, some in fact being the smallest known insects. The "fairy flies" of the family Mymaridae are especially minute, the adults of one species, ironically named *Alaptus magnanimus,* measuring but 0.21 millimeters (about 1/120 of an inch) in length. These and the tiny members of many other families are egg parasites, undergoing their development in a single egg of the host instead of in a larva. The reason for their small size is plain. Some of the egg parasites are among the most useful to man despite, or perhaps because of, their small size. *Trichogramma minutum,* for example, can be reared easily by the millions in laboratories, being available commercially, and then liberated where there is an infestation of some injurious insect that it will parasitize.

Not all of the very small parasitic wasps are egg parasites, however, for many of them merely parasitize very small hosts such as aphids and scale insects. Since many of these insects are extremely destructive, particularly to fruit trees, their parasites are extremely valuable to man. It is quite common to find the empty shell of an aphid with a round hole evidencing the emergence of a parasite, perhaps one of the Braconid genera such as *Aphidius* or *Praon,* or perhaps one of the teeming Chalcids.

Some of the egg parasites are rather large as egg parasites go, but these are the ones that parasitize the egg masses of spiders and various insects, particularly Orthoptera. Some of the curious wasps of the family Evaniidae, known as ensign wasps, specialize on the egg capsules of roaches and as a result are not uncommon in even our largest cities. The common name of these wasps is due to the peculiar abdomen, which is flattened sideways and supported on a long, very thin stalk attached to the top of the rear of the thorax; it protrudes up behind the rest of the wasp like a flag or ensign on a slender pole.

Still other wasps specialize on the pupae of their hosts (Plate 137), ignoring the larvae. An interesting example of this is a small Chalcid, *Pteromalus puparum,* that parasitizes cabbage butterflies. A female will wait, sometimes for hours, near a caterpillar that is getting ready to pupate. Not until it has completed its transformation will she approach, stab it with her ovipositor and lay her eggs within it.

The phenomenon of parasitism is enormously complicated by the fact that many of the parasitic species are themselves the hosts of still other parasites, which we therefore term "secondary parasites" or "hyperparasites." These are often just as specialized in their host relationships as the primary parasites, attacking only certain species. Thus the Braconid *Apanteles,* which we have mentioned as a primary parasite of cabbage butterfly larvae, is itself parasitized by the Ichneumonid *Hemiteles.* Nor does the chain of parasitism end even here, for there are small Chalcids that parasitize the *Hemiteles* larvae. We may thus have a butterfly caterpillar inside of which are *Apanteles* larvae, inside of which are *Hemiteles* larvae, inside of which are Chalcid larvae. It reminds one of a nest of boxes, each containing a smaller one, and in the central, smallest box a rare prize—or perhaps nothing at all!

The existence of such hyperparasites is a matter of importance when primary parasites are being considered for use as a means of biological control of a pest. The presence in an area of a heavy infestation of *Hemiteles* might greatly lessen or render impossible the control of an injurious species by *Apanteles,* since not enough of the latter might survive to do effective work on the pest.

A number of the parasitic wasps reproduce quite regularly by the development of unfertilized eggs. This phenomenon, known as parthenogenesis, is really quite widespread among insects as well as other groups of animals. In some of the wasps the male sex, in fact, appears to be vanishing, and may in time disappear completely, leaving only the females to carry on the species. The very striking-looking wasp *Pelecinus polyturator* is a common parasite of June beetle larvae. Females may be two and a half inches long, of which the larger part is the incredibly long, slender abdomen. The males, which have short, club-shaped abdomens, are extremely rare.

In these wasps the course of larval development is relatively ordinary. In many species, however, it is much more unusual and, perhaps, subject to grave hazards. In many groups the larva undergoes a complex development, passing through two or more stages so different from each other that at first glance they would seem to be totally unrelated. Such hypermetamorphosis especially characterizes many of the Chalcids. The larva of *Perilampus,* for example, begins its life as an active creature that bores into a caterpillar of a moth such as one of the web-worms (*Hyphantria*), and waits there without feeding. If the caterpillar is not parasitized, it dies. If, however, it is parasitized by either a Tachinid fly or an Ichneumon wasp, the *Perilampus* larva bores into the body of the parasite larva and feeds and lives there for a while. It then leaves the parasite larva (all this is inside the moth caterpillar) and, changing to a totally different, maggot-like form, spends the rest of its larval life as an ecto-parasite. With so many chances of failure compounded, it is a wonder that any *Perilampus* survive.

An equally complex development is shown by the Scelionid wasps of the genus *Riela,* which develop as larvae in the eggs of the European *Mantis religiosa.* The adult wasps seek adult mantids, alight upon them, cast off their wings and live as external parasites on the mantids. Those that happen to land on male mantids soon die. Those on female mantids, however, move to the genital regions, and as the mantid lays her egg mass they lay their eggs within it. The wasp thus parasitizes the adult mantid as an adult and the mantid eggs as a larva, a most advanced form of double parasitism.

Few insects, if any, are secure from parasites. Even aquatic species are parasitized by many specialized forms such as some of the Chalcid family Trichogrammidae. The female of the tiny *Hydrophylax aquivolans* even uses its wings to swim beneath the water (like a penguin or cormorant) to seek the eggs of the damselflies of the genus *Ischnura* in which it lays its own.

Most of the parasites that we have mentioned have been those that live inside the host. A great many others, however, live on the external surface of the host, feeding from it through punctures. This is not practicable for the soft-bodied larvae of Hymenoptera when the host is an active animal living out in the open; but it is very feasible when the host is itself soft-bodied and relatively helpless and lives in a confined and sheltered cavity or nest. Thus a great many parasitic wasps parasitize insects that live within galls, or in nests or cases prepared and provisioned for them by their mothers; and in the majority of such cases the parasites feed from the external surface of their hosts.

A great many other species live as invaders—as guests "who came to dinner"—in such galls or nests. These are in general termed inquilines. A true inquiline does not attack the host—that is, the primary inhabitant of the gall or nest—but merely shares with it the food available. It is often impossible to draw a sharp line, since many species may begin as inquilines but, growing faster than the host or legitimate owner (to use a human term), may either monopolize the food so as to cause the death of the host or else may end by eating the host.

The problem of straightening out the relationships of the species we may find in a single gall or nest is, of course, enormously complicated by the fact that both the host and the inquilines may be subjected to the attacks of various parasites that feed directly upon them; and that these parasites in turn may be attacked by secondary parasites and these in turn by still others. A single gall, or a nest of a solitary wasp or bee, may thus be a little community in itself, consisting of half a dozen species entangled in a complex web of life that includes the original source of food, the rightful owner of this, one or more uninvited guests, parasites, hyperparasites, predators and scavengers.

THE SEED and GALL WASPS

A great many of the wasps belonging to these essentially parasitic groups are relatively normal eaters

Oak leaf galls caused by a **Gall Wasp** (*Cynipidae*).

the gall. The galls are quite specific, all those formed by a plant in response to the larvae of the same species of gall wasp being uniform enough to enable identification of the species of wasp. It is usually, in fact, much easier to recognize the particular type of gall than to recognize the insect. Those of closely related species of wasps tend to be similar; but those of distantly related species may be extremely different. One may be a smooth pealike swelling on a twig; another on the main vein of a leaf may be similar in size and shape but covered with a fine network of raised lines. Still another may be a smooth sphere two inches in diameter, filled with spongy fibers; that of a related species may look the same externally, but within may have a central sphere no more than one-eighth of an inch in diameter in which the insect lives, supported by many rods radiating to the outer shell. Many of the large galls on oak contain a high percentage of tannic acid and are consequently much used, although less than formerly, for making inks and for tanning leather.

Certainly the most unusual of the gall insects are the wasps of the Chalcid family Agaontidae, which live in galls on wild varieties of figs, but are essential for the formation of fruit on the cultivated varieties. The males are wingless and otherwise unusually modified, while the females are winged. Both sexes are produced in galls in the male flowers of "caprifigs," which do not bear fruit usable by man. The male emerges from the pupal stage first, crawls to a gall that contains an unemerged female, bites a hole in the gall and inseminates the female within. The female then emerges and flies about looking for fig flowers. Finding the female flowers of an edible (Smyrna) variety, she enters them and crawls about in them. Although they have attracted her, they do not stimulate her to lay eggs in them. She will eventually leave them in search of other flowers; but meanwhile she will have pollinated them with pollen from the male caprifig flowers. As a result they can then form fruit, which will be the type edible by man. Since time immemorial fig-growers have known that it is necessary to have some of the caprifigs growing among the edible varieties, and even to cut branches of the caprifigs at the right season and hang them in the edible trees. Their knowledge was purely empiric, for it has been only relatively recently that we have found out about the significance of the male caprifig flowers, the edible variety female flowers and the essential part played by the gall-making wasps, the only natural agencies that can pollinate the fig.

THE HUNTING or SOLITARY WASPS

If we were following a formal sequence of classification we would take up the ants at this point. These insects are, however, so extraordinarily set apart from all the other Hymenoptera by their so-

of plant material. Thus many members of at least two families of the Chalcidoidea, the Torymidae and Eurytomidae, bore within the seeds of a great many plants. Some, such as the apple-seed chalcis, *Syntomaspis druparum,* and the clover-seed chalcis, *Bruchophagus funebris,* are serious pests.

By far the majority of these plant-eaters are gall-makers; and the majority of these belong to the family Cynipidae, perhaps the best known of all of the groups of gall-making insects. The most important work done on these insects in North America, incidentally, was done by Dr. Alfred Kinsey, who is more widely known for his statistical research on human reproductive and sexual activities. About 86 per cent of the known species of Cynipinae produce galls on oaks alone, about 7 per cent on various species of the genus *Rosa*, and about 7 per cent on a wide variety of other plants.

In these gall wasps there is little doubt that it is the presence and presumably the secretions of the larvae that stimulate the plant to form the gall. The egg laid by the female in the plant tissue, and any secretion injected by her as she does this, seem to have no effect; for it is often not until months later, when the egg hatches, that the plant begins to form cial habits that it is best to complete the more normal wasp and bee series without interruption, and then to treat the ants separately.

The superfamily Vespoidea contains a large number and a great variety of wasps, which show almost every possible gradation from quite ordinary parasites to relatively highly specialized nest-building and society-forming species. It is, in fact, perfectly possible to trace out the probable course of the evolution of the social species by studying a sequence of the solitary and semisocial ones.

The larvae of the family Dryinidae live as parasites within the nymphs of various Homoptera, and in this do not differ materially from the other parasitic wasps. They are unusual, however, in that they cause the growth of a prominent tumor on the abdomen of the host. In some cases they also abort the development of the reproductive organs of the host, thus, in effect, castrating it.

A number of families live, as larvae, as inquilines in the nests of various solitary wasps and bees. Sometimes the larva merely eats the provisions that have been laid up for the rightful inhabitant of the nest, but more frequently it eats the "owner" of the nest also. The most widely known of these wasps are the so-called "velvet ants" of the family Mutillidae (Plate 146). The males of most of the species are winged, but the females of all are wingless. Since the latter in particular are usually covered with a short velvety pile, often richly and brightly colored, the origin of the common name is obvious. The females of many of the species are black and scarlet or black and orange, and may attain a length of nearly three-quarters of an inch, although most species are considerably smaller. Some species of the arid regions are densely covered with long, whitish hairs. The females are often very conspicuous as they run busily about on the ground with little or no attempt at concealment, seeking the burrows that solitary wasps and bees may be stocking with provisions. Slipping into such a nest, the Mutillid lays an egg that will hatch before that of the host, thus enabling her larva to eat not only the provisions but the host larva itself. The exoskeleton of the velvet ants is extremely thick and hard, a feature that is doubtless of great value when a female is attacked by a bee or wasp whose burrow she has invaded. It requires a surprising amount of force to drive even a sharp, stiff, steel insect pin into one of these wasps, so that the stings and jaws of their opponents must have little or no effect upon them. The Mutillids themselves are equipped with a most extraordinarily efficient stinging apparatus, the sting being curved and sometimes nearly as long as the abdomen; with it they can give an injection of a very potent poison. This is responsible for such local names for them as "cow-killers," "mule-killers" and others unprintable.

Similar to the Mutillids in many ways are the "cuckoo wasps" of the world-wide family Chrysididae (Plate 136). They are doubly appropriately named, for like the cuckoo they lay their eggs in the nests of others; and their scientific name, which means "golden," is well deserved because of their brilliant, metallic, iridescent colors. The most characteristic are emerald green, often shading into a deep cobalt blue or an intense ruby, in which changing lights bring out an incredible play of colors. They have little or none of the velvety pile of the Mutillids, but like them have extremely thick and hard exoskeletons, which doubtless stand them in good stead when they are caught in the act of laying an egg in the nest of a solitary bee or wasp. The females are winged and are rather fast fliers, and in the majority of species are unable to sting.

A few other small families have somewhat similar habits. The majority of the Vespoid wasps, however, are solitary hunting wasps that seek insects or spiders, which they paralyze or kill by stinging. The prey then is used as food for their larvae and, to some degree, for themselves. In general each species and group is relatively exact as to the type of prey attacked and the method of storing it for use of the larvae; but within the whole group we find almost all possible gradations from primitive hunters that merely leave the prey where it was found, paralyzed and with an egg attached, to others that prepare an elaborate structure before they begin hunting, and bring the prey back to this.

The world-wide family Scoliidae includes the largest of the Vespoid wasps, some species being nearly three inches long. The wasps are often black with bands or spots of yellow, orange or red, and frequently have dark wings with a green or blue iridescence. The females of at least the majority of species hunt the underground larvae of Scarabaeid beetles, burrowing after them in loose soil, leaf mold or sand. The larva is stung in such a way as to paralyze it but not to kill it, a very important matter since this insures that it will remain fresh and edible for the future Scoliid larva. The wasp then lays an egg on the prey and leaves it where it was found. The wasp larva lives as an ectoparasite on the Scarabaeid. Except for the paralyzing of the prey by stinging, this is little, if any, more advanced a technique that that of an ichneumonid parasite.

Another world-wide, large and important family is that of the spider wasps, variously known as Pepsidae, Psammocharidae or Pompilidae. The wasps (Plates 133, 134) are black or metallic blue, with long legs and transparent salmon-colored or iridescent bluish wings. Many of the species are extremely large, being as much as three inches long, but others are no more than one-quarter of an inch in length. The prey is almost exclusively spiders, ranging from extremely small ones up to even the

(Above) A **Potter Wasp** (*Eumenes*) working on its partly finished juglike mud nest, and (below) bringing a ball of clay to the nest.

largest of the so-called tarantulas. There is considerable variation between the different species as to the type of nest in which the prey is stored and in the technique of stinging it. Some species are extremely primitive in these respects, doing little more than stuff the prey into a convenient crevice or hole. Others, however, construct vaselike receptacles of cemented earth, which are attached to stones or walls. Some species apparently sting the prey so as to kill it, but others sting it so accurately in the large nerve centers that it may remain alive as long as forty days, ensuring fresh food for the wasp larva.

The big tarantula-hunters of the North American Southwest put on a most impressive show with their chosen prey, the enormous and powerful "tarantulas" that abound in these regions. Prying about in likely places, a wasp locates a tarantula. Often she

goes down its burrow, where one might think she would be at a frightful disadvantage. After considerable sparring around and feinting, she closes with the prey. Occasionally there is a regular rough-and-tumble in which it would seem impossible for the wasp to avoid the powerful poison-laden jaws of the spider. Almost invariably, however, she emerges as the victor, managing to slip her sting into the right point on the lower surface of the tarantula where it will hit the large nerve center. Some wasps apparently give the first sting in the spider's head and thus immobilize its jaws.

A number of other families of the Vespoids contain wasps with a considerable diversity of habits. Some are parasites on various groups of insects; others are inquilines in the nests of various wasps and bees; and still others are hunters. By far the largest and most important family, however, is the Vespidae. It contains a number of subfamilies, some of which are solitary, while others show very instructive gradations to a social condition, and still others are the most highly organized socially of all the wasps. Within the limits of a single family we can thus trace out the evolution of wasp societies.

The subfamily Masarinae is an interesting group of solitary wasps, which may be recognized by their strongly clubbed antennae as well as by the fact that unlike the other Vespidae they do not pleat their wings when they hold them over their backs. They construct nests in the form of tubular cells placed side by side either in the ground or in hollow stems, provisioning them, in most unwasplike fashion, with a paste of pollen and nectar, which they collect from flowers. This is a curious parallelism to the habits of the bees, which evolved from an entirely different group of wasplike ancestors. Unlike the bees, however, the Masarine wasps have no special pollen-carrying structures. Only one genus of the subfamily stocks its nest with caterpillars.

The large, world-wide subfamily Eumeninae contains many species of solitary wasps common in all the temperate regions as well as in the tropics. The two chief genera, each with many representatives in North America and Europe, are *Eumenes* (Plate 145), the potter wasps, and *Odynerus*, chiefly burrowing wasps. The potter wasps are easily recognized by the shape of the abdomen, which has a long, slender, bulging petiole attaching the almost spherical terminal part to the thorax. They are noted for the beautifully shaped little clay pots that they construct and fasten, sometimes quite high up, in plants. These are often almost globular and have a short, thin neck with an expanded lip, so that they look like miniature jugs. They are provisioned with paralyzed caterpillars, and are then sealed after an egg has been laid in each.

Odynerus contains many species that make burrows in the ground, others that tunnel in plant stems (especially in those with a soft interior pith) and others that use tunnels or holes already made by solitary bees or wood-boring insects. One can never tell when almost any small hole in wood, brickwork or cement will be pre-empted by one of these wasps. One of them plugged with paralyzed caterpillars and packing material the mouthpiece of a tin horn hanging outside a farmhouse door, to the great surprise of the farmer's wife who tried to blow the horn to call the workers in to dinner. Another, which we ourselves watched, provisioned a nest, from which her offspring emerged successfully, in a crevice in a brick fireplace on our lawn. But the most unusual *Odynerus* nest that we have seen was made in a round drainage hole in the wooden paneling of our station wagon. The wasp managed to stock the nest completely with caterpillars, and to lay her egg in it and seal it, during the periods when the station wagon was standing in its usual place in between trips to town. Unfortunately the egg did not hatch, as we found out when we finally opened the nest, or we would have been able to report perhaps the most widely traveled wasp larva ever recorded.

Some of the wasps of this group depart from the simple pattern of provisioning the nest, laying an egg in it, sealing it and leaving the larva to hatch and grow alone. *Synagris spiniventris* does this when there are plenty of caterpillars; but when game is scarce the female is unable to accumulate a sufficient store for the larva's entire growth. She then lays the egg in a nest with an inadequate supply of provision, but leaves the nest unsealed and brings in more caterpillars from time to time. In the meantime the larva will have hatched and begun eating; and so it comes to pass that the mother feeds the growing larva directly. Such "progressive provisioning" is the essential first step toward the evolution of a society; for all insect societies are based upon a family group consisting of mother and offspring. Another species of *Synagris* (*S. cornuta*) does the same thing regularly instead of only occasionally. So, also, do certain other related wasps such as the African *Odynerus tropicalis,* a member of a genus that contains chiefly solitary species that practice wholesale mass provisioning, and the little *Zethus spinipes* of eastern North America. Some of these wasps prepare the food for the larva by chewing it into a paste, another move toward the intimate contact of parent and offspring that typifies the true insect society.

In such species as these, however, the offspring do not stay around the nest after they have completed their metamorphoses and become adult wasps. We cannot therefore regard the short contact of the mother and her larva as sufficient to justify calling them anything more than subsocial. In the subfamily Stenogastrinae, however, and in fact within the single genus *Stenogaster,* we find subsocial and truly social species. These slender wasps of the Old World tropical regions generally make nests that may contain twenty or more separate hexagonal cells constructed of a delicate paper formed by chewing decayed wood. The mother feeds a number of larvae simultaneously. In the subsocial species the young wasps leave the nest when they transform to the adult condition. But in some others they stay around the nest and thus, with the mother, form true societies, albeit only of a temporary nature. The daughter wasps are fully developed and functional females, showing no evidence of the sterility that characterizes the worker caste of more advanced insect societies. In a short time they leave the nest and make nests of their own, their place being taken by younger sisters.

The two great truly social subfamilies of the wasps are the Polybiinae and the Vespinae. The former group, which is much the larger and more diversified, occurs chiefly in the New World tropics but has some members in Africa and a few in southern North America. The Vespinae form a world-wide group that includes the familiar (sometimes much too familiar) hornets and yellowjackets of Europe, Asia and North America. In each of these subfamilies we find some genera consisting of species that, although truly social, form only small and temporary colonies and build primitive nests; and in each there are other genera containing species that form colonies of thousands of individuals, housed in large, elaborate and long-enduring structures.

Thus the African *Belonogaster* and the New World *Mischocyttarus,* both Polybiine genera, seldom form societies containing more than a few dozen individuals. Their nests, like those of all other truly social wasps, are formed of wood chewed to a pulp and moistened and cemented with saliva. They are merely open combs, unprotected by any outer sheath, and are hung from various plants or, perhaps, beneath some projecting shelter. Since they have little or no protection from rain they must be oriented so that the cells will not catch and hold water; and so the larvae and pupae hang head downward. In *Belonogaster* there is something of a primitive division of labor, the older female offspring laying eggs and the younger ones foraging. In *Mischocyttarus,* on the other hand, there is to be found in each colony only one queen, presumably the original mother; and except when a colonizing swarm is produced (which occurs in rather haphazard fashion) the daughters are sterile workers. There is not, however, any structural distinction between the fertile females and the sterile workers, the latter being merely the females whose ovaries fail to develop because of malnutrition. This is only the first step toward the development of castes; but it is definitely the most important step.

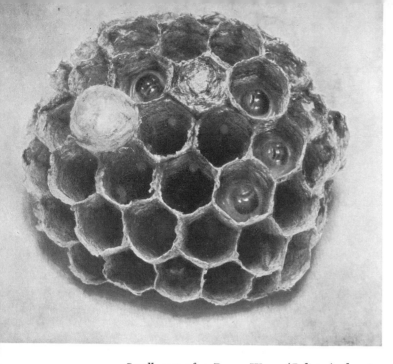

Small nest of a **Paper Wasp** (*Polistes*) showing eggs, small and mature larvae and cocoons containing pupae. In a cell at bottom right is a fly larva living as an invader (inquiline) in the nest.

Nest of a **Paper Wasp** (*Polistes*) being raided by **Army Ants** (*Eciton hamatum*). The wasps are helpless against these invaders.

The Vespine genus *Polistes* (Plate 150) has an almost world-wide distribution. It contains the often large, slender paper wasps of Europe and North America which so commonly build their open-celled paper combs beneath eaves and sheds or wherever some projection gives shelter from rain. They are extremely well known to nearly everyone except the dwellers in the largest cities as invaders of our houses in the autumn. At this time the young queens, leaving their dying natal colonies, scatter widely and seek sheltered places in which to spend the winter. Large numbers may gather in attics and in houses that stand vacant during the winter. We have even found them occupying the deserted globular nests of yellowjackets and hornets as winter refuges. Fortunately these young queens are not at all aggressive, stinging only under strong provocation; and their sting, although temporarily painful enough, is in no way comparable to the more serious ones of yellowjackets and hornets.

The species of *Polistes* differ from each other with respect to whether more than one queen may occur in a colony. The common *Polistes annularis* of eastern North America appears to have no set practice. Sometimes a single young queen starts a nest all alone in the spring and carries on alone to found a successful colony. She may, however, be joined by one or more other young queens, with the result that the colony grows faster and more securely; or she may, for no reason that a human can see, desert her small nest with young in the cells and join another colony that is starting elsewhere. This gregarious tendency of *Polistes annularis* queens is in direct contrast with the intolerance of a honeybee queen for the presence of another queen in her colony; and is all the more remarkable since the queens of most other Temperate Zone species of *Polistes* do not welcome other queens seeking to attach themselves to their colonies.

In describing the lives of termites we mentioned the great amount of mutual licking and grooming that both nymphs and fully grown individuals carry on continually, the body secretions being apparently highly relished. This is also a very important feature of wasp societies but in a quite different way. The larval wasps, hanging head downward in their cells, are fed by the queens and workers, chiefly with mouthfuls of caterpillars or other insects chewed to a paste. When thus stimulated, or even when simply prodded, the larva emits a drop of saliva, which is greedily taken by the adult wasp. Pleasant though it may be for us to imagine that the wasps feed the larvae because of a tender maternal instinct, we are forced to realize that nothing of the kind seems to exist. The wasps merely feed the larvae because when they do so they receive automatically in return a drop of much relished liquid. The adults often, in fact, exploit the larvae unmercifully by stimulating them again and again to produce the desired drop of saliva, without giving them any food in exchange.

This phenomenon of mutual feeding by larvae and adults, which is known as trophallaxis, is believed to be the chief, perhaps the only, mechanism that builds up and holds together the wasp society. It is the attraction of the larval secretions that keeps the daughter wasps attached to their natal colony, and insures that they will pay constant attention to the larvae and will feed them. Nor is the undue exploitation of the larvae without its benefit to the colony, since it is perhaps largely by this means that the larvae are so handicapped that they are unable to complete their growth normally and develop into sterile workers instead of queens.

Despite a great deal of study, we do not understand at all well what forces change the routine of a *Polistes* colony as the summer wears on. In part, food may become more abundant; and in part, the workers, satiated with plenty of sweet nectar and fruit juices, may exploit the larvae less. In any event, larvae begin getting enough food to be able to develop into fully sexed females. The queen, too, begins to change her habits, laying some eggs without permitting any of the sperm, which she stores in a special sac in her abdomen, to fertilize them. Such unfertilized eggs develop into males, who fecundate the young queens. As the season progresses fewer and fewer workers develop. Eventually the old queen ceases laying eggs and the colony disintegrates. Only the young, fecundated queens live on, to spend the winter in sheltered places and, if they survive, to found new colonies in the spring.

HORNETS and YELLOWJACKETS

Conventionally these wasps are regarded as members of the single genus *Vespa* (Plate 149); but many entomologists split this into three or more subgenera or genera differing from each other in the distance between the eyes and the mandibles and also, to some degree, in nesting habits. All three of the groups occur in Europe and Asia and in North America as well; but in the last-named continent the only representatives of the true *Vespa* group is the introduced European hornet, *V. crabro*.

All of the groups make nests that are far more extensive and better constructed than those of *Polistes*. The combs are entirely surrounded by a sheath except for a small entrance at the bottom or side; and especially in the nests that are built above ground, usually in trees or shrubs, the sheath may consist of many layers of tough, weatherproof paper with air spaces in between. Such a nest gives excellent protection to the colony within. A number of tiers of combs, each one horizontal, fill the space within. The nest grows by the constant con-

The paper combs of this large **Hornet** nest are encased in a sheath and suspended in a tree.

An underground nest of a **Hornet** (*Dolichovespula*), opened to show the tiers of paper combs in which the young are reared.

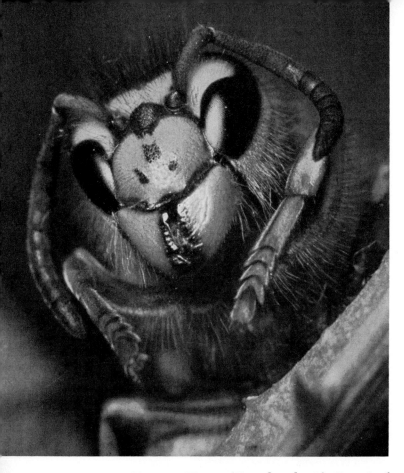

European Hornet (*Vespula vulgaris*). Portrait of a common species.

struction of new combs below the old ones, each suspended from the older one above it, and by lateral enlargements as well, with consequent tearing down and enlargement of the outer walls. The subterranean nests are far less strongly constructed, but are strengthened by many buttresses extending out to the walls of the cavity; and here, too, almost constant enlargement is the rule during most of the season.

These wasps form extremely large colonies, even though it is most unusual for more than one queen to occur in a nest. At the height of its development a large colony may consist of five thousand individuals, but during the entire season as many as twenty-five thousand may be produced, including the males, which fecundate the young queens and then die, and the young queens, which live through the next winter. It is not surprising that the original queen, the mother of such a throng, becomes battered and worn toward the end of the season. She and her daughter queens are far larger than the workers, the latter forming a well-marked caste.

There are, however, no subcastes among the workers, a feature in which the societies of the wasps are more primitive than those of both ants and termites. The earliest-produced workers are quite small, probably merely because the unaided queen was not able to feed them enough. As more workers mature and take up their tasks, the size of the later arrivals increases to normal. A certain division of labor, though not of structure or size, now appears among the workers, the older ones going out to forage for food and wood pulp, while the younger ones remain in the nest. Here they receive the materials brought in by the foragers, feed each other and the larvae, enlarge the nest, guard the entrance and, by fanning their wings, ventilate the colony. Sometimes, toward the end of the season, incompletely sterile workers are produced which are able to lay eggs. As far as is known, these workers are never fecundated, so that their eggs develop only into males.

As in *Polistes,* the adult wasps feed primarily on nectar, fruit juices, fermenting sap and similar sweets, which they gather wherever available. They are also, however, extremely active predators, since the larvae are fed with insects, spiders and other animal food that has been thoroughly chewed to a pulp. They typically pounce upon small insects in flight, apparently not using their stings but crushing them with their strong mandibles. Even large, powerful predatory insects such as robber flies and dragonflies are captured, and some of the larger hornets may kill others of smaller species. In the economy of nature they are thus of dual importance, since they cross-pollinate many flowers (although they are not nearly so efficient at this as the bees) and also act as predators of great consequence to other insects. They also act as scavengers, having no hesitation at carving up any dead animal that they may find. They are, in fact, nearly as inevitable visitors at a picnic as the proverbial ants, and will busily snip off mouthfuls of any meats available as well as gorge themselves on sweets.

We have several times remarked upon the wide extent of parasitism as a way of life among animals in general and insects in particular. It should therefore be no surprise that among the social wasps there are in nearly every group some species that have abandoned the self-supporting habits of their relatives and ancestors and have become parasites upon their congeners. This is certainly true of some European species of *Polistes* and is suspected, but not yet proven, of some of these wasps in North America. Each of two subdivisions of *Vespa* contains at least one European and one North American social parasite. The queens of these slip into the nests of closely related species and deposit their eggs in the cells. When the eggs hatch, their larvae are cared for by the workers. Eventually they develop into queens (for no workers are ever formed in the parasitic species) or males. There is also a North American species, *V. squamosa,* that exhibits a very mixed behavior, sometimes having independent nests of its own, complete with workers, and at other times acting like a social parasite upon a closely related, normal species. Perhaps it is in the process of evolving the socially parasitic habit. As we will point out later, similar habits of social parasitism have evolved among the ants and the bumblebees; but they are notably absent among the termite societies.

HONEY WASPS

Although the adult social Vespids feed largely upon sweets and the foragers often bring home a cropful for the stay-at-homes, they make no effort to store either honey or any other food. In the New World tropics, however, there is a most interesting group of Polybiine wasps, best known by the appropriate generic name of *Nectarina,* that do this. The nests of some of the species, which are made of conventional wood pulp and are hung in trees, may form ovals as much as twenty inches long containing as many as fifteen thousand individuals. Nectar, concentrated to form honey, is stored in large quantities in the paper cells, a feature of special interest since it is not at all sure that it is used to feed the larvae. Natives of the regions where these wasps occur often collect the honey, a simple matter because the wasps are singularly nonaggressive and, when the nest is opened, may sting very little or not at all. Barring such attacks, the colonies are perennial, since these wasps exist only in tropical regions where there are no cold winters with which to contend. New colonies are apparently formed by swarms consisting of a number of queens and workers. In both forming and maintaining colonies a number of queens cooperate, a feature which explains the large size a colony may attain.

THE SPHECOID HUNTING WASPS

It may seem like something of an anticlimax to turn from the social wasps back to another group of solitary hunters. The Sphecoid hunting wasps (Plate 144), however, far exceed the solitary Vespoid wasps in numbers, complexity and interesting habits and are well worth separate study for themselves. They show us, as the Vespoids also do, some transitional stages toward the evolution of social life. They do not include any clearly social species; but they are so evidently related to the bees that we may regard the latter as cousins that split away from the ancestral wasp stock many millions of years ago.

Some authors regard the entire group as forming but a single family; others split it into a dozen or more families. Whatever rank may be given them, the various groups are not always very distinct from each other in habits; and some groups contain members that differ greatly from each other in the prey selected and the type of nest used and the method of preparing it. Perhaps the small family Ampulicidae shows the most primitive habits. These wasps hunt roaches, which they sting into insensibility and then stuff into a convenient crevice. In humans we would stigmatize this failure to prepare a

A **Mud Dauber Wasp** (*Tripoxylon politum*) and its "organ pipe" mud nest which it stocks with paralyzed spiders.

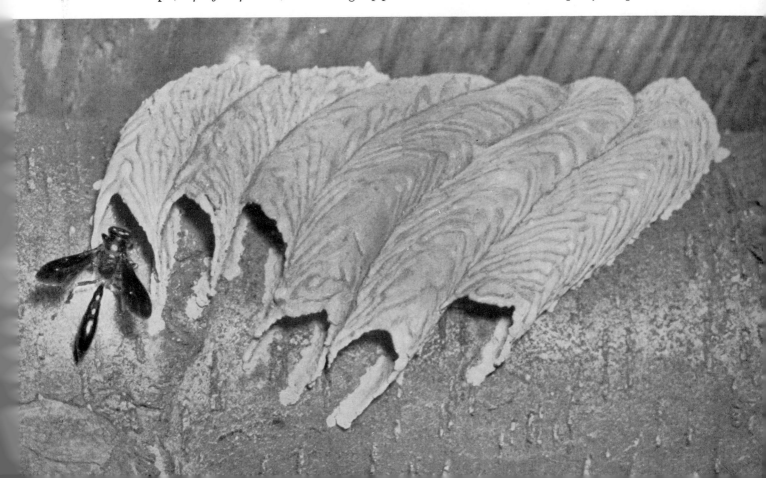

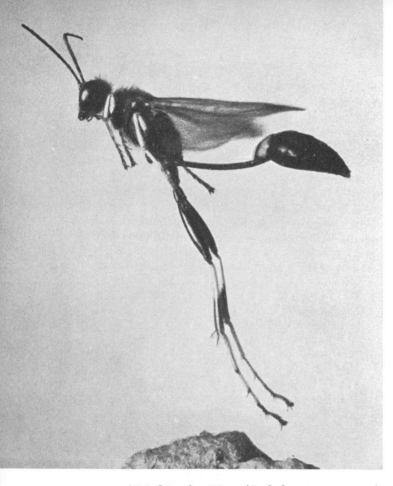

A **Mud Dauber Wasp** (*Sceliphron cementarium*), noted for its long hind legs and the extremely long stalk of its abdomen.

nest in advance as "lack of forethought." It would be highly improper to apply such a phrase to insects, since they cannot be said to think at all; but the net result is the same.

The great majority of Sphecoids, however, definitely prepare the nest in advance of going hunting. This has the obvious advantage of enabling the wasp to get the prey into its eventual destination, the sealed nest, as expeditiously as possible. Parasites, we must remember, are always about, on the watch for an opportunity to lay an egg on the prey or in the wasp's nest. It is not at all uncommon for a Tachinid fly to find the prey that a wasp has left while it looks for a suitable nesting site. Ants, too, sometimes make off with unguarded game. By transporting the prey immediately to an already prepared nest, the wasp minimizes such dangers. It is not, however, entirely safe even then, for parasites often enter an empty nest while the wasp is hunting and lay their eggs in it as though in anticipation of its being stocked with provisions in the future. If the wasp seals its nest while it is out hunting, it must lay down the prey in order to reopen it, and in those few moments parasites may manage to slip in an egg. In truth there is no security in a world full of parasites, thieves and intruders.

252]

A major disadvantage of preparing the nest in advance lies in the necessity of transporting the prey when it is obtained at some distance. A great many wasps catch insects smaller than themselves which can be carried easily in flight, but this is disadvantageous in that it leaves the incompletely stocked nest unguarded while a sufficient number of this small provender is captured. Others make use of large prey, sometimes heavier than themselves, and may have a long and arduous task dragging the load over rough terrain and through dense, tangled vegetation. Some species carry such a heavy prey some distance up from the ground by climbing a tree trunk and then, taking off in flight from such a lofty starting point, are able to make most or all of the journey to the nest through the air. A great many drag the prey for what, translated to a human scale, would be the equivalent of a man carrying two hundred pounds for some miles over the roughest possible sort of obstacle course.

One of the most familiar groups is the genus or genera known as *Sphex* and *Ammophila* (Plate 143). The wasps are long-legged and slender, with extremely thin abdomens that enlarge gradually to a terminal club. Some species are all black, others are black with grayish silvery patches, many others are black with red on the abdomen. The largest are nearly two inches long. The wasp first prepares a burrow in a suitable spot, and while doing this scatters widely the soil which she brings to the surface, leaving no telltale evidence of its excavation. She may fortify herself from time to time by visits to flowers to sip nectar. Before beginning hunting she makes a complex series of short flights around and above the nest site, undoubtedly fixing in her mind a visual pattern of its location and of prominent landmarks by which it can be located from afar. This done, she begins hunting. The chief prey of her group is caterpillars of Lepidoptera, sometimes far heavier than the wasp herself. On finding such a one she at once closes with it and stings it a number of times, puncturing quite accurately a number of the large nerve ganglia that lie along its lower or ventral surface. Although some very exaggerated and highly anthropomorphic claims have been made that the wasp has an instinctive knowledge of the caterpillar's anatomy, it is undeniable that in the majority of instances she does succeed in paralyzing the prey and not killing it. She also squeezes its neck vigorously with her jaws, a process (known as malaxation) that cannot fail to disrupt the nerve connections there and may also enable her to feed to some extent on the caterpillar's juices. Finally she grasps it in her jaws and, straddling it with her long legs, drags and carries it to the nest. The way may be long and tortuous, so that she may occasionally have to leave the prey and make an orientation flight to set herself on the right track. Eventually she reaches the prepared burrow and drags the caterpillar down to the chamber that awaits it. Laying an egg on it, she leaves it and commences filling in the opening of the nest. It is now that *Ammophila* distinguishes herself; for as she packs dirt in the opening she chooses a pebble a little smaller than her head and, holding it in her mandibles, uses it as a maul with which to tamp the dirt down hard. By this act she allies herself with man and the exceedingly few other animals that habitually use a tool.

The closely related, more stockily built wasps of the genus *Chlorion* do not use a tool to tamp down the dirt, and they catch grasshoppers instead of caterpillars, but otherwise behave much as does *Ammophila*. We have often watched the big black and orange-red *C. ichneumoneum* dig, provision and seal its burrows on our back lawn in Connecticut. Approaching the burrow astraddle its victim, an *ichneumoneum* customarily lays the grasshopper down almost touching the entrance of the burrow, runs in headfirst, turns around in the chamber, comes up headfirst, seizes the prey and backs down the hole with it. We occasionally interfere with its routine by pulling the grasshopper away some inches from the mouth of the burrow while the wasp is turning around down below. Coming up, the wasp reaches for the prey but is forced to emerge completely in order to grasp it. Invariably she then goes through the same set routine, leaving the prey at the entrance while she goes down and turns around. Again we move the prey away, and again the wasp comes up headfirst, finds it out of reach and is forced to emerge completely.

Such interference with the set, hereditary routine of most insects usually results disastrously because the insect, which is unable to change the fixed pattern of its behavior, becomes what we would call "frustrated" in the human sense and abandons the whole performance. Occasionally this happens with *ichneumoneum*. Usually, however, the wasp eventually manages to adapt to the new situation and either dashes straight down the burrow with the prey, headfirst; or else switches itself around without letting go of the prey and backs down with it. Sometimes this happens after only three or four interferences; sometimes the wasp will not vary its behavior until a dozen or so trials have been made.

Our own experiences with *ichneumoneum* and similar wasps have been so casual that they prove nothing. A great deal of very thorough, carefully controlled work of this nature has been done by others, however, on insects of many orders and families; and new experimental work is constantly being planned and carried out. From it we are learning much about insect psychology. A rational opinion is being developed that lies somewhere between the extreme beliefs that insects have no minds and

(Above) A **Hunting Wasp** (*Ammophila sabulosa*) carrying a paralyzed caterpillar to the burrow it has prepared in advance, and (below) dragging the caterpillar backward into the burrow.

that insects have minds of a human type. The present attitude cannot be summarized better than in the words of Dr. T. C. Schneirla of the American Museum of Natural History: "Although learning contributes in many ways to environmental adjustments in insects, and may often be complex, it is not on the psychological level of mammalian learning. Claims that insects are capable of intelligent adjustments of a high psychological order seem to depend upon limited evidence which leads to exaggerating superficial similarities to mammals at their best."

One group of Sphecoid wasps, the family Bembecidae, departs from the general pattern of solitary hunting and mass provisioning in a direction that points toward a rudimentary social evolution. These are short, chunky wasps, rather "hornet-shaped" and often banded with yellow and black or greenish gray and black. Some, at least, are definitely sociable in their nesting habits, a considerable num-

[253

ber of the females often digging their burrows in close proximity to one another. Each one, however, manages her own affairs independently. The Bembecids practice progressive provisioning, laying the egg in the completed burrow before accumulating any prey and then feeding the larva with flies. In some *Bembex* more than one larva is thus reared at one time; one species, *B. rostrata,* may support five or six larvae each of which requires fifty to eighty flies during its development. The young wasps, however, do not remain around the nest and aid the mother in any way, so that these wasps cannot be said to have made more than the first step toward a true society.

THE SOLITARY and PARASITIC BEES

The majority of people have a concept of bees based on the highly social honeybee and are therefore greatly surprised to learn that the vast majority of these insects are neither social nor even sociable. Only the bumblebees (a rather small group), the stingless Meliponid bees of the tropics and the honeybees (of which there are perhaps four species) can be said to be truly social, although among solitary bees we can trace a few species that are more or less semisocial.

The bees arose as a group of wasps, related to the Sphecoids, which became adapted for visiting flowers and utilizing the rich, concentrated foods that are offered by these plant organs. Undoubtedly there were flowers before there were bees, since pollination by wind is a very ancient plant characteristic. But there can be no doubt that as the bees evolved, so did the flowers of a great many plants. Today a very large number of plants are essentially dependent upon bees for the transfer of pollen from flower to flower, and many of the distinctive structures of the flowers of these plants represent modifications to ensure successful pollination by this means.

Many other groups of insects also visit flowers regularly and have become more or less specialized for this, but none has become so thoroughly adapted for flower-visiting or so completely dependent upon flowers as the bees. The chief characteristics of the group all evidence this. The lower lip (labium) has become more or less elongated, sometimes extremely so, forming a tubular structure through which nectar can be sucked. The body hairs have become plumy or feathery, excellently adapted to entangle and hold pollen grains. And pollen baskets (corbiculae) consisting of brushes of special pollen-holding hairs are located on the legs or body. On these, large masses of pollen, first entangled among the hairs, are molded by the action of the legs and carried. In addition there have evolved a great many complex behavior patterns that, no less than their structural specializations, adapt the bees for their lives of dependence upon flowers.

Cells in the nest of a **Leaf-cutter Bee** (*Megachile*) lined with pieces of leaf cut by the parent.

The great majority of solitary bees (Plates 147, 152) have fundamentally the same pattern of life, which is essentially like that of their relatives the Sphecoid wasps. After having prepared a nest the female stocks it with provisions, lays one or more eggs in it, seals it and departs. Her offspring eat the accumulated stores, pupate and in time emerge as adults. Sometimes there are two or more generations annually, sometimes only a single one.

There are nearly as many minor variations of this pattern as there are species of solitary bees, which run into the thousands. The majority make their nests in the ground, frequently on banks or along the edges of old borrow pits where there is exposed soil and good drainage. Sometimes a local dearth of suitable places brings about considerable concentrations, in such a spot, of species that are normally entirely solitary; but many species seem to be more or less sociable by instinct, although each female takes care of her own affairs alone and may be quite intolerant of any close encroachment by others.

Sometimes the nests are quite small and primitive, containing only a few cells, in which larvae feed individually; in other groups the larvae feed from a common store. Occasionally we find the females of some species sharing a common entrance chamber from which their individual burrows open separately. This is an important step toward the evolution of a type of bee society that is quite different from that of other social insects.

A considerable number of solitary bees make their nests of earth cemented to form a masonry that may be surprisingly strong. All types of nests are found, ranging from the single, completely solitary cells of some species, perhaps fastened to the side of a pebble, to many-celled structures joined to those of other individuals of a large colony to cover large areas of a cliff or of the wall of a building. The latter type includes the nests of the famous mason bees, the Osmiinae, of southern Europe and Africa, about which the great French naturalist Fabre wrote some of his finest essays.

Closely related to these sociable mason bees are the leaf-cutter bees, the Megachilidae, a large and widely distributed group that has the pollen-carrying hair brushes on the lower surface of the abdomen instead of on the hind legs as in most bees. Their nests are often built in ready-to-hand spaces such as the pith cavity of a dead twig. Oval pieces of leaf, cut from the living plant, are used to line the chamber and make partitions between the cells. This is perhaps the one group of bees that does definite damage to man's plants, since some species use pieces cut from the petals of flowers and may thus render many blossoms unsightly and unsalable. Roses are often thus attacked and seriously marred.

A goodly number of solitary bees bore their own tunnels in wood, some cleaning out pith cavities in stems and others boring extensive nests in hard wood. The lesser carpenter bees (Ceratinidae) are quite small, seldom more than one-quarter to one-third of an inch long. Most of the species are black with faint metallic green high lights. The large carpenter bees (Xylocopidae), on the other hand, are among the largest and most powerful of the bees, some of them being more than an inch long and making deep holes half an inch or more in diameter in hard wood. They resemble very large bumblebees, often having considerable yellow fur on the thorax, but have flatter, usually black or faintly metallic abdomens, and a much faster flight. They are often sociable, but despite this are quite quarrelsome.

There are many other groups of solitary bees, each with its distinctive characteristics, but none shows any outstanding differences of habit from those that we have mentioned. Perhaps the most noteworthy are the long-tongued Euglossidae that abound in the New World tropics. Some of these are among the largest of all bees; and many have extremely brilliant, iridescent and metallic blue and green colors that quite rival those of nearly any other insects. "Handsome is as handsome does," however; and the Euglossids are equipped with stings more than adequate to protect them against anything with a hide thinner than that of a rhinoceros. We write feelingly, from painful memory of an Amazonian amazon.

It should come as no surprise, after the wasps, that a good many solitary bees have evolved habits of parasitism upon their relatives. The degree of their parasitism varies somewhat; but fundamentally the egg is laid in the more or less provisioned nest of another solitary bee. Many of the parasitic forms look like ordinary bees, often resembling their hosts quite closely. One group, however, *Sphecodes* of the family Andrenidae, has the vesture very inconspicuous but the body brightly colored with red and yellow in wasplike fashion. The families Panurgidae (what is Rabelaisian about a family of bees?), Stelidae and Nomadidae are partly or entirely composed of such parasites.

We mentioned above that among the ground-nesting solitary bees are some species that have more or less communal nests, a number of females sharing a common entrance from which their individual burrows open. These are Halictids, members of a very large, world-wide group variously classified either as a family or else as a subfamily of the Andrenidae. Even the sharing of such a common entrance, of course, is the simplest sort of socialism. It has recently been shown, however, that some species go far beyond this, engaging in communal labor to gather soft insulating material or to prepare air spaces that act as insulators for the whole group. Furthermore, one member of the group acts as a guard at the entrance, keeping out Mutillid wasps and such parasites, while the other members are performing their routine tasks. In some species of the genus *Augochlora* only one or two of the females may be in egg-laying condition at any one time; and while they are laying eggs in the cells the others are collecting pollen and nectar. Unfertilized or sterile females may be found in such colonies doing a share of the chores. Sometimes, in fact, these unmated females seem to do most of the foraging. We cannot call these females a worker caste, since they show no differentiation from the fertile ones and may be potentially fertile themselves, lacking only the presence of males. But in one Brazilian *Lasioglossum* there occur small societies of a fertile female, the queen, and four to twelve sterile workers. The queen is short-lived, but is replaced.

Although small and not long enduring, these Halictid bee groups are true societies—groups of individuals sharing a communal nest, carrying on their community duties with a division of labor, and differentiated from each other into castes. But they differ strongly from all other known insect societies, since they arise by the coming together of mature individuals not necessarily of the same parentage; for in all other social insects the society is formed by the continuing association of parent or parents and offspring—that is, of a family group.

THE SOCIAL BEES

There are only three main groups of truly social bees: the bumblebees, the tropical stingless bees, and the honeybees. Although at various times believed to form three families, these are now usually considered as being no more than different subfamilies, or perhaps only tribes: the Bombinae, Meliponinae and Apinae respectively, of the family Apidae.

The ordinary bumblebees are all members of the genus *Bombus* (Plate 148). Although practically world-wide, they are most characteristic of the Temperate Zones, both North and South. In the New World they occur from Tierra del Fuego to the northernmost limit of land in Greenland and Ellesmere Island. A few of the tropical species maintain all-year-round colonies; but in most species, including all those of the temperate and arctic regions, the societies do not survive the winters and, like the social wasps, must begin anew each spring.

Young queen bumblebees, unlike those of the wasps, usually hibernate underground. In the early spring they awaken and seek the first blossoms, and then begin hunting for suitable nesting sites. These are either on or in the ground, old mouse nests, small rodent burrows or dry tussocks being favored by different species. Hollowing out a small cavity, the queen makes a honey pot, using the wax that is formed by glands in her abdomen and exuded on both upper and lower sides. She fills this with honey, and more or less simultaneously makes also another cell for her first small batch of eggs. When these hatch she feeds the larvae in their common cell, using either a mixture of nectar and pollen or else (in certain species only) dry pollen alone. The larvae finish their growth, spin their cocoons and pupate, and in due time emerge as workers. Their total development takes from three to four weeks. Meanwhile the queen has been making additional brood cells and laying eggs in them, as well as collecting more nectar and pollen as opportunity permits. The first workers are very small because of underfeeding, but soon begin their tasks of gathering nectar and pollen, enlarging the nest and caring for the brood. The queen can thus devote more of her time and energy to egg-laying, although she still makes occasional trips to visit flowers.

The colony therefore may grow rapidly, although those of the bumblebees seldom attain very large size, a thousand individuals being exceptional. The species differ considerably from each other in this respect, as well as regarding favorite species of flowers, disposition, flight habits, the amount of nectar stored etc. Toward the end of the season begins the production of males and young queens, the former developing from larvae from unfertilized eggs and the latter from larvae from fertilized eggs that have received adequate supplies of regurgitated liquid food. Eventually, as autumn comes, the colony disintegrates. The males, the old queen and the workers die, and the young queens scatter and seek places underground in which to hibernate.

Although in the mass they are not so important for the pollination of most flowering plants as are the small solitary bees, the bumblebees play an essential part in pollinating such plants as red clover, since their long tongues enable them to reach the deep-lying nectar. The introduction of European bumblebees was found to be necessary during the settlement of New Zealand, since the native bees and the honeybee either did not visit clover at all or else were inadequate for pollination on a large scale.

The stingless bees (Meliponinae) are a tropical group of wide distribution in both the Old and New Worlds, although the majority occur in the latter. A few species are as large as small honeybees, but the great majority are much smaller, some being less than one-eighth of an inch long. It is somewhat of a misnomer to call them "stingless," since some of the species have a definite though vestigial sting. Let no one suppose, however, that the loss of power to sting leaves these bees defenseless, for they bite hard and are unpleasantly sticky, and some species wet an attacker with a burning fluid that may cause a severe rash.

The size of the colony differs greatly in various species, ranging from no more than a few dozen in some to several thousand in others. The social life of a colony is highly organized, representing in some ways a stage of development intermediate between the more primitive bumblebees and the more advanced honeybees. Each colony contains only one egg-laying queen, presumably the original founder, but a considerable number of young queens may also be present. At least some of these young queens will leave, each accompanied by a swarm of workers, to form new colonies. A colony may last for several years, but it is not known that there is any mechanism for the replacement of the old queen by a younger one. Such propagation of colonies by swarming is an advanced characteristic that also takes place in the honeybees, although with them it is the old queen who leaves with the swarm. The young stingless bees, however, are fed in a very primitive fashion like that of solitary bees, the brood cells being mass-provisioned and sealed, leaving the larvae to feed themselves. When the young bees emerge as adults their brood cells are

[continued on page 273]

123. A **Syrphid Fly** (*Milesia virginiensis*). This flower-visiting fly is a good mimic of large, boldly marked wasps and may be found visiting the same flowers.

124. A **Syrphid Fly** (*Spilomyia fusca*) that mimics the big black-and-white Bald-faced Hornet.

125. A **Syrphid Fly** (*Eristalis tenax*) that mimics the Honeybee. The maggot of this worldwide species lives in decaying organic matter as a scavenger.

126. A wasp-mimicking **Syrphid** (*Milesia virginiensis*).

127. A **Syrphid** (*Merodon equestris*) that mimics a Bumblee. Its maggot bores in the rootstocks of iris and gladioli and is often harmful to them.

128. A **Green Bottle Fly** (*Lucilia*). Some members of this genus breed in carrion; others lay their eggs on the wool of sheep, the maggots then boring into the host.

129. A **Robber Fly** (*Bombomima*). It doubtless benefits from its mimicry of bumblebees since the latter are shunned by insect-eating animals because of their sting.

130. **Housefly** (*Musca domestica*). The most serious carrier of human disease and the commonest fly in homes everywhere—except for igloos.

131. A **Thick-headed Fly** (*Physocephala*). The wasplike appearance of these flies appears to protect them from the attacks of birds that have learned to leave wasps alone.

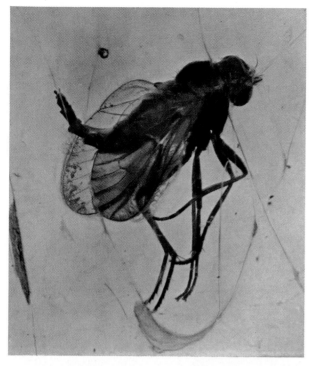

132. A Fossil **Fly** in Baltic amber. The preservation of insects in amber is often so good that even identification of the species is possible.

133. A **Tarantula Hawk** (*Pepsis*). Members of this genus are among the largest of the wasps, some species attaining a length of nearly three inches.

134. **A Tarantula Hawk** preparing to attack its enormous and dangerous prey, a tarantula.

135. **A Mosquito** (*Aedes sollicitans*). A salt-marsh species that is abundant and pestiferous.

136. A **Cuckoo Wasp** (Family Chrysididae) that is a social parasite in the nests of solitary bees and wasps.

137. **Chalcid Wasp** parasites swarming over chrysalis of **Mourning Cloak Butterfly** (*Nymphalis antiopa*).

138. **Ichneumon Wasp,** female, showing the long, piercing ovipositor through which she lays her eggs in caterpillars.

139. **Pigeon Tremex** (*Tremex columba*), female, a common American Horntail. She lays her eggs in wood, where her larvae bore destructively.

140. Leaf-cutter Ants (*Atta*) carrying leaves which will be used in an underground nest as a medium for growing fungi to feed the colony.

141. Army Ants (*Eciton hamatum*). A number of workers are attending the queen, whose body is heavy and swollen with eggs.

142. **Ants** and **Aphids.** The larger ants milk the aphids for their honey-dew and in return often protect the aphids by taking them into underground nests during the winter.

143. A **Hunting Wasp** (*Ammophila*), female, in sleeping position. This group of the Solitary Wasps is noted for consistent use of a "tool": when the female has provisioned her nest she seals the entrance and tamps down the soil with a pebble held in her jaws.

144. **Cicada Killer** (*Sphecius speciosus*). One of the largest of the Hunting Wasps, it provisions its nest with adult Cicadas.

145. A **Potter Wasp** (*Eumenes*), female, finishing her juglike nest.

146. A **Velvet Ant** (*Dasymutilla occidentalis*). Although the females of these brightly-colored wasps are wingless, they are agile runners and can inflict a painful sting.

147. A **Solitary Bee.** Such small, non-social bees, which occur in great numbers, are the most important cross-pollinators of many valuable crops.

148. A **Bumblebee** (*Bombus*) with a ball of pollen on its hind leg.

149. A **Yellowjacket Hornet** (*Dolichovespula diabolica*), female, on the nest comb. Most Yellowjackets make their paper nests in the ground, often under rotting stumps.

150. **Paper Wasp** (*Polistes*) workers crawling over the small nest comb, where eggs and larvae as well as capped pupal cells are exposed.

151. A **Hornet** head, showing the large compound eyes and strong jaws.

152. A **Solitary Bee** (Family Andrenidae). These small, metallic bees are among the most effective cross-pollinators, especially on flowering tree crops such as apple.

A **Honeybee** worker (*Apis mellifera*) visiting a Sage flower.

[continued from page 256]

abandoned and never used again, a primitive and seemingly inefficient procedure that is also followed by the bumblebees but not by the honeybees.

The nests of many of the species are built in the open in trees or on walls or cliffs, while those of many others are constructed in hollow trees or other crevices. A few nest in the soil, and quite a few regularly use the nests of termites. The nests are made of varying mixtures of clay and of a wax-resin mixture called cerumen. Some of the species of *Trigona* are noted for the tubes, perhaps as long as fifteen inches and expanded in funnel form, that project outward from the entrance hole. It is sometimes possible to locate an otherwise concealed nest by seeing this prominent entrance tube. Within the nest are built series of horizontal combs, the lowest being the oldest. The combs open upward, a much more practicable-seeming feature than the downward opening of wasp combs and the sideways opening of those of the honeybees. The brood cells, like those of the wasps and honeybees, are regu-

larly hexagonal. The honey and pollen pots are specially built separately from the brood combs and are distinctive in shape.

The honeybee is a native of the Old World that did not occur in the New World until brought over by European man. In pre-Columbian days, however, at least one stingless bee, *Melipona beecheii,* was widely domesticated by the natives of Central America and Mexico as a source of honey and wax. Even today many colonies of this bee are kept by the natives of Yucatan, the hives being short sections of hollow logs with the ends stoppered and a small hole for the bees bored in the center.

One very exceptional stingless bee, *Lestrimelitta limaõ,* while not by any means such a social parasite as *Psithyrus* is on bumblebees, lives very largely, or perhaps entirely, by robbing *Trigona* bees. They make well-organized raids on a *Trigona* colony, stationing some guards at the entrance to prevent *Trigona* workers from entering while the mass of the robbers are looting the colony of honey

[273

Swarm of **Honeybees** on a branch of an apple tree.

and wax. This they carry back to their own nests, which are characterized by specially prominent entrance tubes.

THE HONEYBEES

For all practical purposes there is only one honeybee, *Apis mellifera*. It is a bit uncertain just where the original home of this species was; western Asia or Asia Minor is as safe a guess as any. There are two other species, *A. dorsata* and *A. florea*, both natives of southern Asia, but neither has proven susceptible of domestication. Both hang the nest, which consists of a single comb, from the branch of a tree. That of *A. dorsata* is sometimes very large, perhaps a square yard in area. This rather large bee has an exceedingly "vicious" disposition (most people, we fear, regard any animal that defends itself bravely as "vicious") and has been known to sting to death men who were merely walking beneath the nest. All of its cells are of the same size and shape, whereas *A. florea* makes different types of cells for honey storage and for each of the three types of brood; this is more advanced than the habit of the domesticated honeybee, which does not have special honey cells.

The honeybee (hereafter by "honeybee" we refer to the domesticated *A. mellifera*) occasionally hangs its combs in trees when in a wild or escaped state, but most frequently seeks the shelter of a hollow tree or cave. It places the combs vertically so that the cells open sideways, each cell being slightly tilted upward at the edge. The worker brood cells are slightly smaller than those used for drone brood. Queen brood cells are relatively enormous structures, much the size and shape of a peanut and fastened irregularly about the edges of the combs. Honey is usually stored in drone-sized cells and pollen in worker-sized cells, quite consistently in the back or upper part of the nest. The beekeeper makes use of this habit by placing empty comb in "supers" or tiers stacked in layers above the main hive.

New colonies are formed by a type of swarming unique with these bees; in it the old queen leaves the hive, accompanied by a large number of the workers. The task of mothering the future populations of the hive then falls upon a young queen who emerges from the pupa at or about the time of the departure of the swarm. This technique insures the continuity of the colony, replacing the old queen by a new one at intervals. It also gives greater assurance of success for the new colony, since this is mothered by a queen of proven fertility. If, as occasionally happens, no young queen is available at the time of the exodus of the old one, the workers can feed up young worker larvae and thereby produce queens. The female larva develops into a queen if fed royal jelly, a special mouth secretion of the workers, for its entire larval life; but if fed this for only the first two days and thereafter fed a mixture of honey and pollen, it develops into a worker. Drone (male) larvae receive the same food as workers. The queen is considerably larger than a worker and has a much larger abdomen. This befits her enormous egg-laying capacity, which may reach a figure of several thousand daily. Drones are heavier-bodied than workers and have relatively much larger eyes.

It is the colonizing swarm that most often "makes the newspapers," sometimes giving the most unlikely people an unexpected and intimate acquaintance with several thousand bees. The swarm is merely a temporary gathering where the bees that will accompany the queen rally about her. Meanwhile, and very likely for several days before, "scouts" are seeking a suitable place for a permanent home. Eventually, perhaps after one or more false starts, the swarm will move to this. Blowing horns, ringing bells, flashing lights and all the other devices of folklore will not influence its course.

Left behind in the old hive, the young queen goes on her marriage flight high in the air accompanied by the drones, who pay no attention to her if she is not flying. Mating takes place in the air and ends with the queen tearing out the drone's genital organs, so firmly are they affixed to her. This, of course, kills the drone. After her return to the hive, workers remove these encumbrances, but she retains in a special storage sac the seminal fluid with which she will fertilize her eggs. Techniques have been developed for the artificial insemination of queens, making possible controlled breeding of bees of known pedigree. Such an artificially inseminated queen can be introduced into a hive in a small screened box, the exit from which is stopped with candy. It takes the workers some days to eat this away, a period long enough for the queen to develop the characteristic odor of the hive and thus become acceptable. A new queen can thus be introduced only in a queenless hive, for otherwise she would be attacked immediately by the old queen, who will not permit the presence of a rival.

The life of the bees is as busy as it is proverbially supposed to be. It is quite efficiently organized, despite the fact that each bee merely acts according to its instinctive pattern of behavior. No bee ever "tells" another what to do, at least in the human sense of "telling," although as we shall see, there is communication between them. It is the age of a worker that automatically determines what it will do. A day or two after emerging from the pupa a worker takes up such household duties as tending the larvae; this may continue for a week or so. The bee then leaves the hive for its first flight and, incidentally, its first defecation. For a number of days it makes short flights, thereby building up a mental pattern of the neighborhood that will aid it later in homing. During this period it also secretes wax, which it kneads into usable form and applies where it is needed in building new comb. It also cleans the hive and acts when necessary as a guard. Finally, after about three weeks of life as an adult, the bee begins foraging, not only visiting flowers for

(Above) Worker **Honeybees** on brood comb. Developing larvae can be seen in the cells. (Below) Pupae of the **Honeybee** in brood cells.

nectar and pollen but also obtaining the sweet honeydew of aphids and similar insects, water, and various plant waxes and resins (propolis) that are used along with beeswax in the construction of the hive. During the busy, hot summertime a worker may live for only six weeks.

[275

Once it has started visiting a particular species of flower, the individual bee tends to be conservative and to continue visiting that same species as long as any nectar and pollen are available, ignoring equally rich sources in the flowers of other species. Much experimental work has shown that the bee possesses powers of smell, color discrimination, form perception and location "memory" which, although differing widely from those of the human, are adequate for its recognition of different flowers. This tendency of the individual bee's to specialize is of great importance to plants and often to man, since it does more to insure the cross-pollination of the species visited than if the bee were visiting a number of species indiscriminately. Nowadays many beekeepers transport their hives about for considerable distances, keeping them in contact with the best "honey flow." Such traveling apiaries are particularly common sights in alfalfa- and citrus-growing regions.

Experimental work has shown that in remembering the location of a group of flowers with a good honey flow, and orienting itself in respect to this and the hive, a bee relies chiefly upon the relative position of the sun and on a definite, though not very accurate, sense of direction and of distance. It can probably sense the position of the sun even on dull days, since its eyes are sensitive to the ultraviolet waves that penetrate even a cloud blanket. The bee also has a fair sense of time, for it can be conditioned to return to a source of food during the

A queen **Honeybee** emerging from her large, opened brood cell.

same period each day. It has been shown that the bee can not only return accurately to a source of food but can also direct other members of the hive to the same place, without accompanying them. In 1923 Dr. Karl von Frisch published a paper that will always be a classic, telling about this "language of the bees" and describing how, with perceptiveness and ingenuity worthy of that other distinguished apiarist, Mr. Sherlock Holmes, he had learned its details. During his studies von Frisch had marked for individual recognition many thousands of bees, whose actions were then studied and recorded both at food sources and inside their hives.

Upon arriving at a hive with a cropful of sweets, a bee begins a definite set of activities. A so-called "round dance," which is really a series of figure-eight loops, is performed by running rapidly on the surface of a comb, and repeating the gyrations on other combs. This attracts the attention and stimulates the activity of other workers, which, scenting the announcer with their antennae, identify the type of flower or other source of food. Such a dance indicates no direction but is performed only when the food source is within about one hundred yards. The vigor of the performance corresponds approximately to the abundance of the food. Other bees, stimulated by the dance, rush out. Upon their return, laden, they too perform the dance, thus in effect sending out others. As the supply diminishes, returning workers perform less vigorously or not at all, so that fewer and fewer others are stimulated to go forth.

When the food is farther away, the returning bee performs a modification of the round dance, called the "tail-wagging dance" because it switches its abdomen from side to side while running about on the comb. It also makes a straight run between the loops of the figure-eight. The greater the distance away of the source of food, the smaller and fewer are the loops and the faster the tail-wagging. Finally, the direction to the food with respect to the position of the sun is indicated by the direction of the straight run between loops. If the food is directly away from the sun, the straight run is directly downward on the surface of the vertical comb; if directly toward the sun, the straight run is directly upward. Directions at various angles toward or away from the sun are indicated accurately to within a very few degrees, by the angle of the straight run upward or downward. Since bees subsequently returning from the same food sources go through the same performance but change the angle as the sun's angle changes, the information is always relatively accurate. Here again, as the food source diminishes so do the number and vigor of the returning dancers, so that fewer bees go out.

An interesting activity is the so-called "clustering" of the bees during cold weather. In a cold environment an individual bee is quite unable to keep its body temperature high, partly because of its small size, partly because it lacks sufficient insulation, and partly because of its lack of such an internal high-speed heat-production mechanism as that of a bird or mammal. It can, however, produce some heat by constant muscular contractions. When the hive temperature falls below 57 degrees Fahrenheit the bees begin forming a dense ball, half on one side of a sheet of comb and half on the other. The central bees, being insulated by the layers of individuals outside of them, are very warm, since a temperature in the interior of the cluster may be maintained as much as 100 degrees F. higher than that outside of the hive. A continual change of position goes on, so that each bee gradually rotates from the cold outer space to the warm interior of the cluster and then back again. Throughout the cold season the formation is maintained, gradually moving about on the surfaces of the combs and feeding on the stored foods. Extremely low temperatures may, however, immobilize the bees so that they starve to death even though food is available nearby. Finally, long before the actual coming of spring, some premonition warns the bees that winter is drawing to a close. In January or February the queen begins egg-laying, so that by the time spring arrives there are many new bees ready to emerge from the hive and take advantage of the spring blossoms.

It is not to be expected that so rich a source of food as a thriving colony of honeybees could long exist without being exploited by many other organisms. Perhaps the most injurious of these is the infectious disease known as "foul brood," which often completely wipes out thriving colonies. Curiously enough, the Italian type of bees, preferred by beekeepers also because of their mild disposition, are more resistant to this disease than the German type. Insects of many groups manage to invade the nest and survive in its crevices, some of them merely scavenging on the debris, some stealing wax and honey, and others (like the larvae of the wax moths and bee moths) actually destroying the comb and thus indirectly killing the larvae. The wax moth larvae also spin messy webs all about, thus still further complicating the bees' economy. One very large moth, the giant death's-head sphinx of Europe and Africa, has a short, strong tongue with which it pierces the comb and sucks honey. The fondness of bears for honey is of course proverbial. Outside the hive many enemies specialize on bees. Some of the flycatchers, such as the kingbird, have a very bad reputation with beekeepers, as also do certain large dragonflies and robber flies. There is even a most extraordinary, minute, wingless fly, the bee louse (*Braula caeca*), which lives as an adult clinging to the bodies of the bees, after having developed as a larva that burrows through the combs. Beekeepers have learned how to combat such pests, but in a state of nature the bees are often seriously hampered or imperiled by them. They can survive only because of their great individual and communal efficiency and the matchless fertility of the queens.

THE ANTS
—*Superfamily Formicoidea*

It is almost obligatory to consider the ants last of the Hymenoptera, for after them any other group would seem like a decided anticlimax. Perhaps they are not quite as advanced structurally as the highest bees, although that is open to doubt. They are without equal, however, in numbers of individuals, in the unparalleled effects that they have on nearly all other forms of land life and in the extent and intricacy of their social development.

No more than a single family of ants is recognized. This is divided into at least eight subfamilies, of which the majority are world-wide. Three of these, the Cerapachyinae, Pseudomyrminae, and Aneuretinae, are relatively small and contain few members with distinctive habits, although they are of great importance and interest. Others are: the Ponerinae, the most primitive ants; the Dorylinae, the famous army and driver ants; the Dolichoderinae, the stink ants and their relatives; and the Myrmecinae and Formicinae, the most specialized and most numerous groups. We shall consider the Ponerinae and Dorylinae separately because of their distinctive characteristics and habits, but will take up the other groups more or less together, treating them in terms of what they do rather than in the sequence of their formal classification.

All known ants are social, although the societies of some groups are very small and primitive. All are organized, as in most other insect societies, in groups consisting fundamentally of an association of mother and offspring. In many, however, this relationship may be obscured by the presence of more than one fertile female (queen) in a colony. In most instances this happens by the coalescence of two or more colonies of the same species, or by the adoption into an established colony of young queens of the same species. Some ants, moreover, form societies consisting of more than one species, which may become very complicated.

In their methods of founding new colonies, too, ants show many differences. Basically their way of doing this is rather like that of the termites. From a well-established colony a mass exodus of young winged males and females takes place, sometimes to the number of scores of thousands. During what is thus a combined marriage and dispersal flight, the matings take place. After this the males die, for the ant society, like those of the other Hymenoptera, is a pure matriarchy. This is one of the ants'

Opened mound nest of **European Wood Ant** (*Formica rufa*). Such mounds are sometimes several feet in diameter and the colony may consist of more than 90,000 individuals.

chief differences from the termites, in which the male accompanies and aids the female in founding and maintaining the new colony.

After the flight the fecundated young queens drop to the ground, remove their wings and begin searching for places in which to set up housekeeping. Usually this is done immediately, although in some primitive ants the queen may wander about for some time. In a suitable spot, sometimes in the soil, sometimes in a crevice or under bark, the queen prepares a small chamber, in which she usually seals herself away from the world. She lays a small batch of eggs, which she tends assiduously until they hatch. Both during this period and also subsequently while she is feeding the first batch of larvae with salivary secretions, she exists on the nourishment obtained by absorbing her flight muscles, now otherwise useless to her. Eventually the small brood of workers reaches maturity. Developing from fertilized eggs, they are females; but being undernourished, they are both sterile and un-

dersized. They then take over the work of the colony, freeing the queen for a life of egg-laying. Future batches of workers, better nourished, will develop to normal size but will likewise be sterile. In time, perhaps in four or five years, the colony will grow large enough and strong enough to produce a batch of winged males and females; and these will emerge as a swarm and leave on their marriage flight. The old queen remains in the original colony, living for many years if no accident intervenes, instead of leaving with a swarm, as is the rule in the honeybees.

Be it noted that there are actually hundreds of variations from the general pattern of colony-founding described above. The "normal" ant colony no more exists than does the statistically "average" man.

A most characteristic feature of many ants is the longevity of the individual, in strong contrast to most other insects in which the individual lives for only a few days or weeks after attaining maturity.

Queens have been known to live for as long as twenty years in captivity, and workers for nearly half this long. Moreover, the workers of some species have been shown to possess considerable capability for individual learning and memory, although on a different and much more limited plane than our own. This undoubtedly has contributed enormously to the great success of many ant societies. Because of it older workers can, and are known to, pass on to younger ones by precept at least some of the fruits of their experience. As a result the society gains greatly in stability and efficiency.

The ants, then, have a highly efficient social organization coupled with some ability to transmit "knowledge" of a sort by precept. They have long lives and very fecund queens. They possess considerable adaptability and a dynamic behavior that have enabled them to penetrate nearly all possible land environments and to exploit nearly every possible opportunity. It is no wonder that they are one of the most widespread and successful groups of animals, and are nearly everywhere to be reckoned with as one of the major forces of nature.

Structurally the ants are differentiated from the other higher Hymenoptera by their elbowed antennae and by the presence of a knob, node or swelling on the slender stalk or petiole that connects the thorax and the enlarged part of the abdomen. This may be a mere inconspicuous bulge or a prominent upright scale. Although the great majority of males and fertile females are winged (in a few species they are not) none of the workers ever possesses wings. In all other characteristics the ants show enormous range of variation. Some have well-developed compound eyes as well as simple ocelli; others are blind. Some have stings; others have lost this weapon but have replaced it with the ability to secrete powerful burning acids. Some of the largest species have workers more than an inch in length; in others the workers are no more than a millimeter or two long. Some species form societies consisting of no more than a dozen or so individuals; others exist in vast communes with populations of a million or more. Some are rapacious predators; others are general eaters and scavengers; others live on seeds, of which they accumulate great stores in their nests. Still others live on sweet honeydew secretions of various insects; and some live on fungi that they plant, grow and tend in extensive underground galleries. Most species are self-supporting; but many are parasites on others, some for food, some for shelter, and some, the most advanced slave-makers, for nearly everything.

Ant Senses and Communications

In the earth-bound lives of the workers, smell and the very closely allied sense of taste are preeminent, while sight plays a relatively minor part.

The workers of some ants are blind, although they have vestiges of eyes; and numerous others have greatly reduced eyes that can be of little use for seeing even simple images, and function only for distinguishing light and darkness. To the species that forever remain beneath the surface of the ground, or come up into the open only at night, this blindness is no handicap. Even to those that forage aboveground during the daytime it is far from serious, so keen are the senses of smell and taste, as well as touch. In the workers of many other species, however, the compound eyes are well developed and fully functional for definite image perception; but even in these sight is of lesser consequence.

So great an emphasis on smell and taste makes the characteristic odor of each colony a matter of major importance. This is a compound of the basic scent of the species and many details of soil and food chemistry. An ant from a strange colony, even of the same species, will be instantly set upon and killed or driven off if it intrudes into a nest. But if it can be kept in the nest, perhaps by some experimental human artifice, long enough to acquire the local odor, it may be accepted without question. It is this reliance upon odor alone that makes possible the return of so many young queens to the home nest after their marriage flights, and facilitates the lives of so many other insects as guests or intruders in ant colonies.

The sense of taste is inseparably involved with the colony odor because of the mutual caressing, feeding, licking and grooming of each other that constantly goes on in a colony. This far exceeds the needs of feeding, for two completely full-fed ants often meet, exchange antennal strokings and then pass from one to the other a drop of fluid from the mouth. The eggs and larvae, too, are frequently licked, an act that is not without its use in keeping them free from fungus infections. The continual food exchange, trophallactic in its nature, acts as a common bond that insures the continued interest of the workers in the brood and in each other, just as it does in the social wasps and the termites. And, as with the termites, there is evidence that it is by this means that inhibitory "social hormones" are passed about the colony—which hormones, eventually reaching and affecting the developing larvae, regulate the proportions of these that will develop into workers or soldiers. Perhaps the same mechanism affects the production of broods of males and females, much as it seems to do in the termites. The ants have not been so well studied in this respect, but at least one very suggestive piece of experimental work done on the small ant *Pheidole morrisi* almost conclusively showed that the presence of a certain proportion of soldiers in colonies inhibited the development of additional individuals of the same subcaste.

The sense of touch is extremely acute, chiefly through the presence of a great many short, tactile hairs with sensitive nerve endings at their bases. These, as well as many taste-smell organs, are particularly abundant on the antennae. Closely bound in with the sense of touch is that of hearing, for although ants seem to lack any specific hearing organ they are very sensitive to sound-produced vibrations of the surfaces with which they are in contact. Many ants make sounds, such as squeaks and grating noises, that are definitely audible to the human, and doubtless many others that are above the range of our audition. Some have sound-producing structures on the first segment of the abdomen, others click their mandibles or knock their heads against a solid object.

Some ants show considerable ability to form and retain definite memory patterns, although none shows any evidence of mental powers that in any way approach the consciousness of the human mind. It has been well stated that ants are capable of *learning,* but not of *recollection;* they cannot, that is, recall an image or even form a mental image of anything concrete, much less of an abstraction. The foraging ant will return accurately to the place where it recently found food, following exactly the same path as before, even though its odor trail has been obliterated, thus showing that it possesses a sense of distance, direction and elapsed time. In doing so it will lead other ants to the source of food—not, as the human would, by telling them to come along, but simply by precept. There is no evidence in ants of anything like the "language" of the honeybees. The other ants, smelling and perhaps tasting the food brought in, and perhaps sensing special excitement secretions, merely follow automatically. Even after a winter's hibernation an ant will show that it has retained something like a memory of last year's trails and foraging grounds. Such a veteran will function as a leader and trainer of others less perceptive or less experienced. There is evidence, too, that a small proportion of workers, otherwise indistinguishable, differ from the others in being consistently the first to start doing something. Such a "work-starter," especially if an experienced veteran, may be a very important member of the community because of its effect on the others; but we must remember that it is never in the human sense a leader giving directions or orders or, in fact, telling the other ants anything. It starts off first because it is by nature a quick starter; its experience and prior conditioning make it do certain things and go to certain places; and the other ants follow it because to do so is inherent in ant nature. Such "work-starters" have been observed and carefully studied in some species of ants; they probably occur in many and possibly in most ant colonies.

Some Unusual Ant Activities

Many ants have established relationships with plants that result in great benefits to the ants and, in some cases, probable advantages to the plant. In most of these instances, special structures formed by the plant attract the ants and often induce them to take up residence. Since in many such cases the ants have powerful stings or poisonous secretions with which they drive away other animals, the plant is more or less recompensed for the food and shelter that it provides. Various acacia shrubs in both the Old and New World tropics have peculiar large thorns with swollen bases that are frequently inhabited by colonies of ants (*Pseudomyrma, Crematogaster*). During their development the thorns are filled with a sweetish pulp that the ants eat; and in the cavities thus formed the ants take up residence. Unquestionably the ants resent any intrusion and retaliate effectively, as anyone who has ever stumbled into a bull's horn acacia can testify. Some observers claim that the ants thus protect the plants in the New World from defoliation by leaf-cutter ants, and in Africa from browsing animals. This is probably partially true; but there is no real evidence that the peculiar thorns, or other food bodies on leaves, were evolved by the plants as "an attraction to the ants." Neither is there evidence that special nectaries and peculiar food bodies formed by other plants were evolved for that reason.

It is, however, of great interest to see how many ants have developed habits of regularly visiting or nesting in plants that offer these special opportunities. Some ants, in fact, such as the *Azteca* species that nest in the hollow stems of cecropia trees in South America and feed on special bodies formed by these plants, are practically dependent upon the plants, whatever may be the benefit derived by the cecropias.

Among many others, the *Azteca* and *Pseudomyrma* of the New World and the *Oecophylla* of the Old World are mostly arboreal, many species building their nests a hundred or more feet up in the trees of the tropical forests. The tree ants *Oecophylla longinoda* and *O. smaragdina* are widely distributed from Africa to Australia. The nest is made of silk and is contained in a tight structure made by fastening leaves together, also with silk. Since adult ants cannot secrete silk, their main source of this material was for a long time a great mystery. We now know that these ants, as well as a few in other genera such as the Oriental *Polyrhachis* and the South American *Camponotus senex,* thus utilize the silk that their own larvae normally secrete and use in the formation of their "cocoons." While a number of the ants pull the edge of a leaf into position, others pick up mature larvae, squeeze them so that they secrete liquid silk, and use them, just as we would a tube of glue or plastic cement, to fasten the leaf down. Other larvae are similarly used as shuttles to weave the nest itself. As far as is known, this extraordinary habit is unique in the animal kingdom, the nearest thing to it being the exploitation of child labor by humans.

Among the ants that nest in hollow stems or twigs, the North American *Cryptocerus* and *Camponotus* (*Colobopsis*) are noted for their unique method of closing and guarding the nest entrance. The heads of the major workers of these ants are specially strengthened and shaped like corks or plugs. One of these individuals simply takes her stand inside the nest entrance, facing out, and plugs it with her head, or head and thorax. Only the proper password in ant language, a scent stimulus of the characteristic colony odor involved, causes the door-keeper (who is also the door itself) to open the way and admit the returning forager.

PRIMITIVE ANTS

The most primitive ant subfamily, the Ponerinae, is almost world-wide but is especially well represented in Australia, the refuge of so many other primitive forms of animal life. In North America there are only a relatively few inconspicuous species. Structurally the Ponerines are more like their Vespoid wasplike ancestors than are the other ants, having the abdominal petiole merely swollen and lacking the distinct node or scale of most other ants. In their social and caste development, too, they are very backward, for there is often practically no difference in appearance between the queen and the workers; and the queen often must go out and forage for herself instead of remaining in the nest and having all her needs attended to by her sterile daughters. In some of the species, in fact, some of the workers also lay eggs. In the genus *Leptogenys* no truly recognizable queen exists, although one worker-like queen or queenlike worker does most of the egg-laying for a colony. There are very few genera in which occur recognizable soldiers distinct from ordinary workers. All of this shows very primitive social status.

The Ponerines are all predatory, a primitive food habit among ants. Some, however, tend to be rather narrow in their choice of prey, catching only millipedes or sowbugs or termites. One species of western Australia specializes on the young queens of other ants when these are abundant during the swarming season. Some of the termite-feeding species carry out quite organized-appearing raids on termite nests, seemingly being led by a single individual who presumably discovered the nest. Despite the defenses of the termite soldiers and nasuti, the attacks may be successful enough for each raider to carry home several termite bodies.

The Ponerines also show primitive habits in feeding their larvae, for the prey is merely more or less bitten into pieces and tossed to them. There is none of the thorough predigesting and mouth feeding that occurs in the social wasps and bees, and that also characterizes the higher ants. Instead, the larvae must scramble and fight for the food and grind it up themselves. In this respect it is also noteworthy that the Ponerine queen does not immure herself in the first brood chamber and feed the larvae with her secretions, but instead goes out on hunting trips much like one of the solitary progressive-provisioning wasps.

Perhaps the most notorious of the Ponerines are the members of the genus *Myrmecia,* almost confined to Australia and Tasmania (there is one species in New Caledonia) where they are known as bulldog or jumper ants. The larger species may reach a length of an inch or more. Almost all are extremely fierce and active, swarming out to the defense of their nests in a series of leaps that may be several inches long. In the genus *Odontomachus* the mandibles can be opened so wide as to project outward at right angles. These are then brought together on a slanting stick or pebble off which they slip, hurling the ant forcefully into the air. Since the bulldog ants are equipped with extremely powerful stings they can be not merely intensely aggravating, but actually dangerous to humans, especially when it becomes necessary to clear away their nests.

THE ARMY ANTS

The famous army ants or legionary ants of the New World and the equally famed and feared driver ants of Africa compose the subfamily Dorylinae (Plate 141). In its own peculiar way this is one of the most extraordinary groups of the ants. Contravening all of the rules of proper ant behavior, these insects have no fixed place of abode but wander gypsy-like about the country, occupying only temporary bivouacs. Since they are savage predators, nearly every form of small animal life in the path of a hunting column is instantly attacked, and killed and torn to pieces if it cannot make good its escape. Neither humans nor penned or cooped livestock are by any means immune, so that the cry announcing the approach of a column of the African driver ants (which are especially rapacious) may well bring about a mass flight of the inhabitants of any village that lies in the path of the insects' advance.

Although the existence of these ants has been known for centuries, comparatively little was understood about their habits until rather recently; and much of what was formerly supposed to be fact is now shown to be fancy. Studies of species of *Eciton,* for instance, have shown that the colony in this, the most prominent genus of the New World army ants, does not keep forever on the move,

Major part of a bivouac of **Army Ants** (*Eciton burchelli*) under the end of a large log. Midnight flashlight photograph shows the beginning of emigration to a new site.

making only "one-night stands" in any resting place. Instead, the life of the group is divided into two phases, each of which succeeds the other: a statary or static period during which a single site may be occupied for as long as nineteen to twenty days; and a nomadic period of seventeen days during which the colony moves about and occupies a fresh bivouac each night, weather permitting. The basic factor that determines the duration of these periods is not, as was formerly supposed, hunger, but the timing of the periodic growth of the ovaries and the consequent egg-laying of the queen. This does not act as a direct stimulus, however, as much as it merely touches off a wave of stimuli among the workers by causing the presence of young larvae after the eggs hatch, coincident with an additional stimulus presented by the presence of young workers, just out of their cocoons, that developed from the previous batch of eggs.

During a nomadic period the queen can keep up with the movements of the group, since her abdo-

men is not distended with a heavy burden of unlaid eggs. During this period, too, the workers are carrying along the young larvae that recently hatched from the last batch of eggs; and very likely the stimulus of the larval secretions, received in trophallactic exchange, aids materially in keeping the workers active and on the move. At this time, also, most of the workers are hunting and more ground is being covered, so that food enough is brought in for all. In time the larvae mature, spin their cocoons and pupate; and this ends the trophallactic exchange between them and the workers. The workers now cease their active migration and the colony goes into the static phase.

At the same time (and this synchronization is very important) the ovaries of the queen become active again, so that about a week after the colony has settled down her abdomen is enormously swollen and she begins to lay eggs once more. Over a period of about six days she may lay 25,000, after which her ovaries become inactive for another period. In a few days the eggs hatch; and by the nineteenth or twentieth day from the beginning of the sedentary period most of the young workers from the previous batch of eggs have emerged from their cocoons. The colony is now full of both very young larvae from the recent lot of eggs, and of young, callow workers from the previous lot. A wave of trophallactic stimuli touches off a burst of activity and the next nomadic phase begins.

During both the one-night stops and the longer periods of egg-laying and cocoon-hatching, the ants construct no nest or shelter. Instead, they form a clustered mass, perhaps in the shelter of an overhang, and during the longer stops in a hollow tree or log. This living mass, which may be very sizable since it can consist of 100,000 to 150,000 workers, actually *is* the nest; for inside it are passageways and chambers where the queen lays her eggs, the larvae are fed, the eggs and pupae are stored and the other business of the colony is carried on. It is curiously reminiscent of the winter cluster of the honeybee, in which the members of the colony form a mass for mutual protection against cold weather, with the queen at the center, perhaps laying her eggs.

The queens of these ants, as already noted, are wingless from the start, an exception to the general rule for ants. Even when not distended with eggs they are many times the size of even the largest workers. The males, too, are relatively enormous. They, however, have wings and are so different in appearance from the other members of the species that for a long time some of them were supposed to be wasps. The workers show a high degree of caste differentiation, not only in the presence of a considerable range of sizes among the ordinary workers, but also in the development of many large soldiers with enormous, hooked, single-toothed jaws.

A raiding group of such workers and soldiers not only methodically covers the ground in their path but also climbs high into shrubs and trees where much additional game is found. Young birds in the nest are killed and cut to pieces. Even large animals such as lizards, snakes and mammals may be killed if they cannot escape. Ferociously stinging wasps can do nothing but buzz about impotently while the ants pillage their nests of the brood and everything else edible. Even African pythons, rendered sluggish by distention with a full meal, are said to have been killed by the ferocious drivers of the genus *Dorylus.* The New World *Ecitons* are not as rapacious and so are often welcomed by natives whose villages they invade, for they clean out the hordes of cockroaches, bedbugs and other pests that have been accumulating since the last raid.

The lives of the African drivers show a pattern of alternating nomadic and static phases like that of *Eciton* described above. They and many other *Ecitons* differ considerably in the durations of the phases. Like the *Ecitons,* the drivers have enormous wingless queens (which, incidentally, are blind) and extremely distinct-looking, winged males.

Although these ants are fundamentally tropical, quite a few species of *Eciton* range northward in the United States to North Carolina and Colorado. These northernmost species hunt in small files instead of in large, conspicuous armies. They appear to prey chiefly upon the brood of other ants; but one species has been recorded as peculiarly fond of nuts, a very unusual diet for this group.

AGRICULTURAL and HARVESTER ANTS

Many ants have been credited with practicing agriculture, but modern observations have shown that a large proportion of them do no such thing but are merely harvesters (Plate 140). In the New World, however, is a tribe of Myrmecine ants, the Attini, the members of which are really farmers, though of a most specialized kind. The principal genus, *Atta,* contains many species. One occurs in Texas, others in Argentina and many throughout Central and South America. Its species and those of the other chief genus, *Acromyrmex,* are especially noted for polymorphism of the workers, which occur in a very great range of sizes from tiny,

A **Leaf-cutter Ant** (*Atta*) carrying a piece of leaf back to the underground nest. The manner in which it holds its bit of leaf aloft has earned it the name "parasol" ant.

small-headed minors to relatively gigantic, large-headed majors. Other genera occur as far northward as Long Island, New York; but the northern species are small and timid, and form only weak colonies. The principal center of the tribe is in the deep tropics of Central and South America.

There is a most curious account of South American natives using the heads of *Atta* soldiers to suture cuts. We cannot guarantee that it is not apocryphal; but we can say from personal experience that the long, hooked jaws grip together quite strongly enough to draw and hold together the edges of a cut, and will continue to hold long after the body of the ant has been removed.

Our first acquaintance with the "saubas," as the Brazilians call them, was under the happiest auspices. We had finished a day's hard collecting in scrub jungle near Belem, Brazil, the great seaport near the mouth of the Amazon River. Here it was that Wallace and Bates, two of the greatest field collectors and naturalists of all times, first worked in 1848; here Bates began the incredible collecting and field studies in the Amazon region that covered a period of eleven years and first made known to science much of the teeming life of that region. It was near Belem that he first met the saubas. Returning to the city, we relaxed where a very pleasant outdoor café offered tables under the shade of great mango trees. Happening to glance down at the pavement we saw, in the heart of the modern city, our first saubas. Completely unconcerned with man and his works, they were busily snipping pieces from fallen mango leaves or picking up pieces dropped from the trees by other workers overhead. Each ant would then start away with its burden, a single piece of leaf, which was sometimes increased en route when another ant climbed aboard, apparently just for the ride. The long file of laden workers passed along the curb to a spot no more than thirty feet away, where there was an entrance to an underground nest. Down this they scurried to add their contributions to the hoard of leaf fragments below. Often the piece of leaf quite hid the ant carrying it, bringing to mind the name "parasol ants" often used for the saubas. In the interest of first seeing the ants, we forgot that we were supposed to be relaxing.

These ants do not eat the leaves, as was once supposed, but use them as a medium on which to grow fungi; they then eat the peculiar small bodies (bromatia) formed by the fungi. Not only may each species of ant have its own species or genus of fungus, but the bromatia are special structures formed by the fungi only when cultivated by ants of that species.

Before leaving the nest a virgin queen equips herself (quite unconsciously) with a pellet of fungus, just as human brides used to carry along a "starting" of yeast for breadmaking in the new home. This is accumulated in a special cavity below her mouth; it is a dower essential for the life of the colony that she may found. After the marriage flight she drops to the ground and excavates the first small brood chamber. Here the fungus is manured by her feces, so that by the time her first eggs have hatched it has grown to form food for her larvae. This is the colony's subsistence.

In time an *Atta* colony may reach gigantic size, perhaps extending underground for hundreds of feet with galleries and chambers many feet down in the earth. The excavated soil will be piled aboveground as a spreading mound; in a common Brazilian species this may contain more than 280 cubic yards of earth, and the colony may consist of as many as 600,000 individuals. All about, for great distances, well-worn trails mark the routes taken by workers. Such colonies may be extremely detrimental to the work of human gardeners, since the ants often defoliate trees and shrubs or large areas of garden plants. It is impossible to eradicate a large colony by ordinary means; and even with the aid of explosives, bulldozers and modern insecticides it is extremely difficult and often too expensive to be worth while.

Not all of the Attine ants are leaf-cutters, for instead some of the more primitive genera collect the fecal pellets of other insects, particularly those of large caterpillars; and most or all species use some miscellaneous plant debris. Some species steal human provender such as farina meal; this, like the leaf pieces of the saubas, is carried to the nest and serves as the medium on which the fungus grows.

Since the days of Solomon many ants that really do nothing of the sort have been regarded as engaging in agriculture. The truth is that they reap but do not sow, for although they are actually specialized seed-eaters, the seeds that they collect and store in their nests are not from plants that they cultivate. It often happens, however, that some of the stored seeds get wet and start to germinate; and these, carried up out of the nest and discarded, may grow to form a ring of plants about the nest opening. It was these gardens, springing up fortuitously, that gave rise to the belief that the ants deliberately planted the seeds and harvested the resulting crop. Among these ants is the Near Eastern *Messor barbatus,* the one to which Solomon refers. In the genus *Pheidole* are found soldiers or major workers with enormous heads and very powerful jaws and jaw muscles. These individuals seem to act as seed-crushers for the colony. The genus *Pogonomyrmex* contains various North American species, some of which build conspicuous mounds, surrounded by bare areas, in the plains and desert regions. Certain of the *Pogonomyrmex,* such as the bearded ant, *P. barbatus,* have powers of stinging that are almost unequaled among ants. We can vouch from personal experience that a single sting on the ankle may nearly incapacitate a man temporarily. Since finding this out the hard way we have collected *Pogonomyrmex* with the utmost caution.

THE PASTORAL ANTS

Many insects, some of which are extremely abundant, have sweet secretions or excretions that they often pour forth in great quantities. Most noted for this are perhaps the majority of Homoptera: aphids (Plate 142), jumping plant lice, scale insects, mealy bugs and leafhoppers. Also noted for the production of honeydew are the caterpillars of many butterflies, particularly hairstreaks and blues. In addition, a great many plants produce abundant supplies of nectar, not only in their flowers but also in organs located elsewhere.

Quite as we would expect of members of so dynamic and opportunistic group, a great many ants make the fullest possible use of these secretions, especially of the abundant insect honeydew. This has certainly been going on for a long while, since many specimens have been found in Baltic amber showing that ants then, as now, regularly attended aphids. A great many ants do not confine themselves merely to visiting the honeydew producers, but have evolved definite, often intimate, relations with them.

Much honeydew is collected from where it has fallen from the producers, sometimes abundantly enough to wet the surfaces beneath as from rain; but much more is received direct from the aphids and other insects themselves. These not only show no fear of ants but actually welcome them, if the term is permissible, for upon being stroked gently by the ants' antennae they respond by voiding a drop of honeydew, sometimes upon a special structure that holds it in a convenient position for the ant to imbibe it. It has been shown, moreover, that aphids thus continually stimulated by ants secrete much more honeydew than they do when left alone, a matter of concern to man when aphids are feeding upon plants valuable to him. While thus attending the aphids, most ants protect them from molestation or attack. Some of our large species of *Formica* are especially fierce, rushing at an intruder and biting it or discharging volleys of formic acid spray. Other ants pick up threatened aphids and carry them away to safety, just as they would do with their own brood if their nest were disturbed.

Many other ants go far beyond such simple defensive tactics and thus definitely pass over into a pastoral way of life. A good many species build shelters, which may be simple, rooflike coverings or may entirely enclose the "livestock" and the stem upon which they feed. Sometimes cemented earth is used, sometimes a paper-like substance made of chewed plant materials and known as "carton." Some of the species of *Crematogaster,* small, active and very widespread ants, are especially noted for their use of carton for making aphid shelters as well as building special brood chambers in their nests.

Still other ants carry their care of the aphids or other honeydew-producers even further by transferring the insects themselves, or their eggs, from one plant to another where the pasturage is better or less crowded. Among these a large group of soil-living ants belonging to *Lasius* and related genera are particularly well known and widespread. The abundant *Lasius americana* is famous, or rather infamous, for its care of a root-feeding aphid, *Anuraphis maidi-radicis*. Since this aphid is destructive to both corn and cotton by sucking great quantities of sap from the roots, *Lasius* is responsible for serious damage to these crops. There is reason for believing, in fact, that in at least two localities it is only through the activities of these ants that the aphids are able to survive the winter. In the autumn the ants carry the aphid eggs down into their deep underground nests, where they care for them during the winter. In the spring they carry the young aphids that hatch from the eggs out of the nest and set them on the roots of various early grasses. A little later, when the young corn plants have begun to grow, they transfer the aphids to these, along with others more recently hatched. A field of corn may thus be a perfect meshwork of *Lasius* burrows extending from plant to plant. Later in the season, when the aphids grow up and begin to reproduce, the ants transfer the mature wingless females to other plants, but pay no attention to the winged ones, which fly away to colonize other areas. The ants' actions are thus beautifully adjusted to the complex reproductive activities of the aphids as well as to their general needs. Certainly no human could take better care of his domesticated animals than such ants do of their aphid "cattle."

The relationship of some ants with certain blue butterfly caterpillars is a similarly close one, although the majority of such caterpillars that secrete honeydew are merely visited and protected upon their food plants. In the case of certain species, however, such as the large blue, *Maculinea arion,* of Europe, the ants visit and protect the caterpillars for a time and then take them down into the nest. Here, we are sorry to say, the caterpillar of *arion* ill repays its hosts' kindness by eating some of the ant brood, although it does give honeydew in exchange. Similar relationships have been discovered, or are suspected, between ants and butterfly caterpillars in Australia, Africa and North America. In some cases the relationship appears to have evolved so far that at least the butterfly is dependent upon the ants, although the ants can get along very well without the butterfly.

"Repletes" of an **Australian Honey Ant.** These special workers are incredibly distended with honey and serve as living storage pots for the colony.

Unusual though they may seem, all of the activities that the ants carry on in attending, protecting and caring for their "cattle" are really not at all outside of the normal pattern of ant activity, and so represent nothing essentially new. Within the colony an ant is constantly caressing other members of the group with its antennae, receiving a trophallactic droplet of liquid for doing so. When, therefore, small insects with neutral or pleasant odors are found to respond in just the same way that the ant larvae and sister workers do, these insects simply become, by what a human psychologist would term "transference," fellow members of the society. As such they are visited, caressed, protected and moved about according to the dictates of necessity, and in general treated no differently from the way the ant's own larvae would be. With this pattern established, the stage is set for the further refinement of taking the creatures down into the nest when winter threatens and returning them to their proper feeding places when weather permits.

HONEY ANTS

Probably no ants live entirely on honeydew, but many use it as their chief food. Among such ants certain groups have evolved a most extraordinary

One **Carpenter Ant** worker grooming another, a common and important activity in the ant society.

method of storing the liquid food. Bees and honey wasps manage this by means of waxen or paper combs; but the manufacture of these appears to have been beyond the power of ant evolution, although some ants do make other structures of paper carton. The so-called honey ants have solved the problem of honey storage in a most extraordinary way, by utilizing certain of the workers as living honey pots or honey bags. Such a worker, which is called a "replete," is fed by the returning foragers until its abdomen, which houses its capacious crop, becomes incredibly distended to many times its normal diameter. In this condition the replete is usually unable to walk about normally, and does little but hang from the ceiling of an underground chamber. Here it remains, perhaps for months, until a time comes when its contents are wanted. Then, when properly stimulated, it gives up its contents in normal trophallactic fashion. Just what happens to it when it is emptied is not known. Probably it dies, to be replaced by the creation of another replete from a callow worker when the nectar and honeydew sources again yield abundantly. The sacrifice of a few workers is a very small price to pay for such storage facilities.

A number of ants belonging to various groups of the Camponotinae and Dolichoderinae have independently evolved this unique habit. They include *Melophorus* and *Leptomyrmex* of Australia and New Guinea, *Plagiolepis* of Africa, *Camponotus inflatus* of Australia and *Myrmecocystus* of northern Mexico and the southwestern United States. In the last genus the most widely known species is *M. mexicanus,* of which the subspecies *horti-deorum,* discovered in the Garden of the Gods (hence its name) near Manitou, Colorado, was described in 1881. The nests are usually in dry ridges and notably where the soil is very hard and difficult to dig. It is surprising that the rather slender, delicate-looking ants can excavate as much as they do, for the tunnels may go down three feet or more, with many lateral branches leading to the brood and storage chambers. In the latter the repletes hang from the firm ceilings. As many as three hundred, their abdomens swollen to the size of peas and golden from the contained honey, may be found in a single colony, although we ourselves have never found more than about fifty. Even with pick and shovel it is hard digging; but it is well worth it when finally, perhaps head down in the excavation, one can look along one of the horizontal galleries and see the repletes massed along the ceiling, gleaming like amber beads in the rays of a flashlight.

A chief source of the honeydew of this ant is the abundant secretion from galls caused by a Chalcid wasp on the scrubby shin oak twigs, but certainly much also is collected from aphids and scale insects. The honeydew in the repletes is extremely sweet and delicately flavored, far surpassing, in our opinion, honeybee honey. Following the custom of the country, one simply eats the whole replete or, if particularly fastidious, the swollen abdomen only. The repletes of *M. mexicanus* are sometimes sold in Mexico as a special delicacy. Those of another honey ant, *Camponotus inflatus* of central Australia, are greatly prized by the Australian natives, who dig up large areas to obtain them. We can think of no more worthwhile buried treasure.

Prenolepis imparis, a very common ant of much of the United States, is a notorious visitor of aphids and other sources of honeydew. Its workers have unusually distensible abdomens so that individuals are frequently seen swollen to a "semireplete" condition, especially when they are busily exploiting a rich source of sweets.

MIXED SOCIETIES

It is not at all unusual to find a colony of ants in which two different species appear to be living together amicably. Knowing something of the jealousy with which most social insects protect the sanctity of their nests by killing or driving out even other members of the same species, this may seem surprising. Such mixed societies are, however, a perfectly natural phenomenon among many ants. They may arise in a number of different ways, which are of great interest in showing us many of the ways in which ants have deviated most strikingly from the "normal" pattern of colony foundation and maintenance, and evolved some highly abnormal societies.

Sometimes a close look will show that each species in a supposedly mixed colony actually has its own tunnels and runways, separate from those of the other although with only a thin wall between. Such closely adjacent groups often arise when two young queens of different species happen to excavate their first brood chambers near each other, perhaps under the same flat rock. The growth of the two colonies may then result in contact with each other or in coalescence. Trouble may ensue, with the stronger exterminating the weaker; or an amicable adjustment may take place whereby the two societies exist as peaceful neighbors.

Thief Ants

Again, it may be that one of the species has evolved habits that enable it to live close to larger, stronger and more prosperous neighbors, not only undisturbed but with profit. Such are the many species of thief ants that often live chiefly or entirely by pillaging other ants. Typically these ants have very small, agile workers capable of penetrating the galleries of larger species in search of refuse, food or even the brood of the other ants, or of actually snatching food from the jaws of workers of the larger species and escaping with it safely. Sometimes the little ants are protected by a rank odor, like the *Dorymyrmex* which build their tiny crater nests in the big mounds of the fierce harvester ants (*Pogonomyrmex*). Sometimes they seem to be too small and neutral to be worth notice, like the tiny yellow European *Solenopsis fugax* and the North American *S. molesta,* which freely enter the nests of many larger ants to glean, steal and even kill the brood. *S. molesta* also frequently invades our houses, where it is a decided, though hardly a critical, nuisance in the pantry. *Carebara vidua* of South America is a similar species that infests the nests of termites. It is an extraordinary ant in that when a young queen leaves on her marriage flight she carries, clinging to the tufted hairs of her tarsi, a number of the minute blind workers. These aid her in founding a new colony near a suitable termite nest. A dozen of them would add up to no more than the weight of her head alone.

Tolerated Guests

Other mixed colonies may arise from the presence of one species as a tolerated or even welcome guest in the nest of another. The classic case is that of *Leptothorax provancheri* (formerly known as *emersoni*) of New England and Canada, which lives in the nests of the common *Myrmica brevinodis.* The little *Leptothorax* maintain their own separate brood chambers, which they defend vigorously against trespass by the *Myrmicas.* They are, however, welcomed in the nest of the *Myrmicas,* since they climb on the backs of their hosts and groom them, a process apparently so pleasing that the *Myrmicas* solicit it by feeding the *Leptothorax.*

Social Parasites

The young queens of a good many species of ants do not found their new colonies in the conventional way by independently preparing a brood chamber and rearing their own first workers. Instead, they somehow gain acceptance to an already established nest, in which their eggs and brood are cared for by the workers. In many cases the queen simply returns to her own home nest, or perhaps enters a different nest of her own species. Such occurrences account for the great majority of ant colonies in which there are more than one queen, a common phenomenon. The young queens of many species, however, enter the nests of ants of a different species; and in various instances of this, all sorts of curious things happen.

The young queen of the common Alleghanian mound-builder, *Formica exsectoides,* an ant that makes mounds as much as five feet high and twelve feet in diameter, enters a colony of a related *Formica,* the abundant black ant, *F. fusca.* Somehow she manages to escape being thrown out or killed;

and in time she also by some means presumably brings about the disappearance of the *fusca* queen, although whether this is done by the *fusca* workers or by herself is not certain. In any event the *fusca* workers then care for her brood. The colony becomes a mixed one and eventually, as the *fusca* workers die off without replacement, a pure one of *exsectoides*.

In Africa the young queen of *Bothriomyrmex decapitans* coyly hangs about the nest entrance of *Tapinoma nigerrimum* until some of the *Tapinoma* workers, little knowing what a serpent they are taking into the bosom of their colony, seize her and drag her into the nest. There she takes refuge either among the brood or on the back of the *Tapinoma* queen, where her strange odor is not noticed. After a few days she has acquired the colony odor and has become acceptable. Meanwhile she occupies herself by sawing off the *Tapinoma* queen's head, thus well deserving her scientific name, *decapitans!* She is now the sole fertile female; the *Tapinoma* workers care for her and her alien brood; and in time the colony becomes one of *Bothriomyrmex* alone.

Slave-makers

The phenomenon of slave-making among ants is intimately tied in with that of social parasitism in getting a new colony established, for a great many of the ants that get their start by taking over an established colony of another species are slave-makers after their colonies have become established and strong. Perhaps the best-known slave-makers are the small ants of the European and North American genus *Harpagoxenus,* which at the start parasitize, and later raid, colonies of *Leptothorax;* the blood-red slave-maker *Formica sanguinea* and its close North American relatives *F. subintegra* and others, which doubly attack other species of *Formica;* and the famous amazons, *Polyergus rufescens, lucidus* and others, which also make double use of *Formicas*. Established colonies of these ants make regular raids on the nest of their victims, killing or driving off the workers and seizing the larvae and pupae. These are carried back to the raiders' nest, where in due time they emerge as workers and automatically take their places as normal, productive members of the society. They are not, of course, slaves in the usual human sense of the term, since they occupy no inferior status and within the organization of the colony share equally in the rights and privileges of the community.

In the case of the amazons, but not of the other slave-makers listed, the habit of slave-making is completely obligatory, since these ants are totally unable to feed themselves or care for their brood. Partly this is because their mandibles are long, sharp and sickle-shaped, terrible weapons but poor tools. Even more important, they are psychologically barred from doing things for themselves, so that they will stand about and starve in the presence of food if there is no slave worker to feed it to them. From the viewpoint of modern human morality they might well be regarded as "degenerates," but we have no right to apply human standards to them. The scientist may use the same term and say that they show degeneration of certain structures and habits; but he uses the term objectively to signify that they have undergone a reduction or loss of certain structures or capabilities that their ancestors possessed, a quite justifiable statement.

Similar evolutionary degeneration is shown by some of the social parasites, which have lost the worker caste altogether so that only queens and males are produced. These, like all the individuals of the amazons, are entirely dependent upon the workers of the host species. In the European *Anergates* the reduction has even extended to the males, who are wingless and pupa-like and unable to leave the host nest. They fecundate the young queens, who are almost necessarily their sisters, before the latter depart from the nest to seek one of a potential host elsewhere. Such degenerative species represent one culmination of ant social evolution.

GUESTS AND INTRUDERS

An ant colony is a rich source of shelter and food, available to any other animal that can solve the problem of coping with the ants' defenses. It is not to be supposed that such possibilities would have remained unexploited in the dynamic world of evolution—and such indeed is the case. Probably more than three thousand different kinds of animals (some estimates run as high as five thousand) have adjusted their lives to take advantage of the ants in one way or another, often living in the ant nests in the utmost intimacy with their hosts. It gives us something of a measure of the relative ecologic importance of the ants and the termites to note that the latter, the other great group of social animals that forms a similar target for exploitation, have been subject to the attentions of less than one-third as many such guests and invaders.

Technically the animals that live in the ant and termite nests are known as myrmecophiles and termitophiles, terms that would be translated as "ant-lovers" and "termite-lovers." We must commonly refer to them as "guests," although in truth many of them are unwelcome ones, and still others are like the man who came to dinner. They show a great many gradations, from species that merely scavenge in the nests, to others that steal food or baby ants, to still others that have entered the trophallactic pattern of the colony and are fed and tended by the ants. Many are actually harmful to the ants, but others perform services or have ways of gratifying their hosts that make them highly welcome.

A considerable number of roundworms (Nematoda) and parasitic wasps (Chalcids) are out-and-out parasites on, or in, the ants. Among the real guests a few Crustacea and a considerable number of mites (Acarina) are present, but the majority are other insects. Even the primitive Apterygote insects are represented, and in the Orthoptera there is one whole family of ant-guest crickets and another of roaches. A small number are the larvae of moths and flies, but the vast majority are beetles of a number of families. From such a large group we can mention but a few representatives.

Such genera of the rove beetles (Staphylinidae) as *Myrmoecia* and *Myrmidonia* lurk in or near ant nests and eat dead or disabled ants or attack solitary living ones. They are not tolerated by the ants, but are able to defend themselves by means of a repellent secretion.

Many of the guests steal food from the ants, a favored method being that of many small mites, silverfish and springtails, which snatch a bit of the droplet of liquid that one ant is feeding to another. Some of the very tiny mites ride around on the ants without apparently disturbing their hosts. Their technique is particularly interesting, for no matter how many of them may be riding on a single ant, they always arrange themselves symmetrically in such a way as to keep the load from being lopsided.

The minute, wingless crickets, *Myrmecophila*, and roaches, *Attaphila*, the smallest of the Orthoptera, often browse on the ants' legs and bodies so persistently that the ants are annoyed and lunge at them; but their small size and superior agility permit them to escape. They also feed around in the nest as general scavengers. The roaches live, as their name implies, in the fungus gardens of the leaf-cutting Attine ants, being the only ant guests known there.

Although the flies are not commonly represented, some very curious members of this order live with ants. In both Europe and North America the large larvae of *Microdon*, a genus of flower flies (Syrphidae), are oval, leathery and unsegmented-looking creatures that resemble insect larvae so little that they have been described various times as molluscs. They appear to live as scavengers, usually tolerated by their hosts and more or less protected by their hard integument. The tiny larvae of *Metopina*, however, a genus of humpbacked flies (Phoridae), cling about the necks of the ant larvae by means of a special suction disc and steal food while the larvae are being fed.

We have already mentioned the larvae of some of the blue butterflies that secrete honeydew, as a result of which they are taken down into the nests by the ant. Some, at least, eat the ant brood. Other butterfly and moth larvae are scavengers and predators upon the brood, but must get into the nests by

themselves if their mothers did not succeed in entering it to lay eggs.

The most advanced and unusual of the guests are beetles of many families, chiefly of the rove beetles (Staphylinidae), scarabs (Scarabaeidae), Paussidae and Pselaphidae. Like the aphids and butterfly larvae, these give something in return to the ants—not in their cases honeydew, but the equally relished secretions of certain glands. These are discharged through bundles of special short hairs, called trichomes. The ants spend much time gnawing at these, so greatly do they relish the secretions. The little beetles are fed by the ants by regurgitation just as other ants and ant larvae are, and are treated and protected as valued and full-fledged members of the community. The European *Atemeles* and *Lomechusa* and the North American *Xenodusa cava* will often be found very commonly in the autumn in the nests of carpenter ants (*Camponotus*), where the adult beetles spend the winter. In the spring they move to nests of *Formica*, where they breed. The ants rear the beetle larvae with even more care than they do their own, sometimes neglecting their own larvae to an extent that interferes with their normal development.

ANT MIMICS

Many insects such as various bugs and beetles, and even some small spiders, definitely mimic the appearance, postures and behavior of ants. Even an experienced entomologist may have to look very closely at one of the mimics before he can be certain what it is. The spiders, such as *Myrmarachne* and *Synemosyna* of North America for example, have very un-spider-like narrow waists. They also make up for the fact that they have eight legs and the ants only six by holding their first pair of legs out in front and waving them about like antennae. Supposedly the mimics are benefited by being mistaken for ants and are therefore left alone by predators that would otherwise catch them. It is probable that to a certain extent this is so, although the protection cannot be complete because of the great number of birds, lizards and other animals that consistently feed on ants. But the mimetic resemblances seem too extreme to be due to mere chance.

ANTS AND MAN

The space that we have devoted to the ants is warranted by their almost infinite variety of habits, societies and relations with other organisms. Widespread and all-pervasive, they have also an incalculable secondary effect on nearly all other forms of land life; and it is here that they chiefly concern man. In the temperate zones of the world and in the deserts, where termites are scarce or absent and where earthworms often do not occur, their activities in turning, mixing and aerating the soil are of im-

A predatory ant (*Daceton*) with a small locust that it has caught.

measurable importance. It was Darwin who first called major attention to the work of the earthworms, pointing out that in England as much as 1300 tons of soil per acre will be brought to the surface in 100 years by their efforts. In Brazil, where there are no earthworms, we know that the ants will comparably move more than 1600 tons of soil per acre in 100 years; and in North Africa a *Pheidole* has been found to move more than a ton of soil in an area of only fifteen square yards in a hundred-day period! The ant hills and craters on our lawns, no less than the worm casts on our putting greens, are minor nuisances to most people; but they are signs of an unending activity in the soil that is usually of the utmost agricultural benefit.

Nor must we forget that all of this activity is of critical importance in making the soil pervious to water. More and more, as subterranean water tables recede deeper and deeper, are we becoming conscious of the need of drastic water conservation. Much or most of the rainwater that falls upon impervious ground merely runs away over the surface, to evaporate or spill into streams and be lost to the area. But where ants are abundant, and the soil is

A **Carpenter Ant** (*Camponotus herculaneus*). A queen with larvae.

consequently loose and absorbent, the water soaks in quickly, replenishes the local water table, and is available for both plants and shallow wells.

The activity of ants in killing other insects is also constant and great. Many of the insects are, of course, beneficial or neutral as far as man is concerned, but the great majority are harmful; for it is the abundant plant-eating insects that most damage man's crops, and these are the ones that the ants most commonly destroy. In every hayfield are literally millions of insects feeding at the bases of the grasses and in the turf and roots where they are never noticed; yet they consistently reduce the crop by large percentages, a steady but usually unnoticed drain. It is upon such insects the ants largely feed. One large ant colony in Europe was observed bringing in insects at the rate of 100,000 daily during the most active periods. We can be sure that man is a heavy gainer from such activities.

On the other side of the ledger there is no gainsaying that in many ways the economies of ants and man are antipathetic, and that great harm to man is wrought by ants. We have mentioned the heavy damage to such crops as corn caused by aphids for which the attendant ants were responsible, and a long list of such instances could be compiled. Equally serious in many areas of the tropics is the damage done by the leaf-cutting Attines.

Our houses are often invaded by many species, for our nests are just as wide-open invitations to exploitation as the nests of the ants themselves are to other insects. The big carpenter ants (*Camponotus*) may be household nuisances as well as destructive tunnelers of wood. The worst household pests are the very small, ubiquitous and cosmopolitan Pharaoh's ant, *Monomorium pharaonis,* and the tiny thief ants such as *Solenopsis molesta.* In the southern United States the aggressive, imported Argentine ant, *Iridomyrmex humilis,* is a serious household pest as well as a very destructive ant to many crops outdoors and in greenhouses. The fire ants, *Solenopsis geminata* and *saevissima,* the latter also an importation from Argentina, also cause much trouble in the South by their savage dispositions and extremely painful stings, sometimes seriously handicapping fruit-pickers and field workers, especially in citrus groves. Other fire ants in the tropics make outdoor work extremely hazardous, as everyone will agree who has ever brushed against a bush covered with them. The vicious bulldog ants of Australia are proverbially unpleasant in this way.

Such things are really, however, relatively minor. Modern man has equipment and techniques to control even the worst ant pests when they become bad enough to warrant it. And the cost of this is very small compared to the enormous, largely unseen benefits that he receives from far more members of the group.

Some Details of Insect Structure and Growth

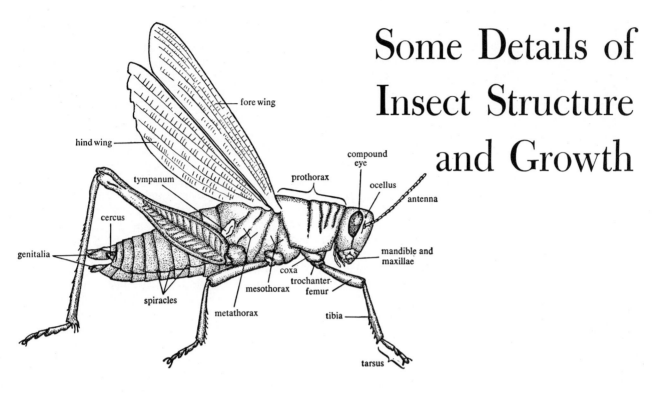

THE insects share many fundamental characteristics with the other arthropods, and have evolved others of their own. An awareness of these is important, not only for understanding the complex behavior and great success of insects but also as a tool in recognizing them.

Insects are jointed animals, being composed of a series of ringlike segments that are usually plainly visible in at least part of the body. An insect consists of three main divisions: the head, the thorax and the abdomen. The head is composed of at least five segments, but these are so fused together, forming a compact capsule, that they are no longer distinct. The next region, the thorax, consists of three segments that are usually easily distinguishable, although they are subject to considerable modification. The first of these, immediately behind the head, is the prothorax, the next is the mesothorax, and the last is the metathorax. The third region, the abdomen, consists of eleven or twelve segments, of which the terminal ones are so joined together that they are not distinguishable in most adult insects, although they usually can be seen in embryos or immature insects.

The head bears a single pair of antennae that serve for touch, taste and smell; the eyes; and a set of mouthparts that are used for biting and chewing in the more or less primitive insects. These consist of a front lip, or labrum, usually a simple, hinged flap; a pair of sidewise-moving jaws or mandibles; a pair of first maxillae, complex appendages used for picking up and holding food as well as for tasting; and a pair of similar second maxillae at the rear of the series, usually joined together to form a rear lip, the labium. Each maxilla bears a jointed sensory structure, the palpus, used for tasting. Finally there is a central tonguelike structure, the hypopharynx, located between the maxillae. Such a set of biting mouthparts is fundamental, and is possessed by insects that are relatively primitive in this respect. A good many of the orders of insects, however, have evolved mouthparts that function as tubes through which liquids are sucked, often in combination with a piercing apparatus. These are not fundamentally different structures from the biting mouthparts but are formed into a tube by the lengthening and fusing together of some or all of the separate mouthparts. This has been accomplished in different ways by different orders. We may thus say that biting mouthparts are, in general, primitive; that tubular sucking mouthparts are more advanced; and that the latter type has been evolved independently and quite differently by a number of orders.

In addition to the antennae and mouthparts, the head bears the single pair of compound eyes, each of which consists of a number of close-packed units called ommatidia. Each ommatidium has its own lens and system of light-sensitive cells, like a single eye; yet the whole mass of them on each side functions more or less as a unit. In some dragonflies there are as many as 28,000 or more ommatidia in each compound eye. The typical adult insect has also three separate simple eyes, or ocelli, situated in a triangle on the front or top of the head. Young insects may have a somewhat greater or lesser number of similar simple eyes only, or may have the compound eyes as well.

Each of the three segments of the thorax bears a pair of jointed legs. Each of these has a quite consistent pattern, consisting of five divisions which are, from the body outward, coxa, trochanter, femur, tibia and tarsus. The coxa is typically the ball of the ball-and-socket articulation with the body. The trochanter is usually very small; the femur is typically the largest segment and contains the most muscles; and the tibia is often the longest. The tarsus, the functional foot, is usually divided into a number of segments, typically five, although especially in very primitive insects and in many larvae there is but one. The last tarsal segment bears one or a pair of claws; and this and often other segments have glandular sticky or hairy pads, the pulvilli.

The thorax also bears the two pairs of wings, which are outgrowths, but not true appendages, of the mesothorax and metathorax. They develop as small flat pouches that eventually expand greatly to form the wings. Most of the area of a wing is thin and membranous, but the strong tubular veins give it an astonishing strength and rigidity. The size, number and arrangement of these veins, both of the longitudinal ones and of the cross veins, is of greatest importance in insect identification and in the study of the interrelationships of the groups. The wings are moved during flight chiefly by muscles that change the shape of the thorax. The angle at which they are held, either during flight or at rest, is determined by the pull of other muscles attached to small structures at their bases.

Stemming from a common, primitive pattern of very simple flaplike structures, the wings of various orders of insects have evolved great differences from each other. We can almost always see that their special characteristics are highly adaptive, i.e. efficient in the particular environment and way of life of each group. In some, the wings have been partially or entirely lost, so that these insects have returned to the condition of their primitive wingless ancestors. This has happened most notably in such groups as the fleas and lice, which have adopted a life of parasitism, living on the bodies of larger animals such as birds and mammals. The wings are also considerably reduced or absent in many groups that lead a digging or burrowing life during the adult stage, or that live in confined spaces. In various other groups we find members in which the wings have been lost or greatly reduced for reasons at

which we cannot even guess; in a number of moths, for example, the females have lost the wings but the males are strong fliers. It is interesting to note that a large proportion of the insects of small oceanic islands, and of other regions where flying may be unusually hazardous because of the constant danger of being blown out to sea, have lost the wings, whereas their close relatives in more normal environments have retained them.

In one of the largest insect orders, the flies (Diptera), the hind wings have been transformed into a pair of small, knobbed organs that are used in equilibration during flight, all of the actual flying being done with the front pair. In some other orders the front wings have become so thickened and heavy, or else so reduced, as no longer to serve actively for flight, which is carried on solely by the hind wings. In the beetles (Coleoptera) these thickened front wings protect not only the hind wings, but much of the body of the insect as well.

Various groups show enormous differences in flying ability. In some the wings serve merely to keep the insect in the air for a relatively short distance, perhaps after a take-off assisted by strong jumping legs. In some others, however, notably the dragonflies, moths, butterflies and flies, the power of flight has been evolved to as great a degree as in any animals—sometimes for speed and endurance, and sometimes for delicate control and the ability to hover in one spot or even to fly backward. A few of the insects make long, transoceanic flights of several hundred and perhaps of a thousand or more miles.

In most modern insects the abdomen is without obvious appendages, although the primitive ancestral forms had a pair on each segment. The majority of insects today, however, have lost most of these, at least in the adult stage, although as larvae they may have several pairs. Some of the more primitive orders have one pair of appendages, the cerci, near the tip of the abdomen, and these usually have a sensory function; and in most of the orders two pairs near the end have been highly modified to serve as genital structures. In females these are used in connection with egg-laying and are therefore called the ovipositors; in males they are used for copulation. The structure of these organs, which are known collectively as the genitalia, are of the greatest importance in classification.

Many special sensory structures and organs have been evolved in various groups, serving chiefly for touch, taste and smell. Organs of hearing, of which the most fundamental part is a tightly stretched membrane analogous to our eardrum or tympanum, are most widely known in the locusts, grasshoppers etc. (Orthoptera) and in a large part of the moths (Lepidoptera). In one group or another these are located on the front legs, the thorax or the abdomen. A great many other special organs occur in various groups, ranging from glands that secrete and distribute nauseous or poisonous defensive substances to special structures for offense, defense or locomotion.

Insect respiration is managed so differently from that of the vertebrates that a word about it is necessary. Air is drawn into the body through a number of pairs of openings, known as spiracles, which are located on the sides of some thoracic and most abdominal segments. From these it passes along a complex system of thin-walled tracheae. These branch and rebranch many times, their smallest branches reaching the immediate vicinity of all the tissues. The exchange of oxygen and carbon dioxide, which in us is carried on in the walls of our lungs, thus takes place directly between the tissues and the tracheal branches. The blood of insects plays little or no part in their respiration, whereas in our bodies it is the essential carrier.

Growth and Development

An extremely important and characteristic feature of insects, as well as of all other arthropods, is the presence of a shell-like outer skeleton, or exoskeleton, and the absence of an internal skeleton such as our own. The exoskeleton is formed by glands in the skin as a liquid which soon hardens and is thus molded closely about the entire outer surface. It is relatively thick and rigid over most of the segments and joints, but thinner and more flexible along the lines and sutures between segments. Like a suit of armor, it affords protection to the rest of the insect within, while permitting all necessary freedom of motion. It is complex in its composition but owes its strength chiefly to an organic compound, sclerotin, which is chemically allied to the materials of our hair and nails. We often use the terms "heavily sclerotized" or "lightly sclerotized" to refer to parts that are unusually strong and hard, or weak and flexible, respectively. The muscles attach to the inner surface of the units of the exoskeleton, often to inward projections that form a sort of functional endoskeleton.

No other feature of the insects and other arthropods has had a more profound effect upon the activities and evolution of these animals. Like the armor that it resembles, the exoskeleton serves excellently for mechanical protection, especially in the aquatic groups where its weight is a negligible matter. To the terrestrial forms it is also a most efficient protection against desiccation, one of the great hazards of land life. Furthermore its position, surrounding the muscles that move it, confers a mechanical advantage in the matter of leverage that results in greater muscular efficiency.

The arthropods have not, however, managed to evolve any method of adding gradually to the exoskeleton as the individual grows in size, as we are able to increase the size of our bones. As a result an arthropod must periodically molt the entire exoskeleton as it is outgrown, and then quickly form a new and larger one. This molting is not only costly in material (although many arthropods thriftily eat the old exoskeleton); it is also a serious periodic interruption of the activities of the animal, which is condemned to an interim of almost total inactivity by being temporarily deprived of its firm muscle attachment and of whatever protection the exoskeleton affords.

The process of molting has only recently been shown to depend upon a complex series of endocrine activities involving special hormones that are formed by various glands and carried about the body by the blood. This is strikingly analogous to the endocrine gland mechanism that controls our own growth and so many of our activities. One set of endocrines in the insect causes loosening and disintegration of the old exoskeleton, which is then cracked open and molted; while another set controls the formation of the new, larger exoskeleton by glands in the skin. The growth of an arthropod is thus seen to be a series of starts and stops, rather than such a smoother, more continuous process as ours. Increases in size take place chiefly after the old exoskeleton has been molted and before the new one has been formed and has hardened. Each molt is called an ecdysis; the molted exoskeleton is called the exuvium; each period of activity between molts is called a stage or stadium; and the form that the animal has during a stadium is called its instar.

Metamorphosis

More than any other animals, the insects have evolved a series of changes during the development of the individual, which are sometimes profound, and which are collectively known as its metamorphosis. No feature is of greater importance to the understanding of the life and activities of an insect.

Most insects undergo embryonic development in eggs that usually have a hard, sclerotized shell and are laid by the mother. However, a surprisingly large number of species of quite a few orders do not lay eggs, the young being retained and nourished, sometimes for a considerable period, within the mother. Upon hatching from the egg or being born, the young insect is usually quite different from the adult of its species and is therefore known as a larva. The caterpillar that will eventually grow to be a butterfly and the maggot that will become a fly are examples of larvae. Some types of larvae are given special names: nymphs are larvae that gradually transform to the adult condition, i.e. have an incomplete metamorphosis (see below); naiads are aquatic nymphs; but it is perfectly proper to refer to all as larvae.

The larva eats and grows, molting a greater or

lesser number of times in the process. In addition to its larval structures it begins to form some others, such as the sex organs and wings, that will not be fully developed or functional until it is an adult. Finally the larva reaches maximum size, after a period of life which in some insects may have lasted as little as ten days or even less, and in others may have required as long as seventeen years. The time has now come for its transformation to the adult. It is here that we have a simple measure of the different types of metamorphosis shown by various insects.

In some insects there is practically no difference between the larvae and the adults, save in size and the sexual inactivity of the larvae. The two stages live in the same environments, obtain and eat the same foods in the same way, and behave and look alike. Such insects are said to have no metamorphosis. They are all small, primitive forms that are primitively wingless and show a notable lack of advance in most other ways as well. They represent primitive "holdovers" that have somehow managed to survive from ancient days despite their archaic condition, as have similar "living fossils" in other groups of plants and animals. They constitute only a fraction of 1 per cent of all the insects.

A great many insects show a definite, although not a very marked, metamorphosis. In them the larva and the adult may or may not be quite similar; but at least they do not differ profoundly. They almost invariably differ in that the adults have functional wings while the larvae do not. In these insects the wings, which begin development during larval life, do so as external pads that are quite plainly visible on the larva's thorax. These insects are therefore collectively known as the Exopterygota (that is, "outside wings"). In practically all of them the larva simply changes to the adult in the course of a single molt. The last instar larval exoskeleton cracks open and the adult emerges, expands its wings, hardens its exoskeleton and goes about its business. Even though in some orders the larvae, such as those of the dragonflies, live in the water and respire by means of gills, while the very different adults are wholly terrestrial and aerial, there is obviously no fundamental difference between the two stages. If there were, the change from the one to the other could not be accomplished during a single molt. Such a metamorphosis, involving a definite but not a profound difference between the larva and adult, so that the larva transforms directly into the adult, is termed "direct" or "incomplete." The insects that show it are obviously more advanced in nearly all ways than the primitive Apterygota and constitute about 12 per cent of all insects.

Finally there is the great majority of insects, in which the larval stage is exceedingly different from the adult. The larvae of many of these orders, such

as the maggots of the flies and the grubs of the bees and wasps, have, in fact, become so strongly modified that they are scarcely recognizable as insects at all. Far more often than not, the larvae live in an entirely different type of environment from that of the adults and feed very differently. The difference between the larva and the adult is too great for the one to be able to change into the other and carry on "business as usual" in the meantime. Accordingly there has evolved another stage in the life cycle, the inactive pupa. This is typically a mummy-like creature that does no moving about or eating but merely lies quiet, often inside a protective cocoon. We like to think of the pupa as resembling a shop that has been temporarily closed for extensive alterations. Externally there may seem to be very little going on, but inside there is great activity. Some of the old structures are being remodeled to fit into the new plan; others are torn down and scrapped; others are brought out of storage and prepared for use for the first time; and still others are complete innovations. So it is within the pupa as the larval structures give way to those of the adult, many of which are extremely different.

Finally the reorganization is finished and the adult is ready. The last molt takes place as the pupal exoskeleton cracks open and the adult crawls out, expands and hardens itself and begins the last stage of its life. It will grow and molt no more. As a larva it concentrated upon eating, growing and storing reserves of food in its tissues. As a pupa it concentrated on remodeling itself from the prosaic, earthbound larva into the winged, mobile adult. Now it can concentrate upon the final great task of the individual—to multiply and reproduce itself and to populate the earth with its kind. Such a metamorphosis, in which the pupal stage is present, is termed "complete"; and because the larva does not transform directly to the adult it is often called "indirect." The insects with this type of metamorphosis constitute some 87 per cent of all insects. Since their wings develop internally during the larval stage, not becoming external until the pupa, they are known as the Endopterygota (that is, "inside wings").

There are so many exceptions and fine degrees of difference that it is difficult to generalize safely about a million or so different species of insects, each of which follows its own pattern of growth and development. But in general we can distinguish a pattern of utility or benefit in this type of metamorphosis—the benefit gained from an efficient division of labor. The egg stage of the insect is a small, inexpensive, easily transported unit for multiplication in numbers, as well as an inconspicuous and well-protected structure in which the delicate embryonic development can take place. The larva is an utterly practical and prosaic nutritive stage; untroubled by thoughts of travel or sex—in fact, untroubled by thoughts—it concentrates upon eating, digesting, growing and storing reserves of food. The pupa, like the egg, is fundamentally inactive and concerned with internal changes and reorganization. And finally the adult, often not eating at all but living on what it ate as a larva, concentrates upon reproduction—upon finding a mate, and moving about to deposit its eggs in the most suitable places and to colonize new areas. Each stage has its appointed tasks, for which it is efficiently adapted, in the overall pattern of the survival of the species.

In summary, let us remember that in the primitive Apterygota, which lack wings, there is little or no evidence of metamorphosis. In a number of more advanced orders, which are classified as the Exopterygota because their wings develop externally, there is a distinct metamorphosis but the larva transforms directly into the adult. In this type, which is called direct or incomplete metamorphosis, there are but three stages during the life cycle: egg, larva (or nymph) and adult. Finally, in the most advanced orders, which are classified as the Endopterygota since the wings develop internally, there is an additional stage, the inactive pupa, during which the larva becomes transformed into the adult. In this type, which is called indirect or complete metamorphosis, there are then four stages in the life cycle: egg, larva, pupa and adult. Metamorphosis represents, in varying degrees, a specialization of the larva for one set of tasks and a specialization of the adult for others.

Classification

The insects are regarded as members of one of the great divisions, or phyla, of the animal kingdom, the phylum Arthropoda. They constitute one of the classes into which this phylum is divided, the Hexapoda (that is, "six-legged") or Insecta. A class may be (and in the case of the insects is) divided into subclasses; but its fundamental divisions are orders. Orders are divided into groups known as families; families consist of genera; and genera are composed of the smallest units, species. The species consists of a population of individuals that have certain characteristics in common and reproduce naturally, perpetuating their own species. We say "naturally," since many species can be crossed under artificial conditions, producing hybrids—such as mules and tiglons among mammals—which would never be produced in a state of nature or which, if they were produced, could not reproduce their kind.

All of these categories are often split into "subs" and "supers," such as superfamilies (a division of an order) and subfamilies (a division of a family). A common insect would be classified as follows:

Kingdom—Animalia (Animals)
Phylum—Arthropoda (Joint-legged Animals)
Class—Hexapoda (Insects)
Subclass—Endopterygota (advanced insects with complete metamorphosis)
Order—Lepidoptera (Butterflies and Moths)
Superfamily—Papilionoidea (Butterflies)
Family—Papilionidae (Swallowtail Butterflies)
Genus—*Papilio* (True Swallowtails)
Species—*glaucus* (Tiger Swallowtail)

In referring to a species we use a double scientific name—a combination of the genus and the species names. The tiger swallowtail is, then, *Papilio glaucus,* and the spicebush swallowtail is *Papilio troilus.* The papaw swallowtail is *Graphium ajax;* its placement in a different genus indicates that it is a somewhat distant relative.

Bibliography

SCORES of thousands of articles and thousands of books have been written about insects. Any bibliography that attempted to include even the modern works dealing with specific orders, families and smaller groups would have to include several hundred titles at the very least. However, such a list would be out of place in a book of this nature. We have given, therefore, only the chief modern works dealing with insects in general, as well as a few classic titles. In most of these can be found extensive bibliographies, so that the person interested in securing additional information can easily go as much farther as he wishes.

BALACHOWSKY, A. and L. MESNIL (1935–1936). *Les Insectes Nuisables aux Plantes Cultivées*. Paris.

BEIRNE, B. P. (1955). *Collecting, Preparing and Preserving Insects*. Ottawa, Canada Department of Agriculture.

BERLESE, A. (1909–1925). *Gli Insetti*. Milan, Società Editrice Libraria.

BLUNCK, H. (1953). *Tierische Schädlinge an Nutzpflanzen*. (Band 4, *Handbuch der Pflanzenkrankheiten*.) Berlin and Hamburg, Parey.

BORROR, D. J., and D. M. DELONG (1957). *An Introduction to the Study of Insects*. New York, Rinehart.

BRUES, C. T., A. L. MELANDER, and F. M. CARPENTER (1954). *Classification of Insects*. Cambridge, Mass., *Bull. M.C.Z.*, Harvard College.

CARPENTER, F. M. (1930). A Review of Our Present Knowledge of the Geographical History of Insects. *Psyche*, Vol. 37, pp. 15–34.

———. (1947). Early Insect Life. *Psyche*, Vol. 54, pp. 65–85.

CHAUVIN, R. (1957). *Physiologie de l'Insecte*. Institute National de la Recherche Agronomique, Paris.

CHOLODKOVSKY, N. A. (1923–1926). *Manual of Entomology, Theoretical and Applied*. 2nd ed. Moscow-Leningrad. (In Russian.)

COMSTOCK, J. H. (1940). *An Introduction to Entomology*. Ithaca, N.Y., Comstock Publishing Company.

CURRAN, C. H. and others (1945). *Insects of the Pacific World*, New York, Macmillan.

EIDMANN, H. (1941). *Lehrbuch der Entomologie*. Berlin.

ESSIG, E. O. (1947). *College Entomology*. New York, Macmillan.

———. (1926). *Insects of Western North America*. New York, Macmillan.

FABRE, J. H. (1879–1891). *Souvenirs Entomologiques*. 10 vols. Paris, many editions.

FROST, S. W. (1942). *General Entomology*. New York, McGraw-Hill.

GRANDI, G. (1951). *Introduzione allo Studio dell'entomologia*. Bologna.

GRASSÉ, P. P. (ed.) (1949–51). *Insectes* (in *Traité de Zoologie*). Paris, Masson.

HANDLIRSCH, A. (ed.) (1926–38). *Insecta = Insekten* (in Kükenthal and Krumbach, *Handbuch der Zoologie*). Berlin and Leipzig, Walter de Gruyter.

HENNEGUY, L. F. (1904). *Les Insectes*. Paris, Masson.

IMMS, A. D. (1957). *A General Textbook of Entomology*, 9th ed. revised by O. W. Richards and R. G. Davies. London, Methuen.

LAMEERE, A. (1929–1938). *Précis de Zoologie*. Brussels, H. Cauwenberg.

LUTZ, F. E. (1948). *Field Book of Insects*. New York, Putnam.

MARTYNOV, A. V. (1928). Permian Fossil Insects of Northeast Europe. *Trav. Mus. Geol. Acad. Sci. URSS*.

METCALF, C. L., W. P. FLINT, and R. L. METCALF (1951). *Destructive and Useful Insects*. New York, McGraw-Hill.

OLDROYD, H. (1958). *Collecting, Preserving and Studying Insects*. London, Hutchinson.

OMAN, P. W., and A. D. CUSHMAN (1946). *Collection and Preservation of Insects*. Washington, U.S. Department of Agriculture.

ROEDER, K. D. (ed.) (1953). *Insect Physiology*. New York, Wiley.

SCHRÖDER, C. (ed.) (1925–1929). *Handbuch der Entomologie*. Jena, Gustav Fischer.

SHVANVICH, B. N. (1949). *A Course of General Entomology*. Leningrad. (In Russian.)

SNODGRASS, R. E. (1935). *Principles of Insect Morphology*. New York, McGraw-Hill.

SWAIN, R. B. (1948). *The Insect Guide*. New York, Doubleday.

TILLYARD, R. J. (1926). *Insects of Australia and New Zealand*. Sydney, Angus & Robertson.

WEBER, H. (1954). *Grundriss der Insektenkunde*. Stuttgart, Gustav Fischer.

———. (1933). *Lehrbuch der Entomologie*. Jena, Gustav Fischer.

WIGGLESWORTH, V. B. (1956). *Principles of Insect Physiology*. London, Methuen; New York, Wiley.

INDEX OF INSECTS

Note : A numeral in parentheses refers to a color plate; a page number followed by an asterisk indicates a black-and-white illustration.

SUBJECT INDEX